The Riddle
of Autism

The Riddle of Autism

A Psychological Analysis

George Victor

Foreword by
E. James Anthony

JASON ARONSON INC.
Northvale, New Jersey
London

THE MASTER WORK SERIES

First softcover edition 1995

Copyright © 1995, 1983 by George Victor

Library of Congress Cataloging-in-Publication Data

Victor, George.
   The riddle of autism : a psychological analysis / George Victor.
       p.   cm. -- (The Master work series)
     Originally published : Lexington, Mass. : LexingtonBooks, c1983.
   Includes bibliographical references and indexes.
   ISBN 1-56821-573-8 (alk. paper)
   1. Autism in children. I. Title II. Series.
RJ506.A9V53   1995
618.92'8982--dc20
                                                       95-31218

Manufactured in the United States of America. Jason Aronson Inc. offers books and cassettes. For information and catalog write to Jason Aronson Inc., 230 Livingston Street, Northvale, New Jersey 07647.

Dedicated
to the memory of
Charles Ferster
1922–1981

Contents

    Seizures   235

Chapter 16   **Retrospect and Prospect**   241

              The Basis of Autistic Development   241
              The Development of Autism   243

              Endnotes   249

              Bibliography   277

              Index of Names   323

              Index of Subjects   334

              About the Author   336

Foreword

Autism is a sphynxian riddle: an enigmatic challenge to the projections of the clinician who is driven to understand the underlying, unexpressed meaning of the condition and whose understanding is only too likely to be colored by the preconceptions imposed by training, experience, and scientific persuasion. The word itself has been used variously, which has added to the confusion. For some, it has represented a phase of normal human development following birth; for others, it has been regarded as a conserving mechanism, under the general rubric of withdrawal, that permits the organism to retire from a stressful environment until better equipped to deal with it. This latter usage connects it to the freezing or sham death evinced by many species.

Nonclinical psychologists have tried to make better use of the concept by defining it more carefully, scrupulously, and workably, in order for it to become susceptible to experimental investigation. They have described it as a movement of cognitive processes in the direction of immediate satisfaction, short-circuiting the more elaborate modes of thought. The movement is essentially inward: there is an excessive susceptibility to such inner determinants as memories, residual traces from previously experienced dangers, an overload of anticipatory reactions before any real threat of danger, or magnified feedback bodily mechanisms that have increased inner awareness. From an experimental point of view, the possibility of autism could be maximized by an increase in the intensity of inner determinants, an impoverishment of the outer environment, or by excessive choice imposed by the attractiveness of a rich milieu.

The nonclinician, mainly the learning theorist, has postulated three stages in the development of autism. First, life satisfactions or frustrations yield affects that are fused with cognitive dispositions; second, the cognitive structure becomes dominant in the process, and primitive meanings of acceptance and rejection are assigned; and third, the affective components are integrated with the cognitive elements into a whole experience. This final stage represents autism. True autism appears when the affective ingredients markedly distort the cognitive picture of reality. Moreover, the truly autistic individual is unaware that reality is being distorted. In line with this conception, Piaget spoke of autism as "thought in which truth is confused with desire," in which every desire evokes immediately "an image or illusion which transforms this desire into reality" (pseudo-hallucination), in which "no objective observation or reasoning is possible" and where everything is "in accordance with the subject's pleasure." There is basically confusion between the self and the non-self. All these ideas are enriching in the theoretical sphere and useful in the laboratory, but the clinician is likely to find them unhelpful, and there is good reason for this, as Solley and Murphy remind us:

The richest ideas about autism, in the most general sense, are those based upon the observation of patients. Although such materials are not repeatable in the sense of laboratory repetition, they are based upon countless vivid, independent observations which represent stronger effects than can probably ever be produced in the laboratory. The motivations, drives, and experiences which produce the "autistic effects" are more intense than almost anything we can duplicate in our experiments. In a real sense, life is a better experiment than anything we copy. For a penetrating picture of autism we can turn to the writings of clinicians. (*Development of the Perceptual World* by Charles M. Solley and Gardner Murphy, 1960, pg. 69.)

What Dr. Victor has compiled for us does represent a very rich mine of ideas regarding autism, and there is no doubt that he does present us with a very penetrating picture coupled with a wide variety of etiological explanations.

Bleuler, who coined the term *schizophrenia*, described autism as one of its most important symptoms and defined it as a "preponderance of inner life with an active turning away from the external world," mirroring the fulfillment of wishes and strivings. Autistic thinking, independent of logical rules, is directed by affective needs and is prominent in psychosis, in dreaming, in mythology and superstition, and in normal neurotic and poetical fantasy. It is largely governed by the pleasure principle.

There are, therefore, two conclusions about autism that can be drawn from the considerations of Bleuler and subsequent clinicians:

1. It is related to a mechanism that is extensively used throughout the phylogenetic series.
2. It is a mechanism that finds expression in normal, neurotic, and psychotic states.

The autistic response and behavior seen in infants and younger children may disappear as outward forms but continue in a perceptual and cognitive mode in the adult.

Recent studies in the field of child psychiatry have tended to place a special emphasis on the developmental point of view, redefining childhood psychopathology as a developmental psychopathology. This approach has already borne fruit with regard to the pre-adult affective disorders in which the different stages of development have been shown to produce different symptomatic and behavioral profiles. So far, autism has not been subjected to a detailed, developmental scrutiny, and it is, therefore, gratifying to note the author's tendency to look at the genesis of autism against the background of normal, developmental stresses. I believe that in calling attention to this he is opening up the possibility of systematic observation and research in the longitudinal study of autism. Follow-up investigations are also proving useful in establishing linkages between the childhood and adult psychopathologies, and providing some limited answers to what happens to autistic children when they grow up. Many of them enter institutions for the retarded or psychotic where eventually the institutional effect adds its own pathogenic coloring to the ongoing clinical picture.

If one chooses the developmental route, one is forced to select established developmental theories to provide an explanatory framework for evaluating observed or experimentally elicited data. Learning theory tends to be ahistoric in this respect. When the psychologists, Solley and Murphy, began to examine the phenomenon of autism, they turned understandably to two theorists who, more than any others, have been responsible for the massive knowledge that has accumulated on the developmental aspects of cognitive growth, namely Piaget and Werner, and both contributed heavily to the understanding of the role that autism played in long-term growth patterns. Curiously enough, Dr. Victor has not turned to these sources. One can sympathize with his need to trim his theories in the face of providing material that is almost overwhelming in its complexity. In general, I like his flexible attitude to the help provided by theory, and although he deals extensively and predominantly with operant systems, he is by no means rigidly bound to theory. In the course of his book, he refers to theories resting on hard data as well as to hunches with only a few findings to support them. In fact, he states very clearly that consistency and the development of a unitary explanation have not been his goals. Rather, he has tried to include whatever seemed promising. In considering the state of the art, he feels that it is premature to choose among the hypotheses, all of which need to be verified by systematic inquiry.

What he does and must be commended for doing is delineate for future researchers the most promising areas of study in which firm foundations have already been laid. The areas would include attachment and separation theory, operant theory dealing with reinforcement schedules and contingencies, theories dealing with ritualism and compulsive behavior in relation to stressful training, and concepts deriving from animal studies dealing with gentling. He realizes that the integration of all these in a unified theory of autism would be tantamount to a conceptual breakthrough, and this certainly does not seem to be at hand at the present time.

However, what he tries to do for us is to provide a fairly clear pattern of the development of autism during the first two years of life, indicating that it is a pervasive developmental handicap characterized by heightened attachment behavior, compulsive preoccupations, conditioned helplessness with selective attention to cues, diffuse inhibition with negativism, and self-stimulation.

All this is envisaged within the context of a railroad analogy in which a train of events may start on one of several branch lines, representing different kinds of autistic development, that merge into the main line. This explains, according to the author, how autistic development may begin at different ages, follow different paths but eventually end up looking the same. The analogy resembles the Waddington-Piaget theory of the "genetic landscape" in that one is following a developmental pathway with both genetic and environmental determinants, but whereas the railroad analogy ends up with the individuals all looking the same, the landscape analogy tries to account for differences in development.

Dr. Victor is not overly concerned with the organic substratum of clinical autism or with the merits or demerits of organic theorizing; he is content to present powerful explanations furnished by psychological theories and approaches. However, he is quite aware of the other end of the spectrum. For example, in talking of the early sequencing already mentioned, he points out that it may account for the development of autism "entirely on the basis of psychological knowledge;" that is, "If the average neonate had these experiences, autism would be the likely outcome." Nevertheless, he adds: "This is not meant to suggest that all causes have been identified here or that all causes of autism are psychological. . . . The psychological paths to autism are also physiological in that all behavior is behavior of organisms. . . and responses are all mediated by parts of organisms." Furthermore, "the beginnings of the paths may be physiological."

To attempt to explain the symptoms of autism is not easy, but the author does it most ingeniously and convincingly through the use of both attachment-separation and operant theory. Recently, others, such as Frederick Stone (*Psychotherapy and the Practice of Child Psychiatry,* 1982) have taken a different tack, and it is interesting to see the convergence of different viewpoints.

> [Autism] is almost certainly a heterogeneous disorder, a profound handicap whose nature is still not fully understood. . . . What is perceived here is chaos, especially the chaotic attempt to understand spoken language. It is not surprising that the child seeks to create for himself or herself what I choose to call 'perceptual monotony.' When the impressions coming in from the outside world produce turbulence, it is not surprising that the child tries to regulate sensory input by, for example, perseverative and ritualistic behavior. These are not rituals to be analysed and interpreted. They are the child's desperate coping with terror. . . . Many of these children seem to be struggling to function with a vestigial ego.

Dr. Victor sees the same phenomenon as an attempt on the part of the child to cope with the unpredictability of his environment, which is far from average or expectable.

Yet, although these are seriously disturbed children, there is no attempt on the author's part to segregate the autistic child from the human race of children. Everything, he tells us, that the autistic child does is also done by the normal child. What the autistic child does is to carry the normal behaviors of development to their extreme. Some clinicians might perhaps take exception to this, especially if they have been confronted by severe self-mutilations, yet it seems to me that the good practitioner practices best when he can locate his patients on the same scale and vary his practice accordingly. With this in mind, it is easier to understand some of Dr. Victor's paradoxes: The autistic child does not exhibit nonattachment behavior; he is attached to his mother but shows this negatively by being selectively detached from her (and perhaps not from the father), not recognizing her, or else treating her as a nonhuman object.

Finally, let me add a few words of appreciation of the author's beautiful descriptions of the mythologies that build up around psychiatric disorders and seem to be equally shared by parents as well as practitioners (as evident in the fascinating exposition on the evolution of Kanner's ideas regarding the parents of autistic children). What the author suggests, taking his cue from Goldfarb, is that the mothers of autistic children may not have narcissistic character disorders but are depressed and that this maternal depression has its counterpart in the depression that is near the core of both the separated and autistic child (who is often subjected to the cumulative traumata of separations). This is an engaging hypothesis, and a surprising one for me, since with all my experience of the families of autistic children, I have never thought of depression as being salient in either parent or child. The mothers often seemed desperate as they shopped around for clinical opinion but not hopeless or helpless as in a depressive disorder. Nor would I have discerned hopelessness and helplessness in the autistic child. I am now encouraged to go back and look again. In fact, I am much beholden to this book. It has made more sense of the autistic state than any other text that I know, and the huge range of symptomatic behaviors that previously had appeared randomly on checklists now fall into place as intelligible manifestations of the parent-child relationship gone awry in its attachments and in the training and learning experiences.

E. James Anthony, M.D.
Blanche F. Ittleson, Professor of Child Psychiatry,
Washington University School of Medicine

Introduction

Whether or not a child is diagnosed as autistic depends upon who makes the diagnosis. Inconsistent practice has led to criticism of clinicians as willful—as making words mean whatever they want them to mean.[1] Although severe, the criticism can be extended. The basic data of autism—descriptions of autistic children and their symptoms also shift, depending upon who describes them. Things said flatly by some workers have been contradicted no less flatly by others. For example, the children have been described as having defective senses, as pretending to have them, and as having superior senses. To say that "Every aspect of childhood autism is at present a subject of acute controversy" is an exaggeration but suggests the turmoil in the field.[2]

The turmoil centers around issues that stir powerful emotions and draw people into warring camps. The scholarly forums in which the wars have been conducted and the scientific language used lent credibility to positions taken. People wrote that there was increasing evidence for whatever they advocated. Some went so far as to assert compelling evidence or definite proof. Speculations were bolstered by predictions of imminent breakthroughs. However, breakthroughs have not materialized, and evidence for theories advanced remains inconclusive. Much that has been written, including ideas considered established, is questioned in this book. The basis for the questioning and for the new formulations advanced is indicated in rather extensive notes and bibliography.

Claims that there is at least a growing acceptance of one or another position are also questionable because they do not reflect actual consensus. People have put aside disagreements to make common cause on matters that have social consequences, but the disagreements that were put aside remain. Clinicians have come together mainly in advancing the position that autism is an organic condition, but what they mean is not agreed on. Some workers mean that autistic behavior is a manifestation of organic impairment. Others mean that the behavior is a psychological adaptation to an organic impairment. Still others mean that the behavior is a psychological adaptation to certain experiences or lacks of experience that were occasioned by a temperamental peculiarity (not an organic impairment). Similarly, while most clinicians agree on the general idea that autism has an organic cause, they disagree about what type of organic cause is involved. In specifying the nature and cause of autism, they contradict each other and refer to observations that are so inconsistent as to be irreconcilable.

The phenomenon of autism extends beyond clinical and scientific boundaries. Professionals as well as parents describe mystical experiences in their contacts with autistic children. Some have left their established careers as a

1

result, undertaking heroic and religious missions. The writings of many are colored by supernatural ideas.

Whether fascination with autism is a passing fad or a significant point in the extension of knowledge remains to be seen. At present, autism occupies a large part of the stage: "I know of no parallel in psychiatry or medicine where so much attention has been given to a relatively uncommon disorder."[3] Although autism has received more attention than its incidence would warrant, it is more common than has been reported. Analysis of diagnostic practice and of children's behavior shows that the diagnosis of autism overlaps with other diagnoses and, specifically, that many children diagnosed as retarded are intelligent but autistic. Using narrow definitions of autism, its incidence has been estimated at 4 or 5 in 10,000. The number of autistic children now listed as retarded, while difficult to estimate, may raise the incidence of autism to a far higher number.[4]

The identification of autism in 1943 as a distinct clinical entity spurred its study. Unfortunately, when a subject is defined first as a clinical phenomenon, workers tend to study it in isolation from general knowledge. This has been particularly true of autism. A quarter of a century ago, Phillips noted that "virtually none of the theory of autism is related to extant developments in general psychological theory."[5] That is still true.

Books and articles on autism have grown out of writers' experiences in treating children. Many writers have stayed within the frameworks of their experiences, their treatment orientations, and their theoretical disciplines. Others who have gone beyond their own frameworks have not gone beyond a clinical perspective. Little integration of ideas and data generated by researchers with different approaches has occurred. The lack seems a reflection of the tendency to view autistic children as quite different than other children and adults.

To illustrate, compulsivity has been considered a primary feature of autism since Kanner's early writings. Nonetheless, the compulsive behavior of autistic children has been discussed largely without reference to the psychological literature on compulsivity, ritual, and superstition. Similarly, muteness, echolalia, and other language peculiarities of autistic children have been discussed independently of what is known about these behaviors in children or adults not diagnosed as autistic.

The clamor, inconsistency, mystification, and fragmentation indicate a need for an integrating perspective. The integration presented here is designed for researchers, clinicians, teachers, and others who work with autistic children. The need for progress is urgent. "Childhood autism is the most overwhelming psychiatric disturbance of childhood."[6] Besides the children's suffering and handicaps, their parents are burdened severely by trying to rear them and by the guilt of having them. "No emotional disorder...has been more completely attributed to a mother's personality than autism."[7]

My method has been to review and analyze the observations and theories of others to see what consistencies emerged and how discrepancies could be reconciled and to interpret the data on autism in the light of general psychological knowledge. That review and integration have contributed much more to this book than my clinical experience with autistic children and their parents years ago.

Inaccuracies from being close to the subject were touched on here and are detailed in the text. Errors from my perspective will be clearer by hindsight than foresight, but it is possible to identify sources of error. Any viewpoint or focus sharpens some aspects of a phenomenon and blurs others. Working with other people's material means filtering it—omitting some elements, changing others, and giving what remains greater emphasis. Transformation of their material was necessary here in developing new formulations. In some places, the change made in what an author meant has been indicated. To have done so in every place and to have given full contexts would have lengthened the text greatly. To have omitted such material would have reduced greatly the data on which this book is based. Reinterpreting and taking out of context are common in scholarly writing. Nonetheless, it is disconcerting to have one's words used in a way one did not intend. I apologize to any writer who regrets the use made here of his or her material.

Additional sources of error in the book inhere in the inflammatory and taboo qualities of subjects covered. A number of the topics are so surrounded by prejudice and animosity that much that is written about them may be viewed with skepticism. That is particularly true of the broad topics of motherhood and infancy. When they come together in discussing infant rearing and disturbance, the likelihood of distortion is high. "Infant handling . . . is still a subject on which many different specialists use the full weight of their professional authority to back up their private prejudices."[8]

There are major advantages in taking a perspective. Working with patients involves pressure to come up with therapeutic ideas immediately. When the need is great, as it is in autism, the pressure is considerable. Clinicians are constrained also by the personal effects that their ideas have on their patients and on their patients' relatives. Freedom from the constraints of working with autistic children and their parents has enabled me to go at my own pace and to follow a large number of threads as far as they led. Some were followed outside the area defined as autism. In addition, I have not tried to maintain a set theoretical viewpoint but have shifted from behaviorism to psychoanalysis or other approaches whenever it seemed advantageous to do so. The result is that material on autism has been combined here with material from mental retardation and schizophrenia, from field observations and laboratory experiments with animals, and from nonprofessional sources—myths and the richly detailed biographies written by parents of autistic children. Much of the material has been neither used in connection with autism nor brought together before.

To include as much from psychology as seemed useful, I employed a broad definition of autism. Distinctions between subtypes of childhood psychosis—between autism of insidious and sudden onset, between autism present very early and autism after a year or two of normal development, between autistic and symbiotic psychosis, or between autism and schizophrenia or even retardation—have not been stressed.[9] Thus, I have not always maintained distinctions among classifications considered well established. Strictly speaking, those distinctions cannot be said to rest on fundamental differences because the basic natures of autism and schizophrenia are unknown. The basic nature of mental retardation, although considered self-evident, is also unknown. A scientifically satisfactory definition of retardation has yet to be developed. The current definition is a catchall, covering rather different kinds of children including many who are intelligent but autistic.

The scientific validity of a tentative classification is demonstrated eventually by its usefulness in organizing data and generating hypotheses. Its clinical validity is demonstrated by its usefulness in the development of treatment for people designated by it. By these criteria, autism has not been a useful classification up to now. Lovaas and Newsom concluded that theoretical formulations based on the concept and derived from the study of children so designated have not proven valid.[10] My experience with the concept is similar; it has served to draw attention to a number of psychological problems, but solving the problems seems to require changing the concept.

Dissatisfaction with the concept has fostered proposals to narrow and broaden it. Some workers have suggested that varieties of autism represent distinct conditions with different causes that may have to be studied separately. Others have argued that autism is not distinct from schizophrenia or retardation. Whether narrowing or broadening the concept proves useful will not be known for some time.

This book is based mainly on psychological knowledge because I am a psychologist and because my impression of what has been done up to now indicates that psychology has much to offer in explaining the behavior of autistic children. Knowledge in various fields of psychology provides a basis for tracing the beginnings of autism to transient characteristics of neonates combined with parents' fantasies, aspirations, and reactions to neonates. Unresponsiveness and aversion to handling are common in neonates. When they occur in conjunction with certain kinds of infant care, unresponsiveness and aversion are reinforced. Their persistence, together with other factors, interferes with the growth of infant attachment after the third month. In turn, disturbed attachment leads to fears, intolerance of novelty, and compulsive behavior. Such developments bring an infant to the formal training that occurs in the second year at a serious disadvantage. Consequently, training is met by increasing negativism and fixed and regressive responding, leading to a pervasive learning handicap. The combination of various kinds of knowledge on early development provides a basis for explaining much of the range of autistic behavior, including features of autism that have not been addressed in earlier theories.

Almost all autistic children's caretakers are women, although men sometimes have critical interactions with them. I refer to the adults who participate in the interactions as mothers, parents, and caretakers in order to suggest that they are usually women, but not necessarily, and that they need not be parents.

Theories, Parents, and Guilt

Along with its advantages, a psychological approach raises a serious problem. Parents already suffer much guilt about having autistic children, and psychological interpretations of autism arouse more guilt than other kinds of interpretations. That is partly because psychology and psychiatry have roots in religion and are associated with the detection and punishment of evil.[11] The association is too strong to be broken by assurances from writers that, in identifying causes, they are not assigning blame. The connection affects clinicians too. Efforts to free the mental-health professions from moralizing have not succeeded fully.

In the 1940s and 1950s, the field of autism was dominated by psychological theories, with unfortunate results. Kanner's theory—the best known— explained autism as the result of a lengthy process of "emotional refrigeration" of infants by selfish parents. This and other psychological theories became weapons in the hands of clinicians inclined to blame parents for children's problems. The blame was part of a wave of psychological criticism of parents that swept over the United States beginning in the 1920s. The most famous and influential voice was that of John B. Watson, the first American behaviorist, who went so far as to suggest that every mother ruined her children psychologically.

By the 1960s, misuse of psychological theory against parents generally and particularly against mothers of autistic children led to a turnabout. Writers advised against psychological theories of autism as pernicious to parents and as unfounded. The injunction usually was accompanied by statements that psychological causes had been disproven and that autism had been shown to be an organic condition. Occasionally, the argument was carried beyond saying that specific psychological theories already advanced had been disproven to the point of saying that no psychological theory advanced in the future could be valid.[12]

Injunctions against psychological theories of autism were associated with two trends. Behaviorists who worked with autistic children avoided discussing causes of autistic behavior.[13] This avoidance limited the scope of treatment strategies developed and hindered behaviorist contributions to the nature and prevention of autism. The other trend was an acceleration of the search for organic causes. The result was similar to the result of the search for organic causes of schizophrenia in adults—an outpouring of disconnected facts. Workers had examined the bodies of adult schizophrenics microscopically, going literally from the hair on the head to the capillaries of the cuticles on the toes. Hundreds of positive findings had been reported—some seized on with enthusiasm for a time, but most forgotten quickly. Reports on physical abnormalities in autistic children are more recent and have not reached the sheer volume of such reports on schizophrenic adults. The similarity is indicated by the abnormalities in autistic children reported in only one year (1977) in the *Journal of Autism and Childhood Schizophrenia:*

Celiac,

Cytomegalovirus (a virus associated with organic retardation),

Extra bisatellated marker chromosomes,

Fingerprints,

Hypertelerism (abnormally wide spacing of eyes),

Low seating of ears,

Lack of righthandedness,

Varicella (chicken pox),

Webbed toes,

Serotonin,

Serum calcium,

Serum zinc,

Depressed lymphocyte responsiveness,

Whole-blood 5-hydroxyindole concentration,

Syphilis.

As writers have pointed out, such findings are not useful in explaining autism because they result in too many factors and because each factor applies to too few of the children.[14]

Heredity and Environment

In the past, people found it meaningful to state simply that the cause of a pattern of behavior was hereditary or that the cause of another was environmental. Hereditarians and environmentalists opposed each other vigorously over the determinants of mental abilities, character traits, and emotional disturbances. The most protracted struggle developed over intelligence—over whether it was inherited or acquired and over whether its association with sex and race was inherited or acquired. Many psychologists came to think of the controversy as meaningless. The core of their analysis was that heredity and environment were so interdependent that their effects could not be separated. Every pattern of behavior (beyond the simplest reflex) was seen as a result of the interaction of heredity and environment. And to say that a pattern was due primarily to one was unscientific.

Such causal statements can be questioned on more-fundamental grounds: the concepts of heredity and environment are not as distinct as people consider them. Other distinctions, long held by scientists and philosophers to be basic and self-evident, have been challenged in this century. The best known is Einstein's reformulation of the basic distinction in physics between matter and energy into a unified theory in which matter is energy. His analysis altered physics, mathematics, and adjoining areas of philosophy. Pending a formal analysis of the concepts of heredity and environment, the idea that they blend into each other may be illustrated by the following hypothetical case.

A pregnant woman and her husband believed that the fetus she carried was male. The belief coincided with their strong wishes and ambitions. Caught up in fantasy, they chose a male name, bought male infant clothes and toys, and planned a typically male career for the child to be. Momentarily crushed by the subsequent birth of a girl, they did not give up their fantasies. They gave her the name already chosen and the clothes and toys and reared her as if she were a boy. As the years went by, the child experienced cognitive problems attributable to the discrepancy between her parents' treatment of her and treatment by people who viewed her as a girl. Let us assume that no other facts were relevant. Were her problems due more to her heredity or her environment?

Even though the relevant facts are not in dispute in this case, traditional concepts of heredity and environment do not provide a basis for answering the question. How it is answered may depend on the point in time on which one chooses to focus. The years in which she grew up make an obvious focal point and support the idea of a purely environmental cause—discrepant treatment. Had she been born a boy, however, the discrepancy would not have occurred. Therefore, the environmental cause of her problems was caused by a hereditary factor—her sex. Also, insofar as the hereditary factor occurred first and caused the discrepant treatment, it may be considered a primary cause.

Sex is determined during fetal life by the action of a gene. Therefore, sex is determined by a purely hereditary cause at that time. If the focus is shifted to the moment before conception, sex is determined then according to which of the sperm ejaculated becomes attached to the egg out of which a fetus develops. Determinants of sperm selection remain to be worked out. Some of them seem to be environmental. Therefore, the sex of a child may be determined environmentally, or its determination may be unspecifiable as between heredity and environment, or its specification may depend upon the point in time on which one chooses to focus. Similarly, which of the many eggs in a woman gets fertilized depends upon the functioning of her reproductive system and her overt behavior (when and how she has intercourse). In short, genetic causes are determined by sperm and egg selection. In that respect, genetic causes are also environmental.

Some of these points may be illustrated by material that bears on autism. A number of studies in recent years have found distinctive temperaments in neonates and distinctive styles of infant rearing in mothers (see chapter 6). Chess and her associates concluded that autism resulted from the combination of one type of neonate with one type of mother. Other combinations did not produce autism. Thus, a neonate who became autistic if reared by one type of mother did not become autistic if reared by another, and a mother who fostered autism in one type of neonate did not foster it in another. Assuming the theory to be correct, is autism caused by constitution or experience? Again, science provides no basis for choosing one over the other.

The nature-nurture controversy has moved away from heredity and environment. Instead of *hereditary*, the words *congenital, organic,* and *constitutional* are used increasingly. While not synonymous with *hereditary*, they represent the nature side of the controversy. On the nurture side, the words *acquired, functional,* and *psychological* often are used. These words are less polarized: a congenital or organic factor may be due to environmental causes. A constitutional factor often is understood to result from a combination of heredity and environment. Nonetheless, the newer words continue to reflect the idea that causes of behavior can be separated into two types, with one said to be primary. Therefore, use of these terms carries over traditional ideas about separating causes.

Nothing said in this book is intended to add to the nature-nurture controversy. Parts of the book, nonetheless, may be used to further the controversy. Therefore, it may be worth emphasizing that by explaining autistic behavior in psychological terms, by focusing on children's experience, I am not saying that autism is primarily a psychological condition as distinct from an organic one. Similarly, the explanations advanced at a few points of physiological causes of autistic behavior do not mean that autism is an organic condition as distinguished from a psychological one.

One may speak of a psychological condition that is not organic, of behavior independent of physiology, of a mind without reference to a body in common parlance, science fiction, and the realm of supernatural events. To take such ideas literally as scientific is misleading. In that sense, all psychological conditions are organic.

Identification of the causes of autism is needed badly. Little advance in treatment or prevention is likely without it. The nature-nurture controversy and the problem of blame and guilt are major hindrances to the scientific study of autism. That is reason enough for setting aside the controversy.

Unfortunately, the controversy can be set aside only intellectually at present because its roots run through centuries of language habits and of training children by arousing guilt. Clinicians use the word *etiology* to refer to causes. It is derived from a Greek word that means both cause and guilt. Arieti found the two meanings confused in a number of primitive languages.[15] It may be a long time before scientists can talk about causes of behavior without implications of guilt.

Acknowledgments

In trying to bring as much psychological knowledge as feasible together in explaining autism, my coverage necessarily has been selective. Selection was easier in areas with which I was familiar before beginning this book—for example, conditioning and learning, experimental neurosis, compulsive behavior, separation, and schizophrenia in adults. My limited knowledge of pregnancy, childbirth, infant development, attachment, speech, mental retardation, epilepsy, and mythology made sampling those literatures more difficult. Their potential for illuminating autism seemed worth exploring, even if only to a preliminary extent. To help with resultant errors, people from a number of fields read drafts. They did not necessarily agree with my formulations. I am grateful to the following people for their help: Sharon Bailly, Alan Bell, Sidney Birnback, Lewis Brandt, Elizabeth Claire, James Feather, Marjorie Gelfond, Joseph Geller, Howard Gruber, Edward Haupt, Alan Jacobs, Paul Kennedy, Milton Kleinman, Seymour Kuvin, William Mason, Barbara McCormack, John O'Connor, Edward Plimpton, Ammon Roth, Teresa Schachter, Jonathan Steele, Gloria Steiner, Robert Stern, Manny Sternlicht, Stephen Victor, Irene Williams, Ilana Zarafu, and most of all, to Benjamin Lichtenberg, Cheryl Roth, and Janice Victor (my wife).

Part I
The Mystery

Behavior that defies convention is baffling and threatening. Through the centuries, only limited efforts have been made to understand gross deviance. It has been attributed mainly to supernatural causes like possession by divine or satanical spirits. Modern thinking emphasizes scientific explanations for emotional disturbances, but deviance still evokes irrational explanations. Autistic behavior is extremely deviant and threatening to parents and other adults. More than any other mental disturbance, its study has been hindered by the persistence of supernatural and other unscientific ideas. These ideas occupy a large place in the field of autism (chapter 1) and need to be distinguished from objective phenomena before autism can be defined. Even after unscientific ideas are set aside, an unmanageably large number of symptoms remains so that further narrowing and reformulation of the concept of autism are needed, as is discussed in chapter 2. Analysis of the meaning and causes of autistic behavior begins with an exemplary case presented in chapter 3. The main threads in the case are generalized and the literature on autism is surveyed in relation to them in chapter 4.

1

The Child of God: Forerunners, Mysteries, Controversies, and Myths

Autistic children are enigmas. That is not because their behavior defies analysis but because study of their behavior has been hindered by misleading descriptions of it and by bitter conflict surrounding the children. Parents find themselves embattled with their extremely difficult children on one side and with clinicians on the other. Their situation is not conducive to objective reporting; nonetheless, their reports continue to be the primary source of data on the children. Clinicians and researchers also have been less than objective because of their role in the conflict. The biases of those who participated as attackers or defenders of parents were often obvious. Many who stood aside from the battle were also influenced by it.

The literature on autism is permeated by mystical ideas that obscure the nature of the condition, but the mystical ideas also provide leads toward an explanation of autism. Therefore, analyzing them can be doubly useful.

Classification

The occurrence of psychosis in children has long been denied and still is minimized. Maudsley, the first to write at length about it in 1867, was criticized severely by his colleagues for considering children psychotic. (Before the eighteenth century, the occurrence of any mental disturbance in children was denied, and mention of it is lacking in medical writing.)[1] Pressure against discussing psychosis in young children remained so strong that few writers dealt with the subject. Those who did tended not to mention psychosis but to use euphemisms.

In this context, the question of how to fit autism into existing classifications, and specifically whether or not it was a form of psychosis, was left hanging more often than answered. Writers who addressed the question usually identified autism as a form of psychosis (with a minority identifying it as a form of retardation). They stated that autism was an uncommon form—that most psychotic children were not autistic. But the actual diagnostic practice was to use autism as the diagnosis for almost all young children considered psychotic. Theoretically, psychosis was divided into a variety of types. In practice, however, other types of psychosis in young children remained largely undefined or undiagnosed.

Among the euphemisms for avoiding reference to psychosis were atypical development, ego defect, weak ego boundaries, borderline, and schizoid. These terms have largely been replaced by *autism*. The term *childhood schizophrenia* was introduced before *autism* and clearly referred to psychosis. Through the years, many workers considered autism and childhood schizophrenia to refer to essentially different conditions, while many others considered autism a variety of childhood schizophrenia and still others used the terms synonymously. Childhood schizophrenia was the only diagnostic category for psychotic young children in the 1952 and 1968 editions of the diagnostic manual of the American Psychiatric Association. In the third edition in 1980, childhood schizophrenia was replaced by three classifications, of which autism is the principal one. The other two are vague concepts: one (childhood onset pervasive developmental disorder) is new, and its acceptance will not be known for some time; the second (atypical development) is old but has not won acceptance by clinicians until now. In short, the recent practice has been that, when a clinician found a young child to be psychotic, autism was usually the diagnosis given.[2]

Forerunners

Psychosis and retardation, although widely regarded as fundamentally distinct categories, still have not been defined well enough to make the distinction clear. Before the eighteenth century, people did not try to distinguish between them in children. Psychotic and retarded children, including those who would be diagnosed autistic today, were called *children of God.* In Christian tradition, all children were gifts of God. However, these were special children whose peculiarities were considered a mark of divinity, a sign that their mothers had been chosen for rare favor. In rural Europe, where they did not pose a social problem, their births were considered a blessing to the family and a good omen to the community.

Physicians called them *idiots,* a term from Greek, meaning that they were autistic (withdrawn, isolated). Later, *idiot* came to mean retarded, and there was no medical term in general use for psychotic children. A subclass of the retarded possessing remarkable skills, called *idiot savants,* was recognized later. This group has been identified specifically as autistic.

Another line of thought leading to autism came from a traditional medical concept applied to adults. Adult disturbance had long been divided into extremity of mood (melancholia and mania) and loss of mind (dementia). Traditionally, dementia was thought to occur only in elderly and middle-aged people. In the nineteenth century, the concept was extended to young adults and adolescents *(dementia praecox).* Then, at the beginning of this century, the concept was extended to young children *(dementia praecocissima* and *dementia infantilis).* The few writers who dealt with the subject emphasized catatonic behavior in the children. But these extensions of dementia were not accepted, and the presence of any kind of psychosis in young children was not accepted by most clinicians before 1950. The fact that autism now is recognized fully is a major step and has led to an outpouring of research.

While these conceptual changes were occurring, the social situation of autistic children was worsening. They still were called children of God in Ireland at the middle of this century, but in other parts of Europe and in the United States they came to be seen in quite a different light. Growing urbanization, technology, and universal education had created a society with no place for them and held their parents up to shame. It became harder to see them as bringers of good fortune. They often were excluded from schools, and placement in mental institutions was urged on parents. The parents interpreted the position taken by society toward autistic children as hostile, correctly so.[3] Children diagnosed as retarded were treated with open fear and hostility. In the last hundred years, they came to be viewed as a threat to civilization, and measures were taken to control and eliminate them. By 1930, sterilization of retarded people had been legalized in half of the United States. It was carried out on a substantial minority. Euthanasia was proposed but not implemented.

Social changes also have affected the role of mothers in relation to children. By European tradition, mothers had little responsibility for the moral, social, and intellectual shaping of their children. Men defined goals in rearing children and devised methods of discipline and education. Sometimes women did the work under the direction of men. Sometimes they were forbidden even that role. For example, in parts of the United States, only men could be school teachers until the last century.

When responsibility for children's mental development was turned over to women, other changes also were taking place. Developments in science and religion contributed to the growing view that God was not responsible for conceiving children and shaping their character. Conception as well as discipline and education came to be the responsibility of women. No longer gifts of God, children came to be considered a human product. And when they turned out badly, their mothers were blamed.

Autism is now called a disease—something purely negative. Even when called the divine disease, more horror than joy is implied. At the least, parents' lives are made difficult; at worst, they are shattered. Frustration, guilt, bitterness, and social isolation tend to come with having autistic children.

The Nonhuman Child

Ambivalence toward children is normal; to an extent, all parents view their children as both blessings and curses. With autistic children, however, the ambivalence is extreme and colored by supernatural ideas. Clinicians and scientists also connect the children with subhuman and superhuman creatures. For example, autistic children have been identified with legendary and real feral children, fairy changelings, and "Children from Another Planet."[4] The suggestion that the children are not human has been taken seriously enough to be countered by scholarly assertions that they are.

These conceptions of children evoke mixed images of monsters and of people destined for greatness. Feral children are those found in the wilderness, often thought to have been reared from infancy by animals. Among the legendary heroes to whom such beginnings were attributed are Romulus and Remus. In European tradition, changelings were the offspring of fairies and other superhuman creatures. After birth, they were exchanged secretly for human babies and reared by human foster mothers as their own. These children, who passed as human, were described in legend as "remarkably beautiful, but strange and remote from human kind," with superhuman powers. Wing suggested that autistic children were the source of these legends.[5]

Like changelings, the planetary beings to whom autistic children were compared were strikingly beautiful and possessed supernatural intelligence and other powers. Their relationships to their mothers were peculiar. The mothers were unknowingly made pregnant by unearthly beings. Similarities to the beginnings of many legendary heroes are obvious. Also, by definition of parentage, these children were bastards, and according to one European tradition, bastardy destined children for greatness as well as evil. In the Middle Ages, bastardy was attributed to many heroes including King Arthur and Charlemagne.

The feral children, changelings, and children from another planet have in common a number of features associated with autistic children. They are seen as extraordinarily beautiful and capable, inspiring awe. They are reared by mothers who experience them as alien. And they strike people as non-human. It may not be surprising that parents have occult reactions to their autistic children. More puzzling is the uncanny effect on clinicians, reported in scholarly articles and books. "To come face to face with a schizophrenic child is one of the most awe-inspiring experiences a psychotherapist can have...."[6] "The examiner feels dehumanized."[7]

Some of the occult references are metaphorical and made lightly in passing. Others represent serious attempts to describe the uncanny reactions of clinicians who deal with autistic children, as in Bettelheim's description of Joey. The nine-year-old boy seemed like an electrically powered robot. His movements suggested that "he did not move arms or legs but that he had extensors that were shifted by gears." Part of his simulation involved carrying electric wires with him, which he arranged in complex ways, plugging some into a wall socket and attaching others to himself. When the staff of the institution, concerned for his safety, prohibited the use of wires, Joey continued the wiring arrangement in pantomime. The effect was compelling:

He performed the ritual with such skill that one had to look twice to be sure there was neither wire nor outlet nor plug. His pantomime was so skilled, and his concentration so contagious that those who watched him seemed to suspend their own existence and become observers of another reality. . . .

Children and staff took spontaneous care not to step on Joey's imaginary wires lest they interrupt the current and stop his being. . . .

Even our best efforts to relate to him shattered on his machine-like existence. . . all those who tried to befriend him, including his parents, ended up by providing this mechanical boy with the tubes and motors he seemed to need for his very existence. . . .[8]

Elaborate pantomime like Joey's is not necessary to create a humanoid impression. Some workers consider a nonhuman quality to be characteristic of the children.

The attribution of nonhuman traits is a departure from professional detachment. Some clinicians have gone further, becoming so deeply involved that their careers took strange turns, as in the following examples.

The Clinician's Odyssey

Delacato had had a long, well-established career as a pioneer of an innovative treatment for brain-injured children. His Doman-Delacato method was known in many parts of the world, as was his institute in Philadelphia. Writing in 1974, he said that contact with autistic children and their mothers changed his life. He gave up his prior work and the institute "to spend all my time journeying with those mothers and their autistic children." It was "a journey into a strange and alien world," depressing and alienating, but bringing a sense of dedication, of being a savior, and of transcendental gratification in finally having been shown "the way."[9]

DesLauriers and Carlson also identified themselves as saviors. They framed their work with autistic children around a story of Jesus' miraculous healing.[10]

The experience of Kanner, who shaped the era of autism (the 1960s and 1970s), was less fanciful but not less dramatic. More famous than Delacato, he was at the head of his profession before he came to study autistic children. He was the author of many articles and of the book *Child Psychiatry*, which had achieved recognition as the major textbook in the field. As far as I know, he was also the first modern scholar to suggest nonhuman elements in describing autistic children. He barely suggested them, but his reintroduction of the mystery probably contributed to the ensuing fascination with what became known throughout the world as Kanner's syndrome. His first article on autism in 1943 is said to have "altered the course, direction, and, indeed, the history of American child psychiatry."[11]

Contact with autistic children and their parents altered his life too. Over the next three decades, autism was the focal point of his increasingly controversial work. His observations and formulations became the basis of the interest, controversy, and research that followed. Much of the literature can be construed as a defense and extension of his ideas or a refutation of them. His writings are also a major source of the formulations developed in later chapters. Understanding his odyssey is a beginning in understanding autism.

The background of Kanner's involvement was the wave of criticism of parents that spread through the United States beginning in the 1920s, producing theories about parental causes of mental disturbance. The best known were Levy's theory about overprotective mothers and Fromm-Reichmann's theory about schizophrenogenic mothers. Like many mental-health professionals, Kanner was drawn into the conflict. His participation was intense and he fought on both sides, foreshadowing the controversy about the role of parents in autism that was to follow. In 1941, while working with autistic children, Kanner published an article about mothers' destructiveness. He said they intruded into their children's lives, engaging them in wars in which the mothers used surreptitious and dictatorial techniques, crushing the children's opposition. In the same year, he published *In Defense of Mothers,* a book in which he sought to relieve mothers of guilt in relation to their children. He also tried to counter what he saw as the source of their guilt—the psychological criticism to which they were subjected.[12] The ambivalence toward mothers shown in these two publications runs through his work up to his last major publication on autism in 1973.

While Kanner's first article on autism was in press, one of the children described in it was presented at a staff conference by the child's therapist, whose formulation of the case was that the autistic behavior was fostered by the mother. Kanner disagreed vehemently, taking the position that the formulation was not only incorrect but also impossible. He said that no parent, no matter how the parent behaved toward a child, possibly could cause autism.[13]

Nonetheless, in subsequent articles, Kanner began to suggest that parental coldness was the cause of autism. As the number of cases he had studied grew, his statements became stronger and stronger. Among the phrases that he used and that were repeated by colleagues, *refrigerator mother* became the best known.

The purpose of reviewing Kanner's statements is not to add to derogation of parents. Therefore, it seems appropriate to indicate here that, although parents impressed Kanner as if they were cold and had little interest in their autistic children, the impression was misleading. Reasons for this conclusion are given in chapters 3 and 4.

In 1948, Kanner criticized the blindness of colleagues who looked for physiological causes of autism rather than noticing parental behavior. He found the evidence for parental causes over physiological causes to be "so obvious as to force itself on...an open-eyed observer."[14] Over the next fifteen years, he repeated this conclusion often and vigorously. At times, he did so without qualification, but most of the time he qualified the conclusion, as in the following passage, which was to be quoted widely:

> The emotional refrigeration which the children experience from such parents cannot but be a highly pathogenic element in the patients' early personality development, superimposed powerfully on whatever predisposition has come from the inheritance.[15]

Kanner and others argued subsequently about the passage's meaning—about whether experience or heredity was cited as the main cause of autism. The indicated emphasis on experience was supported by its context. In article after article, Kanner gave details of parental behavior that he identified as fostering autistic behavior. He consistently found the parents cold, unloving, affectionless, formal, detached, mechanical, and perfectionistic generally and specifically toward their autistic children. By contrast, his references to heredity or constitution were usually vague and unsupported by details.

Sometimes Kanner did specify a hypothetical constitutional cause. He found the parents to resemble the children in their isolated ways and concluded that the parents were autistic. This suggested the possibility of a genetic link between the parents' and children's autism. However, his study of family trees did not turn up psychotic relatives in significant numbers. Therefore, Kanner considered it more evident that the parents transmitted autism to their children by behavior than by genes.[16]

During this period, Kanner noted over and over that no organic defects had been found in the children. He considered the absence of organic findings to be striking in view of the extensive medical examinations and laboratory tests given them. One of his stronger statements read:

> Not one of the 55 patients studied has had in his infancy any disease or physical injury to which his behavior could be possibly ascribed by any stretch of the imagination.[17]

He added that he did not believe an organic cause for autism ever would be found.

Kanner's most extreme statements about the cause of autism were accompanied by his most vehement remarks about parents. He said that the condition resulted from being "abandoned to vegetation in an impersonal custodial setting" (referring to the home) and that the condition usually could not be remedied because the parents sabotaged treatment. Therefore, unless the mothers could be helped by psychotherapy, the only hope for most autistic children lay in removal from the home and placement with foster mothers.[18]

Then, as Kanner's position on the cause of autism softened in the 1960s, he again defended the parents and turned his vehemence in the direction of colleagues:

> It is recognized by all observers, except for the dwindling number of those impeded by doctrinaire allegiances, that autism is not primarily an acquired, or 'man-made' disease. The fact that many of the parents are rather detached people has been confirmed frequently enough, but this observation cannot be translated summarily into a direct cause-and-effect etiologic relationship, an assumption sometimes ascribed to me via pathways of gross misquotation.

> At no time have I pointed to the parents as the primary postnatal sources of pathogenicity....

> [H]erewith I especially acquit you people as parents. I have been misquoted many times. From the very first publication to the last I spoke of this condition in no uncertain terms as innate.[19]

The extremity of the positions Kanner took is accentuated by his non-recognition of the self-contradictions. He did not retract what he had said or acknowledge having erred. In the book that capped his involvement with autism, he reprinted articles written over three decades, placing contradictions side by side.[20]

The contradictions have been emphasized to suggest that his involvement with autism was intense and irrational. I have not found self-contradictions or mystical elements in Kanner's writings on other subjects.

While Kanner's position was changing, two perceptions remained constant. From first to last, he described the children as rare, beautiful, enigmatic, and talented. Whether attacking or defending the fathers and especially the mothers, he pictured them as cold, haughty, and dehumanized. The image of the children suggests positive awe; the image of the parents, although similar, is negative. My thesis is that both images are derived from ancient myths that are perpetuated in modern yearnings for the coming of a special child and fears of the power of women. Before developing the thesis, other questionable attributions will be described. Evidence for the inaccuracy of some of the attributions will be cited in later chapters.

The Prophet

Autistic children have been endowed by parents and clinicians with extraordinary virtues and handicaps. The virtues include transcendental beauty, ethereal grace in movement, an air of beatitude, fey charm, intelligent looks, extraordinary precocity, supernormal vision and hearing, ability to find their way in unfamiliar terrain and in the dark, memory that exceeds normal or even human ability, and the destiny to be great.

Defects attributed to them include not knowing who their parents are, not distinguishing between animate and inanimate objects, inability to find their way, blindness, deafness, and inability to speak. Speech is of major importance in general and particularly in autism; it is the subject of chapter 14. Inasmuch as autistic children's inability to speak is widely considered an established fact, it may be well to emphasize here Kanner's observation that the children's lack of speech has been exaggerated. For example, the following have been reported to be completely mute: children who spoke rarely, in special circumstances, as in emergencies or when ill; children who sang, recited poetry, or repeated television commercials; children who spoke regularly to people other than their parents.

Paradoxical combinations of superior abilities and defects are attributed commonly to autistic children. The same child may be said to have supernormal and defective hearing, to have shown verbal precocity and inability to speak, and to be bright and retarded. Such combinations, although illogical, tend to be accepted because they are consistent with traditional mystical ideas. Before autistic children were identified, idiot savants personified the combination of mental retardation and superiority in the same person.

In ancient times, such combinations were expected in prophets: "from the day of the destruction of the temple the art of prophecy was taken away [from the professionals] and given to fools."[21] Those destined to become seers were often deaf or blind. Their inability to hear or see mundane things was thought to give them a special inner vision—an extrasensory perception of people's hidden thoughts and of the superhuman forces that shaped events. Consequently, they could foretell the future. In addition, people who did not speak received special attention. They were expected to reveal mysteries when their lips were unsealed.

Autistic children have been seen as prophetic, metaphorically and literally. Kanner said they give the impression of silent wisdom.[22] One child seems to have a "knowing smile".[23] Another's expression suggests a "secret inner power."[24] Wing noted:

> The impression they give of alert intelligence waiting to be released from behind bars....
>
> Autistic children do have a fascination which lies partly in the feeling that somewhere there must be a key which will unlock hidden treasure.[25]

The Myth

Autistic children are not transcendentally beautiful or fey. They are not deaf or blind, and they do not possess superior inner or outer vision. They are not prophets or saviors. Nonetheless, these ideas were shared by many clinicians;

the composite image is a group experience. Therefore, its source is probably cultural. And the image conveyed by clinicians is the same one that many parents have had at the births of their autistic children. Parents' fantasies are detailed in chapter 4 but may be summarized by the myth of the coming of a special child, destined for greatness.

Rimland suggested that autistic children were destined for greatness by conception—by the extraordinary combination of genes that occurred when they were conceived.[26] This idea seems related to the idea of superior parentage and conception associated with the changelings and unearthly beings to whom others compared autistic children. The tradition of extraordinary conception is part of the myth of the coming of the hero.[27] After the hero was born, beauty and prococity often marked him for future greatness. For Rimland, autistic children's handicaps were also related to their superior destiny, and handicaps are common in the lives of mythical heroes. Handicaps and superiorities have been construed in ancient tradition and by modern parents of autistic children as marks of the special child, the future leader.

If traits incorrectly attributed to autistic children are derived from heroic myths, the same may be true of traits attributed to their mothers. In some of the better-known hero myths, mothers had to protect their infants against threats from husbands and others. However, in an earlier set of myths, the threat came from the mothers. According to Harding, these mothers were the moon goddesses of various cultures, and the sons whom they destroyed were their favorite children. Among the mother-son pairs were Isis and Horus, Ishtar and Tammuz, Rhea and Dionysus, and Aphrodite and Adonis. The goddesses were characteristically brilliant, haughty, fickle, icy, and withdrawn. Their attitude toward men ranged from coolness and contempt to destructiveness.[28]

Venerated in early times, the moon goddess was no longer an acceptable model for women when Mediterranean cultures developed into the Jewish, Christian, and Moslem ones familiar today. Her incarnations, known as Gorgon, Hecate, and Lamia, were objects of hatred and fear. Her image appeared later in witches—women who were feared, tortured, and killed. The same image probably underlies the concept of the castrating female, feared and avoided by men in modern Western cultures.

Harding's description of these incarnations—"cold-blooded, without human feeling or compassion.....they do not...experience the passion, the desires, the griefs of instinct"—is much like Kanner's description of mothers of autistic children. Delacato suggested that the cold-breasted image of witches was analogous to the refrigerator image of the mothers. The fickleness of moon goddesses was mirrored in Kanner's idea that the mothers alternated between involvement with their autistic children and ignoring them for long periods. If those myths are the source of projections by Kanner and other clinicians, they also may explain the idea that mothers try to destroy their autistic children.[29].

To conclude, the attack on mothers of autistic children seems rooted in ancient myths and fears of dangerous women. The overwrought controversy about the cause of autism and some of the traits attributed to the children also seem rooted in ancient myths. Parents perceive their autistic children to be special at birth or in early infancy. In particular, the children are perceived as good babies who do not need attention. The myths probably contribute to those perceptions. The thesis that such perceptions and associated parental behavior influence the children's development is explored in later chapters.

2

The Autistic Child: Symptoms, Diagnosis, Definition, and Data Biases

Setting aside the mystical qualities attributed to autistic children only partly clarifies the picture. What remains is a huge number of attributes, with writers disagreeing about which are essential. As few as two and as many as seventy-five symptoms have been said to define autism. Definitions have reflected clinicians' viewpoints to such an extent as to invite comparison to the fable about the blind men and the elephant.[1]

Some traits have been attributed incorrectly to the children. Others occur in so few of them as not to be characteristic. Still others arise when children already autistic adapt to their situations, and may be considered secondary. The symptoms found in the literature are reviewed in arriving at a definition of autism. First, the pattern is exemplified. Although most autistic children are boys, the girl to be described serves ideally as an introduction for what follows.[2]

A Sad-Eyed Cherub

Elizabeth is a sad-looking child of three. She does not talk. Her walk is immature, with poor balance. She does not run at all. Her eating is limited to mashed and finely cut food, eaten in a set manner. If her mother gives her a spoon, placing it in a certain position in Elizabeth's hand, and then holds Elizabeth's hand in a certain way, Elizabeth eats. If her mother is not faithful to the details of the ritual—for example, if she supplies another utensil or if her mother holds Elizabeth's hand too near the fingers or too far from them, too lightly or too firmly—Elizabeth does not eat. Before the mother submitted to this routine, mealtime was extremely trying for both.

In the past, Elizabeth banged her head against hard objects much of the time. Now, she does it occasionally. Her usual activity is rocking, and she chooses to be alone most of the time. If someone enters the room, she moves to a corner, turns to sit facing a wall, or leaves the room. She occupies herself for hours and makes few demands. Partly for this reason, her mother says, "She is too good a child."

A major activity, while sitting and rocking, is scratching the walls, the heating vents, or the grill at the bottom of the refrigerator with her fingers. She does this until her fingers bleed but shows no sign of pain. And under other conditions in which children suffer pain, she does not show signs of distress.

25

She is often unresponsive, seemingly deaf. On the whole, she seems hardly alive, staying in one place, appearing not to give or receive signals or to feel or need anything. Nothing has been found wrong with her senses or any other part of her body to account for her behavior.

In each of these respects, Elizabeth is typical of autistic children. She shows Kanner's two basic symptoms: heavy use of rituals that give daily activities a highly repetitious, unchanging character, and extreme isolation. She also shows the varied symptoms that other writers have listed as criteria of autism.

Symptoms

Ritual and Change

Many rituals of autistic children affect their parents. Eating, dressing, washing, and going-to-bed rituals particularly tend to force parents to involve themselves. However, most of the children's rituals are solitary. A common one is following an undeviating path in going from one room to another. Autistic children also engage in simpler repetitive activities that are not always identified as rituals. Many have objects they carry wherever they go and play with for minutes or hours. An example is a stone on a string, which is set spinning or swinging, over and over.

Autistic children's rituals are similar to those of compulsive and ordinary people. Rituals usually have the functions of maintaining self-control and of keeping the environment from changing. That is true of autistic children's rituals. The difference is that theirs are more bizarre and are clung to with more tenacity.

Ritual is not the only way autistic chidren prevent change. If parents buy new furniture, rearrange furniture, or even move a chair slightly from its usual position, the children may protest so much or be so unhappy that their parents may feel compelled to restore the original situation. After a number of such episodes, parents may stop making changes.

Isolation

The nature and function of isolation are less clear and reflect opposition between proponents of psychological and organic causes. Kanner, to whom isolation was the most basic symptom, also called it aloneness, detachment, withdrawal, and inability or disability to relate. These terms had different meanings. By withdrawal, he meant a reaction to negative parental influence, as when he said:

Regardless of the problems of heredity and constitution, life experiences have confused these children, made normal relationships impossible, and driven them to withdrawal and schizophrenic behavior.[3]

When Kanner spoke of inability to relate, however, it usually was coupled with the phrase "from the beginning of life," implying an innate cause.

As different writers use it, the concept of isolation refers to a variety of behaviors including preoccupation with nonsocial activities, altered consciousness, unresponsiveness, simulated lack of awareness of surroundings, and avoidance of people. The behaviors probably arise at different times in a child's life and have different functions.

Communication

After ritual and isolation, language deficiency is the most commonly cited feature of autism. The usual report is that speech is lacking or peculiar and not used to communicate. Kanner gave increasing emphasis to language deficiency, in time raising it to be the third major symptom. But he also repeatedly emphasized that autistic children seemed more lacking in speech than they were. He said they could communicate effectively by speaking and that they did so at times.

Those children who are verbal show many peculiarities of grammar, pronunciation, and usage. What they say is often baffling. Common words are not used (*I, yes,* and *mama*), while rare ones may be. Many of the children mimic adults' speech and television commercials. Sometimes the mimicry is extraordinarily accurate in content and tone. Words may be recalled verbatim months or even years after they were heard. Less-common communication peculiarities include:

Answering a question with a question;

Pedantic language;

Literalness;

Metaphor;

Tone that is flat, singsong, or atypical;

Singing but not talking;

Fragmentary speech, trailing off;

Use of grunts, clucks, and other sounds in place of words;

Requesting things by gestures, although able to speak.

Autistic children's writing may contain letter and word reversals. Some write simultaneously with both hands—ordinary writing with one and mirror-image writing with the other.

Sensation

Autistic children's peculiar use of their senses also has baffled adults. By appearing not to hear, some have been diagnosed and treated medically as deaf. Many appear not to feel pain. On the one hand, these and other nonuses or selective uses of senses have led to inferences that autistic children had defective senses and to hypotheses that the defects were the cause of autism. On the other hand, autism has been explained on the basis of supernormal acuity.[4]

When clearly using their senses, they do so in odd ways. A child who shows no reaction to loud noises may jump at sounds so faint that others do not hear them. Another who seems oblivious to nearby events watches distant ones that others are not aware of. In addition, the children often rely on peripheral vision rather than looking at the object to which they are attending. Such behavior misleads adults into concluding that autistic children are self-absorbed and out of touch when they are attentive. The children also deliberately avoid sensation, as by covering their eyes or ears with their hands.

Another oddity is the impression given that they do not rely on the customary senses—vision and hearing—for apprehending their environment. Instead, they seem to prefer to explore things by touch, smell, and taste.

Testing autistic children's sensory functions is often difficult and sometimes impossible. Abnormal acuities have been reported, but when audiometric and other laboratory tests can be done effectively, normal acuities are found.[5] Therefore, sensory defect is not considered a symptom of autism here. Many writers have interpreted the apparent deafness and blindness of autistic children to be feigning. Some proposed that feigned deafness be considered a symptom of autism.[6]

Eating

Autistic children's eating disturbances are often dramatic and put extreme pressure on a mother. If she does not comply with her child's food preferences and rituals, the child may refuse to eat at all and starve without forced feeding. Malnutrition resulting from eating disturbances probably accounts for the slenderness and shortness of some autistic children.

Disturbed eating is reported in the great majority. It is almost as common as ritual and isolation and more common than other behaviors that have been considered symptoms of autism. Nonetheless, it has been neither considered a symptom nor dealt with in theories about autism.

Sex

Elizabeth, the quiet child described earlier, has another side. She lacks animation when with her mother. But with her father she plays actively, and her wild excitement resembles seizures or orgasms. The clinicians who described Elizabeth suggested that she enjoyed fantasies of impregnation by her father, but they did not elaborate.[7]

In a book about her autistic child, a mother pointedly described the:

> Quivering tensing of all muscles in a kind of passing paroxysm—that response to intense interest or pleasure which has been with her ever since [eight months of age] yet which no doctor has ever seen....[8]

But she said no more on the subject. Like these, most references to sexual behavior in autistic children are brief, vague, incomplete, or noted without comment. Such references are infrequent, and the children often are described as asexual.

Sexual taboos may account for the fragmented reporting of plainly sexual activities. By contrast, symbolic or quasi-sexual behaviors are reported more fully and are said to be characteristic of the children: a variety of rhythmic movements, including rocking and self-stroking, that commonly are called autoerotic. In addition, autistic children sometimes are described as very sensual. Adding the different kinds of erotic and quasi-erotic behavior, it would seem that autistic children engage in more sexual activity than others. Kanner said hypersexuality was characteristic.[9]

Movement

Other peculiarities of movement are also common:

Whirling on their own initiative,

Whirling when given a turn of the head,

Running to and fro,

Bouncing,

Walking on their toes and in other peculiar ways,

Banging or rolling their heads,

Mouthing and licking things,

Grinding their teeth,

Blinking,

Wiggling their fingers near their eyes,

Grimacing,

Allowing themselves to be molded by others (waxy catalepsy),

Moving their fingers as if double jointed or made of dough,

Moving constantly,

Sitting or standing in one place for hours.

Occasional reports include dancing around an object and "strange, repetitive dance steps, body gyrations, and intricate hand movements."[10] Many of the movements are done repetitively for long periods of time. In addition, autistic children tense their muscles or go limp at unexpected times, especially in infancy.

Interests

Still other activities are associated with objects that fascinate autistic children. They may watch simple rotary or swinging movements of objects for hours. The children play phonograph records or spin wheels, tops, or dishes. They flick strings or rubber bands. Some turn light switches or faucets on and off; others open and close doors. Still others rattle stones in a can or tear paper. Many autistic children devote themselves to hobbies involving arithmetic, music, electricity, geography, astronomy, and meteorology and attain extraordinary skills in them. In general, mechanical objects are said to interest the children particularly. They may collect worthless items (bits of lint). Television commercials interest many and are mimicked repeatedly. In addition, absorption in the activities and sensations of their own bodies (breathing, heart beat) is common.

The converse of their unusual interests is the lack of ordinary ones. Autistic children seem unresponsive and indifferent to their environment. Some seem concerned with nothing beyond their daily routine; others seem not even to care about the necessities of life. But the indifference is more apparent than real.

Miscellany

Toilet training is usually a problem with autistic children. In most, it takes long to accomplish, and relapses are common. Play with feces is also reported.

Unusual, intense fears are common but may be accompanied by reckless behavior. For example, the same child may be described as fearing heights and as often climbing to the tops of bookcases or ledges. Fear of strangers and strange surroundings is common, as is wandering away from home.

Sleep is usually a problem. Many resist it vigorously or wake in terror or in other unusual mental states. Nocturnal laughter, wandering, and screaming are said to be common.

The following also have been mentioned as typical of autistic children:

Imitating animals and inanimate things;

Not imitating people;

Adhering firmly to principle;

Being negativistic, stubborn, resistive to learning, and incorrigible;

Being unaware of people, indifferent to them, or treating them as inanimate objects;

Averting gaze and looking through people;

Staring;

Being intensely vigilant;

Scowling, frowning, and looking sad or puzzled;

Laughing without apparent reason;

Lacking expressiveness;

Having "pale alabaster complexions and a remote trance-like expression"[11];

Being immobile, lethargic, or stuporous;

Having violent tantrums;

Throwing and destroying things (not necessarily during tantrums);

Mutilating themselves (especially self-biting and hair pulling);

Being accident prone and making suicide attempts;

Lacking overt aggression and competitiveness;

Concentrating poorly;

Concentrating unusually well;

Being indifferent to possessions;

Being upset by things that are broken and incomplete;

Being inconsolable after a loss (as of a toy);

Panicking at a slight change in the environment;

Being indifferent to cataclysmic changes.

Another group of behaviors associated with autism occurs in early infancy, long before the diagnosis of autism is made:

Being uncuddly, manifested in

> not wanting to be picked up;

> stiffening, squirming, or crying when picked up;

> not molding to the adult's body when picked up;

> not assuming an anticipatory posture for being picked up;

Being a good baby, manifested in

> being content alone for hours;

> making few demands on mother;

Clinging desperately to parents;

Scanning the room.

Finally, traits that cannot be classified as symptoms have been associated with autistic children. For example, the children are disproportionately boys and, in some reports, disproportionately Jewish and firstborn or only children.

Despite the length of this list, there is more. "The list of symptoms could be extended to very great length, for no two autistic children display exactly the same symptoms.[12] A number of contradictory pairs were juxtaposed above, and the opposites of other traits could be added. Some of the contradictions reflect disagreements among clinicians, but a number of writers believe that paradoxical or self-contradictory combinations of behaviors characterize autistic children. Szurek suggested that such paradox is the chief symptom of autism.[13]

Some of the variability among autistic children reflects age of onset. In general, the older they are at onset, the more their behavior resembles that of schizophrenic adults.

From a scientific viewpoint, the list of traits is unsatisfactory—much too long. The aggregate is not a good basis for defining a disease, a mental condition, or any kind of category. It has been suggested that autism is not an entity but that it consists of a number of disturbances. Attempts to subdivide the category, as into autism of insidious or sudden onset, have not proven useful so far.

Wing suggested that some behavior associated with autistic children be thought of as conditioned to particular relationships or contexts rather than as properties of the children.[14] That idea seems applicable to much of the behavior. Before suggesting which behaviors may be basic and which incidental, the course of autism and its relationship to other handicaps is discussed.

The Course of Autism

More controversial than the symptoms of autism is its course. The issue is whether autism is present at birth, implying organic causes, or whether it arises later, implying psychological causes. The argument is oversimplified: a congenital, organically caused phenomenon need not be manifest at birth or even in childhood. Nonetheless, the question of when autism occurs has become a battleground.

The age at which a specific diagnosis is made depends upon on how soon parents bring a child to a clinician who uses the diagnosis. Pediatricians and family physicians have not ordinarily used the diagnosis of autism, so that referral to a psychiatrist, psychologist, or clinic was necessary for it to be diagnosed. Since referrals seldom are made before the age of three, autism usually has been diagnosed after that age. Then, using the histories given by parents, clinicians have estimated age of onset retrospectively, the estimates reflecting their leanings about causes as well as the accuracy of the histories given them.

Histories given by parents about the development of autism may be divided into three patterns:

1. Gross deviance from birth, with a number of behaviors never having developed;
2. Mild to moderate disturbance in infancy, followed by severe disturbance;
3. Fairly normal or precocious development at first—sometimes for a year or two—and then a decline, sudden or gradual.[15]

Each pattern has been accepted by some workers as the true course of autism. However, each is oversimplified since autistic children develop rather unevenly. At any time during the first few years, an autistic child is likely to be learning some skills, not showing or avoiding use of other skills already learned, and regressing in still others.

The question of whether or not autism is present as early as the first months of life cannot be answered in the form that it typically is posed. Autism usually is defined by a set of symptoms that include some—

particularly speech—that are not ascertainable in the first months.[16] In that respect, autism cannot be diagnosed or said to have begun in the first months without altering the meaning of the term. The occurrence of some autistic or autisticlike behavior can be ascertained in the first months but is not a reliable indicator that autism will follow. This does not mean that autism is not present in the first months. As noted, the concept of autism is in need of revision. How it is redefined will determine whether it can be identified that early.

While some workers have claimed cures of autism, they are rare. Without treatment, some improvement is common. As they grow older, autistic children speak more, have better contact with adults, and become more tractable. Some are able to attend ordinary classes. However, even with such amelioration, most fall further and further behind their peers and do not achieve independence.

The improvement that occurs with age or treatment usually is viewed as a change within the basic, permanent condition of autism. Most are considered autistic for life. But the diagnosis they carry, "early infantile autism" as Kanner called it, has been limited by name and by diagnostic practice to the early part of life. As the children grew older, most were given another diagnosis—schizophrenia (as defined for adults) or retardation. The new diagnosis occasionally reflected a change of symptoms, but for most children it meant that they had reached an age at which autism was not used as a diagnosis.[17]

By usage, autism is a diagnosis of extreme disturbance. The usual classification of diseases into mild, moderate, and severe is applied rarely to autism. The symptoms of autism in themselves can be rated from mild to severe and thus do not preclude the occurrence of mild or moderate autism. But such diagnoses are not used. Many moderately autistic children are diagnosed as compulsive. Many others, together with mildly autistic children, are not diagnosed at all. Most children in these groups grow up to lead independent lives, although a substantial minority suffer breakdowns by the time they reach adulthood and then are diagnosed as schizophrenic.

As those diagnosed as autistic grow older, institutionalization becomes increasingly likely. The devotion of hours each day to caring for the children and educating them, with little to show for it, becomes harder and harder to sustain. School may offer the hope of relief, especially for those children who are verbal and intellectual. But most autistic children do not fit into regular schools; many are rejected by special schools also.

At about eight, perhaps after a couple of years in special programs or special day schools, residential placement is likely to be considered. At first, placement in quasi-institutional schools is tried. Relatively few of the children return to the family for long from these schools or graduate to lead independent lives. Some leave the schools to live with a foster family or in a boarding home and may hold jobs. Others, on approaching adulthood, are placed in sheltered facilities that combine work and residence. Most eventually are placed in institutions for the psychotic or retarded. Those who stay with their families are most likely to achieve a measure of autonomy as adults. Marriage is rare among them.

Definitions and Diagnoses

There are many definitions of autism. The lack of a scientific foundation for identifying basic symptoms has resulted in a proliferation of symptom sets based on what has impressed different workers as essential and on factor analysis. Until a definition can be validated by functional or structural data, the operational meaning that autism has for clinicians may be useful in considering how to define it. The operational meaning may be seen in clinicians' diagnostic practices.

Whatever stated definition clinicians use, the fact that autistic children eventually are rediagnosed as schizophrenic or retarded adults indicates a relationship among the three groups. The idea of such a relationship goes against traditional beliefs, however. The dilemma was resolved for Kanner and many other clinicians by concluding that autism and schizophrenia were the same. They suggested that the form a disturbance takes depends upon the age at which it appears. Specifically, their view was that the symptom differences among autistic children, schizophrenic children, and schizophrenic adults were due to the stage of mental development already present when the disturbance appeared.[18]

The idea that schizophrenia and retardation are closely related goes against beliefs that have a longer history and are held more strongly. How they may be related cannot be specified until retardation is defined better. Problems in current definitions of retardation are greater than in definitions of autism and schizophrenia. Nonetheless, a few points may illuminate the relationships between schizophrenia and retardation and between autism and retardation.

For convenience, retardation may be divided into two categories: organic and other. Organic defects associated with retardation usually are discovered at birth or soon after. When that occurs, a diagnosis of retardation is made in infancy. Autistic children cannot be diagnosed at present as autistic or retarded in infancy in this way because relevent organic findings are lacking.

About 90 percent of children diagnosed as retarded have no identifiable organic defects and are not given the diagnosis in infancy. They are diagnosed later on the basis of failure to learn and of low performance on intelligence tests. If the same standard were applied to autistic children, the great majority would be diagnosable as retarded during their preschool and early school years.

Despite limited learning and low scores on intelligence tests, autistic children are considered intelligent by most clinicians. If they are intelligent, that does not necessarily distinguish them from children diagnosed as retarded. Unconventional measures of intelligence have shown that a large minority of people diagnosed and institutionalized as retarded are intelligent.[19] Most children diagnosed as retarded behave autistically, and some workers consider retardation and autism to be much the same.[20] At present, it is questionable whether autistic children can be distinguished objectively from most children diagnosed as retarded.

Although official definitions of retardation were broadened in recent decades, with less emphasis on organic defects, most clinicians continued to believe that undiscovered defects were usually present. The belief was consistent with their diagnostic practices. If a child had been diagnosed as retarded in the absence of organic findings, a subsequent finding of brain impairment usually was taken as confirmation of the diagnosis.

The opposite was true in diagnosing autism. The majority diagnosed it when organic factors were absent. "Usually, only after clearly identifiable, direct physical causes have been ruled out is a diagnosis of autism considered."[21] The diagnosis usually has meant "the complete absence of any evidence of physical or neurological defect."[22] Also, if a child had been diagnosed as autistic in the absence of organic findings, a subsequent finding of organic impairment was taken as disconfirmation of the diagnosis, and the diagnosis was changed.[23] (A minority of clinicians followed the opposite practice. For them, organic findings confirmed a diagnosis of autism.)

In this respect, the practice in diagnosing schizophrenia in older children and adults has long been the same as in diagnosing autism. Many clinicians believed that undetected organic defects caused schizophrenia, but when they were found in people diagnosed as schizophrenic, the diagnosis usually was changed.

These practices imply a conceptual distinction, with retardation on one side and autism plus schizophrenia on the other. Despite official definitions, the concept of retardation that underlies diagnostic practice is that it is an innate, lifelong limitation on intelligence. Despite the beliefs of most clinicians, they diagnose autism and schizophrenia only when they cannot find organic factors.

Some implications for differential diagnosis follow. Differentiating between autism and schizophrenia may not be necessary. The idea that autism is schizophrenia of very early onset is consistent with enough data to be accepted tentatively. If equivalence is confirmed, the fact that autistic children are rediagnosed as schizophrenic when they grow up no longer will raise a question.

Autism may be distinguished from retardation that is diagnosed in infancy insofar as autistic children do not have the diseases associated with organic retardation. The finding of one of the diseases in a child already diagnosed as autistic probably would indicate changing the diagnosis to retardation.

Retardation has been attributed to sensory deprivation and subcultural deprivation, as in ghetto children. Autism seems distinct from such retardation and would not be diagnosed in children whose behavior is due to those experiences.

Familial retardation refers to the inheritance of low intelligence without disease. Autism is associated with parents of average or superior intelligence and, thereby, is distinct from familial retardation.

What remains is retardation attributed to psychological causes—to experiences other than deprivation that result in a pervasive disturbance with low intellectual functioning. This category, which may contain the largest number of people diagnosed as retarded, is not defined well enough to be identified with or distinguished from autism or schizophrenia. The ambiguous category of psychological retardation allows for autistic children to be rediagnosed as retarded even though there may be no indication for a change of diagnosis.

A Pervasive Developmental Disorder

Autism seems more than a disease or disturbance as those terms are commonly used. It is more than a set of symptoms that together comprise a handicap in limited areas of functioning. Autism seems better described by a term in widening use—*pervasive developmental disorder.* It seems to be a general adaptation or personality organization that affects all major aspects of life.

Writers have noted that all autistic behavior is found in nonautistic children.[24] The adaptation known as autism is made up of ordinary behavior that is extraordinary because of its timing, frequency, fixity, and persistence. A very large number of behaviors is associated with autism because the adaptation is extended into many activities and situations. As the children develop, any new experience can be incorporated into autistic operations, any new skill can develop in an autistic mold. Because autism begins early, few patterns of behavior are sufficiently established to develop independently of it.

It should be possible to identify a core of autism—a set of operations that become pronounced early, that influence subsequent development, and that recruit other behaviors into the eventual organization of personality. Reasons for choosing some behaviors as primary, for considering others derivative, and for adding some that are not traditional are found in analyses in later chapters. Thus, the following list of primary features of autism is part of the conclusion of the book.

Disturbed attachments,

Negativism and inhibition of many actions and sometimes of all action,

Ritual,

Peculiar learning,

Self-stimulation and altered consciousness.

Isolation is certainly characteristic, but the idea that isolation refers to a group of functionally different behaviors was touched on and is elaborated later. For that reason, isolation is not included. Defective speech can be interpreted as a result of negativism, inhibition, and peculiar learning. This and other derivations are discussed in later chapters.

If these five features define a pervasive developmental disorder, is it the only one in early childhod? Spitz defined two disorders in infancy that he called *marasmus* and *anaclitic depression*.[25] Marasmus gained little acceptance among clinicians. It referred to a condition more extreme than autism, found in neglected institutionalized infants and not in home-reared ones. Anaclitic depression, or simply depression, attributed to separation from mothers, had more-general application and gained some acceptance. The relationship between depression and autism hardly has been explored. They seem to overlap. Of the features suggested as primary in autism, ritual and negativism may not be pronounced in depressed infants and young children, while disturbed attachment, inhibition, and peculiar learning seem likely to be pronounced.[26]

Negativism and inhibition may be identified in the first weeks of life, but other features in the list may not be. Thus, this definition, like its predecessors, does not refer to a condition identifiable that early; but it is identifiable in the first year.

Biases in Developmental Histories

The analyses to be presented rest on an interpretation of available developmental histories of autistic children. The more-detailed clinical histories come largely from the first two decades after Kanner's formulation of the concept of autism, when interest in psychological explanations was at a peak. At that time, before checklists of autistic behavior were used, clinicians relied heavily on parents' impressions. They relied particularly on parents' reports about the sequence in which behaviors appeared in infancy or failed to appear, which was considered critical in diagnosis. Psychiatrists and psychologists usually did not see autistic children during the first three years of life. In addition, the main features of autism were not necessarily observable in the clinician's office. Some autistic children showed their rituals in the office, but others were immobile there. And their unresponsiveness in the office was an ambiguous sign. Many speaking children are mute in the clinician's office. Therefore, even when clinicians saw unresponsiveness, they still relied on parents to know if the children were unresponsive at home. In addition, psychological tests cannot be used ordinarily with autistic children, and medical tests are not relevant except to rule out other conditions. Therefore, clinicians relied more on information given by parents in diagnosing autistic children than in diagnosing others.

The inaccuracy of developmental histories furnished by parents had been considered a problem before autism was identified. Nonetheless, histories furnished by parents of autistic children were accepted because the parents impressed clinicians as much more accurate than other parents. The impression of accuracy was not based on verification of parental accounts but on the wealth of minutely detailed information that parents of autistic children gave clinicians. Often, the information was supplemented by extensive notes or diaries the parents had kept since the births of the children. In addition, the parents often spoke in a detached, impersonal, unemotional way, conveying an impression of objectivity and precision. However, research indicates that histories that sound objective may not be more accurate than disorganized, emotional histories.[27]

High accuracy in parental accounts is not to be expected. Even nonclinical interviews with parents of normal children have yielded rather inaccurate information. Studies show that the more disturbed a child is, the less accurate is the information a parent gives about the child. Also, the more emotionally laden a subject is for a parent, the less accurate is the information given. Particularly likely to be inaccurate is information about the nature of the relationship between parent and child, the child's personality in relation to the parent, and the rearing methods used by the parent. Least accurate of all is information bearing directly on causes of mental and psychosomatic disturbances.[28]

While little verification has been done on parental reports about autistic children, a number of inaccuracies have been found incidentally. Most often noted is the attribution of unresponsiveness to a responsive child, especially during the first months of life. Another is the attribution of unmanageability.[29]

The basis of inaccuracies is sometimes inferable, as in the following excerpt: "For a time the mother felt certain that vision was impaired because the infant refused to look at her."[30] Inaccurate perceptions may be held in the face of compelling evidence for a long time. When an autistic boy was three, his mother decided to consult a specialist. She did not choose a psychologist or psychiatrist but a hearing specialist. Her reasoning was:

> Deafness could account for his inattention, lack of speech, and unhappiness. True, Peter paid no attention to what we said, but he could locate an aeroplane before we were aware of its approach. And he could pick out any note on the piano that my husband played on the violin. Perhaps his deafness was in a high range, which would make speech unintelligible....

(The last hypothesis was contradicted by the prior observation.)

Peter's parents considered him a wonder child. They were intelligent and had long been aware of his bizarre behavior. Some abnormalities had been discounted in the first three years as unimportant. Others had been construed as marks of his superiority.

The hearing specialist did not find Peter deaf. The parents then took him to a speech clinic, hoping to be told that he had a speech defect. When the clinic diagnosed him as psychotic, "I was aghast and unbelieving," the mother reported. Eventually, she accepted the diagnosis, and in writing about her experiences she pointed out the lengths to which she and her husband had gone to misconstrue her son's behavior.

These parents shared a conscious fantasy—that their child was special, superior. In the next case, no fantasy was described, but a similar one is inferable. A mother believed during pregnancy that no man had impregnated her. She reported that her child was born with one foot reversed (heel to toe). Supernatural conception and physical defect are prominent in the tradition of the special child. The child's foot appeared normal, and the clinicians doubted the mother's report of clubfoot. They checked hospital records and stated in their article that the mother's report was untrue. This mother made other incredible statements that were not checked and were presented by the clinicians without question.

Checking histories furnished by parents is rare; reproducing unlikely histories at face value is the common practice. That does not mean clinicians necessarily believe what parents report. Nonetheless, publication of such histories without comment has contributed to the supernatural image of autistic children.

In addition to biases in reporting, much critical information is not given because parents are not aware of it. Some of it involves behavior that is so subtle and quick that it has been observed only by slow-motion study of film with repeated replay.

Inaccuracies found in histories of autistic children do not show a simple trend. Parents report what they consider abnormal, and that depends on attitudes that vary from one to another. Serious physical illnesses and mental symptoms in infancy have been omitted by some parents. In contrast, children who appeared normal during the first year have been described as grossly defective from birth. Probably, the histories parents give at any time reflect their current perception of the child. Fabian concluded that use of the first history given by parents of autistic children was always questionable. Key facts were omitted and were revealed only after rapport with parents was established, which took from one to three years.[31]

Omissions often reflect taboos that affect the questions clinicians ask as well as the answers parents give. Clinicians and parents also are biased by prevailing theories. Negative parental attitudes and rearing practices are thought to cause mental disturbance in children, while positive ones are not. Consequently, negative data are inquired for and, when found, are likely to be reported as significant.

Probably the main bias has been to view behavior as an isolated trait of a child rather than as part of an interaction with the environment. Complex behavior of children develops in the context of relationships with caretakers. Histories given by parents tend to minimize that context. This is particularly true in cases of autism, as is illustrated in the next two chapters.

3

A Retarded Genius: A Case and Interpretation

The next case illustrates three ways of looking at autism. It shows the effects of circumstances and of rapport between clinicians and parents on histories parents give, and it shows how different histories can be reconciled. The material is from a book entitled *Dibs*, which has become the best known in the field.[1]

The Case

When Dibs was three, he was isolated, unresponsive, and seemingly oblivious to people much of the time, not talking and appearing deaf. Most of the time, he was immobile or engaged in quiet, repetitive, ritualistic activities. When interfered with, he became violent, creating serious management problems. On the whole, he was stubbornly oppositional.

His mother, less and less effective in caring for him, in desperation put him in a day school. After two years in the school, he was somewhat improved— more active and speaking a little—but not enough to participate adequately in class. The school staff doubted that they could help him or keep him further and were frustrated by his parents' lack of cooperation. On being informed that the school was considering not keeping him on, the parents proposed that he be sent to a residential school for retarded children. As a last alternative, the school staff proposed consultation with Axline, a child therapist.

The mother agreed, provided that Axline accept certain conditions. When they met, the mother spoke about her son in a cold, detached, scientific way, giving minimal information about him. Then she said:

> I can only refer you to the school for any more details of Dibs' case history. There is nothing more than I can add. And I will not be able to come in for any interviews myself. If that is one of your conditions, we will forget the whole arrangement right now. There is nothing more that I can add. It is a tragedy—a great tragedy. But Dibs? Well, he is just mentally retarded. He was born that way. But I cannot come in for any interviews or questioning.[2]

Dibs' mother was a doctor, known for developing innovations in heart surgery. Her husband was a famous scientist. He was less cooperative than she, refusing to speak at all to Axline, as he had refused to meet with school staff during the time that Dibs had been in the school. No one at the school had even met him.

Thus, the mother and father personified Kanner's image of parents of autistic children—brilliant, haughty, cold, selfishly absorbed in their own affairs, and refusing to alter their ways to benefit their son.

Axline did not press the parents and agreed to treat Dibs without their cooperation. After Dibs had been in treatment a few weeks, his mother asked to see Axline. This time, she gave a much fuller and more-emotional account. She spoke of Dibs as a sad, tragic child, who seemed to want something from her that she felt incapable of giving. He was her first child, and she had felt at a loss with him because of her lack of "real experience as a woman."[3] Axline's impression was that the mother had not experienced love before Dibs' birth, and it seemed that she had not wanted to. She said that she and her husband had been well established in their careers and happy in a marriage based on mutual respect. They had not wanted children or other changes in their lives.

She had conceived accidentally when she and her husband were well on in years. The pregnancy had been unusually difficult and had caused marital problems. Her husband, resenting her for having gotten pregnant, had withdrawn increasingly into his work. They had stopped doing things together.

"And then Dibs was born and spoiled all our plans and our life." He made his parents miserable. "He was such a heartache, such a disappointment from the moment of his birth," inasmuch as "he was so different. So big and ugly. Such a big, shapeless chunk of a thing!" His behavior was also distressing, for he stiffened and cried when picked up; "he rejected me from the moment he was born." Worst of all was his evident defectiveness. "I felt that I had failed miserably. I decided that I would give up my work.....I had lost all confidence in myself....I knew that I would not be able to perform an operation ever again!"[4]

As the months went by, Dibs developed slowly. He did not talk. With her medical training, his mother did not need a pediatrician to tell her that Dibs was grossly retarded. Her husband concurred. Apprehensive about being asked to show the monstrous baby, they stopped having people in and cut themselves off from their friends. They felt humiliated.

Persistent efforts to train and teach their son were unsuccessful. Reluctantly, they began to seek help. A neurologist found nothing wrong with Dibs. They consulted a psychiatrist, but he was quite unhelpful and the consultation with him "very nearly wrecked our marriage." He insisted on a full work up—a searching examination of the parents as well as the child by a team of clinicians. "They probed without mercy into our personal and private lives.....They seemed to take a sadistic pleasure in their insensitive and cruel persecution." Then, the psychiatrist presented the findings: there was nothing fundamentally wrong with Dibs except that he was "the most rejected and emotionally deprived child he had ever seen." He said it was the parents who were badly disturbed and in need of psychological help.[5]

In the face of this indictment, the parents were bolstered by the fact that they had had a second child, a daughter who had turned out well. "Certainly she is proof that the fault is not ours."[6] Nevertheless, the psychiatrist's words shook them badly, adding to the animosity that had been growing between husband and wife. The marriage continued to deteriorate and came near the breaking point.

This history resembles many given by parents of autistic children. Because it is incomplete, it lends itself to different interpretations. One is that Dibs' condition was innate and was the cause of his parents' distress. Their reactions were fairly typical of parents to whom a handicapped child is born. And their problems were complicated by the failure of clinicians to understand the child's handicap and the parents' situation.

However, if one discounts the mother's statements that she had done everything possible for her child, the history may be interpreted as showing that Dibs' autistic behavior was due to rejection by his parents. The psychiatrist they consulted did discount her statements, and it is easy to speculate about his reasons. The mother's haughty emphasis on the value she and her husband placed on intellect and achievement over home and intimacy probably would have impressed most clinicians adversely. The statement that Dibs rejected her from birth lends itself to the interpretation that she rejected him and then projected her attitude onto him. Such an interpretation is supported by her statement that she had not wanted children. The attribution of physical and mental monstrosity to a child who appeared normal to others also supports an interpretation of parental rejection. Many details of the mother's account that have not been included here are consistent with a picture of a child rejected by parents whose interests were centered in their careers.

After some months of psychotherapy, Dibs began to improve. At first, both parents interpreted this development as a change for the worse.[7] The father became particularly alarmed because as Dibs talked more, what he expressed was animosity toward his father. Nevertheless, the parents allowed therapy to continue.

After further improvement, increasing contact and warmth between Dibs and his mother were noticeable when she brought him to therapy and came for him at the session's end. The mother began to express pride in Dibs. At the end of one session, Dibs told her that he loved her and he hugged her. She responded with tears, clutching his hand tightly. Then she asked to speak to Axline again. To this meeting, she brought things that Dibs had made. She boasted about her son's talent, which she considered "superior and unnatural." In addition, she volunteered further information about the first three years of Dibs' life. Her manner was very different from the haughty coldness of the initial meeting or the tears and bitterness of the second talk. The content was also very different.

She said that she always had known that Dibs was not retarded. Nonetheless, there were times when his unresponsiveness worried her and when she doubted his ability. When he had been an infant she had begun to cram him with knowledge. She had given him a "vast collection of records" and played them over and over to him. "I have read hundreds of books to him. . . I have talked to him constantly, explaining everything around him." And he showed extraordinary precocity, but his achievements did not satisfy her. She added, "I don't think any child was ever so tormented with the constant demands made upon him that he pass this test and that test— always, always he had to prove that he had capacity. He had no peace."[8]

Dibs began to resist his mother's training and testing and to hide from her when she pressed him. At first, he would go under a table; later, he would run out of the room or hide in his room; but she followed him. In time, his evasiveness generalized: he hid from her when she was not training or testing him as well as when she was, and he hid from other people. Finally, he developed more-effective avoidance—ignoring her so much that she no longer knew whether or not he heard what she said to him. In addition, he balked at new learning tasks. As he grew, he narrowed rather than extended his areas of competence to the extent that people outside the family came to look on him as retarded. This second history suggests a basis for understanding Dibs' isolation, seeming deafness, lack of speech, and incompetence generally.

In interpreting both histories, additional data will be used. First, Dibs had been responsive to his grandmother all his life. Second, his sister was conceived deliberately. The mother's decision to have another child was made shortly after Dibs' birth. Her reason was that Dibs would need a companion. Third, when his sister was a toddler, she was sent away to boarding school to give the mother more time with Dibs.

Interpretation

The first version of Dibs' history (combining the first two conversations between his mother and Axline) holds together superficially. The explanations given for actions and events seem plausible. However, much of what the mother said does not make sense from a psychological viewpoint. (Similarly, most people's accounts of their own and their children's lives are plausible only on a superficial level.) Five themes in what Dibs' mother said occur in many cases of autism.

1. The circumstances of Dibs' conception. Accidental and other untimely or unlikely births are frequent in the literature.
2. The mother's perception of Dibs as retarded when he was an infant.
3. The mother's rather extensive training of Dibs.
4. The mother's giving up her career.
5. The mother's isolation of herself from society.

Dibs' father had been furious with his wife over the pregnancy, which he considered a betrayal. He reacted as if she had gotten pregnant deliberately. She justified his reaction to an extent by saying that her pregnancy had ruined their life plans and the basis of their relationship. She even suggested that getting pregnant was a violation of the code of the social-professional circle of which she and her husband were members. Her defense was that no one was responsible for the pregnancy—that it was a chance occurrence. Such arguments have been common, especially in the past when conception was more strongly thought to be in the hands of God or fate. But accidental conception hardly can be argued by a doctor to a scientist—people who consider fertilization a matter of cause and effect. It is not surprising that Dibs' father was dissatisfied with his wife's explanation.

No one questioned the statement, vigorously reiterated by Dibs' mother, that she had not wanted children. In the past, women who claimed to have wanted their children were not always believed. Social pressures on women to conceive and not to abort were heavy. Clinicians suspected that women who really did not want their children said that they did because of social pressures. Recently, the opposite idea has been gaining acceptance: to conceive and to carry a fetus to term, a mother must want a baby, consciously or unconsciously. According to proponents of this view, women who do not want a baby rarely conceive. If they do, they miscarry.[9] While the theory remains to be proven, it has enough support that one may question a statement about a baby who was born not having been wanted.

A more-compelling reason for questioning this mother's statement that she did not want children is the fact that shortly after Dibs was born she decided to have another baby. This decision went against her emphatic statements about her husband's and her attitudes and life plan, the bad effect her pregnancy had had on her marriage, and the disaster that Dibs' birth had been. Against such considerations, her explanation—that Dibs would need a companion—does not contain a sufficient motive. A resolution to have herself sterilized so that no further accidents could occur would have been more consistent with the current crisis, the values she espoused, and her prior life pattern. The abruptness with which she decided to have another child also seems uncharacteristic. In short, her brief explanation does not explain a decision that turned her life around, risked loss of her husband, and risked having a defective baby because of her advanced age. The decision appears to have been impulsive; the gamble it amounted to was extraordinary.

If we assume that, despite her strenuous protest, Dibs' mother wanted children, a number of otherwise puzzling events fit together: her accidental pregnancy, her husband's sense of betrayal, her abrupt and lasting abandonment of her career, and her decision to have another child.

The assumption of such a wish requires more than discounting her statement that she had not wanted children. It also calls into question her assertions that she had been happy in her career and marriage. Perhaps she had been in the early years, but the readiness and permanence with which she gave up her career may be a measure of the limited value it had reached. In addition, frustration in her marriage was indicated more directly in the picture she gave of her husband as extremely insensitive, inconsiderate, and selfish. She suggested that her son had suffered as a result of her frustrating marriage. "Why have I taken out on Dibs the strained relationship that grew up between my husband and myself?"[10]

Probably, she had changed during the years they were married, while her husband had not. She evidently never mentioned any wish for children to him. "I thought the role of a mother wouldn't interest or hold a man of such brilliance."[11]

Women who have little interest in children, who are committed to careers, and whose life plans are jeopardized by an unplanned pregnancy are likely to consider an abortion. If they have a baby, they are likely to turn the care over to someone else when they can and resume their careers. Dibs' mother seems not to have considered an abortion, although her social-professional class was the most accepting of such a solution. She was also in a position to have had others care for Dibs but did not do so. In the circumstances, devotion to her son was not to be expected. Nonetheless, devotion was what he received and more of it than wanted children ordinarily receive. She poured her time and energy into him; she restructured her life with him as its focus.

Much of her effort went into training Dibs. In his second year she devoted herself to teaching him to read. With a storehouse of educational materials, she spent a great amount of time instructing him step by step, and she succeeded:

> His father said that I was out of my mind when I told him Dibs could read. He said no two-year-old could learn to read, but I knew he could. I had taught him to read.[12]

She was able to do this because her husband made few demands on her time, leaving her with her son. When her second child's need for attention interfered, "We sent his sister away to school... so I could concentrate on Dibs.[13]

She built her life around Dibs, and he did not satisfy her. When at four he did not talk, seemed incompetent, and was a management problem, her disappointment was understandable. The question is why he was "such a disappointment" when born and why he still did not satisfy her at two, when he talked, read, and had an extensive knowledge of music and plants and extraordinary craftsmanship in drawing. In his second year, he learned at an astonishing pace (consistent with an I.Q. of 168 that he scored after treatment). What his mother expected is unknown. She seemed to expect more than an ordinary child.

Dibs' mother did not consider a psychological explanation for conceiving him or that she might have erred in taking contraceptive precautions. She adhered to the idea that conception had been an accident. This idea is related to the idea of supernatural conception. It derives from primitive thinking in which all accidental events are attributed to the intervention of supernatural beings. That is particularly true when a woman conceives accidentally after many years of childlessness, as was true of Dibs' mother. In addition, she thought of his powers as unnatural. These are the indications that she expected a special child with supernatural powers.

Most women have expectations and fears during pregnancy of bearing a supernatural creature—a monster or savior or a combination of the two. The fantasies may persist after birth and explain the disappointment that some women experience at the first sight of their babies (chapters 5 and 6). The fantasies also contribute to misperceptions of their babies. Then, within days or weeks, the fantasies, misperceptions, and disappointments fade. They may be forgotten or remembered as curious ideas of no importance. For Dibs' mother, the experience did not fade; when he was five, she remembered her disappointment vividly.

On the one hand, Dibs' mother explained much of the rather extensive intellectual training she gave him by her concern that he was retarded. On the other hand, she said that she knew he was not retarded. When she doubted his intelligence, she must have known as a physician that congenital retardation occasionally can be treated medically. However, she did not seek medical consultation during his infancy. In addition, she probably knew that overtraining retarded children is harmful, not helpful. And when Dibs later did function at a retarded level, she stopped training him. She did most of the training when he was clearly precocious—when she knew that he was precocious and was proud of him for it. Therefore, the idea that he was retarded does not account for the extensive training given him.

Some of the biographies by parents of autistic children describe even more-extensive training than Dibs received.[14] The usual explanation is that the children seemed defective, and the training was designed to bring them up to the average. In some cases, subnormal functioning did lead to training, but in others the training came first and was associated with precocity. That was Kanner's general finding: parents devoted enormous efforts to teaching their autistic children to identify musical pieces and to memorize prayers, catechisms, and the names of presidents and state capitals during their infancy.[15] The parents were training for superiority.

Dibs' mother said that she gave up her medical career because of the loss in self-confidence that resulted from bearing a defective child. However, he was not defective at the time she decided to give up her career, and later, when she knew that he was precocious, she did not resume her career. Therefore, the idea that he was retarded does not account for her giving up her career.

Many other parents gave up careers to devote themselves to their autistic children. Some regretted the loss, but others said that their relationships with the children were the most valuable parts of their lives.

Dibs' mother explained her self-imposed seclusion as a reaction to having borne a misshapen, retarded child. Again, he was not misshapen or retarded, and the reason given does not explain the action taken. Probably, the mother's seclusion and her perception of her infant son as misshapen had a common source—the myth of the birth of the hero.

The wish to have a child was suggested as an explanation of a number of events surrounding Dibs' life. The wish to have a special child could explain more of them, including the mother's sacrifice, misperception of her child, shame, and seclusion.

The situation of career women is still difficult. In the past, following a career usually required going against considerable social pressure and overcoming serious obstacles. Few women attempted it. Of those who did, fewer still persevered long enough to transcend the limits society placed on them, to gain distinction through achievement. Most who started careers were tempted strongly to revert to what they had been raised for, to follow the easier path to a potentially higher goal—immortality through motherhood. The more brilliant, talented, and highly trained they were, the more they tried to substitute for career achievement the creation of a wonder child. The ambition, energy, resourcefulness, and tenacity that earlier had carried them against societal obstacles were redirected into the child.

When one seeks to transcend one's life through another person, one tends to endow the person with beauty and other virtues beyond reason, as in infatuation. Probably that is the basis for parental attribution of beauty and grace to autistic children.

The perception of an autistic child as ugly is rare. More common is parental attribution of an animal quality. Usually it is an unattractive quality, associated with sensuality, wildness, and lack of inhibition or socialization. The mother's description of the infant Dibs as "a little wild animal" is so common in the literature of autism that it has been considered characteristic.[16] Monstrousness, ugliness, and animal wildness suggest a negative side of the awe of the children, perhaps a reaction formation against infatuation with them.

Dibs' mother and father seemed at first to fit Kanner's phrase, "refrigerator parents." Coldness and detachment from their son were what they portrayed and seemed to explain his behavior. Only one of the clinicians and teachers to whom Dibs was brought got to know the passionate side of Dibs' mother and her devotion to him and how they affected his development. None got to know his father.

Dibs' nonperformance and stubborn oppositionalism have been interpreted as a reaction to extreme training pressure. And the pressure was seen as a result of the redirection of the mother's energies from her career into her child's life. Such redirection occurred in the lives of many parents of autistic children but not in all. A number of circumstances can bring a parent to seek immortality through a special child. Different conditions at or about the time a child is born—including peculiarities in the child—can foster the effort. The parent's motives are background. The training given directly influences the infant's development. The kind of training broadly described here need not lead to autism; sometimes it leads to genius. Assuming that a child is well endowed, the difference in outcomes depends upon details of the training and upon other experiences in growing up.

4

The Special Child: More Cases and a General Interpretation

The interpretation of Dibs' case may be put in the form of a broad hypothesis. During infancy, autistic children become extremely important to one or both of their parents, and some aspects of the resultant devotion foster autistic behavior. Extreme parental involvement has been noted as a reaction to autism. Parents commonly react that way to a handicapped infant, and such reactions account for some of the devotion seen in parents of autistic children. What is hypothesized here is involvement that precedes autistic behavior. In many cases, the involvement precedes the birth of the child.

The hypothesis is made more specific and qualified in later chapters. Here, it is applied in its broad form to the literature on autism, beginning with book-length cases—those richest in interpersonal data. The idea that parents are extraordinarily involved with their autistic children while portraying themselves as cold, indifferent, callous, or rejecting toward them is best illustrated in a number of biographies written by parents.

Rejection and Devotion

After learning that her child was autistic, one mother read Kanner's description of refrigerator parents and concluded that it fit her and her husband rather well. She described herself as compulsive, inhibited, awkward, and uncomfortable with sensuality. Some of her body's reproductive activities seemed a joke that feminine biology played on her, particularly her unintended pregnancy.

She had two girls and a boy, all planned. When she completed their early rearing and was preparing for a career as a college teacher, she accidentally became pregnant. Depressed and resentful, she postponed her career indefinitely.

The girl who was born to her then, Elly, was an immediate disappointment. The mother had wanted a boy "because you can dream bigger dreams for a boy," and she thought she had given birth to one. Then, at the first sight of Elly and the realization that she was a girl, the mother sadly felt that "they took my little boy away."[1] Elly became a problem infant, requiring more attention than the other three children had and making her mother feel imprisoned.

So far, the history suggests that Elly was an unwanted child of a cold mother whose interests lay outside the home when Elly was born. In addition, Elly may have become the object of her mother's resentment over the unplanned pregnancy and postponement of career plans. That was the impression the mother gave. She described her care of Elly as given grudgingly.

Despite the mother's deliberate characterization of her relationship with Elly in these negative terms, Elly was the child to whom she became most intimately and powerfully attached. The attachment began in the first months—long before Elly's symptoms appeared. Some details of their early relationship are in sharp contrast to the picture the mother gave of herself as rejecting and as uncomfortable with sensuality and her body. Instead, those details suggest a picture of a sensualist whose care of her baby approached a poetic idealization of motherhood.

She breastfed Elly and in doing so, she experienced an alteration of consciousness with rare feelings of intimacy and serenity. The secluded, blissful periods with Elly were extended until breastfeeding occupied a large part of each day. These days were extended into nine months—beyond the average. This period of unaccustomed sensuality and serenity seems to have been one of the happiest of the mother's life. She seems to have fallen in love with Elly, as indicated by some of her descriptions: a bronzed, gold baby of unusual beauty; a golden child; a fairy child; the dancing grace of her body; her fairy purity. Understandably, "it broke my heart to wean her."[2]

Weaning also seemed to affect Elly badly, and by the time she was two, her mother perceived her as retarded and began an intensive program of training in basic skills. Mother and daughter were to spend hours a day at it—an experience distressing to both and sometimes excruciating. It was to go on for years.

Like Dibs' mother, Elly's was not particularly constrained by economic factors or class values to follow the course she took. Rather than being made a prisoner, she chose to have the baby, to seclude herself with Elly, and to make Elly the center of her life. When she concluded that Elly was retarded, she made the decision to devote herself to Elly, aware that it would be at the expense of family and career. The decision was her own, without solid encouragement from others and without any basis for knowing that the training would be successful. Elly became her career. She did not hire someone to take over Elly's care—neither in the first year when things were going well nor in the second year when they went badly. She did not turn Elly's care over to a grandmother. In short, she did not do what many other women in her social class have done about a child conceived untimely.

In another case, an unplanned pregnancy led to prolonged deliberations about what to do because "we did not want Noah."[3] The woman expected that having the baby would be disastrous (and events proved her correct). She therefore insisted on having an abortion. Her husband agreed. Nonetheless, they decided not to have one on the grounds that they could not afford it. They were, indeed, short of money, but having a baby costs far more than an abortion.

The decision to have a baby or not is one of the most important in a parent's life. When people make such decisions for seemingly irrelevant or trivial reasons, they are unaware of more-serious reasons. In this case, the father found transcendental gratification in his love of Noah, and both parents entered new careers as a result of having the baby.

Another mother said after the premature birth of her autistic child, Joan, "Even though I had looked forward very much to having this baby, I only wanted her to survive if she would be healthy and normal in every respect." The idea that the mother did not want the baby was supported by the fact that she avoided contact with her for weeks and declined to give her a name for three months. She said, "I do not really know why we had not named her until now. . . . . Perhaps, for us, the giving of a name would have denoted acceptance of her as a member of our family." This seemingly callous rejection of Joan was a last-ditch resistance against a powerful desire for her. "Despite my attempts to control my feelings, I loved her a little more each time I saw her."[4] And the mother developed an attachment to Joan that was exclusive and all consuming. Her husband and sons were left to themselves. The achievements of Joan—the autistic child—became the mother's greatest source of pride and the basis of her life's meaning.

In the case of Dibs, Elly, Noah, and Joan, the mothers encouraged people to see them as callous toward their autistic children. In three of the cases, their apparent coldness and rejection of the children were seriously misleading. (Whether the fourth mother's apparent rejection of her infant was also misleading is difficult to ascertain because the account was written by the father and reveals much more about him than his wife.)

The extraordinary attachment and devotion of Dibs', Elly's, and Joan's mothers go against the women's stated intentions and seem out of character with their past lives. Many mothers of autistic children—especially in Kanner's sample—came from social settings in which women commonly hired nursemaids to care for their children while they pursued careers, community service, or leisure activities. They were not compelled by the conventions of their subculture or by economic limitations to give up their educational interests or careers when they became pregnant. Nonetheless, they did so. Despite protests of how grim and depressing they found motherhood and claims that their interests lay elsewhere, motherhood was what they did not give up.

Conformity accounts for the behavior of many women who put aside their individual choices under social pressure to be mothers, but conformity does not explain the behavior of these women. Many of them were nonconformists—individualistic, courageous, stubborn, accustomed to making their own decisions. The biographical accounts show remarkable tenacity in defying authority and social pressure. And they seem to have been unusually free of demands from husbands to give up careers or to have and keep the children.

In these cases, strong parental attachment was reasonably evident. In others it was not. My hypothesis is that in many cases attachment was masked by what appeared to be indifference. Most parents are ambivalent toward their children, and extreme ambivalence may appear as indifference. That is, indifference may be the outward manifestation of a combination of love and hate. Contradictory impulses often immobilize a person, giving an impression of unemotionality when strong emotions are present. Attachment also may be masked by depression and denial.

Hope and Despair

The devotion of the parents described earlier combined hope and despair in their children. They perceived the children as superior, even superhuman, and tried to rear them accordingly. They also perceived the children as defective, sometimes hopelessly and permanently so, while trying to remedy their defects. These contradictory perceptions were intertwined, sometimes in conscious ideas of defects as marks of superiority. The combination of these ideas with devotion to the children seems to develop along the following lines:[5]

> A child is born at a turning point in a parent's life or the birth causes a major change.
>
> The child is perceived as special and is treated accordingly.
>
> The parent's interests and energies become focused in the child, to the exclusion of other people and activities.
>
> The parent is disappointed in the child.
>
> The parent's energies continue to be focused in the child but in a more-negative vein.

These elements suggest a sequence of events over a period of months, and in some cases that happens. But the events can overlap; all of them may begin on the first day after a child is born. The elements are also too general. Many times in a person's life can be picked out as critical, especially by hindsight. Which truly were turning points may be hard to ascertain. In addition, the birth of a child may in itself be critical in a parent's life, particularly when it is a first, only, last, or handicapped child. Many parents perceive one or more of their children as special, particularly in small families. The role of parents, especially mothers, is to devote themselves to their babies, foregoing other interests to an extent. And all parents are disappointed in their children to an extent.

Elly's mother clearly described a turning point. She was reorienting her life from being a homemaker toward an outside career when Elly was conceived. Noah's parents were both going through turmoil and change, attempting to resolve major conflicts about their identities, when Noah was conceived. A considerable number of the cases in the literature similarly involve conscious, identifiable turning points. In some, the mothers were moving toward or away from outside careers when they became pregnant with their autistic children. In others, the mothers thought their marriages might be ending and, therefore, were anticipating major life changes.

In still other cases, as in the case of Dibs, a turning point is inferable, but no deliberate or conscious change was occurring. When a major change is taking place unconsciously, it may be indicated by peculiar behavior, the meaning of which is not clear to the person involved. For example, a person who has no conscious wish for a change may have a vision or perceive omens of a change and then embark on a new career. By inference, leanings toward the new career were present earlier and contributed to the vision or omens but were not conscious then. If detailed information about the person is available, less-dramatic indications of the coming change usually are found.

In myth, turning points are identified by omens or prophecies. Subsequently, the mythical figure begins an ordeal, which ends with a transformation of identity, role, or status or the assumption of a mission. When people sense inner stirrings without realizing that they are moving toward change, they become more alert to omens. They may look for meaning in events to which they otherwise would pay no attention.

Some of the biographies contain suggestions made in passing of omens around the births of autistic children. Others are more explicit and dramatic. One mother left her family when pregnant, had a bizarre experience with a stranger, and was terrified. She seems to have regarded the experience as an omen about the child to come. Later, she began consciously to wish for the coming child to be divinely special and to anticipate that it would be diseased.[6]

Another wrote that, while nursing her eight-week-old child:

[Q]uite suddenly I had a very strong feeling—call it a premonition or what you like—that for some reason or another this child was to be very close to me, would need me very much, perhaps a great deal more than either of my other two children would. At the time I simply attributed this feeling to the fact that he bore my father's name. Perhaps if I were wise enough, it might be my privilege to help him develop into a great spiritual leader.[7]

Perhaps a wish for that to happen had been involved in naming the boy after her father.

A father described his horse, Kahlil, who had a defect that was considered a mark of divine possession:

[S]ociety calls it an imperfection which supposedly often characterizes a more skittish and unpredictable animal. In some stables, an imperfect horse such as Kahlil would be destroyed . . . . . It was this beautiful mark of difference that was this horse's specialness.[8]

Because of the defect, Kahlil was the father's favorite. He was perceived as superior, embodying transcendental spiritual values.

The man's autistic son was born a year after the purchase of the horse and was given the same name. Later, the father thought:

> [H]ow odd and foreboding, to find much of this horse in my special son. Like this statuesque animai, [my son] too had a profound beauty that others found problematic and wanted to discard.[9]

The father endowed his horse and son with the same name and transcendental qualities and then took their similarity as an omen. The father's wish for such a horse and such a son were clear.

The two women and the man began new careers in relation to their autistic children. Their omens are interpretable as unconscious leanings toward the new careers.

The most common omens about special children are unexpected conceptions and peculiar experiences during pregnancy. Accidental pregnancies were discussed earlier. Others that may be taken as signs of a special child to come are conceptions by women who because of age or other reasons consider themselves infertile and conceptions by women whose husbands have been away for extended periods or have become emotionally estranged.[10] Any unexpected pregnancy raises the question "Why now?" which may be answered along supernatural lines. Many autistic children were the result of unexpected pregnancies. Omens during pregnancy are discussed in the next chapter.

A life change need not be desired to give a birth special meaning. In itself, change is disorienting and leads to a search for guidelines—for meaning in events. In addition to the changes mentioned, a birth may be given added importance by a move to a new locale, a spouse getting sick or losing a job, and birth complications. These are so common that their impact can be underestimated. They are reported frequently in histories of autistic children, but they may be equally frequent in histories of other children. The following seem more frequent before the births of autistic children than other children, although comparison data are limited:[11]

Sudden loss by the mother of an idealized lover;

Hasty marriage to an unsuitable or dull husband (often preceded by the first change);

Absence of the husband in unusual or unexpected circumstances;

Regular absence of the husband due to business trips or separation;

Serious illness of the husband or the mother;

An affair by the husband;

A long period of no sex between the parents;

Extreme marital strain, impending breakup of marriage;

Death of the mother's husband, mother, or father;

Abandonment of career or education by the mother;

Abortion, miscarriage, stillbirth, and neonatal death.

These events tend to foster depression in mothers.

Depression

Whatever its causes, depression is so common in women after giving birth that, when not severe, it has been euphemistically called baby blues. Though common, it is often partially disabling and may have serious effects on an infant's development. More than any other disturbance in mothers, severe depression disrupts infant development.[12] For the moment, depression will be discussed as a global condition. Later, the specific behavior of depressed mothers in caring for their infants will be discussed.

Elly's and Noah's mothers were already depressed when the children were born. Joan's mother became depressed during the first months after birth. These cases exemplify the depression in mothers preceding and during their autistic children's infancy that has been reported by a number of clinicians and that is thought to cause autism.[13] Other writers have not reported depression, but their descriptions of the mothers implied it. For example, one suggested that autism was due to maternal rejection that was manifested in neglect. He found that mothers did not call a doctor for sicknesses that, when occurring in nonautistic siblings, did result in calling the doctor. He found autistic children in "unchanged underwear, hair matted with mucus. . . . Parental inattention or carelessness allows the child to get hurt or lost."[14] Most clinicians consider such inattention and neglect to be signs of depression.

Another report also did not mention depression in the mothers but described them on the basis of film analysis as having fixed expressions, subdued voices that were usually flat and sometimes inaudible, and restrained large body movements. In addition, "They frequently seemed immobile if not rigid. Animated behavior was not observed," but much fidgeting was.[15] Depression is also suggested in descriptions of "perplexity" and "paralysis" in mothers of autistic children—confusion, hesitancy, and lack of decisive action.[16]

Similarly, Kanner's descriptions of the parents as cold and mechanical suggest depression. Specifically, the kind of stiff, distant, perfunctory infant handling that he and others found to be characteristic of mothers of autistic children is associated with postpartum depression.[17]

Still other writers neither reported depression in the mothers nor gave details suggesting it. Some of them did not touch on the question; others did not find the mothers depressed before their children's autistic behavior became apparent.

The occurrence of depression in parents of autistic children is not controversial in itself. It is to be expected that, if parents were not already depressed, the grinding experience of having an autistic child would cause depression. The question is whether the parents' depression came before the child's autism and contributed to it or was a consequence of the autism. In many of the cases, depression evidently came first and was intensified later by the child's autistic behavior.

When a mother is depressed—whatever the cause—a common effect is extreme devotion to her infant. The following was cited as typical of the attitudes of depressed mothers:

> I'm glad that God gave me...the privilege of being a mother...and I loved [the children]. In fact, I wrapped my love so much around them....
>
> They were my whole life....

Depressed women were often supermothers, self-sacrificing, with high career aspirations for their children. When asked what they were proudest of in life, they referred to their children. "None mentioned any accomplishment of their own, except being a good mother."[18]

The idea of devotion to an infant may suggest eagerness and enthusiasm. However, devotion, like love, can be desperate and grim. That is usually the case when depression accompanies devotion.

Dedication

Being at a turning point, with or without depression, means that a child born then tends to assume extraordinary importance in one's life and to become the subject of devotion. A boy usually fits with the lofty ambitions that emerge at such times, and a defective child is likely to receive more-intense devotion than a talented or ordinary one. But maleness or defect are unnecessary; any infant born at a turning point in a parent's life is likely to receive special devotion.[19]

It is common in modern Western cultures (in contrast to Spartan ones) for mothers to favor a handicapped child. They also tend to favor a normal child if they consider the child to be handicapped, sickly, or delicate. Clinicians have identified a need for a handicapped child.[20] Despite the burdens of such a child, and despite complaints and protests by mothers, the child so perceived usually has the most intimate contact with them and is their favorite.

10

One of a pair of twins, identical in health and other respects, is sometimes chosen as the sickly one. Actual and imagined sickliness may be taken as an omen of greatness to come because belief in such omens is part of the folklore of many cultures.[21] In addition, many parents feel that something rare and precious is added to their lives by a defective child and that they have been chosen divinely to receive it. Ideas like the following, more common in the past, still are voiced by parents of retarded children:

> Nobody in the world ever really needed me except this one little child. Thank God that he will need me forever.
>
> I love this child and this child loves me. Nothing else in the world really seems to exist.[22]
>
> [P]arents of mongoloids have...joys unknown to the parents of normal children.
>
> [W]e accepted Nigel as a gift from God which we were greatly honored to receive.
>
> [W]e deemed it a great privilege that we were entrusted with this precious soul in a somewhat handicapped body.[23]

The presence of such joys in parents of retarded children—and of autistic children—does not mean the absence of sorrows. For some, the sorrows contribute to exaltation above their prior lives. A mother described her son's autism as "a tragedy which is more grievous than death, more awful than any physical aliment that can strike." Nonetheless, she concluded her book with lengthy expressions of gratitude for the enrichment of her life and for the vocation she found in having this child. Comparing her son and herself to Jesus and Mary, she related a visionary experience:

> [A]t this split-second moment I had found the answer to the reason for my own being as well as that of our small son: that the two of us together were destined to use whatever gifts we might possess for the glory of God and for the good of His millions of mentally retarded children so long as we both should live.[24]

A father wrote that his autistic child brought enrichment, excitement, love, and purpose into his life. "Loving this little boy brought the best in me alive."[25] Another father said his autistic child was the only thing in life he ever really loved.[26] A mother said, "I only live for Chaim."[27]

The biographies written by parents contain the detail of what is touched on or implied in many of the clinical histories. The children are perceived as rare, precious, spiritual, heroic, or awe-inspiring. They may be seen as incarnations of dead ancestors or of gods. Boasting about them is common.[28] In addition, the parents' lives are enriched by the children, given purpose or meaning, or made more spiritual. At the extreme, the parents may become missionaries or speak as prophets.[29] Of their accomplishments, those involving their autistic children are most important to the parents.

Some of the parents described consulting one expert after another about the children and rejecting the advice given them. They went against clinicians, educators, administrators, and statistics. One couple was told that their daughter was severely and hopelessly defective and that she probably never would learn even to recognize her parents. They were urged repeatedly to institutionalize her. The parents seemed hardly to have wavered in the face of this advice and of repeated failures in trying to help her. The father, unschooled for the task to which he set himself, devised his own method of training and socializing his daughter. He and his wife worked with the child daily, often to the point of exhaustion, for years. Their success against all odds might explain their pride in telling the story.[30] However, parents whose efforts met with failure also wrote with pride.

In short, the perception of a defect in a child may lead to devotion that reaches the level of dedication to a cause. Whether a child is considered defective realistically or on the basis of imaginary qualities may not matter. The designated child is more likely than a sibling to receive disproportionate attention and intimacy and to be expected to achieve distinction. Twin studies indicate that the designated child is also likely to become schizophrenic.[31]

Rearing the Special Child

Clinicians have been impressed by the detailed histories parents gave about their autistic children. The detail was often made possible by extensive records the parents had kept, often since birth.

> Few children have ever been observed by their parents with such minute precision. Every smallest detail of the child's development, utterances, and activities had either been recorded in voluminous diaries or were remembered by heart.[32]

The reason often given for starting the diaries was that the parents expected the children to become famous as adults. The records were to serve as source material on the early years for biographies that the parents intended to write about the children after they had achieved fame. Parents who had more than one child chose the one who turned out to be autistic for this project. Rimland suggested that no other group of parents kept diaries.[33]

To implement their expectations, many parents began early to prepare the children. In addition to cramming them with vocabulary, music, poetry, and various lists, according to Kanner, the parents attempted the "earliest possible control of elimination" and even training to walk as early as three months.[34]

Training the infants and testing them on what they had learned required extensive effort. If time used for observing and recording is added, many of the parents seem to have had little time left to do anything else. They gave up other activities. In addition, devotion to the children often was facilitated by going into seclusion with them.[35]

Parents explained the seclusion by their embarrassment over the children's defects or eccentricities.[36] In many cases, however, seclusion began before defects or eccentricities appeared. The pattern has points in common with the phenomenon of hiding children away. In recent folklore, infants were thought to be hidden away because they were monstrous. In reality, when so-called attic or closet children were examined, they were found to be bizarre—retarded, psychotic, or physically defective—but the defects were usually the result of having been kept in closets, not the cause of it. The hiding of children is probably traceable to myths in which infant heroes were hidden for protection against their mothers' husbands. Some mothers have kept their husbands away from their autistic children during infancy.[37] Inasmuch as the mothers' actions were not explained by immediate circumstances, they may have been rooted in mythical ideas.

Sacrifice and Love

Elly's mother gave the impression of sacrificing for her daughter as a duty and not of devotion based on love, tenderness, affection, or joy. The descriptions many other parents gave also indicated duty without love, and the impression was reinforced by statements of not having wanted the children.

In contrast, love was suggested in the portrayal of Elly as extraordinarily beautiful. Parents typically have described their autistic children in such extravagant terms, suggesting that attraction or infatuation was present.

A mother said she was detached from her autistic son, had rejected him since the first time she saw him, and had turned his care over to a nursemaid. In fact, the mother spent considerable time with him, and they shared intimate experiences in which he was sexually aroused. She seems to have been denying their mutual attraction.[38]

A father's avoidance of physical contact with his autistic daughter was extreme. "He never touched her. He confessed that he had to force himself to walk past her outstretched arms with averted face and eyes squeezed shut." Unlike Dibs' mother, he did not describe the girl as repulsive but said she was a "Lovely girl with golden hair. The most lovely hair you ever saw. Gee, I'm crazy about Laura."[39]

Searles suggested that parents who treated their autistic children mechanically, as if the children were nonhuman, did so as a reaction against rather intense feelings toward them.[40] Cases of autism in which personal details or observations are available tend to confirm Searles' hypothesis. Cases that have been reported at length, as in biographies, show evidence of intense parental attachment. Affectionate and sensual components in the attachment often are denied but are indicated nonetheless, as in the previous examples.

Several reasons for denial and underreporting of parental love seem likely. Elly's mother described herself as awkward and inhibited about sensual matters. That does not mean she lacked sensuality but that she was not comfortable with it. Consequently, she avoided some sensual activities and avoided talking about such matters, giving an impression of lack of sensuality and passion. In this respect, she was typical of many parents of autistic children.

Minimizing sensuality toward one's children is probably attributable to powerful taboos. Some parents tell of anger and cruelty toward their children more easily than of love, especially insofar as erotic components are involved. Sexual desires and fantasies involving their children, even when conscious, are the last things parents speak of and arouse the greatest shame in them when they do.

Besides reticence, what parents tell reflects forgetting and reinterpretation. After years of the frustration of living with an autistic child, when parents are close to giving up and placing the child in an institution, they may have forgotten their earlier adoration and the endearing qualities they once saw in the infant. In memory, the whole of a relationship tends to take on the color of its last phase.

Ancient taboos on parent-child love and sex were reinforced by Puritanism in recent centuries and by the stern teachings of psychologists and physicians on child rearing in the first half of this century. Professionals warned that playfulness, affection, eroticism, and even attentiveness toward children were harmful. The old taboos and the newer injunctions did not prevent all parents from being demonstrative, but many who were demonstrative felt that they were doing wrong. In the circumstances, some of them needed special justification for following their inclinations toward children whom they loved. Many felt free to be attentive or demonstrative only when their children were ill. In that context, the perception of a child as sick or defective, supported by a physician's encouragement to devote oneself to the child, provided the justification many parents needed to express themselves. They hid their passion in dutiful or spiritual devotion.

The events described here—life changes, depression, perception of a neonate as special, expectation of future greatness, seclusion, and devotion—may be interpreted as a context within which autism develops in many cases. Parents react differently, and the fact that a parent has experienced some or all of these events does not tell how the parent will behave toward an infant—how attentive, responsive, consistent, or demanding the parent will be and what training the parent will provide. These specific determinants of infant development are explored in relation to autism in later chapters.

Part II
The Unfolding of a Pattern

The interpretation of case material in the last two chapters provides a guide for the analyses that follow, in which a sequence of events leading to autism is hypothesized. The idea that a child will be special is determined by events preceding and during pregnancy and after the child is born. Little is known about events prior to conception (other than traumatic losses) that foster the idea. This part begins with a focus on events during pregnancy that foster expectations that the child to come will be special (chapter 5).

Chapter 6 describes mother-infant interactions during the first months that have disproportionately large effects on infant development. Interactions that bear on the development of infant attachment and on disturbances of attachment are discussed at length in chapters 7 and 8. Disturbed attachment in itself is a major component of autism. In addition, attachment determines socialization and learning.

Parental conditioning of infants, both deliberate and unintended, is analyzed in terms of reinforcement schedules, contingencies, demands, and difficulty of cues in chapters 9 and 10. Autistic behaviors are interpreted as reactions to stressful training. Then autism is interpreted as a general adaptation involving negativism, conditioned helplessness, cognitive biases, and the development of integrated role patterns in chapter 11.

5

The Coming of the Child: Prenatal Influences

Many of the strange traits attributed to autistic children are traceable to mothers' fantasies during pregnancy. In turn, those fantasies go back to mothers' early years—to ideas about extraordinary conceptions and births of heroes, deities, and supernatural creatures in fairy tales, mythology, and religion. Those ideas, often long forgotten, are revived during pregnancy and shape the whims, fantasies, and fears that are common at the time. They are aroused most strongly when pregnancy coincides with the wish to alter or escape one's circumstances or to transcend oneself. The result may be an effort to recreate oneself through the creation of a special child.

Events preceding and during pregnancy can give a child to come added importance in a father's life, stimulate his fantasies, and affect his subsequent behavior toward the child, but it has seemed self-evident that a woman reacts to pregnancy and childbirth more profoundly than her mate and that her reactions have more impact on the child than his. There are scattered observations on effects of pregnancy and childbirth on fathers—enough to know that the effects can be profound in themselves and in their influence on wives and children.[1] Perhaps life-style changes, including increased participation by fathers in child bearing and rearing, will foster more study of fathers' roles in child development. Probably mothers and fathers are similar in their wishes of having superior children and fears of having defective ones. However, sexual and other fantasies evoked by the fact of pregnancy, the physiological changes of pregnancy, and the birth process are different for mothers and fathers. Almost all that has been learned is about women's fantasies and subsequent behavior, and the following applies largely to them.

The thesis of this chapter is that, for a substantial minority of women, having a child leads to the most profound changes, and what they experience in the process has specific effects on their children. The fantasies of mothers when pregnant with their autistic children and the events that shaped those fantasies have been described in only a few cases. In the absence of data for the rest, the assumption will be made that the mother's fantasies were similar to the fantasies of other women and had the same cultural sources, including recent folklore and ancient myths.

Pregnancy as Crisis

While some fantasies of pregnant women are considered whimsical, others are taken seriously. Relatives join the women in taking precautions against physical harm to the fetus and against malignant influences on its character. Husbands are advised to be understanding and indulgent toward their pregnant wives, sometimes without regard for reality or consequences. Thus, the fantasies of pregnant women are more or less accepted as a phase of the life cycle.

Pregnancy heightens women's sensitivity and suggestibility and lessens their inhibitions. Some matters that would cause them concern at other times seem not to touch them when pregnant. And trivia that might pass unnoticed at other times are taken as omens, elevating or dashing their spirits. They may visit art galleries and avoid deformed people to ensure that fetuses are exposed only to benign influences. However, it is the mothers rather than the fetuses who are susceptible to such influence. Losses, changes, and illnesses during pregnancy (and in the months after childbirth) have greater effects on them than at other times, and they react impulsively. Romans considered pregnant women so prone to commit crimes that the law exempted them from punishment.[2]

Lessened inhibition is shown by some in unabashed demands made of husbands and other people. Women who are reticent at other times talk when pregnant about personal experiences—ideas, emotions, and sexual and other body sensations. Despite concern about being less attractive than before, they may wear more-revealing clothes and encourage acquaintances and strangers to touch their stomachs. Most women have stronger erotic feelings when pregnant, but they get less relief than at other times from intercourse. Some who do not have frequent intercourse turn to masturbation, with heightened guilt as a result.[3]

The fact that the changes are typical does not make them benign. Mental disturbance is reported rarely during pregnancy largely because disturbed behavior is taken as normal at this time. Bizarre ideas and acts are discounted as capriciousness typical of pregnancy. Allowances also are made for inefficient behavior, and responsibilities are taken away from pregnant women. When they voice concerns about their mental functioning to relatives and physicians, they usually are reassured and advised not to seek help. But when given intelligence tests, many score poorly, showing disorganized thinking. They are more disturbed than their outward behavior shows, and their condition has been compared to psychosis. The delusions found in women with postpartum psychosis are extensions of fantasies from early pregnancy. In many cases of postpartum psychosis, "Careful history-taking revealed the onset of psychosis to be prior to parturition."[4]

The disturbance found during pregnancy reflects the importance of having a baby. The changes occasioned by a first pregnancy are often the most significant in a woman's life. Like other major changes of status, pregnancy traditionally has been accompanied by solemn rites that have retained much of their ancient form, although medical rationales have replaced religious ones. Through the ages, pregnant women have gone into seclusion, undertaken special diets and disciplines, and had changes of consciousness induced, including symbolic death. The practices were designed to purify and prepare them for the coming change of status and to initiate them into it.

While the religious significance of pregnancy and its communal function of making the fields and the herds fertile has declined, and changes in lifestyle have altered people's intellectual beliefs about women's natures and roles, traditional values about childbearing still are ingrained and continue to be reinforced by authoritative teachings. The generations of parents who raised the autistic children discussed here were raised according to traditional values and often were reminded of them as adults. As recently as 1966, in the *American Handbook of Psychiatry,* the essence of womanliness was defined by the following words, taken from the poet Rilke:

> The beauty of a virgin, a being that has not yet achieved anything, is motherhood that begins to sense itself and to prepare, anxious and yearning. And the mother's beauty is ministering motherhood, and in the old woman there is a great remembering.

Accordingly, many clinicians believed that women had to accept femininity in these terms, because:

> These words by Rilke are a statement of motherhood with which no psychological difficulties are likely to be associated. [They] contain the purpose of each phase, the yearning and straining toward the next phase that come with mastery at each point, the sense of achievement and pride.

And, if motherhood were not accepted in these terms:

> Its obverse—self-hatred, inability to accept the feminine identity and destiny, and the inevitable consequence and omnipresent component, rejection and (to varying degrees) even hatred of the child—is the condition out of which the problems in relation to motherhood stem.[5]

Despite certain indulgences, women bore children with greater expectations and under closer scrutiny and severer pressure than they did anything else. They were often under specific pressure to bear sons while having no control of their offspring's sex, no recourse other than magic. The pressure fostered superstitious thinking and behavior. And the apparent success of their magic—the birth of a son—tended to confirm their fantasies that they were under supernatural influence and that their sons, therefore, would be special.

The stresses of pregnancy commonly occur at a difficult time. A first pregnancy involves greater change of status than later ones and, therefore, greater stress. In addition, a first pregnancy often occurs after a series of rapid changes. A pregnant woman may have left her parents' home, her old neighborhood, and her friends recently and may have interrupted or ended her education or prior employment, as well as having gotten married. In addition, she may have taken on the management of a household for the first time in her life. If pregnancy occurs before she has had time to reintegrate her life, she is likely to feel desperate. The situation of being newly married has been promoted as ideal for motherhood, but it is psychologically ill suited. In the circumstances, depression is a likely outcome.[6]

The stresses of a first pregnancy are also hard to cope with because women are unprepared for them. By contrast, a twelve-year-old girl may participate in teenage activities and thereby gain experience that eases the transition to adolescence. A woman may live with a man, approximating marriage, and she may care for another's baby. However, no experience approximates pregnancy or delivery.

Finally, a pregnancy carries added weight because of its bearing on a marriage. Marital dissatisfaction is common and raises questions about whether the relationship will continue. A child born at a peak of dissatisfaction tends to be perceived as cementing a shaky marriage and thereby averting the threat of separation or as trapping a woman in an unhappy marriage.[7] In such a context, becoming pregnant contains elements of a desperate gamble.

The impact of a first pregnancy is particularly relevant here because of the preponderance of first and only autistic children. However, the components of a first pregnancy occur to some extent in all pregnancies. To these general stresses of pregnancy, events may add others. An excess of incidental stresses around the births of autistic children has been reported.[8]

The many factors contributing to the stress of childbearing lend emphasis to the fact that pregnancy is a major crisis, that it fosters depression, and that it brings out intense fears and wishes to be cared for. Even women who hate their mothers yearn for them at this time. But the wish only infrequently leads to the help and comfort that earlier generations of pregnant women got from their mothers.

Mysteries of Pregnancy

While a variety of circumstances contribute to the need for a special child, ancient beliefs determine the content of ideas about the child. The most supernatural and dramatic ideas are associated with first children. According to the Bible, God laid claim to all firstborn children; they were sacrificed or dedicated to God by ancient Jews, Phoenicians, Egyptians, and Greeks, who were significant influences on later European cultures. Mediterranean people also believed that firstborn children were not necessarily fathered by their mothers' husbands. Their paternity often was attributed to gods and human strangers, usually of noble status, and occasionally to animals. The extraordinary paternity was thought to destine firstborn children for greatness, and it was an explanation for births of grossly defective children—monsters.[9] The old beliefs recur in pregnant women's ideas of having perfect children and fears of having defective ones.[10] Many parents still dedicate children—usually the firstborn—to divine or other special roles. The status accorded pregnant women perpetuates mythical themes insofar as they are deferred to somewhat as if they were carrying princes or saviors, their whims are indulged as if they were royal, and they are perceived as saintly, enigmatic, and powerful because of their relationship to the child to be.[11]

In the first half of the century, when many of the mothers described here were raised, girls were prepared for such grace by training to be virgins. They were to keep themselves pure mentally as well as physically—to be free of carnal desires and even of such thoughts. Everything they did was to be subordinated to the sacred office of motherhood. Adherence to these injunctions was to be rewarded first by winning in true love husbands of virtue and high status and, finally, by "the direct intervention of God himself and the bearing of a Messiah." Then, when pregnant, they were exhorted to be:

[C]alm, happy and think only beautiful thoughts.....hold themselves above the desires and irritations of the temporal world. They should...act and feel as if they were purely spiritual creatures and should be treated as such.[12]

The potential for women who chose marriage was higher and more taboo than that of nuns. Nuns were limited to a platonic wedding to God and the wearing of a ring. But temporally married women, like Mary, could hope to be impregnated by God and bear a savior.

By the standards of purity associated with childbearing, pregnancy was an especially troublesome time to engage in "evil" acts or even to have such thoughts. However, pregnancy aroused ideas of masturbation and incest, of having conceived by a former lover or nonhuman creature, of infidelity and leaving one's husband, and of engaging in criminal acts. These thoughts engendered confusion, guilt, and expectations of being punished by giving birth to a monster, as are illustrated in excerpts from the diary of a woman who was pregnant for the first time. The first thoughts preceded conception and reflected the woman's decision to become pregnant.[13]

Having a baby would be my chance for self-renewal.

[P]art earth mother, part Madonna.

My love affair with my child would be a pure, beautiful, holy relationship....

[N]o mortal, man or child would ever make me feel contented and happy....

[M]y last chance to become one with nature, to come to terms with my body.

A body that could produce something beautiful must have some beauty itself....

[A] splendid adventure, a grand experiment.

Oh, how desperately I wanted to have a beautiful baby. I wanted to have a baby because I was tired of working.

...I needed time to figure where I wanted to go in my profession. Having a baby is the perfect out.

Better have a child before I am so old people will laugh at me crossing the street with a baby carriage....

...I will never be lonely again.

During pregnancy she dreamed of giving birth to a monster and had waking fantasies of bearing a hermaphrodite and of having been impregnated by the devil. She thought:

My seed will be cursed because of my sins.

I feel arrogant and wanton.

I am now too pregnant for sex. I feel virginal, precious.

I am initiated into the sisterhood....

I want a little boy so that I can stare at his penis without interruption. I am a sex fiend for even thinking of how much I will enjoy looking at my boy's genitals and admire his sexuality.

There is an evil divinity in me. I feel like the blackest of Madonnas, mean, spiteful, murderous....

I feel blessed by something beyond me....

This is my second chance for perfection.... [Marriage had been her first chance.]

This baby is my masterpiece, my creation, my work of art.

Our child will be proof of the love my husband and I have for each other.

The idea of being pregnant and virginal at the same time, contradictory by modern views, reflects ancient beliefs in which all births were virginal. Only gods were thought to have the power to impregnate women and, by so doing, to restore virginity.[14]

In the days after giving birth, women tend to repress the mythical ideas they had during pregnancy and to be uncomfortable when reminded of them. Later, their retrospective accounts differ from accounts in diaries and from interviews recorded during pregnancy. In one study, pregnant women reported:

> [T]he belief that as a result of going through pregnancy and labor they would be changed. They expected to enjoy, thereafter, a new kind of happiness beyond the conception of the [interviewer] or themselves.

> [They believed that they had] supernatural powers to affect their unborn children and that they will have similar powers to understand and control them after birth.[15]

Toward the end of pregnancy, the fantasies become more elaborate and conscious. Women relate ideas and experiences that are not heard at other times except in psychoanalysis, intoxication, or psychosis. Those who are in psychoanalysis report dreams and waking fantasies of having been made pregnant by their fathers and their therapists. The fantasies become harder to tolerate. As the feared ordeal of delivery approaches, some women welcome it as an end to their fantasies and guilt.

The fantasies of pregnancy have been suggested as sources of traits incorrectly attributed to autistic children, but the fantasies need not lead to misperceptions of children after they are born. In most women, pregnancy fantasies are replaced by perceptions based on experience with their neonates and have limited effects on the interactions. Two groups of women in which pregnancy fantasies are retained after delivery, determine perceptions of the infants, and are the basis of the women's behavior toward the infants have been identified: women who suffer postpartum breakdown and mothers of autistic children.[16]

A reason why mothers retain their pregnancy fantasies in relation to autistic children was suggested in the last chapter. Events in their lives before or during pregnancy give them a more than ordinary interest in having special children. The fantasies and the value placed on the children go together; to give up the fantasies means to view their neonates as ordinary. Most women regret the passing of the exaltation of pregnancy, which probably contributes to their blues after delivery. Those who have an extraordinary stake in having a special child are likely to cling to the omens and other fantasies of pregnancy.

In addition, parents of autistic children are unusually tenacious in their beliefs and expectations. As was illustrated in chapter 2, they cling to beliefs about their autistic children despite compelling evidence to the the contrary.

Their writings document the tenacity better than any clinical impression.[17] Most relevant here is tenacity in what they expect of their autistic children. Perhaps they cling to their expectations after the children are born because giving them up would mean losing the keystones of their lives. Repeated disappointments over months that stretch into years do not end their hopes. The main effect of disappointments in the preschool years is to color their expectations with bitterness. When rapport is established, many parents tell how their greatest hopes in life, residing in their autistic children, remain unfulfilled.[18]

Delivery

The extent to which women's fantasies persist after childbirth also depends on what happens in delivery. The worse a delivery experience, the more fantasy is carried over. Delivery sets the stage for what follows. Women and infants who come through it well are ready to interact responsively. They tend to adapt quickly to each other. Women and infants who come through delivery poorly are unresponsive to each other and tend to continue that way. In the absence of responsive interaction, mothers' views of their neonates are determined by preconceptions.

During the first half of the century, many women were unconscious or only partly conscious during delivery from analgesics and sedatives given them. It had been thought that medication during delivery, by sparing women pain and giving them rest, put them in a better mental state for dealing with their neonates. The contrary seems to be true.[19] Hypnotic drugs intensify pregnancy fantasies, fostering grotesque reveries and nightmares during delivery in many women. These experiences are usually forgotten within days, but they are remembered immediately after delivery, causing confusion, apprehensiveness, and suspicion about what may have happened while they were unconscious or dazed. These feelings and nightmarish memories about their infants have made women reluctant to see their infants.

In contrast, women who remain awake find that the distress and fatigue of even prolonged labor tend to lift during delivery. Contrary to the expectation that newly delivered mothers are exhausted and wan, most who stay awake are found to be radiant, energetic, and eager to handle their babies for some time before they want to rest. For them, the experience of giving birth is positive and remains so if they have access to their babies.[20]

It had been thought that long and difficult labor and birth complications fostered negative attitudes in women toward their babies. That idea was supported by mothers' reports and obstetricians' impressions. Many mothers vividly remembered the pain of labor, the damage to their bodies of delivery ("His head was so big, it ripped me open"), the stitches, and the months needed to recover. They explained their unwillingness to look at or touch their neonates, their lasting resentment, and their grim resolutions never to have more children on this basis. Nonetheless, studies using hospital records have given a different picture. Extreme labor and birth complications were found to have the expected adverse effects. However, variations of labor and birth complications in the normal range, in themselves, were not found to affect how women experienced the births of their babies or their initial attitudes toward them. In addition, length of labor was not found to be determined primarily by factors considered decisive in the past—fetal position, fetal head size or its relation to maternal pelvic size, or other physical conditions. Long labor was associated more with first births and with personality factors.[21]

A major determinant of the experience of delivery is how women prepare for it during pregnancy. Stated broadly, active preparation is associated with positive experience during delivery and readiness to interact afterward with the neonate. Active preparation includes obtaining the layette, making arrangements for giving birth, undertaking physical and mental training for labor and delivery, and talking about the experience of pregnancy and about the infant care to follow. Full communication with one's husband, including talking about details of pregnancy fantasies, is particularly helpful. Women who do not talk about such fantasies tend to have unusually long labor and adverse delivery experiences and to become seriously disturbed after childbirth.[22] Whether the presence of the fantasies in themselves or openness in discussing them is benign is not clear.

The question of how mothers of autistic children prepared for their births is hard to answer. From the picture that they and clinicians have furnished, they seem likely to have arranged their hospitalization and obtained the clothes and equipment needed for the coming child. However, they seem unlikely to have talked much about their pregnancies. Insofar as they were intellectual, perfectionistic, and self-controlled, they are unlikely to have given rein to grotesque fantasies. Reticence and limited communication with their husbands about intimate matters seems to have been common. In some cases, communication was limited further by husbands' withdrawal as a reaction to pregnancy or absence from home during pregnancy. In addition, many of the husbands seem to have been hypercritical and forbidding—unlikely people in whom to confide bizarre ideas.

In short, the situations of the mothers did not favor sharing pregnancy fantasies. The clinical vignettes and autobiographies do not indicate that such matters were discussed with husbands or others. Mothers of autistic children as a group seem not to have had the support and participation of husbands during pregnancy, labor, and delivery that is conducive to a good experience in giving birth and a good relationship with the infant afterward.

In addition, mothers of autistic children are likely to have had adverse delivery experiences insofar as they fit Kanner's picture. Adverse birth experiences are common in women who are reserved, overcontrolled, and give the appearance of imperturbability about matters that disturb them.[23]

The most disturbing aspect of labor for many women is loss of self-control.[24] Those who value control highly may be particularly apprehensive about being unable to hold in their amniotic fluid, urine, and feces. Labor is a sequence of body changes with mounting pain, anticipation of being torn or surgically cut at the perineum, and apprehension about the fetus. By childbirth practices of the past, women did not control these events. Pregnancy also had been a progression of uncontrolled body changes, but they were gradual and relatively painless. The onset of labor marked the beginning of a headlong rush to a fearful climax. Women's only control lay in the choice of being conscious or unconscious during the climax. Even that choice often was preempted by the obstetrician. For these reasons, giving birth was particularly stressful for women who relied heavily on self-control. If not given drugs, they tended to maintain their composure until the end of labor and then lose it, becoming childishly impulsive and dependent. After delivery, they felt humiliated. Thus, they were ill prepared to interact responsively with their neonates.

These considerations imply negative delivery experiences for mothers of autistic children. Their experiences of giving birth to the children have been reported in only a few cases; they were largely negative. In addition, negative experiences may be inferred in those women who were upset at the sight of their newborn infants.

Conclusions

The births of autistic children seem to have had more significance to their mothers than other births. They gave up more in having the children, and they expected more as a result of having them. Therefore, the circumstances favored full-blown pregnancy fantasies. But the circumstances did not favor sharing the fantasies with their husbands, having positive experiences in giving birth, and making a transition from pregnancy fantasies about the fetus and its future to reality-based perceptions and attitudes. The evidence is that the fantasies persisted after the children were born, partly in non-human qualities attributed to them, and that the mothers acted upon the fantasies as if they were realistic.

Newborn infants vary considerably in appearance and behavior but not as much as parents think they do. Parents' perceptions of one-day-old babies as beautiful or repulsive, self-sufficient or demanding, alertly attentive or oblivious, and cuddly or untouchable tell more about the parents than about their infants.[25] Pregnancy fantasies are a factor in such perceptions. When they persist beyond the first days, rearing is likely to be affected adversely. Specific effects that may foster autism are discussed in the following chapters.

6 The Beginning: Mother-Infant Interaction

The beginning of a phenomenon is usually its period of most rapid change and, therefore, its period of greatest susceptibility to influence. Living things are more sensitive to the environment when changing than when stable, more sensitive before development occurs than after.[1]

Conception is the human zero point. In the weeks that follow, the embryo grows and undergoes transformations at a rate that will never be equalled. It changes from more-primitive shapes to resemble a fish, a reptile, and a mammal before taking on human form. During this malleable period, the mother's body and the amnion greatly limit the stimulation to which an embryo is exposed. That is why humans are born as much alike as they are.

When born and exposed to the environment, the neonate is changing more slowly and is therefore less malleable. Formerly, psychologists believed that neonates' senses were undeveloped, making them relatively impervious to the environment and incapable of learning. They are, however, still changing faster than at any later time, and their senses are sufficiently developed for the environment to influence them decisively. Maturation will bring increased efficiency in perceiving, coding, and responding, but early experiences have disproportionately great effects because they determine how later experiences will be perceived and coded. Early experiences can make children unreceptive to later ones. Serious effects, including aversion to mothers, can be conditioned the first day.[2] Whether or not the aversion lasts, it can be critical insofar as mothers react adversely to what they take to be rejection by their newborn infants. Many show a disinclination to pursue the relationship further.

Initial experiences are not usually decisive. A third person's encouragement to mothers to try again is often helpful and, with or without help, mothers turn back to their infants after early negative reactions, and most of them try extra hard with unresponsive infants.[3] Nonetheless, as in other relationships, an early experience may initiate a chain of adverse events.

The birth of an infant is the beginning of a prolonged, dramatic encounter between a woman and child. Despite her maturity, the woman also experiences rapid change and heavy social pressure that make her extraordinarily impressionable. She sees her infant for the first time and is expected to engage in intimate activities with it. First impressions are said to be lasting ones. Whether or not this is true for the neonate is a matter of conjecture. For mothers, it is usually true. An infant's development for a year or more is influenced by the mother's first experience with it.[4]

In the past, a minority of mothers who had positive delivery experiences, were alert afterward, and had immediate contact with their neonates enjoyed good first experiences. And their positive feelings lasted if they had continued contact with their babies. But separation after early contact brought out negative reactions when contact was renewed. These reactions were like those of the majority who had no contact with their neonates for the first twelve to eighteen hours after birth. Many of them found their babies repulsive, were frightened, and avoided touching them. Such reactions, most common with a first child, were associated with fears of defects and suspicions that the obstetrician was hiding some terrible fact from them. Some women held back from their babies until assured that such apprehensions were untrue. Recognition of how deeply mothers were affected led to training of hospital nurses to prevent contact between mother and neonate until a propitious moment, in order to avert a negative reaction by the mother that would stand in the way of her becoming attached to the infant.[5] Though common, these negative reactions usually were not reported by mothers or nurses. The reaction of Dibs' mother to her first sight of him was not unusual.

Separation of mothers and neonates had been a common maternity-ward procedure. Besides the function of protecting infants from maternal rejection, separation was considered useful hygienically for infants, helpful to mothers in recovering from childbirth, and convenient for hospital staff.

By hindsight, preventing contact between mothers and infants was a poor remedy. Now it is known that separation reinforces pregnancy fantasies about neonates and fosters mourning of them as if they had died. In turn, these reactions interfere with attachment to them and consequently hinder their development. The most compelling evidence has come from experiments with premature babies and their mothers. Total separation had been considered necessary for premature babies' welfare. Actually the separation caused serious developmental problems that had been attributed mistakenly to the physical immaturity of the babies.[6] In addition, the separation later fostered maternal neglect and abuse of the children.

Use of obstetric drugs in labor and delivery also interferes with the beginning of the mother-infant relationship. As noted, the drugs intensify pregnancy fantasies and keep mothers sleepy or dazed after delivery, hindering contact with their babies. In addition, obstetric drugs pass the placental barrier and have serious effects on fetuses, with residual effects in neonates.[7] For example, drug-depressed neonates tend to suck weakly or not at all. They are hard to comfort and tend to be unresponsive in other ways. The impression on their mothers may be that the babies are uncuddly, rejecting, or defective by nature.

Many mothers described their autistic children as having been inactive, unresponsive, irritable, and hard to comfort in the first days of life. Insofar as other causes were not found, drugs seem a likely cause in the cases in which they were administered. Other occurrences at birth—pounding on the head from long labor, anoxia from strangulation during delivery or failure to breathe afterward—have similar effects on neonates.[8] These effects are usually transient and of no importance unless caretakers react adversely to them. However, these and other common occurrences may set the stage for adverse developments.

Mothers' perceptions of their neonates, whether based on pregnancy fantasies or subnormal neonatal behavior, are ordinarily transient but sometimes lead to a self-perpetuating chain of events. That happens when mothers behave toward their infants on the basis of early perceptions in ways that condition infants to fit their perceptions. For example, if they perceive their infants as preferring to be alone and leave them to themselves, the infants will remain unsocialized.

Anxiety fosters stereotyping. Many parents find the task of caring for their neonates awesome and anticipate severe consequences for mishandling them; yet they lack clear guidelines. In the circumstances, fathers have been able to withdraw and leave the responsibility to mothers. Mothers have sought advice, particularly in rearing their first infants, but what they usually got from their mothers, friends, books, hospital nurses, and pediatricians was a confusing mixture, much of it poorly thought out and some of it plainly contradictory.[9] And mothers had limited experience by which to evaluate the advice and limited time to weigh and choose. Instead, they found themselves under heavy pressure to act and act quickly. Many felt a desperate need to have something unchanging to hang onto.

In such circumstances, people tend to fix on some approach, more or less arbitrarily, and to adhere to it. The main way that a new mother can find constancy is to adopt an idea of what her baby needs and adhere to it. That is done often by stereotyping the baby. Fixed treatment of a baby also may foster actual constancy in its behavior insofar as the baby adapts to its mother. Thus, stereotyping a baby can be self-reinforcing.

Stereotyping also may result from the persistence of pregnancy fantasies or the focusing of a longing for the return of a lost relative on the infant. Such a focus is shown by statements that a neonate is (or will grow up to be) friendly or wise like a specific relative. Traits attributed to neonates often are considered inherited and expected to be permanent, but early behaviors are not fixed:

At no time in its history will the human being experience more dramatic, intense and dynamic change.[10]

The changes of behavioral characteristics in the first three years of life are extraordinarily rapid. Infants' capacities for motoric, physiological, adaptive, and affective behavior alter from day to day in the neonatal period.[11]

Rapid development in neonates results in rapidly changing needs. Flexibility and rapid adaptation by the caretaker are needed for normal development.[12]

The Uncuddly Baby

Probably, stereotyping infants as uncuddly, unresponsive, and preferring solitude has played a part in the development of autism. Many mothers described their autistic children as uncuddly in the first months of life; on being picked up, they fussed, stiffened, squirmed, and did not mold their bodies to the mothers' bodies. Later, they did not learn to raise their arms in anticipation of being picked up. Their aversion to being held seemed innate—a forerunner of the preference for solitude and the lack of socialization that became clear in time.

The impressions of these mothers may have been correct to begin with. Many neonates—perhaps a majority—are tense and difficult to handle in the first days.[13] As noted, however, such behavior is transient unless it leads to a stereotype and to mutually reinforcing interaction. "My assistants and I have made a special point of picking up tiny babies who their mothers say are not cuddly. With us they are cuddly."[14] The idea that autistic children are less cuddly than others during the neonatal period has been specifically disconfirmed.[15]

Mothers of autistic children have been described as uncomfortable with physical contact and stiff, awkward, and distant in handling the children. That is also true of many other mothers, especially with their first children. But most mothers overcome their reluctance and awkwardness and cuddle their neonates, who respond by becoming cuddlier.

Human and mammalian infants that have little body contact early are unresponsive or averse to it later. For example, some monkey mothers hold their infants stiffly, away from their bodies, in the manner that has been described as typical of autistic children's mothers. These monkey mothers have difficulty making a newborn cling and nurse in a comfortable position. Their infants squirm and cry on being held by the mothers but may be held comfortably by other females.[16] Similarly, human infants who receive little cuddling early remain or become tense and hard to hold. "The baby seems to want to squirm out of her arms and the mother is likely to report that the baby doesn't want to be held."[17] For a time, the resistance may be specific to the caretaker. Later, the infant may resist being held by other people.

Mothers of autistic children seem to overcome neither their initial resistance to cuddling the neonates nor the neonates' resistance. The mothers reportedly continue to hold the infants stiffly, at a distance. Their infants are averse to being held by the mothers, but may be held comfortably by other people. Later, they resist handling by others.

Infants who stiffen or squirm on being held, whether or not they are otherwise autistic, need much holding and cuddling to become socialized. Their resistance to being held may be taken as a sign of their extraordinary need for it. When mothers persist, despite adverse responses from their babies, the babies eventually relax and the resistance is overcome. That applies particularly to autistic children, whose parents were advised by Wing:

> [I]f a baby seems unresponsive, his mother should make a special effort to cuddle him, tickle him, carry him around and talk to him, so that he has the same experiences as a normal baby.
>
> A mother with this kind of baby has to be encouraged to do all the work herself, and she is usually only too happy to do this, once she realizes that she will not harm the baby by breaking into his isolation.[18]

However, the opposite maternal reaction—withdrawal from a neonate who is averse to contact—is common and perpetuates the aversion.

Feeding

Other sequences also may contribute to estrangement between mother and neonate. The following has been common among ordinary mothers and ordinary infants on the maternity ward. A baby was sleepy when brought to the mother. Therefore, the baby nursed poorly, getting little milk. Hungry well before the next scheduled feeding, the baby cried long and was given a supplemental bottle by the nurse. Therefore, when brought to the mother for the next feeding, the baby was not hungry and nursed poorly again. In these circumstances, mothers concluded that they had failed repeatedly. They felt rejected, ashamed, worthless, and desperate. In addition, their distress, lack of breast stimulation by nursing, and failure to empty their breasts by feeding caused their milk supply to dwindle. In the circumstances, many gave up breastfeeding with a sense of personal failure.

Bottle feeding produced some of the same difficulties in the maternity ward and at home, and mothers experienced lack of success as personal rejection and failure. But breastfeeding was more personal, making the sense of rejection and failure more painful.

Early feeding also went badly for many women who breastfed reluctantly. Some were disgusted by nursing; others were apprehensive about losing their "shape" or their freedom to get out of the house. Nonetheless, under pressure from relatives, peers, or professionals, they did their "duty." For them, giving up breastfeeding because it went badly brought relief, but it also brought a sense of failure and of having been rejected by their infants.

The sequences leading to poor feeding experiences usually were not remembered long. When asked afterward, mothers often gave explanations

for abortive breastfeeding that were untrue but more acceptable. They said
that they had not had enough milk or that their babies had not been interested in nursing.[19] Therefore, reports of unsuccessful breastfeeding in cases
of autism, explained by lack of milk or of infant interest, suggest that more-
complex events may have occurred and been involved in very early estrangement between mother and child. Reported problems in bottle feeding may
have similar implications.

In short, aversion to cuddling and poor eating, typically reported in
autistic children in the first months, probably are steps in a process of
estrangement. Rather than being manifestations of innate defects, they are
attributable in the first days to obstetric drugs and other birth stresses and to
maternity-ward procedures and other transient factors. Their persistence is
attributable to more-complex chains of events. However they arise, they
affect mothers adversely and may lead to rearing that unintentionally perpetuates the behavior.

Infant Temperament

Neonates have been divided into types by researchers seeking innate traits
bearing on the development of personality, intelligence, and disturbance.
Babies seem to differ in behavior enough at birth or soon after to be classified for scientific purposes. Some are more wakeful, alert, and active than
others. Some are more responsive and easy to feed and comfort. Some are
more content and adaptable over a range of experiences. Others are fussier,
more easily upset. Still others are unresponsive, isolated, and difficult to feed
and comfort.

Neonates in the last group were thought to have abnormally low stimulus thresholds! Consequently, they were considered vulnerable to flooding
by more stimulation than they could process. Their only recourse was a
primitive mechanism, analogous to feigned death in animals, by which they
shut out external stimulation and became inert. The more such infants were
stimulated, the less responsive they became. In accord with this theory,
mothers of unresponsive infants were advised not to intrude on them but to
shield them from stimulation. Studies of human and animal infants have not
confirmed the advice (see chapter 13). Instead, as was touched on earlier,
more-recent advice is to press stimulation on infants who are averse to it.

Escalona divided neonates into two types—active and inactive. Active
neonates were found to respond optimally to mild social stimulation, and
fleeting attention by an adult at a distance was enough to get a social
response from them. Inactive neonates hardly responded to mild stimulation
but responded well (and sometimes more than active ones) to strong social
stimulation. If made the focus of an adult's attention—touched, talked to

playfully, and played with vigorously—they were as responsive as active ones. Escalone concluded that active neonates would thrive under minimal or routine maternal care but that inactive neonates would thrive only with mothers who spent much time actively stimulating them. With caretakers described as mothers of autistic children have been (distant, impersonal, efficient, providing neccessary physical care but little playful stimulation), inactive neonates were slow in developing. Chess concluded similarly that neither neonatal temperament nor any common type of mothering caused disturbance. Instead, particular combinations of neonatal and maternal types produced disturbances. Infants who became disturbed with one type of mother did well with another; and mothers who were ineffective with one type of infant did well with another.[20]

These findings suggest that a mother who provides routine care with mild stimulation to an inactive baby will get little response and therefore may conclude that her baby is innately unresponsive. However, a more-stimulating adult will find the same baby fully responsive. These findings may account for reports of autistic children being more responsive to other adults than to their mothers in infancy.

The idea that autism develops from neonatal characteristics may be outlined as follows:

Certain infants do not provide certain stimulation to their mothers.

Consequently, the mothers do not provide certain experiences to their infants.

Lack of the experiences results in autism.

One theory is that autistic children are born with defective communication systems and, therefore, fail to provide cues for maternal behavior. Consequently, their mothers do not provide care that infants require for normal development. Another theory is that autistic children do not reinforce their parents for giving them certain care. Consequently, the parents do not give the care, and autism results.[21]

Findings of neonatal types were received enthusiastically in the 1960s. Researchers thought they had identified patterns of behavior that were inherited—enduring patterns relatively independent of experience— foundation stones for the personalities, abilities, and handicaps that would unfold in time. The temperaments identified were thought to be hereditary because they were taken to be present at birth, before environment affected infants. Actually, the temperaments were not known to be present at birth because they were based on observations of infants beginning days, weeks, or even months after birth. In addition, evidence of genetic transmission was lacking. Most important, the neonatal patterns observed were not necessarily stable. Whether they persisted or changed depended on subsequent events. In time, the expectation that research on infant types would account for later personality, ability, and handicap waned.[22]

Expectations and Disappointments

Whether mothers' initial impressions of their infants come from preconceptions or from accurate perceptions, difficulties are likely. Women's fantasies during pregnancy tend to be greater than any human child can fulfill, and a problem confronting all mothers is the discrepancy between the expected child and the delivered child.

> The match between the parents' perception of their child and what they wish to see in that child often determines the ratio of positive to negative feedback, of acceptance to rejection.[23]

The greater the discrepancy, the more difficult is the mother's task, and some discrepancies are so great as to pose crises. Most mothers who suffer breakdowns after childbirth do so in the first days. In their delusions, pregnancy fantasies about the child are elaborated and given the stamp of reality. And the core of the disturbance usually involves disappointment in the child.[24]

The emotional stress of birth for a mother has been conceptualized as loss of part of herself, of her world, and of Eden.[25] Added to this is loss of the child of her dreams, the embodiment of her ambition. Its place is taken by an ordinary child. With the realization that the outcome of pregnancy is ordinary come disappointment and feelings of emptiness. Even when delivery brings joy, a sense of successful completion, and relief from fear, these emotions are fragile, readily giving way to despair. The following statement, although exaggerated, was presented as typical of mothers in the United States: "Every expectation about what the baby will do for you and mean to you is bound to be frustrated in time."[26]

Like pregnancy, the period following childbirth is marked by suggestibility and lability. Mothers watch their babies apprehensively for signs and read omens into details of appearance and behavior. Given the changeability of young infants, their movements, smiles, and babble usually have "no sense other than what the mother gives them; whether [the baby] seem charming and unique, or tiresome, commonplace, and hateful, depends on her, not upon her baby."[27]

Although an ordinary baby may disappoint a mother greatly, she may not understand her reaction. The mother of an obviously defective baby or one diagnosed as retarded at birth has clear reasons for being disappointed. But the mother of a normal-appearing child may be baffled by her feelings, especially after her pregnancy fantasies have faded from consciousness. She may look for a defect in her baby to justify her disappointment in it. She may find that she is disappointed in its sex or its resemblance to a relative. She may read grave meaning into its movements, the tone of its cry, or a mark on its body. And she may seek medical opinion about a suspected handicap.

No matter how severe her disappointment, she may find another way of creating her special child. Taking the neonate as clay, she may direct her energy toward shaping it into something wonderful. She may hope the limitations of biological creation, the ordinary or subnormal child born to her, can be transcended by supernormal rearing.

While many mothers try to create a perfect child by special rearing, mothers of autistic children seem to have greater expectations than others and more-bitter disappointments. Whether their hopes or disappointments predominate, they are spurred to undertake prodigious training of the children.

Awe and Distance

As noted, mothers' first contacts with their neonates commonly have been marked by fear and aversion. In the days that followed, most mothers showed a combination of awe and interest. They scrutinized their babies but tended to avoid body contact. Some even avoided speaking to their infants, remaining silent or using a nurse as an intermediary in expressing what was meant for their infants. First children more than others were treated as if taboo objects.[28]

Their awe of their neonates probably had a number of sources. Some of the mothers justified their hesitancy by fear of harming the babies, as by dropping them or poking them in the soft spot on the head. Such reasons did not explain their behavior but may have reflected ideas from old myths and practices of killing and maiming special children. In addition, the neonate was an embodiment of childhood wishes, greatly to be desired but forbidden and never to be realized. And it was the instrument by which women were initiated into motherhood, the agent of their deliverance.[29] As such, the neonate was a talisman, powerful and awesome. Finally, the neonate was compensation for the disadvantages, losses, and disappointments mothers had suffered in being women and in getting married. Insofar as these considerations applied, the neonate was to be guarded as precious and to be avoided as powerful and forbidden.

Awe and avoidance of the neonate have been noted particularly in cases of autism. Some of the clinical records and autobiographies indicate that the mothers did not react with comparable awe and avoidance at the births of their other children.[30]

Ordinarily, mothers soon lose their awe and become less hesitant and distant in handling their babies.[31] Many mothers of autistic children remain hesitant and distant. Some clinicians have concluded that continuing hesitancy causes autism.[32]

Hesitancy and avoidance have a number of specifiable adverse effects on infants. Hesitancy means delay of reinforcement and inconsistency of cues provided to an infant (chapters 9 and 10). Distant handling and avoidance of infants foster isolation and aversion to being handled (chapter 13). In addition, neonates are particularly responsive to their mothers' heartbeats and sense adults' breathing rhythms and other internal sounds when touching adults' bodies.[33] And they respond positively to being squeezed, patted, and stroked. These kinds of stimulation quiet them when they are upset and alert them when they are somnolent so that they are more receptive to other stimulation and better able to learn.

Close contact also provides mothers with stimulation from neonates, including cues needed in giving care. Without the cues, infant care is more difficult and frustrating. Some of the cues given by infants are intuitively meaningful to mothers, while others have to be learned from experience with infants. Limiting the stimulation received from an infant hinders learning such cues. In addition, avoidance of body contact limits sensual stimulation that fosters mutual attachment. Much of the care a mother gives depends upon her attachment to her infant.

Last, contact is helpful in learning to give cues. Much neonatal signaling is inborn, but after several months most of the cues given by infants are learned. Avoidance of contact with neonates and leaving them alone for long periods of time hinder them from learning to signal, and early signaling is the basis for learning to speak later. Thus, limited contact in the first months may hinder development of speech and other aspects of socialization.

Crying and Communication

Human neonates have a number of reflexes for signaling their needs and responding to their caretakers. The reflexes are important because of human infants' immaturity and dependence compared to neonates of other species. Many human infants are born with poorly integrated physiological systems. Their self-regulatory functions are especially poor, and they are disorganized easily by internal and external events, from which they do not recover quickly on their own. If they are not helped, ordinary stresses may leave them irritable, inactive, and somnolent for long periods, and they may suffer respiratory distress. In these states, they are unresponsive or poorly responsive to signals from caretakers. The residual effects of obstetric drugs also hinder stable neonatal functioning. And the change from intrauterine life to a less-dependent and less-dependable relationship with their mothers may tax their adaptive mechanisms. Therefore, in the first weeks, help in ending their stress reactions—restoring them to a calm alert state—can be vital to their physical welfare and their availability for interacting with caretakers and for learning.[34]

Crying is the main reflex by which neonates initiate contact and signal their needs. To be effective in having needs met, crying must elicit appropriate responses by the caretaker. The sequence of crying and being helped is the first basis for learning to initiate communication. When it does not work—when a caretaker's response to crying is something other than giving help—development is hindered. Responses other than giving help arise for a number of reasons.

Parents find crying unpleasant and are reluctant to reward it. In the past, professionals believed that responding promptly to cries spoiled infants and even caused psychopathology. The prevailing view today, however, is that prompt response is best for infant development.[35]

Some mothers try to meet infant needs even sooner, before crying occurs. Whatever advantages this may have, it has the disadvantage that crying is not fostered as communication. In addition, responsiveness by infants to their own needs may not be fostered. Other ways of getting infants not to cry include ignoring their cries, meeting their needs only when they are not crying, and punishing them for crying. The wish of most mothers is reflected in the folk song, "I gave my love a baby with no crying."

Infant crying as a demand for action would seem most unwelcome to mothers who are depressed and therefore find demands burdensome and by those who strive for maximum control of their infants. The depression of autistic children's mothers was discussed in chapter 4. Their highly controlling behavior has been cited frequently by clinicians and is illustrated best in some of their autobiographies.[36] The reactions to crying of mothers of autistic children have not been reported but may be inferred from parental boasts that autistic children were good babies and therefore were left alone much of the time. Probably, crying was not rewarded.

Neonates have limited resources for communicating their needs but are well equipped to learn how their communications are met. As extensive studies show, "from his earliest days, every infant is an active, perceiving, learning, and information-organizing individual."[37] In particular, neonates perceive the speech, expressions, and movements of their caretakers. They observe sequences of events and distinguish between repetitions and deviations. Repetition of prior sequences gratifies them; deviation upsets them.[38]

How a caretaker responds to a neonate's crying determines how well the crying serves as pretraining for verbal communication. Crying now is considered a precursor of language. The same is true of other preverbal behavior by which young infants respond to or initiate contacts with their caretakers— smiles, expressions, gestures, and perhaps the many tiny movements that have been noted in study of filmed interaction.[39]

Caretakers' attitudes toward infant crying and their intentions about what to encourage and discourage provide limited information about the reinforcements they provide. Much reinforcement and failure to reinforce are determined unconsciously and conveyed by behavior that caretakers may not be aware of. In particular, nonreinforcement of infant behavior due to caretakers' depression is unintended.

Mutual Adaptation

Communication is an aspect—perhaps the most important aspect—of adaptation to each other by caretaker and infant. The critical role of their mutual adaptation has been studied only recently. Earlier, researchers believed that the helplessness of neonates aroused the maternal instinct, by which mothers naturally perceived their infants' needs accurately and knew what to do. In fact, few mothers approached this ideal, and maternal instinct has proved a limited concept for describing infant care in many animal species as well as in humans.[40]

Because human neonates are helpless, elaborate synchronization between their behavior and their caretakers' is necessary. Slow-motion analysis of film has shown a subtle interaction between mothers and neonates that had not been observed before and was unexpected. Each responds in diffuse and specific ways to a great many stimuli from the other. One film showed "a one-day-old child synchronizing its hand motions precisely to the voice of a speaker."[41] Also, different words elicit different movements. Many of the cues and responses by both mothers and neonates involve such small, quick movements that the mothers are not ordinarily aware of them.

This interaction seems instinctive and might remain so if neonates remained as they are born. In many species, one infant is like another and remains much as it is born. It may have no more communication with its mother at the end of childhood than it did at the beginning. The cries and movements of guinea pigs, for example, undergo little change from the day they are born until they are independent of their mothers. Their mothers have little to learn in caring for them. And one infant guinea pig behaves much like another. By contrast, human young receive care for a long time, during which enormous development takes place. A one-year-old's communication repertory and mental functions are vastly more complex than a neonate's. Therefore, in order to have given effective care, the mother has had to adapt to many changes and to learn how her infant differs from others of the species. She and her infant have had much to learn. Unchanging behavior by either one hinders infant development.

Learning occurs most readily in neonates who are in a state of mild arousal, with visual scanning of the environment, response to stimuli, and little other body movement.[42] Mildly aroused neonates respond in ways that give the impression that they recognize and are interested in their mothers and thus provide gratification to the mothers. Other neonatal states range from sleep through inactive wakefulness (low arousal) and high activity without distress (moderate arousal) to fussing, crying, and body rigidity or thrashing (high arousal).

Neonates are mildly aroused for a few hours after birth. Probably, that is why contact then gratifies mothers and fosters mutual adaptation. During the rest of the first week, mild arousal is infrequent and brief, occurring spontaneously after feeding.

Arousal and activity levels of neonates had been considered hereditary and relatively fixed, but experience modifes them over the full range. Low arousal due to obstetric drugs and birth stresses was touched on earlier, and a few other factors will be mentioned. Common stresses such as frustration in feeding and changes of caretaking routine often lead to low arousal. Crying neonates are relatively unresponsive to anything that does not bring relief of their distress. If not relieved, they cry louder and become more agitated. Then, many reach a point of not responding to the arrival of their mother or to an intervention that would have relieved distress earlier. Finally, they stop crying and fall asleep or into quiet, unresponsive wakefulness.

Frequent feeding promotes alertness. It also promotes muscular vigor, deep and regular breathing, good skin color, much wakefulness, and relaxed sleep. Infrequent feeding is associated with the opposite. (According to Kennell, the content of human milk is particularly suited to frequent, almost continual, feeding.) Alertness is fostered also by putting a crying or thrashing neonate to the shoulder. In addition to reduction of arousal, heartbeat and respiration become slower and more regular. Neonates who receive little handling tend to be unresponsively inactive. Extra stimulation brings them to a more-aroused, receptive level. Thus, for most neonates, moderate stimulation is optimal. Excited neonates become quieter; inactive or drowsy ones become alert.[43]

Auditory, visual, and tactile stimuli normally are effective in producing mild arousal. However, infants vary considerably as to which stimulation fosters mild arousal in them.[44] Therefore, a mother's report that her neonate was hard to comfort may mean only that the neonate was not responsive to her method of comforting. Similarly, a report that a neonate was hard to arouse may mean only that the neonate was not responsive to the particular stimulation used by the caretaker.

If mother and infant are not well matched to begin with and do not adapt readily to each other, as the weeks go by they will miss and misread many of each other's cues and will not respond relevantly. Little of the infant's social behavior will get reinforced and serve as a basis for subsequent adaptation. Also, the mother will not find her infant easy to feed, comfort, or handle. She will feel ineffective and may experience her baby as baffling, alien, or not needing her, especially if the baby responds better to another adult.

Usually, the first weeks are a time of rapid adaptation by mother and neonate to each other's individuality. The behavior of each becomes reasonably predictable to the other. According to Sander, the infant's adaptation is reflected in increased responsiveness to the mother as compared to other people; and the mother gets to feel that she knows her baby. When that happens, the third month begins a delightful phase that has been called a honeymoon. The mother exchanges smiling, cooing, and other play with her infant in lengthening, more-complex sequences of interaction.[45]

While the honeymoon at three months is the most common pattern, others are also common. Some mothers are most deeply touched by the helplessness of the neonate and find succeeding stages less attractive. Others find the neonate repulsive and the infant of a few months boringly subhuman. They may show little interest until the infant begins to speak.

Each group of mothers is large enough to be considered normal, but the differences in mothers' preferences should foster differences in infant adaptation and development. High interest in a neonate fosters early learning and may make an infant better able to deal with stress, easier to train later, and easier to bring out of refractory states. A honeymoon at a few months fosters bonding, which in turn fosters learning and tolerance for stress. If the honeymoon continues into the second half of the year, it should facilitate speech.

How infant regularity and synchrony with the mother are achieved is controversial. The traditional view, strongly imbedded in religious and philosophical ideas, is that infants achieve regularity and good character by having a regimen imposed on them. Therefore, parents have long been encouraged to discipline their children from the first days of life. Under the influence of Puritanism and the Protestant ethic, indulgence of children was considered the worst parental sin. In the early part of this century, psychologists' and physicians' advice took the same lines. Watson, then the dominant voice on childrearing in the United States, warned that:

> Mothers don't know, when they kiss their children and pick them up and rock them, caress them and jiggle them upon their knees, that they are slowly building up a human being totally unable to cope with the world it must later live in.[46]

Toward mid-century, as child-rearing ideas changed, infant regularity came to be seen as a response to child-centered rearing. Research indicated that regular, predictable infant behavior was fostered by being demonstrative and adapting caretaking to the initially unpredictable demands of neonates. Good eating was fostered specifically by feeding babies as often and as long as they wanted to eat. Babies reared in this indulgent way were found spontaneously to develop lengthening, regular intervals of undemanding wakefulness between feedings and of sleep at night. They also became increasingly responsive to their mothers. By contrast, neonates required to adhere to schedules were found to fuss and be problem eaters and sleepers in the first year and negativistic or withdrawn in the second.[47]

Mothers were described by Kanner and others as trying to discipline their autistic children early and as adhering to rules rather than reacting spontaneously to the children and adapting to them. That was particularly true in cases reported in the 1940s and 1950s and probably reflected teachings of the early part of the century. As noted, Kanner found the mothers more formal, distant, and perfectionistic than other mothers.

They seem to have had more than usual difficulty with the children during the neonatal period, although little detail bearing on this point is available. It is clearer that the honeymoon was uncommon among them. Rather than playful interaction, the mothers reported a different kind of bliss—having good babies who were left to themselves much of the time. This siutation was not conducive to the development of attachment. On the whole, mothers seem to have been disappointed or frustrated by their autistic children at a number of points—at birth, during feeding crises, and then at the end of the year when the children's speech did not develop satisfactorily.

Mothers' disappointments in their young infants tend to turn into depression. At no other time in their lives are women as vulnerable to depression as in the year after giving birth, and their vulnerability centers on their infants. In turn, no mental state in mothers affect infants' development more adversely than depression.

Postpartum Depression

Most women become depressed in the weeks after childbirth. Usually, the depression is mild to moderate and rarely is identified as clinical depression because women rarely obtain clinical evaluations and clinicians do not ordinarily diagnose depression at this time unless it is severe. Mild depression (baby blues), although considered normal at the time, does lower women's responsiveness toward their neonates. Moderate depression usually is manifested in fatigue, disturbed sleep and appetite, loss of interest in sex, and somatic symptoms, which often are attributed to the physical stress of giving birth and caring for a neonate.[48] Whatever the cause, depression is associated with reduced awareness of infant behavior and reduced or delayed response to it. It is also associated with lowered tolerance for disappointments.

A link between postpartum breakdown and autism has been suggested by Goldfarb and his colleagues. They concluded that the breakdown results from rage at one's infant. Insofar as the rage is forbidden, it causes "overcompensated inhibition," flatness of emotion, lack of spontaneity and of awareness of others' needs, and lack of organized activity. The inhibition

also is manifested in giving routine infant care mechanically, with detachment, while challenging or problem infant behavior elicits hesitancy and
perplexity in the mother. In turn, they believe, this behavior fosters autism in
the infant.[49]

Psychological analysis of postpartum depression began in the 1920s with
Zilboorg's reports that "frigid" women with "masculine" ambitions were
especially prone to it. These findings were supported by some clinicians and
challenged by others.[50] The issue was confused by sexism and by biases in
using the terms *masculine* (when applied to women) and *frigid*. Restated in
more-objective terms, a number of findings on breakdowns after childbirth
may be summarized and interpreted as follows:

1. Women who were relatively comfortable in the life-style prescribed
for them in the culture and relatively satisfied in marriage and respected by
their husbands and others before having children were not affected critically
by bearing children.

2. Women who were relatively comfortable with and successful in
career-oriented life-styles also had relatively little at stake in bearing children.
Included here are women who interrupted their careers only briefly at
childbirth, soon turning over care of the young infant to a relative
or nursemaid.

3. Women who were unhappy in traditional life-styles and particularly
anxious about their roles and relationships with their husbands, but who
nonetheless adhered to those life-styles, had much at stake in having children. Included here are those described as seeking in childbearing proof of
femininity or justification for their roles as wives or homemakers.

4. Women who were uncomfortable with career life-styles and had
strong, conflict-laden wishes for the traditional role but who nonetheless
pursued careers also had much at stake in having children. Included here are
those who gave up careers or who interrupted them for long periods upon
having children.

As a solution to a major life problem, pregnancy may be effective temporarily, but when pregnancy and the privileges it brings end, completion of
the solution requires having a superior child. That makes women particularly vulnerable to disappointment, anger, and postpartum disturbance.

Women in the first two groups were less likely than those in the latter
groups to suffer postpartum breakdown. Women in the fourth group tended
to focus on their children as replacements for their careers. They welcomed
the children as justification for giving up careers or blamed them for loss of
careers. They sought fulfillment through the children's accomplishments or
through careers of devotion to the children.

Mothers described in chapter 4 largely fit in the fourth group. Their
character, situation, and behavior toward their children are also like those of
women described in some studies of postpartum breakdown. The comparison

is not intended to suggest that mothers of autistic children suffered post-partum breakdowns but to indicate sources of specific behavior toward the children.

The fantasies and behavior of women who suffer breakdowns after childbirth are often strikingly uninhibited. According to Lomas, the women fear that they are losing control and are becoming psychotic and evil. They try to regain control by projection, perceiving their infants rather than themselves to be entertaining the wild and evil ideas. Therefore, they hide the infants. To avert future disgrace, they also devote themselves to achieving maximum control over the children's behavior. In turn, overcontrol of the children fosters autism.[51]

The case of Dibs fits the pattern. His mother perceived him to be wild and animalistic as an infant. Since this description was not objectively valid, it may be taken as a projection of her thoughts and impulses. She hid him and devoted herself to training him. Her rationale was that he was retarded and needed special training to bring him up to par, but she knew the rationale was not true. Therefore, it may be that the extensive, premature training was partly an effort to control the wildness she saw in him.

Overtraining of autistic children is usual. Mothers' perceptions of them as wild, animalistic, uncontrollable, or untrainable are also common. Data to connect the perception and the training are lacking. Kanner noted what he considered excessive concern for proper behavior as a factor in the early training of autistic children.[52] The other side of concern for propriety is apprehension about improper behavior. If Kanner's observation is valid, the behavior of many mothers of autistic children is comparable to the behavior Lomas found.

Heavy training of an infant is difficult to sustain. A depressed mother tends to lapse in her training even though she considers it necessary. The result may be periods of heavy training alternating with periods in which the infant is ignored. Such alternation was reported by Kanner.[53]

Depressed people tend to be perplexed, to have difficulty learning simple tasks, and to be highly sensitive to rebuffs. Depressed mothers have serious difficulties with their babies and extremely contradictory attitudes toward them. According to Smalldon, they express disappointment, anger, or indifference toward their infants, calling them idiots and degenerates. But they are very proud of them.[54]

These are extreme reactions. Most mothers, mildly depressed in the weeks after childbirth, feel that they have been let down. They may wonder if something is missing in the babies that prevents communication with them. Helpless feelings are frequent at this time, along with the idea that the long-awaited chance has come and gone and now there is nothing to look forward to.

The disappointment and depression of mothers of autistic children seem to fall between the extreme and the average. In ideas that the baby is retarded or monstrous in other ways, many of the mothers are close to the extreme. In perpelexity, failure to learn simple things in relation to their babies, and sensitivity to rebuffs, they are also near the extreme. Interruption of infant care, ranging from ignoring infants for hours to persistent detachment, seems common. So are sharply contradictory attitudes toward the babies. But weeping, total dejection, insomnia, and anorexia, common in very depressed women, have not been reported in mothers of autistic children.

The following case draws some of the threads together. The parents were both scientists. The mother had planned and saved for five years to have her first child and eagerly awaited George's birth. After he was born, she began a diary about him with minute-by-minute entries.

Labor had been difficult, and she had been given medication. The newborn boy was exceptionally difficult. He alternated between unresponsiveness and hyperactivity with inconsolable crying. Inasmuch as no organic abnormalities were ever found, his early behavior was probably attributable to the conditions of his birth—difficult labor and obstetric drugs.

The mother was determined to breastfeed George, but his behavior made feeding extremely difficult. She took the difficulty as a rejection and became depressed, eating little. Nonetheless, she did not give up. In the following weeks, each attempt at breastfeeding was stormy—George screaming, the mother weeping. Each feeding took about two hours—"a nightmare of who would outlast the other."[55]

In the next few months, George spent much of his time staring at a mobile or his own hand. He responded little to her holding him or playing with him. George did respond to his father during these months, but the father said he found George insufficiently interesting, and he withdrew into his work.

At five months, George was examined by a pediatrician, who at first found him so unresponsive that he appeared deaf and blind. The pediatrician spoke soothingly to the screaming infant, and after twenty minutes of this, George gave a brief smile and allowed himself to be held. After another ten minutes, he relaxed and molded his body to the pediatrician's, smiling. This upset the mother, who voiced bitterness that she had not gotten this response from her son. She also became eager to hold George. However, as she took him, he began to scream, which angered her.

When George was seven months old, the mother began psychotherapy, and two months later George began to improve. He did well for over a year. But he regressed when, at age two, his mother gave birth to another son. She found the second child easy to breastfeed and care for. Her relationship with him was easy and pleasant. Nonetheless, she kept reminding people that his difficult brother came first with her.

This case is exceptional in that the infant's behavior and relationship to his mother were documented in clinical records from birth. The details support interpretations that are more speculative in other cases. At birth, George's behavior was abnormal, but it was not atypical for children born after difficult labor with the help of obstetric drugs. Given his behavior, his mother's reaction to him was typical. Any mother who had waited and prepared to such an extent for the coming of a child and had looked forward to it so eagerly probably would become depressed on finding her baby unresponsive. Any mother who was determined to breastfeed might take her infant's persistent balking as a personal rejection. In the circumstances, the mother's depression and resentment were to be expected. In short, George's and his mother's behavior were normal in the circumstances.

The critical factor in situations like this may be what a mother does when congenital factors that interfere with infant responsiveness are no longer present. Ideally, she would reorient her behavior quickly. But it is not to be expected that accumulated resentment simply will evaporate when an unresponsive infant becomes responsive. Also, the infant's change may be gradual, and a depressed parent may fail to notice it, no matter how badly the change is wanted.

The anger of George's mother was apparent. Presumably, it affected George. It is clear that after his congenital unresponsiveness was gone, George responded positively to his father and negatively to his mother. Had the father taken a major part in rearing him, George might have done better in early infancy. The father's withdrawal left the relationship with the mother as the only basis for developing social behavior. By the time he was five months old, he behaved toward others as he did toward her.

Such case studies are rare. Much more information is available about depression in mothers at the end of the first year and its effects on infant development, with particular relevance to autism. Some writers consider the latter part of the first year critical for infant development generally and for autism in particular.[56]

The most striking study involved a group of children who were apparently normal during their first year. Thereafter, they were slow to walk and talk and fearful of trying new things. They continued to get worse and were diagnosed as retarded when about four years old. By then, their most notable lack was speech, and they did especially poorly on whatever was required of them. In contrast, most of them were highly accomplished in a narrow specialty of their own choosing. Other details were also typical of cases of autism.

In each case, the children's decline was traced to depression in their mothers toward the end of the first year. When they became depressed, the care given by the mothers took on "a peculiar contradictory quality." They continued to provide almost all the care the infants received. In addition, the mothers spent all their time with the infants and prevented other people from having contact with them. Nonetheless, the mothers were inattentive and unresponsive to the infants and did little to meet needs expressed by them. The care given was "silent, mechanical, resentful, gloomy, and lacking any spontaneity." Such care is typical of depressed mothers. It is also typical of the care reported by Kanner and others in cases of autism. The effort made by the mothers went substantially into keeping the infants "quiet and inactive" and into controlling them in a "restrictive, negative way."[57]

One case was chosen to typify the group. The mother, a highly compulsive person, had led a rather narrow life. She took very little interest in people, including her husband, had no hobbies, and avoided activities outside the home. The birth of her first child led to a transformation. She became fascinated with and devoted to her baby. However, she cared for the baby in a mechanical way, with little touching or fondling. Then, when the baby was nine months old, the mother became profoundly disappointed and felt that she had failed. It was not because of any defect or slowness to develop in the child but because the mother became aware that "some great and magical change that she expected had not taken place."[58]

In many of the cases in this study, the mothers' discouragement and depression began with a specific disappointment in their children. For example, some mothers were shaken profoundly by their children's failure to be linguistically precocious.

The end of the first year is when children begin to use words. Parents of autistic children have been described as extraordinarily interested in having them be verbally precocious, undertaking intense verbal training of them during infancy (chapter 14). That would make the end of the first year a critical period.

The development of learning generally and of language in particular has been thought to depend upon infant attachment to mothers that develops during the middle of the first year. Attachment is explored in the next chapter.

7

The Relationship: Attachment in Normal and Autistic Development

The phenomena of isolation and unresponsiveness, considered by many writers to be the core of autism, have been conceptualized as an inability to form attachments. Behaviors included in the concept suggest a continuity from neonatal reactions against handling to avoidance of people by autistic children of several years of age. Along the way, the children show a preference for solitude and for nonhuman objects. They put their parents off by actions that give the impression of not being attached to them, not knowing who they are, or perceiving them as inanimate objects.

Much controversy has centered on the issue of whether the children are born without ability to relate and never develop it or can relate but withdraw instead. Ability has been a major concept in psychology; clinical practice developed largely out of the attempt to define and measure mental ability. Nonetheless, the concept has eluded rigorous definition. Some of the controversy about autistic children rests on ambiguities in the meaning of "can" in questions such as Can autistic children form attachments? and Can silent autistic children speak? It is not necessary to answer such questions. For the purpose of the analysis that follows, it is sufficient to state whether or not autistic children do relate and form attachments. To go further—to discuss concepts like innate capacity or potential—is to pursue lines of thought that long have tempted scientists with disappointing results. There is no clear advantage to offset burdening analysis of autism with the ambiguities of such concepts.

Many details of their behavior show that autistic children do relate. By conventional definitions, they do form attachments, particularly to their mothers. The attachments are atypical and include manifestations not easily recognized.

The considerable literature on attachment—much of it recent—is the source of interpretations of autism that follow. Some autistic behaviors are analyzed as normal attachment behavior, others as uncommon attachment behavior that is typical in certain situations, particularly in separations, and still others as disturbed attachment behavior.

Studies of Attachment

Since Aristotle, philosophers have defined attachment as essential to human nature. Without it, people were not considered human and still are not.

"There never was a child who did not need an adult, nor was there a child who did not fear losing an adult he had. It is axiomatic that this conception is the human condition."[1] Attachment has been considered biologically necessary for survival in past ages and psychologically necessary for mental development. Theorists have suggested that without attachment, infants lack a sense of consistency in their experience—a framework by which to organize their knowledge and behavior. Disturbed attachment and separation have been considered primary causes of mental disturbance.[2]

Study of children's disturbances had focused on the parent-child relationship by the 1930s. That relationship was emphasized by behaviorism and psychoanalysis, the two schools that dominated psychology in the United States after World War I and that particularly influenced theories about child rearing. However, there was also a strong reaction against implicating parents in the problems of their children. It is not clear which trend would have prevailed if the issue had not been affected by dramatic developments.

Research in the field of ethology had an impact on clinical thinking after the discovery of imprinting—the sudden emergence of attachment to mother in infant birds and other animals. In England, heavy bombing of urban centers during World War II led to a massive social experiment. To save young urban children from the physical and psychic traumas of bombing, they were sent to live in rural areas, separating hundreds of thousands from their mothers. As a result, disturbances developed in most of the children and were reported in considerable detail. These reports dovetailed with studies of American children separated from their mothers under a variety of conditions. Nurses and others had been writing about how to prepare children to withstand the psychic trauma of hospitalization. Separation of neonates also came under study, and hospitals experimented with keeping mother and baby in the same room after childbirth (lying in). The results were remarkably good with normal neonates after normal births. Also, as noted in the last chapter, more-dramatic results were obtained in similar experiments with premature babies. In this context, the Iowa experiments of the 1930s, long forgotten, won renewed attention. Young children diagnosed as retarded, who had been cared for in the usual way in institutions, were found to be very prone to disease, as was to be expected. Some of them were given "mothers" (retarded young women who were also inmates of the institutions). The conditions fostered mutual attachment, and the result was normal health and intelligence in the children. But the best known, probably most influential studies were by Harlow and his associates of infant monkeys separated from their mothers.[3]

Spurts of research occurred in the middle of the century by workers in different fields, who were largely unacquainted with each others' findings. The results remained fragmented for some time, but then people in different fields began to see connections with each others' work.

Attachment, Survival, and Socialization

Attachment had been thought to rest on feeding. Together with its physiological function in life and growth, food was considered the basic gratifier in
shaping psychological development. Thus, mothers were thought to acquire
their psychological importance to infants by being associated with the food
they provided. Recent findings indicate that the stimulation of receiving
food is less important than had been thought and that tactile and kinesthetic
stimulation from being held, caressed, or rocked are primary in fostering
attachment.[4] In some animals, attachment can develop independently of
feeding, and human attachment seems more to determine what happens in
feeding than to result from feeding. Disturbance in attachment causes disturbance of eating and gastrointestinal functioning; starvation and death
may result.[5]

From an ethological viewpoint, attachment is necessitated by the helplessness of infants. When care or protection are needed, attachment behavior
in infants and mothers serves to bring or keep them together and to engender
caretaking activities.[6] The absence or departure of mothers in many species
is a stimulus for infant calling.

Human infants are like others in this respect, but their mothers may find
such behavior confusing and even perverse. A mother who rebuffs her infant
may find that, instead of letting her alone, the infant is likely to be more
demanding and clinging than before. This may frustrate her, but maternal
behavior that increases distance from an infant is the stimulus for increased
attachment behavior by the infant.

The need for protection is aroused by threat. In monkeys, for example,
the sight or sound of a predator causes an infant to emit cries that bring its
mother. Mother and infant approach each other. She picks the infant up or
helps it climb on her. It clings to her as she flees. The more threats an infant
perceives, the more it tries to be with its mother; and the more it does so, the
more she is affected. Therefore, when predators are common, infants and
mothers seem very attached to each other. They then show more than usual
attachment behavior during intervals when predators are absent. Other
situations that cause fear or anxiety in infants have similar effects.[7]

The function of attachment in different species depends upon how mature the young are at birth and the conditions in which they are reared. In
many species, mothers care for infants of other mothers as well as their own,
and the proximity of an infant or its attempt to feed may be enough to elicit
mothering. If an infant is separated from or rejected by its mother, survival is
not threatened as long as other mothers are nearby. It is not necessary that
an infant know its own mother or that she know it.

In sheep, goat, and other species, mothers care only or primarily for
their own. A helpless infant that loses contact with its mother or is rejected

by her will die. Behavior that is typical for the species and is directed indiscriminately to members of the species is not sufficient for survival. Mother and infant need to respond to each other as individuals, distinct from other members of the species. And they may need to learn this discrimination because their unaided instincts may not tell them which is their own.

In some of these species, mothers show little attachment behavior. They make little effort to be near their infants or to retrieve them if they stray. Infant attachment behavior is the principal mechanism for maintaining contact and ensuring survival, and infants soon become skilled at identifying, following, or clinging to their mothers. In other species, infants show little attachment behavior, and survival depends upon mothers' behavior.

Human mothers rear their own infants primarily, and lack of attachment behavior by mothers or infants has serious consequences. Mothers show recognition and attachment very early, long before infants do. Human neonates cannot find, follow, or effectively cling to their mothers. And their voices do not carry far in relation to the distances their mothers can travel easily. In addition, human infants do not suddenly imprint to their mothers. Some attachment behavior is present at birth, but most of it develops gradually over a period of months. Therefore, in the first weeks, human infants are more dependent on their mothers' behavior than on their own for care and for the development of their own attachment.

Despite these limitations, infant attachment behavior is important in the first months primarily because it reinforces and increases maternal attachment. The cry of the neonate is effective in eliciting care and contact. In that respect, crying is attachment behavior. It does not endear the neonate to the mother. Nonetheless, it can be a step in an attachment sequence, as follows. The neonate cries, the mother comes and takes action, the neonate is quieted by her intervention, and she is gratified by the response. When that is the usual sequence, attachment is fostered in both. To the extent that the mother does not come regularly and promptly and her intervention is not successful, problems in attachment develop for both.

As the weeks pass, more-pleasing attachment behavior develops. Infants show various kinds of recognition of their mothers, to whom being greeted with smiles and happy-sounding gurgles are particularly gratifying. Cooing, laughing, and behavior interpreted as friendly and affectionate are also powerfully endearing. In addition, infants' adaptations to their mothers' routines are very gratifying. By about five months, infant attachment is well developed, but infants still can hardly follow or cling to their mothers and remain dependent on the mothers' actions.

With the evolution of society, attachment became less critical for survival. In earliest times, mothers' awareness that their infants' physical survival depended on them may have served to reinforce their attachment behavior. Consequently, their infants' mental development was promoted. Later, the structure of the extended family or tribe made substitute infant care available, freeing mothers to engage in nonmaternal activities. Their awareness that their infants' survival did not depend on them was reinforced by advice to mothers in recent decades not to do more than minimal caretaking—in effect, not to engage in behavior that fostered infant attachment. Insofar as mothers followed the advice, developmental problems were engendered.

In these circumstances, what mothers did was influenced by their infants. Infant behavior that was very demanding and gratifying engaged mothers despite prevailing advice. Conversely, a good baby—undemanding, content with solitude and inanimate objects—did little to engage them. The pairing of an infant who was not effective in eliciting maternal attachment behavior with a mother who was not inclined strongly to engage in it was likely to produce an isolated, handicapped child. In short, social changes increased the importance of infants' attachment behavior for their psychological well-being.

Modern society protects motherless young children adequately against direct physical threats such as predators and starvation. That is not enough in many cases to insure survival. Attachment is critical because psychological effects of its lack render infants vulnerable to disease. At the turn of the century, few unattached infants in the United States lived beyond the first year. In foundling hospitals, those who became the favorites of nurses survived. Almost all others died.[8]

The concept of attachment has been used to include behaviors, traits, emotions, and bonds. In the following discussion, I use attachment as a trait to describe infants; they will be classified simply as attached or not attached. Distinctions will be necessary later in applying attachment theory to normal and autistic development.

Novelty and Fear

The protective function of attachment seems closely connected to early learning and the development of intelligence. Animal infants identify some predators by their features. Other predators are not identified specifically; infants react to them as they do to anything that is grossly unfamiliar. That is especially true of primate and human infants.

The unfamiliar plays a complex role in their infancy. Objects that are slightly to moderately unfamiliar, that differ somewhat from prior experience, elicit curiosity. An infant may pay attention, approach, and explore them. But highly novel objects elicit fear and flight to mother. Between the two are objects that elicit curiosity and fear at the same time. An infant may make abortive movements toward or away from such an object. The infant may approach it, while uttering cries that summon the mother. The infant may explore the object briefly and return to the mother and cling to her. The infant may stay with the mother and observe the object. Or the infant may turn away from the object completely or close his or her eyes. How much an infant explores such an object depends on how the mother serves as an attachment figure—how much her presence reduces fear and flight responses.

In turn, exploring novel objects makes them familiar, reducing their power to arouse fear the next time. In general, exploration makes the environment a familiar place that does not arouse fear. In addition, exploration fosters learning. An infant that lacks an attachment figure or is attached to a mother in such a way that her presence does not promote exploration (insecure attachment) will tend to be fearful of many things, to stay within a limited, familiar terrain, and to be handicapped in learning.[9]

The fear aroused by novelty is compounded by separation. A moderately strange object elicits crying and running to mother when separated from her. The same object may be viewed without apparent distress from her lap or may be explored if she is close by. Conversely, separation from mother may be tolerated comfortably as long as no strange objects are present.

The fears and extreme avoidance of novelty that characterize autistic children may be explained by attachment theory—by lack of secure attachment that allows for exploration. In addition, the fears and avoidance may be attributed to lack of experience with the environment resulting from being hidden away, left alone, and not having contact with people other than their mothers.

Mothers do not function as effective attachment figures for most autistic children in the third year and thereafter. How effectively the children used them in the first and second years as sources of security and as bases from which to explore novel objects and situations is unclear. Some were more venturesome when accompanied by other adults than by their mothers. The fact that many were left alone in the middle of the first year suggests limited availability of the mothers in dealing with novelty. The children's fears and avoidance of novelty in the second year suggest limited use of their mothers as attachment figures in exploring novel objects. Lack of an effective attachment figure also can perpetuate self-generated fears. Children are frightened by their dreams and waking fantasies. Presumably, the presence of an effective attachment figure helps one to speak about or silently re-experience frightening fantasies and thereby to become less frightened. Data bearing on this are lacking, but it seems likely that children without effective attachments will be more frightened than other children by their fantasies.

Extreme fear of novelty together with rather limited experience makes for chronic apprehensiveness because unexpected change may occur at any time. And chronic apprehensiveness can foster a variety of symptoms. Rituals—particularly those that prevent change—and inactivity are common adaptations. Any behavior that reduces novelty may be conditioned. In addition, vigilance is likely. Thus, disturbed attachment may lead indirectly to a variety of symptoms.

In many ways, a mother's role as an attachment figure determines how her infant experiences the environment and thereby influences basic adaptations to the environment. Rochlin suggested that attachment was necessary for infants to learn to profit from experience and to modify their behavior in view of future consequences.[10] If that is true, disturbed attachment may lead to severe handicaps. It also may foster narrow specialization in learning. By devotion to one activity and ignoring the rest of the world, a child can limit novelty greatly. Concentration of time and effort in one activity leads to expertness in it while falling behind in other areas. Another intellectual disadvantage in avoiding novelty derives from the sequential nature of much learning. Many tasks are difficult to learn if one has not mastered preliminary steps. Therefore, limited experience is a handicap in most areas of learning.

Variations in Attachment

Attachment behavior in human and animal infants has been defined as following or searching for mother, initiating and maintaining contact or closeness with her, eliciting her attention and nurture, and punishing her for staying away.[11] The emphasis in this section is on infant behaviors that:

Foster a bond in mother (inducing attachment),

Bring mother and infant together when separated (seeking proximity),

Keep them together (maintaining proximity),

Deter mother from staying away (deterring absence).

When these functions are effective, an infant is thought to develop a secure attachment, described as the

[C]onfident expectation that when mother leaves she will return, that when she is needed she will be there, that if the infant cries out or searches for her she will be found.

When these expectations are not met, infants are thought to develop an insecure attachment. When extremely insecure, children are "intolerant of separation or change [and] cling too hard to what they have, or, losing it, avoid all human involvement.[12]

In addition to the four categories of attachment behavior, many infant acts are considered indicators of the presence of attachment in infants. These acts include greeting mother on her return (smiling, vocalizing, or clapping) and using mother as a safe base (exploring novel objects when she is present, returning to her when frightened or hurt).

Behaviors that show the presence of attachment, and particularly behaviors that show pleasure in the relationship, are notably lacking in autistic children. That is part of the reason they are said not to be attached to their mothers. In addition, they are said not to have engaged in other attachment behavior as infants. As noted in the last chapter, the accuracy of such observations has been questioned.

In any case, two categories of attachment behavior are clearly present in infancy—maintaining proximity and deterring absence. Protest at mothers' departure or at signs of impending departure are common and sometimes so pitiable or violent that some mothers never have left the children. Others went out only when the fathers were home, and the parents did not go out as a couple for three years.[13] In addition, mothers who left for a weekend or week found their autistic children so unfriendly and disturbed on returning that they avoided further absences.

As in other children, maintaining proximity and deterring absence are directed at the mothers. Rarely does the departure of anyone else cause protest or distress. Even when, as infants, autistic children smile and vocalize at their fathers and can be comforted by them while unresponsive in those ways to their mothers, it is the mothers' absences that upset them. Some of the children seem perverse in that, while actively avoiding their mothers when present, they are terrified by the mothers' absences.

It may be unnecessary to emphasize that reports of autistic children literally not recognizing their mothers, treating their mothers the same as they treat other people, or treating their mothers like pieces of furniture are inaccurate. Autistic children treat their mothers differently than they treat others. Specifically, much attachment behavior that they show is directed at their mothers. The mothers' reports of not being treated distinctively may be an expression of disappointment over the absence of more-gratifying attachment behavior. The apparent indifference and nonrecognition often are experienced by the mothers as hostility, but hostility does not mean absence of attachment. On the contrary, it can be an element of attachment that serves to maintain proximity or to deter absence.[14] Nonetheless, mothers tend not to interpret the behavior as showing attachment.

Infant attachment behavior begins as innate reflexes but soon reflects experience. Reward for smiling can make an infant smile much of the time. If not rewarded, an infant may not smile at all. The same applies to other attachment behavior, and the modifications resulting from experience may be complex, determining the form attachment behavior takes and the person to whom it is directed.[15] These considerations are background to the following specific aspects of attachment in ordinary and autistic children.

Visual Attachment

Visual attachment includes visual following, eye-to-eye contact, concentration on mother's face, and staring at her. Scanning also may be considered attachment behavior insofar as search of one's surroundings precedes fixing one's gaze on an object. Except for scanning, the behaviors involve gaze fixation.

Gaze fixation on mother begins in the first few weeks. Eye contact is likely to gratify mother and, therefore, may be considered attachment-inducing behavior. Visual following of mother as she moves away has been considered analogous to following by creeping or walking in older infants. Thus, it may be proximity-maintaining or proximity-seeking behavior. Concentration on mother's face has been taken as interest in her. Fixed staring at mother appears at several weeks, usually during feeding. The infant's eyes are wide open and the stare is striking. Facial muscles are tensed, and observers get the impression of a strong emotion. The stare often has been interpreted as an expression of love of mother, but Benjamin suggested that it was characteristic of infants experiencing stress in relation to their mothers.[16]

Infants of three to seven months stare much of the time if separated from their mothers. Unresponsiveness accompanies the stare, giving the impression that it is nonsocial. Sometimes the stare is not directed at people, but it is often directed at familiar people, who experience it as contact (being stared at) or lack of contact (being stared through).[17]

Data on humans and animals support considering fixed gaze an attachment phenomenon. Fixed gaze is also known to be hostile but, as noted, that need not detract from its attachment function. People may find being stared at pleasurable and be moved to intimate behavior, or they may find it distressing and be moved to withdraw. Context and prior conditioning influence their reactions. However, whether people wish to be intimate or to withdraw, they find it difficult to withdraw as long as they are stared at. Fixed gaze thus maintains proximity. If maintenance of proximity is assumed to be the primary function of staring, various phenomena and interpretations may be reconciled.

The attribution of love to infant staring is not so much inaccurate as a romanticization of a more-primitive instinct—attachment. Proximity-maintaining behavior should not be aroused by maternal behavior that indicates continuation of proximity but by behavior that indicates interruption of it. An infant stares at its mother when she is leaving. By conditioning, cues of her impending departure come to elicit staring, and such cues come to elicit the distress that her departure causes. An infant who stares much of the time when she is present may have experienced frequent separation from the mother. Perhaps she has withdrawn while the infant was still feeding or immediately after feeding, when the infant was in an alert, playful state. (If she had waited until the infant fell asleep, her withdrawal would not have been perceived.) Thus, Benjamin may be right in associating stress in relation to mother with staring at her.

Autistic children have been reported to stare when their mothers are present but not about to leave and when their mothers are absent. I suggested an explanation of the former; to explain the latter as attachment behavior requires more assumptions. Mothers' absence should be a stimulus for seeking proximity, but staring has been interpreted here as maintaining proximity. The occurrence of maintaining when seeking is called for may be attributable to the failure of seeking.

Although seeking and maintaining proximity are responses to different cues, they are related functionally. Sometimes they occur as part of a sequence: proximity seeking may be followed by a mother's appearance, to which her infant may respond with proximity maintenance. Let us assume that an infant's seeking has been effective. When baby cried, mother came. Let us further assume that seeking is no longer effective. Depressed or apprehensive about spoiling her baby, the mother has stopped responding to his or her cries. Repeated failure of a previously successful act leads to substitution of similar behavior. In this case, other seeking behavior would be expected. If other seeking behavior is not available or not successful, regressive substitution is to be expected—substitution of inappropriate behavior.

Young children separated from their mothers engage in much staring. They also engage in much behavior identified as regressive—notably, in eating, eliminating, and dressing. Their staring is interpretable as inappropriate attachment behavior in response to the separation and the failure of formerly effective seeking behavior. I suggested some reasons why autistic children show the behavior of separated ones—being left alone and the equivalent of being left alone when their mothers, though present, are unreponsive because of depression. The reasons are elaborated in the next chapter.

The apparent normality or bizarreness of a substitute response depends on whether the observer sees a functional relationship between it and the unsuccessful response for which it substitutes. Adults commonly engage in inappropriate behavior when frustrated, as when they fail to open a familiar lock with its key. Whatever the cause of the failure (a jammed lock or not having inserted the key fully into the lock), people commonly do foolish things. They try to turn the key in the wrong direction or try other keys that they know do not fit the lock. Such behavior seems appropriate because people understand it. The behavior may have been appropriate once in that the person may have had a lock that turned in the direction that the present one does not. In addition, the person may have had the experience of possessing different keys and not knowing which of them to use, so that trying different keys was appropriate (reinforced). If the behavior had been appropriate in the past, its present use is regressive.

Let us assume that staring in older children is the same behavior as gaze fixation in neonates. Before neonates learn to distinguish their mother and to know when she is present, they stare at various objects. Therefore, if other attachment behavior becomes unsuccessful, indiscriminate staring might recur. Separated children stare indiscriminately. It is possible that they regress to the extent that discrimination of their mother is lost, and many are said not to recognize her during visits or after reunion. However, as noted, their apparent nonrecognition is misleading and they still distinguish her from other people. Indiscriminate staring may be regressive whether or not the discrimination is lost.

An alternate assumption is that separated children regress to the point of hallucinating the presence of their mother. Psychoanalysts have suggested that normal young infants hallucinate the presence of what they desire when frustrated.[18] Older children and adults do something of the sort. For example, adults who are in love and separated tend to mistake people who bear a superficial resemblance to the absent lover for the lover. Most of the time, the misperception is partial and brief, with only limited tendencies to act on it. The usual reaction is to stare at the look-alike. However, the experience may be so gripping as to result in inappropriate behavior suggestive of hallucination. For example, a stranger who does not resemble the lover may be stared at, followed, or accosted even when the lover could not possibly be present.

Adults whose mates die commonly hallucinate the presence of the lost one and direct proximity-maintaining behavior toward the hallucinated image. For example, they see the lost one sitting in a favorite chair or carrying on an habitual activity. They may converse at length with the hallucinated image. Insofar as such behavior occurs in normal adults after bereavement, similar behavior in separated young children could be a normal occurrence.

Whether or not infants hallucinate is unknown. They do things that, if done by older children and adults, are indicative of hallucinating. For example, they talk or gesture without directing the communication at any present person. If separated infants hallucinate their mothers, staring could be proximity-maintaining behavior directed at the hallucinated image. Much staring by separated infants appears unfocused. The idea that it is directed at a hallucinatory image might account for apparent lack of focus—focus at the distance of the image rather than on objects at hand. The staring of autistic children may be explainable on the same basis.

Autistic young children stare and scan and do other things that ordinary children do when separated. Therefore, the behavior may derive from their attachment repertory even though their mothers do not recognize and respond to it as attachment behavior.

Autistic children also do things that have not been considered in attachment studies but that nonetheless may be construed as having attachment functions. They wander. They get into dangerous positions and have accidents. They bang their heads and mutilate themselves. These activities are powerful stimulants to mothering. Wandering elicits maternal pursuit, search, and retrieval, sometimes followed by holding. Any behavior that causes self-injury or threatens it may elicit care.

If these behaviors have attachment functions, the effect on parents of autistic children is confusing. The children, having gotten their mothers' attention by dangerous or injurious acts, rebuff them. A similar paradox occurs in normal children after long or otherwise traumatic separations.

They call their mothers and, when the mothers come, reject them. They then act as if the mothers were not present and refuse to be fed and cared for by them. Some go as far as to state that their mothers are not their mothers. Also, while rebuffing them, they may continue to seek their mothers. This behavior is confusing and distressing to mothers, especially when the children act normally toward their fathers.

Factors in Attachment

Factors contributing to attachment may be divided into three groups: maternal behavior that contributes to infant attachment; infant behavior that contributes to maternal attachment; and situational factors that affect either one. In addition, maternal behavior may contribute to maternal attachment. For example, giving up a career at the birth of a child may increase a mother's involvement with her baby. Hiring a nursemaid or inviting a grandmother to come and care for the infant may decrease a mother's attachment. Many factors in attachment have been touched on earlier; they will be summarized with additions.

Maternal Factors

Stimulation by mother fosters infant attachment. Within limits, the more stimulation, the more attachment.[19] Quality of maternal stimulation determines quality of infant attachment.

Ainsworth classified infants as securely attached, insecurely attached, and unattached. Unattached infants had received the least stimulation. The insecurely attached had about as much time with the mother and about as much stimulation as the secure. But the insecure seemed desperate rather than content in the relationship. They did not tolerate her absence well and tried harder to prevent it than securely attached infants did. When the mother was present, they cried, fussed, and stayed close to her. Thus, she was not effective in helping them explore the environment, and they interacted minimally with it.

Many forms of stimulation appear to foster infant attachment. These include touch, motion, sound, and light. Tactile stimulation that fosters attachment includes touching, stroking, patting, holding, squeezing, kissing, and hugging. Relevant kinetic stimulation includes rocking, bouncing, and carrying. Auditory stimulation consists largely of mother's voice; particularly effective are her babbling and imitation of her infant's vocalizations. Her heartbeat also seems important. Among visual stimuli, mother's face is most effective, particularly when facing an infant. Her eyes are of the greatest interest to the infant.

In general, moderate stimulation is most effective. Below certain levels, young infants are unresponsive. As intensity rises, they become alert and quiet. Looking may be followed by mouthing, smiling, gurgling, laughing, and other vocalizations. With more-intense stimuli, pleasurable responses are replaced by avoidance and distress—turning away, shutting eyes, stiffening, and crying.

Complex aspects of stimulation probably have as much influence as simple ones on attachment, as was suggested by a study of infants reared in some Israeli communes.[20] They were cared for largely by nursemaids, and their parents spent little time with them. Thus, the parents gave relatively little of the stimulation received by the children. Nonetheless, the children seemed to form stronger bonds to their parents than to their nursemaids. The same has occurred in many affluent homes, in which feeding and other care were given by domestics, while parents spent little time with children.

Stimulation described as intrusive has been reported to cause avoidance of the stimulation and of the adults who provide it.[21] Intrusiveness is a matter of intensity and timing. Stimulation that interrupts infants' activities is resisted. The same stimulation when infants are not engaged may be welcome. Weak stimulation can be ignored without interruption of infants' activities. Intense stimuli are more likely to evoke active resistance. When stimuli are moderate, timing determines infant response.

The average mother spends long periods stimulating her young infant socially. She positions the infant to face her and then smiles and vocalizes. Meanwhile, she moves her face toward and away from the infant's. Such stimulation has been found to be highly effective. Infants respond by becoming still and staring with wide-open eyes. Then they show increasing excitement, vocalize, and smile. That is the effect when "the mother's actions are carefully phased with those of the infant." An element in the timing of her stimulation is pausing to allow infant response. And when a mother presents much stimulation that is unresponsive to her infant's cues, the infant fusses, cries, and shows "prolonged turning away from the mother's face."[22]

These findings may bear on a film study of infants who appeared normally responsive to people during the first half-year of their lives but who later were unresponsive and diagnosed as autistic. During the first half-year, some of the mothers held, touched, and gazed at their infants relatively little. Others provided a great amount of stimulation, but it was relatively unrelated to their infants' cues.[23]

To summarize a variety of findings on infant-caretaker interaction: care that is responsive to initiatives or signals from an infant fosters a strong, secure bond and good development, and intrusive interaction fosters avoidance of the caretaker, avoidance of stimulation provided by the caretaker, and resistance to learning. Avoidance of the caretaker does not necessarily mean lack of attachment, but it does make for problems in attachment, including nonuse of the caretaker in exploring novel stimuli. Observations of mothers with autistic children and books written by them indicate relatively low maternal responsiveness and considerable intrusiveness.

Infant Behaviors

Early infant behaviors that foster attachment by mother include pleasurable and other positive responses to her and expressions of distress. Pleasurable reactions are smiling, laughing, and joyful-appearing excitement in her presence. Positive responses are recognizing her and greeting her on her arrival; turning toward her, searching out her face, and gazing at her face; quieting and becoming alert on hearing her voice; being quieted by her ministrations when in distress; molding to her body when held; clinging to her; readily accepting food from her; babbling at her; and imitating her. Distress includes crying and fussing in her presence and protesting her departure.

Pleasurable and positive reactions make an infant attractive to its mother and reward her for contact with it. Looking into her eyes and smiling at her are dramatic in their emotional effect on her. In general, the more pleasurable and positive responses given by a baby, the more attachment develops in its mother. However, intensely joyful reactions may arouse concern, shame, or guilt in a mother about overstimulating, indulging, or spoiling her baby. If the baby seems excited, she may withdraw. This is particularly true if her baby's response strikes her as erotic.

An infant who does not cry is easy to ignore and may not compete effectively with other interests and demands for a mother's attention. Distress reactions coerce her to involve herself. Crying can be so unpleasant as to motivate her to do almost anything that puts a stop to it. Protesting her departure may prevent her departure. While resenting an infant who makes her a prisoner, she nonetheless may feel needed; and feeling needed is a powerful base of a relationship. Thus, a mother's attachment may be intense, although colored by resentment over the sacrifice she is making.

Mothers interpret what their infants do in various ways, depending on context, mothers' personalities, their moods, or advice they have received. Therefore, infant behavior that fosters attachment in one mother may have the opposite effect on another. The role of mothers' personalities is illustrated by reactions to two infants who stopped crying on being picked up. One mother interpreted the cessation as responsive to herself, was pleased, and therefore often picked up her infant. The other interpreted the cessation to mean that the infant had not needed her. She concluded her infant was spoiled and had cried simply to get picked up. Therefore, she stopped responding when her infant cried.

The accuracy of their interpretations is irrelevant here; but their reactions are relevant to their infants' development. As noted, responding to cries fosters attachment.

Recognizing mother, greeting her when she comes, smiling, anticipating her actions, and cooperating are pleasing to mothers. Presumably, autistic children's mothers would have been pleased because nothing indicates otherwise. Behavior indicating infant excitement or arousal would seem likely to have fostered a mixture of pleasure and discomfort or guilt insofar as the mothers were uncomfortable with sensual feelings and intense emotions. Many of them described excitement in their infants in negative terms (animal wildness). Perhaps, joyful, sensual behavior increased both maternal attachment and tendencies to be cool and distant.

Infant staring is attachment behavior, whether interpreted as showing interest in mother or making a demand of her. Either interpretation may foster attachment in a mother. But many mothers of autistic children report distress at demands they do not understand. Perhaps being stared at evokes distress in the mothers. If caretakers react adversely to being stared at, their own and their infants' attachment behavior may be reduced.

Situational Factors

In addition to the factors discussed there are factors in attachment that may involve behavior of mother or infant but that, for convenience, are listed separately. Having only one child intensifies maternal involvement. So does having waited long for a child, having sacrificed to have one, having recently suffered a bereavement, and other experiences discussed in chapter 4. These factors foster attachment in a mother, and maternal attachment ordinarily fosters infant attachment.

Sickness, frailty, or injury in an infant foster attachment in a mother, provided that she is not separated from the infant. Handicaps need not be real to have this effect. A spurious defect, whether mistakenly diagnosed by a physician or spontaneously imagined by a parent, will serve. Recent bereavement or other loss or threat to a mother will increase her concern about her infant's health. And the added care she gives may increase her infant's attachment. Infants' sickness and injuries also cause infants distress, which is then expressed in attachment-inducing behavior. Animal infants that are in pain or other distress become more clinging and docile.[24]

A connection between real or imagined illness and autism was suggested earlier. A mother of twins, equally healthy at birth, may identify one as sickly. As noted, she is likely to become particularly attached to that child, and the child is more likely than the twin to become schizophrenic. Therefore, what happens between a mother and a sick infant or one thought to be defective may shed light on the peculiar attachments that develop between autistic children and their mothers.

Mothers report different kinds of experiences with sick infants. Some tell of increased dependence in the children. Others, especially under circumstances in which care or treatment cause pain, report that infants become alienated from them. The administration of painful treatment is equivalent to punishment being associated with mothering. A sick infant cries, calling its mother who, in effect, then punishes the infant. In animals, such a situation causes temporary avoidance of the mother. If an alternate attachment figure is available, an animal infant may shift its attachment. However, if no alternate is available, heightened attachment to its mother develops.[25] Whether the same occurs in humans is not known. Theoretically, the circumstances would foster ambivalent attachment in infants.

Many autistic children develop attachments consistent with such a chain of events. Some show more-positive attachment behavior to another adult than to their mother, if one is available. They may smile at the father, play with him, and be comforted by him, while doing none of these with the mother. They may talk effectively to another adult and not to their mother. Nonetheless, they may be attached desperately to their mother and show the primacy of this attachment by the severity of their reactions to separation from her, as compared to separation from others.

To conclude, situations preceding and during the infancies of autistic children are usually conducive to intense attachment. The children tend to be born into nuclear families in which their mothers are their sole caretakers. They tend to be only or first children, and their births often are preceded by significant losses or changes. But, in the first months, the behavior of the infants and their mothers seems to foster mutual avoidance as well as attachment. The involvement of both may be characterized as intense, insecure, and rather ambivalent. In the circumstances, the children's attachment behavior becomes increasingly baffling to their mothers. The development of paradoxical attachment behavior in autistic children is elaborated in the next chapter.

8

The Strained Relationship: Separation, Reunion, and Estrangement

The consequences of failure to develop secure attachment overlap with the effects of separation after attachment has developed. In a variety of species, separation is disturbing to infants and adults. Animals fret, lose interest in things, become less active, and may engage in self-mutilation or indirectly life-threatening activities. Pining away has been found in birds, dogs, and primates, as well as in human children and adults. Animals and people who are separated tend to be withdrawn and unresponsive. They engage in relatively little behavior that can be rewarded or punished and are hard to teach. Separated human children and adults have negative feelings about themselves (worthlessness, helplessness) and about their situation and future (hopelessness). Whether or not infants have comparable thoughts and feelings is unknown, but separation in infancy reportedly is followed later in life by depressive tendencies, limited socialization, and inefficient learning.[1]

Separation is relevant to autism because it precipitates or worsens autistic symptoms and because autistic children show many behaviors found in other children after separation. In the first three years, separation affects autistic children dramatically, and it has been cited as the cause of their condition. O'Gorman concluded that the withdrawal of most autistic children from the world was an extension of their withdrawal from their mothers. In many cases, withdrawal from the mothers followed separation from them, as by vacation, illness, or the birth of a sibling. Erikson concluded that estrangement or separation from mothers was a factor in every case. Mahler said that full psychosis was always preceded and caused by grief and mourning.[2]

Some autistic children become markedly disturbed during separation. A boy, described as normal until then, was left with his grandmother at eleven months: "he screamed constantly day and night, was unresponsive to people and no longer played. He ignored his parents on their return."[3] Thereafter, he stopped speaking and became fully autistic.

Those who are disturbed visibly by separation may not respond to substitute caretakers' efforts to console or distract them. They may also avoid playing and eating and may regress in toileting and dressing. In addition, the disturbance may increase after their mothers return, resulting in a typical autistic pattern.

More often, the substitute caretaker reports normal behavior during the mother's absence, and the mother is unprepared for the changes she finds on her return. As a mother described it:

> I was absolutely horrified when I came home and saw the way he was ... completely different ... like a changeling. ... He looked through me, he just did not know I was there. You could call his name and there was no recognition at all that you were calling his name.[4]

Another child had shown behavior common to autistic children in infancy. Johnny had rocked, banged his head, masturbated often, and was undemanding. But he also had been affectionate toward his parents and had spoken normally prior to the separation. When he was one and a half, his parents took a trip and left him with his grandmother. On their return, the mother went to get him but he seemed not to recognize her. Then, as she tried to take him home:

> [J]ohnny fought her and continued to fight her all the way to the car. While she drove home, he moved away from her and sat ... with his head down and a sulky expression on his face, refusing to look at his mother. When they arrived ... Johnny ... went straight to his room. He closed the door and would not come out.[5]

The description suggests that his behavior after reunion was organized and consistent. In the months that followed, he learned no new words and stopped using those he already knew. He also became isolated and seemingly indifferent to his parents.

In a minority of cases, strong attachment had been clear before separation, as in the following example. Galia was reared largely by her father, who tried to train her to be a genius. She had a very close relationship with him until she was two, when he went to war and was killed. The mother, depressed, sent Galia to live with the grandmother, who also was depressed. Autistic behavior was noted during this period. When Galia was two and a half, her mother brought her home. "On entering the home Galia ran around searching frantically for her father in every corner of the flat, plaintively calling for him."[6] Her mother told her that he was dead, and she hit her mother and cried for hours. Subsequently, she became fully autistic.

The initial reactions of children who showed disturbance after reunion and subsequently developed full-blown autism usually included nonrecognition of their mothers and a decline in speech. Autistic children who became involved effectively in psychotherapy have had similar reactions to separations from their therapists.[7]

All the features of autism may appear for the first time or be intensified during a separation or after reunion, but their appearance at such times is not necessarily abnormal. Many symptoms of autistic children also are found in many ordinary children and the young of various animal species after separation or reunion and have been interpreted therein as attachment behavior.[8] Therefore, the changes in human and animal young caused by separation will be reviewed and analyzed in relation to autistic children and their experience. Although the separation reactions to be discussed are common enough to be considered normal, their severity and persistence vary from one child to another and from one occasion to another. Analysis of what causes them, what makes them severe, and what perpetuates them seems a likely source for understanding autism.

The analysis begins with neonates and ends with children of a few years of age. It is based on observations by parents and professionals made in natural situations and in experiments. Some children remained at home while their mothers were away. Some children were hospitalized or placed in other settings. Thus, the conditions under which the data were gathered varied greatly. The data may be taken as indicating common elements of infants' behavior repertories at different ages.

Separation reactions to be described were found in a majority of infants or in a large minority in the various studies. *Brief absence* will mean periods of minutes to a few hours; *long absence,* several hours to a few days; *brief separation,* several days to two weeks; and *long separation,* longer periods.

An infant or young child who goes to the hospital experiences a number of changes in addition to separation from the mother. These changes include separation from things and from other people in the home, the absence of familiar routines, the trauma of the illness or injury that led to hospitalization and of the medical and surgical procedures done there, and the novelty of the hospital environment. Without other evidence, it is questionable to attribute changes in a hospitalized child's behavior to separation from the mother. However, there is evidence of two kinds that her absence is the main cause of disturbance in most cases. First, when a child remains at home while the mother goes away, disturbance occurs, and the disturbance is much like that of a hospitalized child. The same has been found in animal studies. Second, when a child is away from home in the company of the mother, as when she also stays in the hospital and occupies the same room, little or no disturbance is found.[9]

Effects of Being Apart

Zero to Three Months

In the first weeks of life, when infants are in a contented state, they do not seem to mind their mothers' departure or being left alone. Nonetheless, being apart affects them adversely in indirect ways. After the first week, they are upset by changes in the care they receive.[10] Mothers rarely leave young infants for more than a few hours, and longer absences require caregiving by other people. Insofar as others do things differently than mothers, being apart reduces familiar stimulation and increases novelty.

The stressful effect of a change in routine after the first week seems to be typical of humans for the rest of their lives and has been found in other species. The effects of a single change are usually transitory. A number of major changes within a year causes breakdowns in most people. Consequently, people and animals are thought to have innate mechanisms for preventing change. According to Maris:

> [T]he impulse to defend the predictability of life is a fundamental and universal principle of human psychology. Conservatism, in this sense, is an aspect of our ability to survive in any situation: for without continuity we cannot interpret what events mean to us, nor explore new kinds of experience with confidence.
>
> We could not survive even for a day if our physical environment were not predictable.[11]

This assumption is consistent with the fact that young infants passively observe sequences of events and are gratified by repetition and upset by deviation. Their reactions do not necessarily depend upon the value of what happens. Even repetition of a sequence that ends unpleasantly may gratify them.[12]

This behavior is independent of attachment and occurs in human infants before attachment develops. The importance to most children of preventing change hardly has been studied. Autistic children are obsessed with the prevention of even slight change.

A variety of caretaking changes have been studied in animals. Substitution of a caretaker, if done only once, soon after birth, may not cause lasting disturbance. Animal neonates have been taken from their mothers and turned over to strange mothers for rearing, including mothers of a different species, without serious developmental handicap. However, frequent switching of caretakers has the severest effects. Rats, which do not show attachment in the usual sense but are disturbed by change, were given alternating care by their own mother and another mother rat. Some died in infancy. The survivors were underweight in infancy and disturbed when mature. They were handicapped particularly in dealing with novel situations.[13]

Autism resulting from frequent change of caretaker has been reported in two children.[14] Such experience is rare in children raised at home. The closest to the rat experiment that is found with any frequency is the situation of hospitalized infants. They experience many caretaker changes as nursing shifts rotate. Perhaps that was the cause of the high death rate cited in the last chapter among institutionalized infants. Neonates living at home may have similar experiences if reared by a succession of nurses or by grandmothers who come and go, alternating with mothers in giving care. They also may have such experiences if reared by a mother whose behavior changes markedly from time to time.

A second way that being apart in the first weeks leads to developmental problems is that mothers are disturbed by it, and their residual disturbance after reunion affects their neonates adversely. The main effect on animals and humans is that mothers become less receptive to their offspring or less attached to them. Reports by mothers have been confirmed by observations and experiments. Much of the data on humans is related to premature birth. Partial or total lack of contact creates a state of suspense in mothers. Many avoid visiting their babies. Some do not think of the babies as their own. Others mourn them as dead.[15]

During their first weeks, infants do not distinguish their mothers from other adults. At this time, long absences or separations have not been found directly disturbing to infants if substitute caretakers effectively copy mothers' caretaking routines. Within weeks, neonates do begin to distinguish adults from other stimuli and to associate adults with positive experiences (relief from distress, for example). In conditioning theory, caretakers thereby become generalized positive reinforcers, whose departure may have a punitive effect.

After a few weeks, being apart increases attachment behavior in mothers and infants. For example, after reunion, infants make more demands and mothers are more responsive than at other times. This applies to humans and animals.[16] Most infants still seem not to mind their mother's departure at seven weeks if they are contented when she leaves. But about 20 percent become disturbed when their mothers depart and when they are alone for a few hours. The more absences occur, the more disturbed they become. Effects include increased crying that may not stop when the mothers return, being hard to comfort, losing interest in adults, and altered consciousness with unresponsiveness.[17] The similarity of these effects to separation reactions in older infants suggests how separation behavior may develop in children who have never been separated for more than a few hours at a time.

Benjamin advanced two explanations for disturbance in infants caused by absence at this time: (1) Some infants receive excessive stimulation from their mothers and become dependent on fairly constant stimulation. (2) Others react adversely because when mothers are absent their needs are not met.[18] Presumably, their mothers go so far away that they do not hear their infants cry or, for other reasons, do not respond.

Attention also may influence whether or not infants show distress at their mothers' departure. Older infants sometimes do not notice their mothers' departure, play contentedly until something draws attention to it, and then show distress. By conditioning theory, a negative effect is to be expected when a generalized positive reinforcer is withdrawn. The effect need not appear until much later or when withdrawal is repeated. A mother's departure seems to be such an event, as is indicated by the following experiment.[19]

When a five-week-old infant was playing happily, the mother approached, attracted the infant's attention, and then left. The infant immediately cried. The mother returned, and the crying stopped. She left again, and crying resumed. After a few repetitions, the infant's crying became more vigorous and did not stop on her return. Most infants studied were hard to comfort at this point. A suggestion of autistic behavior occurred in those infants who reacted to repeated approach and departure not by increased agitation but by apparent loss of interest in their mothers.

In another experiment, an unfamiliar adult elicited increasing distress or detachment by repeated approach and departure. The same reaction was elicited by repeated presentation-removal of an infant's favorite toy, particularly if the toy were an animal. Other objects were not effective at five weeks of age. When infants were two months old, presentation-removal of other objects caused increasing distress.[20]

In these experiments, the infants' attention was engaged by the person or object that was withdrawn. When sucking is gratifying, young infants become absorbed. Their responsiveness to the rest of the environment is low, and some stare fixedly at their mothers' faces. If forcibly interrupted while sucking, many react with distress and heightened activity. Others "become limp and hypotonic and pass quickly into a withdrawn sleep state."[21]

Both reactions are common and seem to be basic reactions of young infants to stress. What determines whether an infant reacts vigorously or limply is not known, but the vigorous reaction can be fostered constructively. If a mother responds to it by resumption of feeding, she will be rewarding it. Then, distress cries and vigorous action will tend to become the infant's characteristic reaction to interrupted sucking. The reaction may also generalize to other frustrating situations, becoming an effective means of communicating and interacting with the mother.

Vigorous effort that is prolonged and that does not succeed ordinarily is followed by inactivity in neonates. If vigorous effort fails time after time, it no longer will be made. Inactivity will become the reaction to interrupted sucking, and inactivity may tend to become the reaction to frustration in other situations.[22]

When an infant is intent on continuing to do something, a mother who interrupts often will have a specific reason for doing it. Let us assume her action is deliberate, based on the judgment that the infant has had enough or that her breast is empty or because she planned to do something else at the moment. In the circumstances, her infant's protest may change her mind. Even if not persuaded, she may allow it to suck further in order to pacify it. Either way, the infant's protest is successful and is reinforced.

However, if a mother believes that feeding is best done for a preset number of minutes, her infant's protest may not deter her from interrupting it. Her method of caregiving will fit best with an infant who reacts to interruption with quiescence. In general, a rearing method that stresses objective criteria (scheduled feeding, measured intake, regular naps) fits with having a quiescent reaction to interruption of whatever an infant is doing. Similarly, the goal of early discipline fits with quiescence rather than protest. Whether or not parents think these matters out, their goals are reflected in what they reward and punish. An infant whose protest at interruption is rewarded by resumption will behave differently than an infant whose protest is not rewarded.

An infant who is quiescent when interrupted or when the mother leaves will not seem to be affected adversely by her action, but a delayed adverse reaction is to be expected. Overt, strident distress motivates caretakers to change what they have been doing. Quiet disturbance does not deter caretakers from doing whatever may have contributed to it and does not motivate them to seek any remedy. On the contrary, quiescence tends to reward caretakers for what they have been doing.

In the light of these observations and experiments, the rearing mothers gave their autistic children in infancy may have been significant in the following respects: from birth or soon after, the mothers were inclined to shape or discipline the children according to strongly held fantasies and preconceptions. In addition, early discipline was valued. Consequently, the mothers initiated contact with the children and terminated it to a large extent on the basis of considerations other than the cues provided by the children. The mothers also valued good babies, who are quiescent on being interrupted or left. Consequently, mothers left the children alone frequently for relatively long periods, during which they did not respond to the children's protests and other cues. Such rearing fosters quiescence, loss of interest in the mother, and solitary play. It discourages communication, protest, and the taking of vigorous action to overcome frustration.

Separations after a period of togetherness in the first weeks rarely have been studied because mothers normally do not leave their infants at this time for more than a few hours. Occasionally, a young baby goes to the hospital, but the physical condition leading to hospitalization may be more significant than the separation at this time. Insofar as infants neither have formed attachments nor even have learned to recognize their mothers, separation probably affects infants no more than absence does. Their mothers, however, are affected more by separation than absence.

Four to Seven Months

After a few months, infants recognize their mothers and selectively direct attachment behavior toward them. Infants become less upset by changes due to brief periods of care by substitute caretakers. But they are more vulnerable than before to changes in their mothers' behavior and appearance. For example, a mother wearing a bathing cap may elicit crying, while another person wearing the cap elicits smiling. The sight of the mother without her usual eyeglasses may elicit staring. The sight of the mother weeping may elicit staring and refusal to eat.[23]

From this age on, separation commonly causes eating and sleeping disturbances. The offer of food or other care by a substitute caretaker may increase a child's distress. As attachment grows, being apart becomes more significant and typically elicits:

> [E]xtreme preoccupation with searching and scanning the environment while at the same time being relatively detached from and unresponsive to the persons in it. The facial expression is blank, except for fleeting bewildered or frightened looks, and the infant may spend hours craning his neck ... letting his eyes sweep over all objects without fixing on any one. Sometimes there is first staring, with relative immobility, and the use of toys or other attempts to interest the baby are ignored. There is no response to familiar figures, who may be stared at blankly or passed by in the persistent scanning of the environment.[24]

Searching and watching for mother may not be obvious, particularly in older children who incorporate the behavior into ritual. For example, a three-year old was seen to be

> [A]musing himself with a droll game of bowing repeatedly and twisting his head. When the observer stood near, however, it was clear that, almost compulsively, the child was making the motions of looking toward a closed door and whispering, "My mummy coming soon."[25]

In addition to scanning, children apart spend hours staring at the door by which their mothers left. Their searching tends to upset adults in whose charge they are left and may be discouraged, but it persists.

The searching is not necessarily attributable to failure to understand the situation. Older children, who grasp explanations that mother will be gone for some time, engage in similar behavior. So do adults. And people who have lost a spouse through death engage in "restless movement about and scanning of the environment .... Directing attention to those parts of the environment in which the person is likely to be .... Calling for the lost person."[26] They know their searching is inappropriate, but they do it nonetheless. The persistence of their behavior suggests that it is regressive, perhaps coming from a time in childhood before the distinction between temporary and permanent absence had been mastered. However useful searching for an absent mother may be for animal infants, in humans it seems a poorly integrated activity.

After a time, most separated children and bereaved adults stop searching, but some continue. Some bereaved children persist for years, occasionally wandering away from home in search, and may even do so as adults.[27] The wandering of autistic children, without apparent purpose and despite their fears of going outside and of novelty, may be primitive attachment behavior.

As noted, the behavior of young children after reunion may be particularly baffling to their mothers. While showing some proximity seeking and maintaining, infants are less responsive to their mothers than before separation. They may turn their faces away when their mothers try to engage them and may resist other adults too. Persistent stimulation leads to a brief show of interest and a smile in some, while others remain unresponsive. Some have disturbed sleep, waking in tears and then taking hours to settle back or sleeping a day or two at a time without waking. Some have feeding disturbances.

At five to seven months infants show an "overdependent syndrome" after reunion. They cling to their mothers much of the time, demanding to be fed, crying inordinately when left alone, and acting very fearful of strangers and suspicious of familiar people (father, siblings).[28]

Attachment is well established by the second half-year. At this time, infants react to separation from their mothers with less activity, less interest in their surroundings, and less responsiveness to stimuli than before. They appear bewildered and sad.

The effects of separation described so far are ordinarily temporary. The question of lasting effects has received little study and is controversial. Again, the effects of repeated separations are evidently more serious and enduring than those of isolated experiences.[29]

Looking ahead, separation causes increasingly severe reactions with age, up to a peak in the second and third years. At that time, separated children tend to reject substitute caretakers. Many are inconsolable in their distress and unreachable in their withdrawal. After the age of four, most children are affected less and less by separation.

After Seven Months

The growing complexity of infants adds to their reactions to being apart. The following vignette was chosen as typical of one-year-old children in an experiment. The mothers' behavior followed the experimenter's instructions.[30]

Brian was carried into an unfamiliar playroom by his mother. They were the room's only occupants. She put him down and took a chair. Brian did not resist being put down. He immediately went to the toys, exploring and playing, with occasional glances and smiles at his mother. A woman he did not know came in. He looked at her pleasantly and continued to play. The stranger approached him, holding out a toy. Brian smiled, crept to her, took the toy, and played with it. His mother left while he was engaged with the stranger, and he may not have noticed her leaving. Then, apparently noticing, he abruptly crept to the chair in which his mother had been sitting and looked at the stranger. She offered him another toy, which he took. This time his play was less active and soon stopped. He sat, chewing the string on a toy, glancing back and forth from the stranger to his mother's chair, looking increasingly unhappy. He began to cry.

Brian's mother returned, and he vocalized and crept to her quickly and pulled himself up. She lifted him, and he embraced her vigorously a couple of times. During their interchange, the stranger left. Again, his mother put him down. This time, he clung and protested loudly. Then he threw himself down flat on the floor, his face to the rug, and cried loudly. She came over and comforted him, and he responded well. Then she disengaged herself again. He again threw himself down and cried. She again cuddled him. This time, he responded only momentarily and then disengaged himself, threw himself down, and resumed crying. She picked him up and led him to play with the toys. He appeared happy again but stopped playing from time to time to cling to his mother.

While he was playing, she again left, saying "Bye bye" and waving. He looked up and smiled briefly but soon began to cry. He say crying and rocking. The stranger returned, offered him a toy, and held out her arms. Brian raised his arms to her and she picked him up. He stopped crying and held her tightly, clutching a fold of her clothing. The stranger put him down, and for the first time, he began to scream. She picked him up, and he was lulled. Then he began to cry softly.

His mother returned, but he apparently did not notice her. The stranger drew his attention to his mother. He looked at his mother, still crying, and turned away from her. Soon, however, he began to reach toward her and smile. When she took him, he hugged her vigorously and clung to her for some time.

Few such experiments have been done with humans. Infants rarely have these experiences as a result of planning, but they may happen unintentionally, in the press of circumstances. The experiment shows how behavior associated with autism can be produced in half an hour. This behavior was atypical for Brian. As a result of a sequence of experiences, none of them traumatic in itself, he began to respond negatively to behavior of his mother that formerly had elicited positive or neutral reactions in him.

Like Brian, the other infants studied showed cumulative effects. On the whole, their behavior became more intense and disturbed. At their mothers' first return, most of them approached; none withdrew. At the mothers' second return, a minority withdrew. They turned away or walked away. When held, they struggled, stiffened or squirmed, trying to disengage themselves.

The avoidance may be classified as normal in the sense that it occurred in normal children in the circumstances. At the same time, the behavior shows the beginnings of withdrawal like that seen in autistic children and in ordinary children after separation.

The power of the stimulus of being left and the complexity of infant responses to it have been noted in many circumstances and species. A couple who reared an infant chimpanzee found, "To shut her up in a room by herself, or to walk away faster than she could run, and to leave her behind, proved, as well as we could judge, to be the most awful punishment that could possibly be inflicted."[31] A girl of twenty-one months was being left in a room by her mother. The child tried aggressively to prevent her mother from leaving. Then, after the mother left, the child turned to a picture book and identified every kind of object in it except motherlike figures.[32]

The experiment with Brian and the one in which younger infants were approached by the mothers who then left involved novelty or deviation from expected sequences. The fact that exposure to novelty makes being apart hard to bear was noted in the last chapter. Particularly distressing is novelty connected with mothers' departure. The infants in the experiments were left under conditions in which their mothers ordinarily did not leave them. At home, an infant may show little or no distress when the mother leaves in her usual way. However, leaving by a door that she rarely uses may arouse much apprehension.[33]

Two other studies are particularly noteworthy here. In both, the infants had been reared in extraordinary closeness to their mothers. The mothers were adolescents and young women who gave birth while incarcerated. Thus, they had been separated recently from the people to whom they were attached and upon whom they were dependent and from their accustomed environments and activities. They were living among strangers in a new, hostile environment that sharply restricted the activities in which they could engage. Their situation fostered extraordinary involvement with their babies. Most of the mothers were devoted in the extreme; almost all their time was spent with their babies in infant-centered activities. The babies developed well.

In one study, the infants were separated from their mothers for about three months toward the end of their first year. During this period, the infants remained in their familiar surroundings, and each was given an individual substitute caretaker. A substantial minority of the infants became severely depressed during this period. They avoided people and stimulation presented to them. Many lay immobile and unresponsive in their cots. Only strong stimulation roused them. Others masturbated or played with their feces.[34]

Another group of infants reared in such circumstances did not experience separation, but each one was left alone experimentally in an unfamiliar room for a short time. This happened when they were between one and two and a half years of age. After a while, each of them showed gestures and movements identified with autism. Some became inactive in relation to the environment, engaging in much self-stimulation.[35]

Monkey infants reared in seclusion with their mothers also form intense attachments to them. This is true in nature and under experimental conditions. Separation causes severe depression in the infants. According to Kaufman, their depressions are like those of human infants deprived of their mothers.[36]

These studies involved controlled conditions and systematic observations. Most of the literature on the effects of separation comes from unplanned, poorly controlled events, and systematic observations are usually lacking. The following discussion summarizes a variety of such reports.[37]

The older children are, the more their reactions to a first separation vary. Insofar as separation behavior is part of attachment, the reactions of young infants are determined largely by innate mechanisms. The older children are, the greater role experience plays in their attachment behavior and, consequently, in their reactions to separation. The more common, prolonged reactions of preschool children are:

Searching, scanning, waiting;

Uncommunicativeness, unresponsiveness, blank staring, absence of emotion, indifference to pain;

Inactivity, apathy, periods of immobility;

Reduced interests, loss of interest in one's toys, destruction of one's toys;

Overactivity, sometimes violent;

Food refusal, food fads, overeating;

Reduced sleep, waking in distress;

Frequent illness;

Loss of skills (particularly speech, toileting, dressing, and walking);

Sad appearance, fretting, prolonged crying, screaming;

Resistance of care or attention by adults, general negativism;

Direction of attention and energy to nonhuman things;

Masturbating, rocking, rolling, headbanging, finger and object sucking;

Ritual

Less-common reactions include rocking or shaking one's crib, calling for mother constantly, self-mutilation, and not crying on occasions when children usually cry. These reactions, except frequent illness, are common in autistic children.

The essence of autism has been hypothesized as an attempt to regain mother; the children "are always reaching out for contact without achieving it."[38] If so, their failure may be due to the unrecognizability of their attempts. Few mothers recognize autistic behavior as proximity seeking, even when they feel compelled to respond to it. The items in the list have been identified by researchers as attachment behavior, but they ordinarily are not identified as such by parents.

In some studies of human and animal infants separated from their mothers, infant behavior has been called depressed. Application of the concept of depression to both groups is controversial. Its application in animal studies need not be argued here. But depression seems to be near the core of the behavior of separated and autistic children.[39] And the psychology of depression is fairly well worked out. Therefore, reasons for considering separated and autistic children depressed are given in some detail.

Depression

The usual objection to considering young children depressed has been that they simply do not suffer depression and that it is misleading to describe or explain their behavior by reference to adult behavior. Young infants do not experience depression the way adults do. Not even children of several years show adult patterns of depressed behavior in their totality. However, a number of the differences between depressed behavior in adults and functionally related behavior in children are superficial. Custom calls for certain reactions in bereaved adults and prohibits them in children. More important, the relevance of the concept of depression to infancy depends not upon whether the behavior of infants and adults is identical but upon functional relationships—on related patterns of cause and effect in infants and adults. Finally, the problem of explaining infant behavior by adult mechanisms does not apply here. The adult behavior (except for the conventional, socially learned forms) is explained by infant mechanisms—mechanisms of infant attachment.

The idea that loss of a parent disturbs young children profoundly is not new: "Death of a parent during childhood has been recognized by writers and poets since the beginning of recorded time as one of the worst misfortunes that could occur to a human being."[40] Nonetheless, until recently, the belief that children (especially young ones) were relatively unaffected by separation from or even death of parents was shared by clinicians and lay people.[41]

In 1924, Abraham wrote about a state like depression in infancy. He concluded that it was caused by repeated experiences of lack of maternal love after enjoying the status of favored child.[42] His and other scattered writings on depression in children received little attention for years. As late as the 1940s, reports of severe depression in infants separated from their mothers were largely dismissed. By then, the idea of childhood schizophrenia had been accepted to some extent. But grief and depression were understood to be profound emotions and, therefore, not to be expected in children. In addition, it was simply evident to the senses of adults that children were not depressed.

The idea that separation and loss caused depression in adults had long been established. People believed it so strongly that they assumed the death of a relative caused depression when no depression was evident. For adults, the death was defined as a loss, and behavior that followed was presumed to be a reaction to the loss: "Almost any behavior that is then manifest is regarded as 'grief' . . . and not only as natural but as desirable."[43] For example, if a man whose wife had died behaved as if nothing had occurred, he was said to be numb with grief. If he was found carousing, he was said to be consoling himself, not himself because of grief, or drowning his grief. Thus, behavior opposite to grief was taken as a sign of grief. Sometimes the interpretation was accurate; sometimes it was not. The point is that grief was attributed to adults because it was expected in the circumstances.[44]

Grief in children was not expected, and adults took measures to prevent it. For example, children were hindered from seeing people in terminal stages of illness and were given euphemistic, misleading explanations of what was happening. When deaths occurred, children were sent off or given activities to distract them. The purpose—to spare children distress—often was achieved in that only limited reactions to death were seen. But the absence of visible reactions contributed to the belief that children lacked deep feelings.[45]

Despite the limitations adults put on children's experience and expression of grief, the behavior of many young children who are separated from their parents or who lose them by death suggests depression. They are sad looking and restless, fuss and cry, speak little or not at all, eat and sleep poorly, and show limited interests, responsiveness, and activity.[46] Adults behaving that way are considered depressed. Separated infants also have in common with bereaved adults susceptibility to illness and death.[47]

Attachment to people and vulnerability to their loss are high in cultures in which infants' attachments are directly primarily to single caretakers, in contrast to cultures with multiple caretakers and diffuse attachments.[48] As infants grow up, they pattern new attachments on their early prototype of exclusive intimacy. Thus, the decline of the extended family has made people more vulnerable to separation at all ages. Widows, widowers, and divorcees, as well as separated children, usually become depressed.

In short, separated children show behavior well described as depression. The behavior has the appearance of depression in older people with the exception of culture-bound forms that adults have learned. It is caused by events known to cause depression in older people. Also, as separated children grow up, residual depression is often found. The behavior of autistic children, particularly in infancy—sadness, limited activity, lack of interest in people and in much of their environment, lack of initiative, low responsiveness and communication, poor eating and sleep—is symptomatic of depression. The symptoms appear in many autistic children after separation when depression is to be expected. In others, the symptoms get worse as a result of separation. For those who have not been separated, an explanation is advanced in the section "Equivalents of Separation."

Bowlby's simplified analysis of children's separation reactions makes a convenient framework for much of the material. Under varied conditions of separation, the many behaviors found may be summarized by three phases. First is *active protest* and effort to regain the mother. The children cry for her and throw themselves about without concern for injury. The behavior is dramatic. It would be hard for a mother to resist, if present. In addition, the children watch alertly or stare expectantly, sometimes in the direction in which she departed. The children look "eagerly towards any sight or sound which might prove to be [the] missing mother. All [this] behavior suggests strong expectation that she will return."[49]

Bowlby called the next phase *despair,* reflecting a growing expectation that the mother will not return. The children are now withdrawn, inactive, and undemanding. Quieter and self-contained, they may be mistaken to be getting over the separation. On the contrary, their mental state is one of increasing hopelessness.

If separation lasts long enough, despair turns into *detachment.* Children become less emotional and less concerned with the mother and begin to show interest in their surroundings. In this phase, children may not appear disturbed and often are thought to have recovered from the effects of the separation. Again, such an appearance is misleading.

Children in the protest phase, despite the violence of their behavior, are relieved most readily and quickly by the mother's return. Detached children, who seem to be content, reject their mother on her arrival and later show the most residual disturbance. Their detachment is a precursor of future lack of involvement with people and increased involvement with nonhuman things. In extreme cases, according to Bowlby, the children form no more attachments but are entirely self-centered and interested in people only for the things they provide. Bowlby's description is similar to descriptions of autistic children treating their parents as nonhuman and primarily as instruments for getting things.

Reunion

Even parents who understand the effects of separation are unprepared for the extremity of the rejection they sometimes encounter after reunion, as in the following example. Laura, almost three, had been hospitalized. As her return home approached, she expressed eagerness to be with her mother and spoke animatedly to her by telephone. On arriving home, Laura banged vigorously on the door, calling her mother. When her mother opened the door, Laura looked at her blankly and said, "But I want my Mummy." For two days she did not recognize her mother and treated her as a stranger, or so the mother thought. During this time, Laura recognized everyone and everything except her mother.[50]

Additional behavior common after reunion includes:[51]

Not crying when expected to;

Seeming not to hear, especially mother's voice;

Being more affectionate to father or a stranger than to mother;

Refusing care from mother or contact with her;

Expressing open anger at mother, including hitting, biting, and verbal reproaches;

And after the anger has diminished,

Heightened dependence on mother: crying when left alone, clinging, refusing to be put down, and extreme intolerance of further separation;

Controlling mother's behavior extensively.

Some of the behavior seen after reunion is a continuation of what began during separation, and some of the behavior may appear for the first time after reunion.

Most of these reactions disappear within minutes or fade over months. An exception is intolerance of further separation. Six months or a year after reunion, when a child seems to have gotten over the effects fully, a second separation causes more-immediate and severer disturbance than the first. In addition, apprehension about separation is aroused readily. Indications of a separation to come may cause high anxiety or desperate resistance. And, when no separation is impending, formerly separated children tend to misinterpret events to mean that it is and become disturbed. Thus, there are residual effects not noticeable until further developments elicit them.[52] Long or repeated separation increases the severity and duration of negative reunion behavior.

To experience active rejection or naked anger on being reunited with one's child is so painful that understanding it may not soften its impact. On the contrary, understanding tends to evoke guilt about the separation, making mothers feel worse. Guilt over separation is aroused very easily in mothers. Less painful than rejection is the idea that the child has forgotten the mother during the separation and no longer recognizes her. But the context shows that the nonrecognition is behavior related to the mother. It is a selective response to the person to whom a child is attached.

Although most of the data summarized here came from studies of long separation, short separation has similar effects and poses similar problems to mothers at reunion. Even absences may have similar effects. According to Erikson, mothers' first excursions out of the house without their babies lead to crises on their return. After two or three hours away, they rush back, eager to be with their babies, but find them seemingly indifferent.[53] The more precious a baby is to a mother, the more excited she will be in her greeting and the more hurt by a lack of response. Failure to rouse a baby from unresponsiveness at this time makes it likely that unresponsiveness will be the reaction to further absences and that it may spread to other situations. In addition, the infant's lack of reaction when the mother returns may give her the impression that the infant does not miss her and is content to be alone.

Autistic children act much like others after reunion. Avoidance of their mothers and unresponsiveness are typical and striking in those who had been responsive before separation. Such behavior can be a shock to any parent. Reports by mothers of autistic children indicate that the mothers react more strongly than most, taking the behavior as a sign that their children are peculiar or defective.

Factors in Separation Reactions

The severity of separation reactions has been correlated with mothers' behavior and the quality of the attachment that had developed in the children before separation. The period before separation seemed the obvious one to study, but the results have been ambiguous. Clearer findings have emerged about the effects of mothers' behavior during separation, and their behavior after reunion seems most relevant to autism.

Relationship prior to Separation

An early finding that gained acceptance was that, when a mother-infant relationship was good beforehand, separation was traumatic. This fitted with the idea that something must be desirable for its loss to be disturbing. Researchers had long believed that adults were most stricken by the loss of someone they loved most deeply and wholeheartedly. According to Marris, that is not true. Rather, grief and other disturbances are greatest when the relationship has been most ambivalent.[54] Turning the coin, there is evidence that infants with good early experience do relatively well when separated and that separation after a poor relationship can be traumatic. These observations fit with the idea that good early experience enables a child to withstand stress.[55]

Probably, the contradictory findings are attributable to vague and inconsistent criteria. *Good* and *poor* are broad terms, not clearly related to the factors considered here. More-specific hypotheses taken from a variety of studies are that the following experiences lead to disturbance at separation:

Intense, exclusive, highly dependent mother-infant relationships;

Mood swings and other maternal behavior that make for unpredictable experiences;

Abrupt separation.

Of these, intense, exclusive relationships have been cited earlier as typical in autism, and some indication of mood swings also has been given. Other maternal behavior that made autistic children's experience unpredictable was discussed earlier and is amplified in the following chapters. Whether or not autistic children were separated more abruptly or with less preparation than others is not known.

Separation frequently occurs when mother and child are least prepared for it. For example, if a child has been ill for some time, the illness usually will have heightened the intimacy and interdependence between mother and child. When the child is hospitalized then, the separation occurs at a peak of involvement with each other. Separations at such times are particularly disturbing to mother and child. In one study, all the mothers were disturbed by their children's hospitalization, and half of them suffered breakdowns.[56] The close, exclusive relationships between autistic children and their parents make it likely that separations were particularly disturbing to the parents. Parents' intolerance of separation from autistic children was reported to be typical by Bosch.[57] In general, the more disturbed a mother is by a separation, the less-effective help she is likely to give her child at each point— preparing for separation, taking leave of the child, visiting during separation, and rebuilding the relationship after reunion.[58]

Mother's Behavior during Separation

A mother's behavior during separation is not usually considered a factor in her child's reaction, but it has direct and indirect effects. The general finding is that the more contact there is between mother and child during a period of separation, the less disturbed and hostile the child will be. And the longer the separation, the greater the effect of what mothers do.

Paradoxically, many mothers have gotten the impression that their visits made their children worse. Those who visited infrequently tended to feel tense and guilty and to find their children unresponsive or hostile. In the circumstances, many children turned their backs on their mothers or behaved as if the mothers were strangers and of no interest beyond the gifts they brought. The rejection was sometimes so disturbing to mothers that they did not visit again.[59]

Visits of moderate frequency usually were awaited with eagerness by the children and began pleasantly, but they often ended grimly. As the mothers' departures neared, the children pleaded with them not to leave, cried, and had tantrums. Doctors and nurses, finding the children quiet and mangeable before a visit and disturbed afterward, sometimes discouraged visiting. In the circumstances, mothers concluded that their children were better served by staying away. Nonetheless, the reverse was true in the long run.

When, during separation, mothers give birth to second children or undergo major surgery, it is obvious that their subsequent caretaking is changed. Less obvious are changes caused by distress over separation. The assumption that, after reunion, mothers are prepared to care for their children has persisted because of underreporting of mothers' adverse reactions to separation. Some mothers who had been inseparable from their children beforehand dealt with separation by turning to new interests—jobs, education, or hobbies that occupied their time. Consequently, some visited their children less often. After reunion, they continued the new pursuits, turning over the children's care to others or dividing their time between the pursuits and the children. In addition, many who did not take up new interests nonetheless underwent changes so that their children did not occupy the same place in their lives after separation as before.

During long separations, mothers seem to lose their attachments to their infants. Anna Freud's explanation is based on the idea that maternal attachment depends upon the stimulation provided by the presence of a helpless infant, urgently in need of care. Therefore, a long period without stimulation is conducive to loss of attachment. Freud's observations were of rather long separations.[60] Brief separations when infants are hospitalized have similar effects on some mothers. They become reluctant to see their infants and may stop visiting. Some speak of their infants as dead and in other ways deliberately try to minimize feelings and interests related to the infants in anticipation of losing them. Others mourn their infants unintentionally and unconsciously, thus preparing themselves for loss. Brief separation not involving infant hospitalization probably is less alienating, but concern about alienation is common in mothers. The reluctance of many to allow relatives to take their babies for a day or two is rooted in apprehension that alienation will develop.

Mother's experiences during separation contribute to the mixture of eagerness, reluctance, and apprehension with which they approach reunion. Separation may critically affect mothers' readiness to rebuild the relationship after reunion. What happens after reunion is decisive in whether children get over separation or not.

Mothers' Behavior after Reunion

When children react negatively to their mothers on reunion, mothers respond in very different ways. At one extreme are mothers who force affection and care on the children. They hug, hold, stroke, and talk, undeterred by the children's disregard or hostility. To illustrate, Dawn was sixteen months old when her mother went to the hospital to have another baby. The reunion occurred on the maternity ward, to which Dawn was brought by her father:

> [The mother] rushed toward Dawn and, snatching her from father, clutched her to her and hugged her in a fierce, desperate grip .... Unlike the other children observed during this study, Dawn was given no time by her mother in which to register non-recognition, bewilderment or indifference.[61]

Dawn tried to push away, but her mother did not allow it. During the reunion, she gave Dawn total, exclusive attention, ignoring Dawn's resistance and ignoring her husband and the hospital staff. Then, for days she gave Dawn preference over the new baby.

Some mothers hold back after being rebuffed and wait in readiness for their infants to come around. Others, deeply hurt and angry, withdraw. Still others alternate between active involvement and withdrawal after reunion.

With insistent, intrusive, and even violently demonstrative attention, children are won over within hours or days after a first separation. Their recovery is almost complete, although traces of hostility toward mothers may linger for months, and vulnerability to a repeated separation may last a year or more.[62]

Such care seems the most beneficial, but it seems not to be the most common. There is no apparent basis for considering such a reaction to rejection normal or more normal than the other reactions.

Maternal behavior at reunion most conducive to lasting, severe disturbance seems to be alternate involvement and withdrawal.[63] Data bearing specifically on the remaining two kinds of maternal reactions are lacking. Probably, waiting for a child to come around is more helpful than withdrawing.

Insofar as autistic children behave like ordinary children who have been separated, effusive, intrusive care might make them less autistic. Such care was recommended by Kanner and Wing, and its use is supported by experiments in foster mothering of retarded and autistic children cited in the last chapter. Zaslow and Breger concluded that autistic children's anger at reunion posed a critical test for their mothers. It was necessary that the mothers accept the children's anger and hidden need for physical contact while winning them over. But the mothers, because of their characteristic difficulties in dealing with strong feelings, did not do so.[64]

The task facing a mother at reunion is difficult when at one's best, and reunion is not a time of calm and resourcefulness. Rather, it is a time when mothers feel particularly excited, apprehensive, guilty, and vulnerable to disappointment and rejection. The difficulty facing mothers of autistic children after reunion is at least as great as other mothers face. The children are highly valued. As a result of separation, they tend to regress more severely than other children and to be extremely unresponsive. The mothers' accounts indicate that they are shocked by their children's behavior and do not indicate that they are effusive toward the children at this time. Effusiveness would be out of character for most of the mothers as they have described themselves and have been pictured by clinicians.

Giving up is also out of character for them. After withdrawing, they apparently direct their energy into retraining the children's speech, toilet habits, and other lost behaviors. Unfortunately, children are unreceptive to training after reunion. Training attempted when resistance is high usually intensifies and prolongs unresponsiveness.

In short, mothers of autistic children probably are not effective in winning their children over after seprations; they may do things that prolong separation behavior in the children.

Equivalents of Separation

As noted, separation behavior occurs in infants who have not been separated for long; absence is not necessary either. The effects of being apart physically have been studied because it is easily defined and measured in hours or days. To identify the aspect of being apart that elicits separation reactions in infants is harder.

For neonates, the disturbing aspect of being apart was identified as the absence of familiar stimulation and as deviation from familiar sequences in being cared for. Substitute caretakers may introduce novel stimulation that upsets neonates. However, novel stimulation may not be critical because brief absences by mothers in which infants remain at home without substitute caretakers are upsetting although new stimulation does not occur. Therefore, the adverse effects of such brief absences are attributable to the absence of stimulation from the mothers. On the basis of these considerations, I assume that one critical element in being apart is the absence of stimuli associated with mothers. Consequently, separation reactions may be hypothesized to occur when mother and infant are under the same roof and when they are not in the same room or when the mother's behavior changes so much that, though present, much stimulation that she formerly provided is lacking or much deviation from familiar sequences occurs.

The first type of situation includes the mother shutting herself in a room (as when staying in bed because of illness or depression or to concentrate on some activity without distraction) or leaving the infant alone in a room. Of these, leaving the baby alone is common in cases of autism. (Depression in the mothers has been reported also but not to the extent of staying in bed.)

The second type of situation may result from a profound mood change or a situational change that has a heavy impact on a mother. Of these, mood disturbances in the mothers have been discussed. Situational changes have been reported in some cases during the children's first year but not in enough to be considered significant. Depression in the mothers, as in mothers of other children, seems not to have resulted in failure to care for autistic children in the first year. Nonetheless, it probably resulted in changes in details of the care because of altered perception of the children, reduced awareness of their cues, and reduced responsiveness.

Distraction of the caretaker when with an infant may also have profound effects. At two months, infants were reported to react to deviations in the caretaker's behavior caused by distraction with attachment behavior and "a state of acute depression."[65]

The situation in which a married person is emotionally withdrawn and continues to live with the spouse has been called emotional divorce. Similarly, a mother-child relationship in which the mother is withdrawn has been called emotional separation and has been cited as causing autism.[66] The meaning of emotional separation can be shown best by example. The following is based on observation of a mother and her infant over a long time, and contains data rarely available.

John was born long after his only sibling, and was clearly his mother's favorite. In the first weeks, the mother-infant relationship seemed ideal. The observer found the mother "prettier and happier than at any other time over the four years that I had known her."[67] John was similarly radiant.

Then, when he was eight weeks old, his father suddenly fell ill and doctors suspected cancer. The mother became depressed. She continued to care for John but in a withdrawn manner, with procrastination. She no longer responded to his affectionate overtures (smiles and cooing). Within a week,

John's behavior regressed. He was less active and less responsive to his mother and to other people.

A few days later, cancer was ruled out, and the mother began to recover. Now, feeling ready to interact with John as she had formerly, she complained that he was somber and unresponsive. It took much effort to get him to smile. Remembering his earlier, joyous nature, she complained that he seemed to be deliberately withholding. She did not extend herself to win him over.

John's condition deteriorated until he was four and one-half months old. The observer became concerned seriously about his apparent retardation. She intervened, persuading the mother to take the initiative, to stimulate John more. Within a week, he was improved remarkably. However, the mother then abandoned her effort, again waiting for John to take the initiative. He again became passive, limp, and undemanding.

The observer continued to urge the mother to be more active and was occasionally successful during the following months. Each time, John responded favorably. But his mother did not sustain these efforts, and each time she faltered, John fell back.

Emotional separation, then, may be defined as a period in which a mother and child continue to interact while stimulation from the mother is reduced or altered. Some emotional separations are identified easily, as in this example. Bereavement in a mother is an obvious event to inquire about, and a change in behavior may be inferred as a result of bereavement or pinpointed with further questions. However, changes may occur in a mother's behavior that affect her infant but that are not ordinarily elicited in interviews. In chapter 6, a group of mothers was described who became depressed at the realization that their children, approaching the age of one, were not precocious. Clinicians have not inquired ordinarily about such matters.

To recapitulate, analysis of attachment and separation behavior in human and animal infants brings into focus a paradox about autism. Symptoms of autism that have been taken as evidence of inability to form attachment are attachment behavior. Not recognizing a mother, not talking to her, treating her as an inanimate object, and avoiding her are behaviors selectively directed at mothers. The behaviors may be rooted in primitive attachment behavior that is not well integrated in the human life cycle. Mothers are confused by them, as was illustrated vividly by one who wrote about her autistic daughter, "During her seven years she had never shown that she recognized me." The mother thought her daughter did not understand anything around her. When the girl was seven, the mother took her to an institution for retarded children. A member of the staff tried to discourage institutionalizing the child, saying, "she seems quite normal. What a sweet child! The ones we have here aren't at all like that." The mother was hurt by the comment, could not make sense of it, and went ahead with her plan. On being left, the girl sat in one spot, "her eyes riveted on the glass in the door" through which her mother had left, and banged her head against the wall until her mother's visit a week later. "Now, with her eyes on the door, I was barely over the threshold before she rose quickly .... At once she took me by the hand, pulled me toward the entrance stairs, down the steps, out through the gate, to the car."[68]

The mother was struck by the competence of her daughter's plea to be taken home and realized briefly that she had misconstrued her daughter's past behavior. For weeks, the girl sat staring at the door, banging her head, and at each visit, pulling her mother to the car, but the mother did not grasp fully the meaning of this behavior.

To summarize, much behavior of autistic children is interpretable as attachment behavior that is elicited ordinarily by separation and other situations. Once present, separation reactions are dealt with most effectively by insistent, intrusive attention—behavior that would be harmful at other times. Histories furnished by mothers indicate separation reactions in autistic children are not dealt with effectively and grow worse.

Some autistic behavior is explainable simply as persistence of separation behavior. In addition, separation reactions that are not dealt with effectively cause autistic behavior indirectly. Attempts at training elicit resistance, and the child may learn little. Also, insofar as attachment is disturbed, all learning that depends on attachment is hindered.

9 Stresses in Learning: Reinforcement Patterns and Autism

Training can provide an exhilarating sense of competence or a stress so great that learning ceases. Training usually falls between these extremes and involves minimal to moderate stress. However, a training procedure that is hardly stressful to one person may be beyond the endurance of another.

The success of deliberate, extensive training of infants—usually in the second year—is influenced by the training that precedes it and by the relationship that has developed with the trainer. Most autistic children come to training in the second year handicapped by insecure attachment, limited experience of predictability, and little skill in increasing predictability other than by ritual and by prolonged separation reactions (unresponsiveness, negativism). These adaptations interfere with training. Therefore, training that would be easy for other infants is difficult for them.

Autistic children are trained by people whose devotion and tenacity are extraordinary, whose objectives are very high, and whose frustrations are also very high. As one parent said, "I tried to teach her constantly, but she never learned."[1]

The combination of handicapped infants and zealous trainers exacerbates some of the difficulties that other infants and parents have in training. Formal training experiences shape the course of learning in autistic children and the cognitive peculiarities and handicaps that become established. This chapter focuses on training in the second year. The training that parents undertake to correct their autistic children's deficiencies usually begins in the third or fourth years, after the training to be discussed in this chapter. Autistic children typically have difficulty with toilet training, are slow to master it, and then regress. However, their peculiar learning is reflected particularly in their speech. In addition, verbal learning is what their parents are most interested in and have reported on in greatest detail. It is the focus of the analysis of their training and learning.

Early Training

Learning starts before birth. Simple conditioning has been done with fetuses, but few parents have joined scientists in deliberately attempting it. Mothers' efforts to shape the minds of their unborn children usually have been limited to thinking beautiful thoughts, exposing the fetus to culture as by going to concerts, and avoiding people who are considered evil influences.

137

Serious interest in training usually starts with birth. Separation in the maternity ward prevents mothers from doing much to train their infants until they come home. Nonetheless, whether or not they intend to, parents train their infants as soon as they have contact with them. Some are unaware of it and think of training as something that will start months later, as with holding a cup or using the toilet. Others begin immediately with eagerness and determination to instill habits they consider desirable. Whether deliberate or unaware, however, parents provide cues and reinforcements when they hold, caress, feed, or diaper their babies.

Neonates are responsive, but in the first weeks of life they are erratic. Their response accuracy is low and varies from time to time. Correct responses given a few times are not evidence of mastery. On the next occasion, a deviant response or none at all is likely. Some observers think that the irregularity is due primarily to motor immaturity and that cognitive (associative) functions are accurate already.[2]

After the seventh week, stable conditioning can be achieved—response accuracy of 100 percent—but erratic response to training recurs at later ages when new skills are being learned. A one-year-old may take a few steps and not walk again for weeks or may speak new words that are not spoken again for months. The same is true of adults when they are beginning to learn a new skill; a novel task may be stressful at all ages, making subjects extraordinarily sensitive to failure, correction, or punishment. Trainers' reactions to early errors may make the difference between further learning and failure to learn the task at hand and, to a lesser extent, failure to learn other things later.[3]

Autistic children often behave as if they were impervious to failure, correction, or even severe punishment. In reality, they are quite sensitive when they are beginning to learn something. No others, including retarded children, have been found to be more sensitive. A common reaction of autistic children to correction at such times is screaming and biting themselves. They may also react to praise and encouragement of new behavior with negativism and inactivity, particularly when the praise calls for additional performance.[4]

Early correct response to training can raise parental hopes. The more eager a parent is for precocity, the more likely the parent is to be encouraged prematurely and subsequently to feel let down. Disappointment may shade into a sense of betrayal, which contributes to anger and depression.

The ambitions parents have for their autistic children are expressed in intellectual training that begins in the first year. They talk and read to the children. They play music for them, and they give their children things to look at. The parents provide an extraordinary amount of stimulation.[5] Ordinarily, such stimulation is advantageous. Sophisticated stimulation is not a problem unless responses are demanded. Infants do not need to be able to understand; if stimulation is repetitious, they learn something.

In an unusual experiment, Greek verse was read to infants reared in an English-speaking environment. Thus, the verse was devoid of meaning. Probably, the only organization of the material possible for the infants was to respond to repeated sequences of sounds. After the children were eight years old, they were taught Greek—new verses and those read to them in infancy. The children learned the verses that had been read to them in infancy faster than the new material. They had learned something in infancy and retained it, although that fact was not evident until years later.[6]

Therefore, while reading to young infants or teaching them lists provides them with meaningless experience, such activities probably accomplish what the parents are trying to do. They familiarize infants with sounds and sequences of words, preparing them for language acquisition. Perhaps the precocious speech of many autistic children is attributable to enriched verbal stimulation in early infancy.

Parents may read to their infants with the idea of preparing them to be geniuses when grown, but it is hard to wait patiently for results that are long delayed. Parents have been highly gratified by autistic children's recitation of lists during infancy but nonetheless have pressed them for greater achievements. Impatience is common, as in the following description of mothers of ordinary children:

> [A]lthough in general [they] were aware that it was useless to hope for too much too soon, they . . . gambled fairly heavily in time and patience on the chance that their own babies were different.[7]

Nonreward and Deprivation

The question is: What happens when the gamble fails or seems to—when an infant does not sustain precocity despite zealous training? A combination of high parental expectation and vulnerability to disappointment, described by clinicians and parents, seems to have been typical in cases of autism. When disappointed, the parents corrected the children, gave them extra training, or withdrew into "long, anxiously sullen silences."[8]

Correction (saying "no" or giving the correct response) is not usually considered punitive but has been found to have the effects of punishment. Withdrawal usually involves withholding of positive reactions and was not always considered punitive. In the early part of the century, corporal punishment was advised against as emotionally harmful, and withholding of love and privileges became the approved method of disciplining children. Equivalent to extinction in the laboratory, withholding of positive reactions was considered benign and essential in training. But analysis of training became more complex with the finding that a situation of no stimulus change could be rewarding or punitive, depending upon the circumstances.

Experiments showed that no stimulation when a positive stimulus was "expected" was punitive in its effect and that no stimulation when an aversive stimulus was "expected" was rewarding.

The terms *expected* and *expectation* need not refer to a hypothetical mental process in an infant or animal. As used in this and the next chapter, an expected stimulus is defined as one that has followed a prior stimulus (cue) or a response in an infant's experience. After a number of pairings and an indication that a subject has formed an association, when the cue is presented or the response is made, the stimulus is considered expected. The effect of emotional withdrawal by one person on another is assumed to be mediated by experiences in which a positive stimulus, which formerly has occurred after a cue or response, does not follow the cue or response. Such experience is called *nonreward*. In short, nonreward is nonoccurrence of an expected positive stimulus. *Deprivation* is removal of a positive stimulus or object that is already present. Disturbing effects of deprivation were described in the last chapter. Nonreward seems no less disturbing.

In the laboratory, nonreward has produced the same effects as punishment. A single instance was distressing temporarily, and repeated instances caused depression, ranging from lowered activity to sitting and self-grooming or not moving for hours.[9] Rocking and self-biting also were found.

As noted, nonreward is common as a deliberate form of child discipline, but its unintended occurrence is more common, especially with infants, and is probably more disturbing. Deliberate nonreward usually is signaled in advance to a child because parents consider explanations to be an important part of training, as in, "I'm not going to let you watch TV when we get home because you did that." The statement serves as a signal, modifying the child's expectation of a positive experience; that is, the statement is a cue that counteracts arriving at home as a cue for television watching. When the statement cue is effective, it takes on a punitive function, and the subsequent punitive effect of not being permitted to watch television is reduced. Unannounced prevention of watching would be a shock—more punitive. Unsignaled nonreward is more distressing than signaled nonreward, as has been shown by the magnitude of distress reactions (crying, defecating, inactivity) in infants and laboratory animals. Also, the distressing effects of nonreward are intensified by nonoccurrence of expected neutral stimuli.[10]

People particularly tend to stop smiling, caressing, and talking affectionately when disappointed. If they are also depressed or resentful, they may be slow to start again, especially in relation to the one who disappointed them.[11] More generally, unintended nonreward and nonoccurrence of expected neutral stimuli are frequent when caretakers are distractible, inattentive, or preoccupied, as well as depressed. They are less aware of what is happening; they forget or lapse into inactivity. The nonrewards that result are unlikely to be signaled and are accompanied by nonoccurrence of expected neutral stimuli. Therefore, the nonrewards are maximally disturbing.

Young infants are particularly vulnerable to nonoccurrence of expected events because they organize events simply. In the first weeks, presumably, a sequence of stimuli can be familiar in only one way, and all other sequences are deviations from the familiar.[12] To young infants, only unchanging repetition is expected. In time, alternative sequences are learned. Still later, cues are learned that indicate which of the alternative sequences is likely to occur on a particular occasion. The expectations of older children are not limited to repetition of familiar sequences. On the contrary, they may expect that something that has never happened is going to happen. For example, a parental statement, "When we get to St. Louis, you will see your grandmother," may influence their expectations decisively. In addition, an older child can evaluate whether a parent is serious or joking, whether the words express momentary emotion or are a statement of what will happen. Much data can be brought to bear in knowing what to expect. At the beginning of life, however, monolithic sequences are the only learned basis for organizing experience. Consequently, nonoccurrence of the expected can occur in many ways. And those infants whose schemata remain monolithic because of disturbed attachment or heavy use of ritual remain particularly vulnerable to nonoccurrence of the expected.

Intermittent Reinforcement

Autistic children experience high demand in infancy, both explicit and implicit. They are expected to master skills precociously, to give lengthy performances, and to achieve high levels of precision. Demand is conveyed partly by the criteria used by the trainer for reinforcing behavior. The analysis of demand in relation to autism will begin with an aspect of reinforcement that has been studied extensively—frequency.

A broad generalization is that the more often reinforcement is given, the faster learning occurs, particularly when a subject is learning a new skill. Reward given every time a response is made (regular reward) is highly conducive to learning.

Intermittent reinforcement has more-variable effects. If rewards are intermittent and infrequent when a new skill is being trained, learning proceeds slowly or not at all. A skill learned with regular reward may be trained further by intermittent reward if the transition is gradual, while an abrupt change to intermittent, infrequent reward may disorganize behavior. For example, a pigeon trained to peck at a spot by receiving food regularly and then abruptly switched to an intermittent, infrequent schedule of rewards for pecking may stop pecking and starve as a result. In contrast, a gradual shift to less-and-less-frequent reward will sustain behavior and make it highly resistant to nonreward or punishment.

Use of intermittent reward means that reward alternates with nonreward, and disturbing effects of nonreward are likely (for example, emotionality, ritual, and inactivity). If intermittent reward is used judiciously, phenomenal levels of performance can be achieved. Animals can be turned into circus performers, behaving in ways that are atypical for their species. Children can be turned into superstars and productive geniuses, whose periods of inactivity are infrequent and brief. Such success requires a trainer who is patient and objective about the learner's skills, sensitive to the learners's frustration tolerance, and flexible in adjusting demand to the fluctuating emotional state of the learner.

When training with intermittent reward is optimal, nonreward has limited negative effects. But when training is less than optimal, disturbance that may not be evident at the time accumulates and appears later in proneness to inactivity. Then a single instance of nonreward, criticism, or punishment may result in a period of inactivity. When demand is high and the learner's needs are not judged and dealt with effectively, long breakdowns are common—periods of apathy, inactivity, or rebellion, with subjects sometimes becoming untrainable.

The required touch is not easy to maintain even for professional trainers. Its maintenance in the home is rare. A parent may succeed easily at training in which the more one does, the better the result is. Parents of autistic children should excel at such training because their devotion and persistence are extraordinary. However, in training with high demand and intermittent reward, doing more is helpful only up to a point and then becomes counterproductive. Such training has the added difficulty that moderate deviation from an optimal mix of demand and reward may not produce learning that is a little less than optimal. It may produce no learning at all of the task at hand and may interfere with future learning of other tasks. A training program in which the optimum is near the breaking point is difficult to administer. The thesis that autistic children receive much training near the breaking point is developed in this and the next chapter.

Intermittent reward is not usually a deliberate means of infant training but occurs unintentionally for a number of reasons. Factors that hinder perceiving an infant's behavior and rewarding it were suggested in chapter 6 to be common in mothers during the infancies of their autistic children. A carry-over of pregnancy fantasies, the tendency to adhere to ideas about the children from the first days of life, the determination to rear a genius, and the depression from disappointment contribute to not perceiving infant behavior and not rewarding it. Insofar as these circumstances applied, autistic children were trained by intermittent reward in infancy.[13]

According to Ferster, intermittent reward has not been found effective in training older autistic children.[14] Unresponsiveness to intermittent reward is known to result from prior negative experience with intermittent reward. In addition, injudicious use of intermittent reward may account for the children's general unresponsiveness to training and for their periods of inactivity.

Learning to Speak

High demand also means requiring a level of performance that is at or beyond a subject's limits. This may be done by using a narrow criterion of what is an acceptable response, with punishment or no reward when the subject fails to meet it. Learning to speak is difficult when narrow criteria are used. It may be the most difficult skill for an infant to acquire under such conditions, and the complexity of language is usually underestimated by parents teaching it to infants. Being responsive to the learner is particularly important in training speech.[15] Probably, these considerations bear on the difficulty autistic children have with language.

The suitability of a criterion in training a child depends not on abstract standards but on what a child's repertory is and on whether the child is beginning to learn a skill or already has some mastery of it. Let us assume an infant is just beginning to approximate the word *cup* by sounds like "cub, "gup," and "gub" but does not distinguish among these sounds. Let us assume also that a parent rewards "gup" and not the other sounds. The parent may reward "gup" regularly, but the infant, not making the distinction the parent does, may experience intermittent reward. Similarly, infants may begin to say a word before they distinguish narrowly among cues for the word. In the familiar example, infants first use *dog* to refer to many animals, and language acquisition is fostered by encouraging such incorrect use for some time. In every case, an infant begins to use a word with little understanding of how the parent uses it; their meanings differ greatly.[16] Gradually, the child's meaning approaches the parent's, but for some common words it will take years until the child's use is equivalent to the parent's. As long as their uses differ, what the parent intends as regular reward may be experienced as intermittent reward.

From these considerations, it follows that learning to speak is fostered by using regular reward with broad criteria for acceptable responses when an infant is learning a new word or a new meaning for an old word. Parents and teachers tend to follow this principle.

Educational systems frequently adjust the schedule of reinforcement explicitly, depending on the extent to which the educational reinforcements are maintaining the child's behavior. When the child is "doing very well," we generally withhold reinforcement. When it becomes discouraged ... we reinforce more frequently.[17]

The opposite also happens: parents and teachers increase rewards when achievement is high and punish more at times of failure. The more personally frustrated and disappointed a trainer is by a learner's failure, the more likely punishment is to occur.

Once a child says a new word regularly, progress requires learning when not to use it as much as when to use it, and correction becomes necessary. Learning when not to use a word requires incorrect use. In this respect, speech acquisition is typical of learning that requires trial and error. But it is difficult for parents to appreciate errors and to treat them objectively as steps in learning rather than as failures. The more perfectionistic they are and the greater their eagerness for successful performance is, the less objective and the more punitive they are likely to be. Autistic children's parents may be particularly intolerant of the errors necessary in learning.[18]

In short, parents try to train early speech in autistic children and expect precocity. They tend to be perfectionistic, to expect that once a correct response has been made it will always be made, and not to appreciate the function of errors in learning. In addition, they tend to be particularly hurt by the children's failures. The result is a mixture of reactions to the children's speech attempts that is relatively high in intermittent reward, correction, and punishment. In addition, they are slow to lower their demands when the children fail and may not sustain the children through particularly difficult periods in learning.

Such tendencies also may affect the training of other skills. It has been suggested that little behavior of autistic children was rewarded because their mothers gave rewards

[O]nly when the child's response, more or less by chance, coincided with the mother's conscious and unconscious fantasy of the moment. The possibility of such a coincidence was small, because the mother's unconscious wish was quite often directly in opposition to her idealized conscious wish. Indeed it was rarely that the child could respond "right."[19]

Reviewing various aspects of conditioning, Ferster concluded: "The common denominator among the parents of autistic children lies in their manipulation of the child's milieu in such a way that the child's behavior is weakened."[20]

Many autistic children who fail to learn language from parents succeed when taught by machines. Their success has been attributed to the consistency of the machines in reinforcing them and to the children having more control of the machines than of their parents.[21] Those parents who become successful teachers or therapists of their autistic children modify their training by lowering performance criteria, following the children's interests and cues, and being more consistent.[22]

The speech of autistic children tends to baffle their parents, who therefore may be at a loss about when to reward and when to correct. Errors in using words too broadly (calling various animals *dog*) are easy to recognize. The opposite—using words too narrowly—is more likely to be misconstrued by parents, who may then react counterproductively. Let us imagine an infant was learning to say "foo" when the mother pointed to the infant's food and asked, "What's this?" A large part of the infant's diet consisted of strained food, and the infant associated "foo" with strained food. But the mother was not aware of the narrowness of the infant's use and thought the infant meant food in general by "foo." Then the infant's diet changed and did not include strained food. When the mother again pointed to the infant's food and asked "What's this?", the infant, knowing no words for other kinds of food, remained silent. To the mother, it seemed that the infant had learned a word and then perversely had stopped using it. She reacted by pressuring the infant, pointing to the food and demanding, "Say, 'food'!" The infant complied, saying "foo" when told to.

The infant had now learned to respond with the word "foo" to a new stimulus, the words "Say 'food'." In addition, the infant may have taken a step toward learning to imitate the mother when under pressure to speak. Having learned to say "foo" to a stimulus other than strained food would tend to interfere with the earlier habit. In addition, pressure during an early phase of learning fosters unresponsiveness, which tends to persist after the pressure is removed. Later, if strained food were presented again and the mother asked "What's this?" the infant might not respond.

A difficulty for many young children and their parents is confusion of words with their opposites. All children have periods of such confusion, and autistic children have more than most. To a parent already frustrated by an infant's lack of speech, saying the opposite of what is correct may seem especially perverse.

In short, an infant's use of words can be incorrect from an adult viewpoint for many reasons. A normal adult reaction is to correct errors, but correction is likely to have adverse effects when it occurs at early learning points. When children unaccountably stop using words or seem contrarily to be saying the opposite of what is called for, parents become confused about what their children know and do not know. Therefore, whether parents react to errors liberally or punitively may depend more on subjective factors—expectations and disappointments—than on what is objectively helpful to their infants. These considerations are easier to understand in the abstract than to apply in life. Parents are not trained to recognize or deal judiciously with critical points in their children's learning. They seem conditioned instead to engage in counterproductive behavior at those times, to provide more nonreward and punishment than they otherwise would. Also, if a child's failure seems perverse, heavy pressure to do better is likely.

Language, unlike many other skills, is a matter of convention. There is no objective reality that determines success or failure in an infant's efforts to speak. The adults teaching language to an infant are the sole judges of whether or not a sound made by the infant is acceptable, of whether it is rewarded, corrected, or punished, and thereby of whether the infant has succeeded or failed; and the consequences of their discretion are great. Failure, once considered the spur to excellence, can disrupt the behavior of humans and animals. After failure, older children tend to do poorly on intellectual tasks. Their attention span is reduced, as is their self-confidence. They may make little effort to do what is asked, becoming evasive, uncooperative, antagonistic, somber, dull, restless, easily discouraged, anxious, or impulsive. A similar reaction to heavy demand has been reported in infants. According to Goldstein, behavior on the demanding task and on tasks formerly handled competently comes to be marked by agitation, daze, fumbling, evasiveness, and unfriendliness.[23]

When a criterion is well below the level of a child's highest performance, rewards are frequent and regular. When the criterion is at the level of mastery, successes and failures alternate, and rewards are intermittent. Older children and adults have less difficulty with such situations insofar as criteria can be explained to them. Infants cannot have criteria explained to them and, therefore, are at a disadvantage in finding regularity in what they experience as chaotic.

Language is also difficult because words have multiple meanings. Cues for their use shift with context and the speaker's intention. Autistic children have extraordinary difficulty with common words for that reason and prefer obscure words that always mean the same thing.[24]

Even without extraordinary stress, many children grow increasingly cautious in word use. Children of one to two and a half years overgeneralize readily. Later, they become cautious in applying familiar words to doubtful referents and in learning new words.[25] Whether their growing caution is innate or acquired, it results in periods of apparent nonlearning and of apparent loss of words (nonuse of previously used words). As a result, parents become frustrated and sometimes alarmed. They may increase pressure on children. But the effect of pressure is usually increased caution. Autistic children who speak tend to hold back words and strive for inordinate precision in those they use. Their caution may be attributable to earlier pressure.

Disturbances that result from stressful training in one skill may spread to less-demanding skills. A child may associate parental pressure with training in general and become resistive to training sessions in themselves.[26] Therefore, the effects of high demand for precocious speech may extend beyond language.

Social learning resembles speech in that cues are multiple and shifting, meanings are subtle and elaborate, and rules are conventional (arbitrary).

Therefore, social learning is also likely to be marked by many critical points and to be easily disturbed by heavy demand.

Conversely, memory is least disturbed by pressure or failure. Perhaps that is why autistic children devote themselves to memory skills and do well with them. Children can learn verses, prayers, and lists without understanding, and these are safer against shifting cues and arbitrary reinforcement. In memorizing state capitals, *Massachusetts* is always the cue for *Boston*. When having difficulty, rote learning of words can be a taken response to a demand for intellectual precocity. It minimizes the risk of correction by a perfectionistic trainer. Some of the complex skills in which autistic children excel, including mathematics and calendar tricks, are foolproof operations that depend largely on rote memory.

Delayed Reinforcement

Assuming that criteria are low enough and reinforcement is regular or judiciously intermittent, success in training depends upon timing of reinforcements. Rewards and punishments that follow responses without delay are most effective. The longer the delay, the less effective reinforcement is. A reaction delayed too long after an infant has done something may not be a reinforcement of the behavior at all.

The most general effect of delay is that training is inefficient. It proceeds slowly and less is learned. Delay also can be stressful. In the first weeks of life, delay of feeding has been reported to cause food refusal.[27] At three months, prompt reward is thought to teach an infant that it can control its environment. The outward effect is a high level of activity, particularly in interaction with its caretaker. Conversely, without prompt reward, an infant is thought to experience helplessness and to become withdrawn and lethargic.[28] Among the serious disturbances attributed to delayed reward is retardation.[29]

Reinforcement may be delayed so long that an infant does not associate it with the act the caretaker intends to reinforce. Rather, the infant may experience it as random or as a consequence of another act that is closer in time to the reinforcement. Parents can explain the relationship between response and delayed reinforcement to older children but not to infants. If the infant associates reinforcement with an act the caretaker did not intend to reinforce, superstitious behavior may be fostered.

Superstitious behavior here is behavior that does not meet a parent's criterion for reinforcement but is accidentally conditioned by its proximity in time to reinforcement intended for other behavior. Superstitions conditioned by delayed reward tend to disappear when repeated and not rewarded further. However, delayed punishment may condition avoidance behavior that does not disappear. It tends to become incorporated in larger rituals or compulsions.

The negative effects of delayed reinforcement are exacerbated by anticipation. For example, a parent may respond to a child's achievement with the promise of a gift. The gift subsequently given is an example of a signaled reward. Signals need not be verbal or consciously understood by the learner; they simply may be conditioned.

Delay of signaled rewards causes frustration and the development of a preference for immediate small gratifications over delayed large ones. When that happens, learning that depends upon long-range consequences is hindered. Autistic children's extreme preference for immediate gratification and refractoriness to training with long-range consequences may be attributable to such delay.

Delay of signaled punishment has been identified as a cause of recklessness and incorrigibility, particularly when threats and punishment are used in further training. Such delay also has been thought to foster self-punishment and provocative behavior in order to bring on expected punishment.[30] Such behavior in autistic children may be attributable to delay of signaled punishment.

These speculations hinge on the idea that mothers of autistic children are slow to react to them because of disappointment, depression, preoccupation, perplexity, or the lack of spontaneity said to characterize the mothers.

Noncontingent Reinforcement

Besides delay, a hindrance to a subject's association of a reinforcement with its behavior is impulsiveness in the trainer. Some parents feel moved by their feelings to reward or punish an infant with little regard to what the infant is doing at the moment. Another factor is reinforcement according to a time schedule. Still another is misperception of the subject's behavior. Whatever stimulates a trainer to reinforce, other than the subject's behavior at the moment, hinders the association of reinforcement with behavior.

Reinforcements that do not follow behavior or are not associated by the subject with the subject's behavior have been called *noncontingent, accidental,* or *random reinforcement.* Noncontingent reinforcement has a number of adverse effects. Like delayed reinforcement, it fosters superstition. And a superstition developed in one context may transfer to others and hinder learning when reinforcement is contingent on behavior. Also, the development of a superstition seems to increase the likelihood of forming new ones. The relevance of such findings to autism is suggested by the children's readiness to acquire rituals, which has been traced to noncontingent reinforcement.[31]

Noncontingent reinforcement interferes with learning less directly also. When reinforcement is timely and contingent, a child becomes more attentive generally and can be conditioned progressively to attend to cues relevant to further learning. Reinforcement that is not contingent or not closely contingent on a child's behavior increases the difficulty of perceiving those contingencies that are present and decreases the child's attention to environmental cues.[32] It also fosters attention to irrelevant cues. Inattention to environmental cues further contributes to ritual and to rigid, limited learning, both of which characterize autistic children and are discussed at length in later chapters. Finally, noncontingent reinforcement causes prior learning to be lost and has been considered a cause of retardation.[33]

Noncontingent reinforcement has been suggested as characteristic of mothers with their autistic children. In one description, a mother's interaction with her child suggested a little girl playing with her doll.

> [T]he doll has no feelings or motivations beyond what the "mother" attributes to it.
>
> [M]ost of the mother's acts toward the child were motivated out of needs arising within herself, and rarely responsive to the child's communication of his own needs.
>
> When a child was engaged in some activity, the mother might suddenly go to him and cover him with hugs and kisses . . . .[34]

If a parent reacts to behavior inaccurately attributed to an infant, the result is noncontingent reinforcement. A bias common in parents is to see what they expect or wish to see in their infants and to reinforce accordingly. Parental misperceptions of autistic children, derived from pregnancy fantasies and from impressions of them as neonates that persisted and influenced parents' reactions to the children were described in earlier chapters. Presumably, the misperceptions resulted in noncontingent reinforcement.

Another source of misperceptions and noncontingent reinforcement is the confusing behavior of autistic children. They are unresponsive and evasive, give obscure responses, and misdirect people about what their behavior means. For example, Kanner asked a boy to subtract four from ten and was told, "I'll draw a hexagon." At first, Kanner thought the boy had not given the right answer. Much later, Kanner concluded the boy had been correct (*six* in Greek as part of the word *hexagon*), but so much time had elapsed that no reward could be given.[35] The general effect of ambiguous behavior is to make adults' reactions depend more on their own interpretation than on the behavior. Another effect is to baffle adults and, consequently, to delay their reactions.

In short, the literature of autism contains many references to perplexed, inconsistent, or erratic caretaking. Such caretaking has been interpreted here as training with intermittent, delayed, and noncontingent reinforcement. Scattered reports indicate other ways that mothers hinder autistic chidren from learning or performing. For example, some mothers frequently interrupt their autistic children, even when the children are doing what the mothers want. A number of reports described prevention by mothers of contact between their autistic children and other people in infancy. In an exceptional study, a mother was found to intervene in ways that prevented her autistic child from having an effect on the environment.[36] In another case, "Mike had on a thin sweater ... while she wore a heavy winter coat. ... [Suddenly] she dashed to Mike and removed his sweater, stating that he was too hot."[37] In addition, many of the mothers have been reported to discourage spontaneity and emotional expression in the children.[38] Many of these findings were made by film analysis and other unusually close observations of behavior that had not been noted by ordinary observation and that were not reported by parents. Therefore, the extent to which parents limit their autistic children's learning and behavior is probably underestimated.

Rewarding Autistic Behavior

Many ways for autistic behavior to arise have been presented. It arises readily in infancy; as writers have pointed out, everything autistic children do is done also by ordinary children.[39] Therefore, the question of what maintains autistic behavior is important. Other children stop engaging in the behavior; autistic children do not stop.

The simplest hypothesis is that autistic behavior is maintained in children by rewarding it. Some of the behavior pleases parents and is rewarded deliberately. Earlier, the desirability of quiescence and lack of demands (the good baby) was discussed together with suggestions of how parents maintain such behavior. Parents boast about the autistic children's rote memorization and special skills. Presumably, they reward the behavior. Even seriously disturbed behavior has been praised as virtuous.[40]

Most autistic behavior is upsetting to parents, who try to discourage it. Nonetheless, they may reward it unintentionally. Parents of ordinary children commonly reward behavior that upsets them. The prime example is tantrums. A parent refuses something when a child asks for it, the child has a violent tantrum, and the parent accedes in desperation. In acceding, the parent rewards problem behavior. Ferster suggested that all autistic behavior that is aversive to parents is likely to be rewarded and thereby maintained. Specifically, parental reward has been reported to maintain the children's self-destructive behavior.[41]

Again, the effects of unintended reinforcement are probably more serious than the effects of deliberate reinforcement, as has been found in studies of disturbance. The same is true of the more-stressful aspects of training that are considered in chapter 10.

10 The Impossible Task: Difficult and Shifting Cues and Forced Responding

Extreme, pervasive handicap has been found with training procedures used largely with animal subjects and reported under the heading of experimental neurosis. The behavior of animals given such training resembles the behavior of autistic children in a variety of ways. The idea that such training causes psychosis in children was suggested in 1895.[1]

The first experiments were by Pavlov and his colleagues, who trained dogs by showing them a circle before giving them food and an ellipse when no food was coming. The ellipse was twice as long as it was wide, and the dogs easily distinguished it from the circle. No overt act was required of the dogs. The conditioning made them salivate at the sight of the circle and not at the sight of the ellipse.

Then the ellipse gradually was made rounder and rounder. The dogs continued to be docile, making finer and finer discriminations. When the ellipse came close to a circle (length/width ratio of 9/8) however, the dogs' discriminations did not improve further but became worse. Subsequently, they failed other tasks with easier discriminations that they already had mastered. In addition, "the whole behavior...underwent a marked change."[2] The dogs whined and barked vigorously in the laboratory, attacked the equipment, trembled, refused to eat, and became inactive and somnolent. They were compared to humans suffering breakdowns.

The disturbances caused by this and other procedures are associated particularly with the task being trained but are not limited to it. Many habits already learned seem to be lost and have to be relearned. House-trained animals may urinate and defecate indiscriminately in the house after training with difficult cues, as when they were infants. Relearning and new learning are inefficient; the subjects may appear incapable of learning. New behavior develops that is repetitive, stereotyped, superstitious, maladaptive, and resistant to further training. Some of the behavior is complex and apparently symbolic. Some is incomplete or abortive. Rituals may be done much of the time and particularly when training is attempted. Animals refuse food entirely or become selective eaters. Their sleep is disturbed. They become negativistic and asocial. In general, their activity is reduced, and they have been described as apathetic, self-restrained, depressed, restless, and irritable. (Use of these terms by experimenters is usually meant to convey similarity to human behavior.) The animals may become immobile, assuming peculiar postures or allowing themselves to be molded, and remain in such postures for long periods (the analogy here is to catatonic schizophrenia). Unresponsiveness may be extreme. For example, a cat may not move while a mouse runs by. A dog may seem oblivious to strong electric shock. Stupor also may occur.

Even survival mechanisms once thought to be unaffected by experience become inadequate. Self-starvation and apparent indifference to pain were mentioned. Animals also show heightened vigilance and suspiciousness and are frightened by innocuous stimuli that did not affect them before; but they may fail to protect themselves from gross dangers. They expose themselves to threats that they ordinarily deal with by fighting or flight. Many do not survive without protection and forced nutrition, and some die despite extraordinary care. The disturbance is more analogous to human psychosis than neurosis.

Not all these effects occur in the same animal, but contradictory combinations are often found. According to Kurtsin, paradoxical behavior is common. Little or no response may be given to intense stimuli while a strong response is made to weak stimuli. Dogs alert to faint sounds that others ignore but seem oblivious to loud sounds that ordinarily startle them. They may turn away from food when presented and salivate when it is removed.[3]

Some of the training procedures and their effects are analyzed in connection with autistic behavior and its possible causes. It is questionable to draw inferences about children from the behavior of animals. However, the procedures have been tested to a limited extent on humans with similar results. For example, in a variation of Pavlov's experiment, a boy was trained to distinguish 92 beats per minute from 144. The child was an enthusiastic participant, who easily learned the distinction. Then, the slow beat gradually was made faster. When it reached 132, the boy became disturbed and resisted further training.[4] The development of disturbance under certain stresses in training follows the same pattern in a number of species, including humans.

Severe disturbance has been produced by a variety of procedures. Solomon and his colleagues trained animals with strong electric shock and called their procedure "traumatic."[5] The concept of trauma connotes extreme circumstances such as loss, violence, or terror. It seems to preclude the idea that severe learning handicap and psychosis can be caused by non-violent, seemingly innocuous, and even well-intentioned regimens in the laboratory and in the home. Therefore, it is worth emphasizing that such behavior can be produced without strong aversive stimulation or deprivation, without what ordinarily is considered trauma. In some experiments like Pavlov's, there was no painful stimulation, no threat, and no deprivation—nothing typically considered punitive or even unpleasant. In the experiments with infant goats and sheep conducted over many years at Cornell University, researchers used mild electric shock. It elicited a startle but no bleating and was judged to be below the pain level. Nonetheless, young animals not only became extremely disturbed and remained so for years but some of them died of adrenal damage. Thus, by physiological measures, the training stress was extreme although aversive stimulation was mild.[6]

Difficult Cues

Many of the procedures that caused severe disturbance involved making familiar cues difficult to use. First, animals were trained to respond to one cue and to respond differently (or not at all) to a second cue. (The disturbing effects were similar whether a different response or no response was made.) For a time, the cues were easy to distinguish. Then they were made increasingly difficult to distinguish. Escape or distraction by engaging in other activities was not permitted.

When cues that no longer could be distinguished were presented, subjects were under pressure to respond without a basis for making one response over the other. Conflict between alternative responses has been considered a key element in training that causes disturbance.[7] Response conflict in an impossible task is postulated as the cause of schizophrenia in the double-bind theory. If simplified, the theory may be considered a special case of response conflict in a task with impossible cues. In a double bind, a person is given two cues at the same time that call for incompatible behaviors and is required to respond.[8] Experiments along such lines have resulted in behavior that is particularly suggestive in relation to autism, as follows.

Lashley and Maier trained rats to jump from a perch onto either of two platforms.[9] The platforms were hidden by doors. When a rat made a correct choice, the door fell open when struck by the rat's nose, and the rat landed on the platform, where food was available. When a rat made a wrong choice, the door was locked. Consequently, the rat got a bump on the nose, and instead of landing on the platform, it fell a short distance onto a net. The doors were marked for the rat by geometric forms. For example, the unlocked door had a circle on it, and the locked door had a triangle.

The task usually was mastered with little or no apparent disturbance. Then, the cues were changed. In one procedure, the cues were switched: the circle now marked the locked door and the triangle marked the unlocked door. The rats became emotional and resisted jumping, but they were coerced to jump by an electric shock or an air jet.

The rats learned the changed problem, but some of them behaved as if they had not mastered it and became seriously disturbed. Further switching of cues caused disturbance in others. The more often and unpredictably cues were switched, the more disturbance developed. In a variation, the task was made impossible. After the circle-triangle discrimination was learned, it no longer worked as a cue. The experimenter locked and unlocked the doors randomly, without regard to the location of the circle and triangle. This procedure also led to refusal to jump, and again the rats were coerced, causing serious disturbance.

Although rats varied in the course and severity of their disturbance, there was a common pattern. When forced to respond to cues that could not be used, much nervous behavior such as squealing when touched, refusing food, chattering, and urinating and defecating excessively during training sessions developed. Subsequently, most rats adopted a new pattern of behavior—a fixed habit. For example, some jumped to the platform on the left in every trial, without regard to whether the circle or triangle was on the left and without regard to the consequences of their behavior. Thus, the fixed habit did not have an apparent function in relation to the environment; it did not increase rewards or reduce punishments. In that sense, Maier considered the behavior purposeless. It seems to have functioned as an inner adaptation, however, since once fixed behavior was established, nervous behavior diminished.

Once established, fixed habits were stereotyped and very stable. Severe punishment did not deter them. The circle and triangle were made reliable cues again, but the rats did not follow them. Then the rats were coached. For left-jumping rats, the negative cue was put on the left in every trial and the door on the right was left open, exposing the platform and the food on it. Nonetheless, the rats continued to jump to the left.

The rats were not oblivious to these manipulations. When the cues were made reliable again, the rats were affected by them, as was shown in their speed of jumping. A left-jumping rat jumped faster when the left door had the positive cue than when it had the negative cue. When the door on the right was left open, the rat looked and sniffed to the right but then turned and jumped to the left. These and other behavior details showed that the rats distinguished the cues accurately but did not jump on the basis of the distinction.[10]

Children who receive analogous training also may adapt by peculiar use of cues, fixed responding, and resistance to further change. "[T]he child cannot cope with the situation in any other way but by memorizing some external criteria, by forsaking opportunities for experimentation, by avoiding failure at all costs, and by doing things 'just so' and in no other way."[11]

To compare autistic children to the laboratory rats, it would be helpful to have evidence of similar development—of learning of cues and responses by autistic children, of resistance to making the responses, of nonuse of the cues, and of the emergence of fixed responding unaffected by reward and punishment. In addition, evidence of comparable training would be helpful. There are indications of similarities.

Many parents report that autistic children learn cues that they later seem not to use and learn responses that they stop making. That is particularly true in the area of speech. Many parents get the impression that the children refuse to make the responses. These impressions are supported by the observations of clinicians and experimenters. Autistic children who appear oblivious to cues betray reactions to them by tiny movements that ordinarily pass unnoticed. In addition, they later recall events of which they had seemed oblivious originally. Other autistic children are more obviously aware. For example, when offered an object, they reach for it and then slap their extended hand and draw it back. One child, when asked to pick up an object, reached for it, stopped short, rocked, and then picked up something else. Sometimes he did pick up the requested object, but then "he frequently became very angry, biting his hands or refusing the food reward."[12] When autistic children who are silent much of the time do speak, some then hit or bite themselves or knock their heads against a wall. Experimental verification of their resistance has been reported.[13] The children's incomplete and self-punished acts may show that they discriminate the cues in the way the adult intended but that they complete their acts on another basis.

Fixed responding is characteristic of autistic children and is discussed later. Also characteristic is apparent nonresponse to reward and punishment.

Estimating autistic children's experience with ambiguous, shifting, and contradictory cues is difficult. People are usually unaware of ambiguities, inconsistencies, and contradictions in their behavior.[14] Consequently, parents are not in a position to report such behavior to clinicians. The kind of detailed study of parent-child interaction that led to discovery of the double bind in schizophrenia hardly has been done with young children.

Some reports indicate ambiguous, contradictory cues in the behavior of mothers with their autistic children.[15] Inconsistency in language training was suggested in the last chapter. Some is inevitable because of the ambiguities in languages (homonyms and multiple meanings of words). A mother who teaches the sound of "eye," meaning an orb, and then teaches it to mean herself, may be surprised if her infant responds according to the first meaning. The mother may be intent on her purpose and not realize that the response is one that she taught the child and is correct in that sense, or she may realize it and not know what to do. With an older person, she could explain, "What I said was ambiguous, and you were correct objectively to take it as a visual eye, although I meant myself." Even when addressing adults, people rarly give such full, supportive explanations. Usually they say something like "No, that's not what I meant. I meant myself." Such correction often carries the implication that the responder made a mistake.

No such explanation is possible for a child of one or two. With an infant, a mother's response is limited to rewarding, correcting, or punishing the unsatisfactory response. In the circumstances described, learning may be promoted by disregarding the mother's intended meaning and rewarding the infant because being corrected or punished is equivalent to having cues switched.

If a mother receives an unexpected response that she at first takes to be an error, the chances that she nonetheless will reward her infant will be limited by the extent to which she is critical, eager for precocity, prone to disappointment, and inclined to see things from her viewpoint rather than her child's. In general, a person's proneness to disappointment and depression makes for changeability in the meaning of cues given.

These considerations, along with the reports cited, suggest that autistic children experience more ambiguous, shifting, and contradictory cues than other children. The idea merits study because the children show behavior that results from cue switching.

The disturbing effects of cue difficulty are compounded by lengthy training sessions, coercion to respond, and restriction of activity or prevention of alternative behavior. Reports of lengthy training were cited in chapter 4. Restriction of autistic children's activities sometimes has been reported. In addition, it is implied in the more-frequent reports of secluding the children in infancy, observing them minutely, and holding them for hours at a time.

Coercion to respond has been described by parents after they concluded that their autistic children were defective and undertook remedial training. One mother wrote, "I'm always torn between overprotecting David and pushing him to his limits. And so he suffers."[16] As in the case of Dibs, however, there are indications of coercion earlier, when the children were normal or precocious—indications of what Kanner described as ceaseless urging of the children to perform.[17] Coercion is consistent with the determination and tenacity characteristic of the parents.

Many—perhaps most—of the parents do not see themselves as coercive or even demanding of their autistic children. In one study, the mothers rated themselves as lax and indulgent.[18] But being lax in some ways does not preclude coercion. For example, one mother who was remarkably indulgent in other respects was trying to train stair climbing in a toddler who showed fear of stairs. She put her daughter midway between the top and bottom of the stairs and left her there, beckoning and calling to her from the landing. The girl made no attempt to climb or descend; she screamed. The mother judged the experience to be one of terror for the child, and it was very disturbing to the mother as well. Nevertheless, she persisted.

Adaptations to Stressful Training

In general, stress arouses emotions, including motivation, that are helpful with some learning and that hinder other learning. High motivation interferes particularly with complex learning.[19] The usual effect is that children and adults try hard and tend to quit when they fail. At first, failure is met by intense effort with declining efficiency in which formerly distinctive cues become increasingly confusing to them. Their problem solving becomes disorganized and regressive, and they quit, resist further training, and turn to escapism. Later, they may try again. If resistance and escapism are not permitted, they may keep trying but are likely to become lastingly disturbed.

A specific adaptation of the platform-jumping rats to their impossible task was the development of a fixed habit. They did not solve the task; rather, they stopped paying attention to most of the cues provided and stopped making choices. The fixed habit had "no adaptive value in the sense that it [was] adequate to the situation or . . . [was] superior to any number of other possible responses." Also, by using the fixed habit, the rats did not master anything of use in future learning. On the contrary, the fixity of the habit hindered further learning. The habits were so fixed that they were "repeated without variation for at least several hundred trials, without the animals once attempting an alternative" even when punished every time.[20]

After the fixed habits were established, Maier removed one of the platforms and required the rats to jump to the remaining platform. A minority did so, and seemed undisturbed, but refused to eat and later showed other serious disturbance. Another minority did not jump despite an air blast that was sufficient in other circumstances to drive resistive subjects off the perch. These rats became the most disturbed. The majority jumped toward the platform but not to it. They jumped short, falling into the net below. This group subsequently showed the least disturbance.

To abstract the essentials of the training, first, the subjects learned to respond selectively on the basis of cues. Then, that basis was made inoperative. They adapted by fixed responding. Then, that too was prevented by the trainer. As a result, many became severely disturbed. The majority escaped serious disturbance by responding abortively.

The adaptation that was successful in averting severe disturbance was complex. Maier concluded that the disturbance was caused by pressure to respond without a schema by which to organize behavior. Those who became severely disturbed adapted simply. Some of them did what the procedure called for—jumping to the platform. Others totally resisted the pressure and did nothing. The successful adaptation was a combination of the two reactions—an incomplete jump.

This adaptation was similar to the earlier one that had reduced distress—the fixed jumping. Both involved acts that resembled the behavior called for. Fixed jumping deviated in that the rats did not use the cues they were conditioned to use. The adaptations retained the form of the trained behavior without its substance (meaning). That is why the experiment is particularly suggestive in relation to autism.

Autistic children do things that have the form of required behavior but not the substance. Echolalia is a prime example: words are used, but they do not meet the requirements of speech. To echo what people say involves responding to only a fraction of the cues they provide. If echolalia is analogous to fixed and abortive jumping, it may be a reaction to stress in learning to talk. Let us assume that an infant experiences shifting speech cues and is under pressure to respond to them. Echoing an adult's speech imposes a constancy on the cues. By using only the sound of speech as a cue, the infant renders unpredictability in the meaning of cues irrelevant to his or her behavior. There is no longer a choice of response, a possibility of being right or wrong. The sound of the cue determines the response to be made with perfect regularity. Therefore, echolalia may serve to reduce the distress of dealing with inconsistent cues.

In addition, echolalia may be accepted and even rewarded by an adult eager to hear words from an infant. As was suggested earlier, a frustrated parent is likely to encourage echolalia by telling a child to echo certain words (Say 'food.'"). Training an infant to repeat lists of states and other material that has no meaning to the infant also fosters echoing. Such experiences prepare an infant to use echoic responses later when under pressure to speak. The result is an adaptation by which demands are met partially (token compliance) and behavior becomes fixed despite variations in cues. As interpreted here, echolalia and fixed jumping are similar to behavior found in some adults—the "Yes, dear" of a spouse who is not paying attention or the "Yes, sir" of a subordinate who is being noncommittal.

In the case of fixed jumping, punishment not only failed as a deterrent but the more punishment was given, the more the behavior was adhered to. This result is not accounted for by reinforcement theory. It may involve regression to more-primitive cognitive functioning as a result of the extreme unpredictability of the situation. As was noted, in young infants, predictability of events seems to take precedence over reward and punishment. Lack of predictability is traumatic for members of a number of species. Prior to the appearance of fixed position habits, varying cues elicited varying responses followed by varying reinforcements in no order. After the fixed jumping appeared, the rats seemed not to be attending to the main cues (the circle and triangle). Let us assume that, by selective inattention, the remaining aspects of the stimulus situation remained constant from trial to trial. The fixed jumping made the rats' responses constant also. And the more they were punished, the more constant the effect of their behavior was. When they were punished on every trial, a perfectly regular situation had developed. The same cue, response, and consequence were repeated on every trial. Thus, the change from an unpredictable situation to a highly predictable one may have perpetuated the rats' adaptation.[21]

Abortive jumping differed from fixed jumping and was a reaction to the change made by the trainer after fixed jumping had been established. The trainer had simplified the task by calling for only one response. Under other conditions, the rats would have made it without distress. But the training experiences resulted in maximum resistance at this point.[22] In this simple situation, the conflict evidently was between jumping to the platform and not jumping. The reaction most effective in averting disturbance was to do neither one but a combination of the two.

If abortive jumping was a combination of jumping and resistance, it was like a number of symptoms of neurosis and psychosis. Hysterical disabilities, compulsions, and catatonic behavior have been interpreted as combinations of tendencies to act and to inhibit the action. Anxiety resulting from conflict between action and inhibition tendencies is thought to be reduced by the symptom, thereby perpetuating it.

The symbolic disguise of the act in hysterical and compulsive people is often lacking in catatonics, who commonly begin a movement and interrupt it, begin to speak but remain silent. The more-disturbed rats showed other behavior typical of catatonic adults—immobility and catalepsy.

Abortive behavior is typical of autistic children. Like catatonics, autistic children typically begin acts and interrupt them, and their echolalia may be a combination of speaking and not speaking. Other peculiarities of their speech may have a similar significance (chapter 14).

In Maier's experiments the adaptation of the rats spread. After disregarding the geometric cues, they also disregarded more-basic cues—the sight of a door being open, the sight and smell of food on the platform. Furthermore, they became unresponsive to cues unrelated to training, including loud noises and bright lights. In this respect also, their behavior resembled that of autistic children. In short, the behavior of animals with such training and of autistic children as they develop becomes stereotyped, fixed, and unresponsive to external cues and demands, and it reflects little of what they have learned. The experiments with animals suggest a way in which children may come to disregard cues and to use little of their experience.

The gap between these findings and children's behavior may be bridged partly by another line of experiments with animals and people. The experiments described so far began with an easy task that later was made impossible. The opposite sequence also has been studied.

Predictability and Helplessness

Adults were given an insoluble task first. They subsequently failed to learn a similar one that was easy. Some of the subjects reported that during the easy task they formed hypotheses about cues that proved incorrect. Nonetheless, they continued to adhere to the wrong hypotheses rather than to try alternatives. As a result of the insoluble task, their behavior had narrowed. They also reported feelings of hopelessness, apathy, and negativism while attempting the easy task.[23]

A similar effect was obtained by a different preliminary experience.[24] Before a task, adults were given a number of electric shocks. Some of them had a switch for turning off the shock. Others did not, although they got no more shock than the first group. For the second group, the shock was unsignaled and inescapable (noncontingent punishment). Then the subjects attempted the task, which consisted of learning which of the controls in a panel would turn off a shock. On each trial they were given a cue, after which they had a number of seconds in which to operate the controls correctly to avoid the shock. Once the shock began, operating the controls correctly ended it.

The group that had control over the shock in the preliminary experience quickly learned the task. Of the group that had preliminary inescapable shock, many did not manage a single escape or avoidance of shock. Asked why not, they said they felt they had no control of the situation. It was, therefore, pointless to try. When the cue was presented, they devoted most of their effort to preparing themselves for the coming shock rather than to seeking a solution.

Some subjects did make the correct response and escaped or avoided the shock on one or more trials. However, they did not profit from the experience. On subsequent trials, they again allowed the shock to occur. It appeared to the experimenters that these subjects did not associate what they did with the occurrence or nonoccurrence of shock. The preliminary experience had resulted in a sense of helplessness that was not affected by subsequent success.

Similar results were obtained in related experiments with humans and with fish, birds, rats, cats, and dogs. Dogs given no preliminary experience mastered the task after a number of trials. Thereafter, when the cue was presented the dogs showed no distress. Gracefully and unhurriedly, they executed the movement by which shock was avoided. By contrast, dogs given the same task shortly after a number of unsignaled, inescapable shocks were slow to act—slow to escape the shock and, on later trials, to avoid it. Some did not act at all. Those that did escape or avoid the shock appeared to learn little from that experience. Their behavior on subsequent trials was hardly changed by their success; they continued to allow themselves to be shocked.[25]

A day later, the dogs learned normally. But a second experience of inescapable shock caused lasting handicap with effects outside of the learning situation, including food refusal and weight loss.

Maier concluded that his procedure rendered past experience useless. The same seems true of preliminary noncontingent punishment. Past experience is the basis of learned behavior. When it is useless, the only remaining basis for behavior is primitive and unlearned, as in muscle rigidity and negativism.

A series of failures causes cessation of effort. After a period of inactivity, an animal or person may try again. Theoretically, renewed effort depends upon the availability of behavior that has not been rendered inoperative, as by extinction, suppression, or a cue that it will not succeed. In discussing why animals and people quit or keep trying in a difficult situation, concepts of helplessness and hopelessness have been used—concepts related to the clinical concept of depression. The behavior described earlier in animals and people has been called *learned helplessness* and compared to depression.[26] How much these concepts overlap remains to be worked out.

Experiments with clinically depressed people have yielded results consistent with the concept of learned helplessness. The belief that their efforts have little effect on outcomes is aroused easily in them—and it persists despite their successes.

Hope, the opposite of hopelessness and helplessness, may be defined as the availability of at least one course of action by which prior experience can be used to increase predictability. The other terms may be defined as the absence of such a course. Helplessness and hopelessness may be defined also as mental states in which predictability is not expected. A person experiencing helplessness may or may not be objectively helpless. The situation may lend itself to a solution, but there may be no act in the person's repertory for increasing predictability that has not been rendered inoperative.

Seligman noted that events that typically precipitate depression—death, divorce, loss of job, academic failure, physical disease, and growing old—present difficulties along with the implication that there is nothing one can do about them.[27] That is also true about positive events that precipitate depression—graduation, promotion, and retirement. Changes of both kinds mean that new cues occur, old cues require different responses, and old responses are ineffective. The changes reduce the usefulness of prior experience.

Marris' explanation of the effects of bereavement and other changes is similar to Seligman's interpretation of experimentally induced disturbance and depression on the basis of reinforcement contingencies. The key element is that environmental change and unpredictability of events are disturbing and arouse effort to restore predictability:

> [T]o ignore or avoid events which do not match our understanding—to control deviation from expected behavior, to isolate innovation and sustain the segregation of different aspects of life—are all means to defend our ability to make sense of life.[28]

When the effort fails, grief sets in (helplessness, inactivity, and apathy). According to Marris, loss of predictability and of the efficacy of formerly effective behavior are the key elements of bereavement and other traumatic changes. As effort is renewed, normal mechanisms become exaggerated: much of the environment is ignored or avoided; deviation is not tolerated; and life becomes fragmented.

Drawing together threads from this and the last chapter, maintenance of predictabiltiy can be impaired by:

Noncontingent reinforcement. Reinforcement may be noncontingent in a child's experience when:

Reinforcement varies according to events that affect a parent but are not distinguished by the child;

A parent deals with a child according to schedules, rules, rituals, and misperceptions that bear little relation to the child's behavior;

A parent is depressed, confused, or for other reasons is slow to respond.

Indistinguishable, shifting, or contradictory cues. Cues may be indistinguishable by a child when:

They are subtle, complex, or otherwise beyond a child's understanding;

Their level of difficulty is raised abruptly from an easier level;

They are ambiguous or have multiple meanings, and the child does not know which meaning applies at a particular time;

A parent's ambivalence or mood change results in inconsistency of cues;

A parent is influenced by events that are not perceived by the child.

Coercion to respond. Coercion is likely when:

A parent has high demands, is overinvolved with a child, is easily disappointed in a child, or takes relatively impersonal behavior in a deeply personal way;

A parent adheres to a plan of child rearing with the expectation that the child will respond on schedule;

A child is negativistic, unresponsive, or engages in fixed responding.

These factors combine and have cumulative effects. For example, limited change of cues ordinarily has little residual effect but can be disturbing if preceded by noncontingent reinforcement. The effects of a single experience of any of these factors are likely to be temporary, but a second experience is likely to have severer and more lasting effects, especially if it comes soon after the first.

The importance of predictability of events has emerged from many areas of research: class structure, group rules and conventions, primitive religion, stressful training, attachment, life changes, bereavement, mental retardation, and schizophrenia. Unfortunately, research in these areas has developed separately.[29]

Schizophrenia, which is linked most closely to autism, has been interpreted as an adaptation in which people use rather little of their experience. Therefore, they have little to go by in evaluating situations and choosing actions. They experience everyday events as new and unpredictable. Their need for predictability is great. Therefore, their energies go into making experience predictable by fixed habits and rituals.[30]

White interpreted schizophrenia as starting in childhood with overconcern about assessing cues before acting. Thus, children become hesitant. Some devote themselves obsessively to weighing cues and forego acting. The extreme is catatonia, which "presents the perfect picture of refusal to put forth any action. Vigilant observation may be going on all the time, but there is a vast inhibition" of responses demanded by the environment.[31] Hesitancy to act often is punished, and the children endure the punishment without speeding up their responses. Like experimental animals, they may respond by becoming even slower to act.

Some do eccentric, irrelevant things to cover their hesitancy and to stop others from pressing them for a response. Being distracted is often more acceptable than being hesitant. People tend to reduce their demands, saying the child is off in another world. Thus, the appearance of being oblivious may be rewarded by lessening of demands and of punishment for nonresponse.

Approaching the problem of autism from different directions, the main contributors in the United States arrived at conceptions similar to those discussed previously. Kanner, throughout the changes in his thinking about autism, stressed as fundamental the children's obsession with keeping their environment from changing. Bettelheim interpreted most of the symptoms as attempts to control and predict events, stemming from the core of autism: "the conviction that one's own efforts have no power to influence the world, because of the earlier conviction that the world is insensitive to one's reactions.[32] Rimland saw as the core of autism an impairment *"in a function basic to all cognition: the ability to link new stimuli with remembered experience....The child is thus virtually divested of the means for deriving meaning from his experience."*[33] Similarly, Goldfarb and his associates concluded:

He is first and foremost a puzzled child. His generalizations of both inner and outer experience are primitive, vague, and confused. He is in a state of constant perplexity because he is unable to observe patterns in reality. Though he may have normal biological equipment for seeing, hearing, tasting, and touching, he fails to arrange sensory information in such a way as to give it form, to connect it with past experience, or to appraise it in the light of previous stimuli.[34]

The same basic difficulty and adaptation have been seen as the core of the cognitive behavior of retarded children.[35] Adaptations common to autistic and retarded children and schizophrenic adults are explored further in the next chapter.

11

Adaptations:
Cues, Rituals, and Roles;
Retarded and
Schizophrenic Patterns

Reactions to stressful training in the home are part of the larger relationship between child and parent. The parent tends to see the child's reaction as part of a pattern, reflecting something basic in the child, and to reinforce accordingly. Consequently, the child's reaction tends to be incorporated in an adaptive pattern. Two likely patterns are retarded and schizophrenic behavior. Selective attention to cues, selective responding, inhibition, and failure to learn are hallmarks of mental retardation. Token responding, ritual, inhibition, and negativism are characteristics of schizophrenia, particularly in its catatonic form.

Learning and other mental processes have been studied more in people diagnosed as retarded and schizophrenic than in those diagnosed as autistic. Therefore, these processes will be discussed further in the light of those studies and as aspects of retarded and schizophrenic adaptations. The discussion will explore what people diagnosed as autistic, retarded, and schizophrenic have in common.

Selective Attention

Educators and psychologists have long believed that the most important thing to learn early is how to learn.[1] Subsequent learning and academic success require development of efficient learning methods, orientations, or strategies. Some ways of learning are generally inefficient. Other ways are efficient in one type of situation but interfere with learning in others. Ways in which children learn have been studied experimentally in much detail and provide a basis for understanding the limited intellectual functioning of retarded children.[2]

The words *method* and *strategy* suggest a deliberate, sophisticated approach to a task. When used in analyzing basic learning processes, these terms do not denote deliberation or sophistication. People's habitual ways of learning are largely unconscious and may be as simple as a preference for one type of cue over others. To avoid suggesting more, the traditional term *learning set* will be used in referring to work under the heading of *strategy*.

Learning sets used by people need not reflect their intelligence. Reinforcement easily changes some of their sets. The more sets people acquire, the more prepared they are to learn under varied conditions. Conversely, people and animals that do not acquire or use sets are limited to blind trial and error in dealing with changing circumstances. They have minimal adaptive capacity and are highly dependent on an unchanging environment. In Harlow's words, such a creature remains a "conditioned response robot."[3]

The most effective learning set in tasks requiring higher intelligence is to generate a hypothesis that can be tested by experience. Then, if the hypothesis is not confirmed, efficacy requires that it be replaced by another. Such a set is the foundation of reasoning and adaptability. The importance of learning sets has been demonstrated powerfully in animal experiments. Subjects that had acquired efficient sets continued to learn well in novel situations even after they had suffered extensive brain damage.[4]

Creatures show considerable individual variation in learning sets. In platform jumping, for example, some rats are attentive to visual form cues and readily learn problems with such cues. Others are more responsive to position cues and easily learn tasks requiring choice of one side over the other and tasks requiring alternation of right and left on successive trials. Similarly, some people notice form cues readily and are slow to use color cues. Others do the opposite. Whether their preferences come from heredity or experience is not usually known. But their preferences can be changed by experience. Form-oriented people can be induced to pay attention primarily to color on a task simply by instructing them to do so or by rewarding them for doing so.

The importance of cue selection has been shown in experiments with retarded children. Form and color cues are prominent in ordinary teaching materials and in puzzle items on intelligence tests. Retarded children tend to ignore form and color and focus on position cues. When given problems with position cues, they may learn as fast or faster than normal children.[5]

Cue preferences can be critical in academic learning. For example, poor students have been found to pay more attention than better students to cues unrelated to text. Poor students rely more in answering questions on their teacher's manner and ignore what they have been taught. Many devote their effort to reading the teacher's intention, to ascertaining which answer the teacher expects. The learning set has advantages in dealing with rather inconsistent adults, but it hinders academic learning and leads to handicap in the long run. The set is characteristic of poor students without regard to the underlying cause. It is found in those with subcultural deprivation, perceptual handicaps, and diseases associated with retardation. The more they fail or are punished, the more they distrust their efforts and imitate adults or seek clues from them.[6]

In this respect, autistic children have been considered the opposite of retarded children. The usual view is that autistic children are interested in things and oblivious to people. In particular, they are said to be oblivious to adults in charge of them. Therefore, they are expected to be responsive to cues in learning materials and unresponsive to the trainer as a cue. Careful observation has shown the opposite: autistic children observe adults, but they do it surreptitiously so that the adults do not notice. In addition, seemingly oblivious autistic children do respond to instructions from adults. However, they do it negativistically or in peculiar ways that adults do not recognize as responses.[7] Some evidence indicates that autistic children watch adults for cues more than normal children do. They watch adults at the expense of attending to cues in the tasks set before them. For example, "When we asked him to put colored pegs into similarly colored parts of the pegboard, he paid attention not to the pegs and board but to our face. It was in our expression that he sought the answer to the problem."[8]

Causes of paying attention to the trainer and not to the task cues have not been studied in people as far as I know. An incidental finding of experiments with stressful training is that animals become more responsive to trainer cues as they become less responsive to task cues.[9]

Unresponsiveness to task cues that have proven unreliable is to be expected. Extra responsiveness to the trainer suggests that the trainer's appearance has furnished cues that were more reliable. Despite care to make themselves neutral stimuli and not bias subjects' performance, trainers often have failed. Experiments on experimenters have shown that they convey their attitudes—their expectations of what their subjects will do—by subtle, unintended cues and reinforcements of which they are unaware. School teachers tend to reinforce according to their perceptions of their students' brightness.[10] For example, a teacher is likely to misperceive an incorrect answer to be correct and to reward it when the teacher thinks a student knows the answer. Similarly, a correct answer is likely to be perceived as wrong and corrected when a teacher considers a student to be dull. (The opposite effect also occurs when adults demand more of a bright child and accept poor responses from a dull one.)

The neutrality and fairness that trainers and teachers attempt by deliberate self-discipline resembles what many compulsive people do ordinarily as a matter of character. Such behavior by parents sometimes results in giving overt cues that are misleading or that are contradicted by emotional reactions that are suppressed incompletely.

Infants who are considered superior or retarded by parents are more likely than those considered ordinary to receive misleading, contradictory cues and inaccurate reinforcements. The parents of children who are diagnosed as retarded in infancy are advised to expect little and to accept and reward whatever effort the infants make. The advice and the most lenient attitudes parents have toward these infants do not preclude hopes, expectations, disappointments, impressions that the infants are not trying, and reinforcements that shift with shifting ideas and feelings about the infants. The reported leniency of parents of handicapped children has been called a legendary belief, and observations indicate that parents of organically retarded children make more than normal demands of them.[11] With or without extra demands, misleading or contradictory cues and inaccurate reinforcements are highly likely. Specialists in retardation consider the eventual intellectual functioning of congenitally defective children to be influenced heavily by their experiences in learning.[12]

Parents of autistic children are at a similar disadvantage in giving accurate cues and reinforcements because of their lofty fantasies and impressions of defects in the children. The establishment of a diagnosis of autism does not end the problem. As the mother who remained torn between overprotecting her son and pushing him to his limits noted, inconsistent training with unfortunate consequences continues to be a problem. She also noted that her child perceived and correctly interpreted her body language, including behavior of which she was not aware.[13]

If a parent is confused about whether a child is precocious or retarded, the parent will be uncertain about how high to set standards in training the child and about how much help to give the child. If the parent's view of the child's ability varies from time to time as the parent's outlook swings between optimism and pessimism, a child who is having difficulty with task cues may be best able to control or at least to predict the parent's reaction to his or her performance by focusing on subtle, unintended cues. If the child has been punished for using such cues, the child may learn to look surreptitiously. Whether autistic children's difficulty in learning stems from innate limitations or from stressful training, the difficulty is conducive to reliance on unintended cues and inattention to task cues.

Parents may tolerate resistance during a lesson and indulgently cut the lesson short, but resistance to beginning a lesson is likely to be met forcefully. Autistic children, like the experimental subjects described, tend to resist beginning. In trying to get an unwilling person to do something, the first step is to capture the person's attention.[14] Conversely, failure to get the person's attention makes it unlikely that the person will do what is wanted. Therefore, failure to get the person's attention often leads to abandoning the effort. People who try hard to control others are skilled in capturing attention; and people who effectively resist control are skilled in not having their attention captured. Evasion is most effective when the evader knows what the other person is about to do. For example, when one knows a demand is about to be made, one can absent or busy oneself or be prepared not to hear one's name being called. Therefore, successful evasion is aided by being aware of the other person while seeming not to be. Autistic children are highly effective in preventing others from capturing their attention (in the sense that others know they have the children's attention). Parents have gone to extreme lengths to get autistic children's attention and even then have had only limited success.[15]

Once a learner's attention has been gotten, cues related to the task are presented. Most tasks require responses to multiple cues and are therefore difficult for creatures that attend only to one cue. The learning handicap of animals trained as described in chapter 10 has been attributed to their use of only a single cue.[16] Given a task with multiple cues, autistic and retarded children ignore more of them than other children, and autistic children ignore more than retarded children.[17] Similarly, autistic children make little use of redundancy or other enrichment of cues. Easy problems often differ from hard ones by having extra cues. When that is true, autistic children tend to do as well with hard items as with easy ones.[18]

Besides using few cues in problem solving and learning, autistic children use few in communicating. Kanner's observations about the children's extreme literalness and precision, their intolerance of synonyms and of different meanings for a single word, have been confirmed. As one mother noted, an autistic child "prefers a long word with a single meaning to small words which change unaccountably in different contexts." They seem to make little use of context cues.[19]

Their extremely narrow use of cues makes autistic children overly dependent on the cues they use. If the cues are unavailable, they will be at a loss. This may account for their distress at changes in their environment. Limited changes that would leave other people with cues for behavior or for anticipating what is to come may remove those relied on by autistic children.[20]

In social interaction, judging others' moods is important. A person's mood may be judged by expression, posture, movements, words, and speech tone. If some of the cues are not provided, one still may judge by those remaining. However, if words and tone are the only cues used, one cannot judge the mood of a silent person.

Sometimes people give mixed cues. They may smile and say that nothing is wrong while slouching and speaking in a flat manner. A person who pays attention to only one of the cues will not sense the discrepancy. Discrepancy in itself is often an important cue about what is coming. It may be a sign of ambivalence, a caution that whatever one does will not please the other. In addition, the more cues used, the easier it is to resolve ambiguities or deal with double binds. A person using only two cues can recognize a discrepancy but has no additional information by which to resolve it.[21]

Thus, restricted use of cues could explain the social ineptness of autistic children. It could also explain their avoidance of social situations and their use of ritual and fixed responding to social demands. Failure to resolve ambiguities while under pressure to respond is highly stressful. Haley suggested that in such circumstances, schizophrenics develop skills in making responses that are not responsive.[22] In this respect, their behavior under pressure resembles the behavior of animals under pressure to respond to difficult cues. The behavior of autistic children fits Haley's analysis of unresponsive responses at least as well as the behavior of schizophrenic adults does (chapter 14).

Beyond elementary levels, learning involves an accumulation of nuances and alternate meanings to what originally were learned as single, simple facts. Old meanings must be discarded or modified. More than one meaning has to be retained as usable, and people must be able to switch from one meaning of a cue to another.[23] Autistic children insist that things remain constant. Their observed inflexibility has been confirmed in experiments. Given problems to solve, they adhere to unsuccessful approaches. They have been found less flexible than retarded children. The idea with which they begin a task is used over and over, even though it does not work. Besides lacking initiative in trying alternative approaches, they resist efforts by the trainer to modify their unsuccessful approaches. "Once a rule is learnt, an autistic child tends to keep it under all circumstances."[24]

Narrow, inflexible responding has been attributed to anxiety about ability to perform. Anxiety hinders reflection and consideration of alternatives. Performance anxiety seems most critical on tasks that require rejection of the first, easiest, or most common response.[25] Performance anxiety has been cited as the cause of some of the low functioning of handicapped people. Retarded children are expected to be particularly anxious about their adequacy because they are inadequate—but that is a simplified explanation.

Inadequacy is much more than a reflection of a record of objective failures. An infant may try to stand countless times, falling each time, without being seriously discouraged or turning to ritual. Performance anxiety in infancy is better understood as the result of training stresses. Retarded and autistic children usually do best (and sometimes exceed others) in skills that are self-taught or learned from machines. The stresses that cause performance anxiety are mediated by adults.

Autistic children are less flexible in their approaches to problems than retarded children, but they are not less intelligent than retarded children. Nonetheless, they act as if they are more anxious than retarded children about their adequacy. If objective handicap were the main source of feelings of the inadequacy and helplessness that interfere with learning and problem solving, it would follow that the greater the handicap, the more sensitive to failure a person would be. That is not demonstrably true about handicapped people. Specifically, autistic children were compared to children whose psychosis was associated with gross brain damage. The autistic children did better in problem solving up to the point of failure. Thereafter, the autistic children declined to random guessing, much below the after-failure level of the grossly brain-damaged children.[26]

The autistic children were more adequate to begin with, but failure caused an extreme drop in functioning. The grossly inadequate children showed little anxiety and maintained their functioning after failure. In this comparison, the autistic children's reaction to failure is not accounted for by anxiety due to inadequacy. The experiment confirmed observations about the extreme sensitivity to failure of autistic children. In this respect, they were unlike children with gross brain damage and like people and animals trained with unreliable cues or noncontingent reinforcement.

Token Acts, Ritual, and Negativism

The fixity of behavior that develops under stressful training has been emphasized—its stereotypy and persistence despite external reinforcement considerations. It has been called *token* behavior because it has the form but not the function of the behavior called for. It has been called *compromise* behavior insofar as it seems to combine elements of incompatible responses.

Features of fixed behavior resulting from training with unreliable cues are found also in everyday behavior that is classified as ritual. The more arbitrary or ritualistic an activity that provides predictability is, the more tenacious a person is in adhering to it. Such an activity seems to become essential to the user's integrity. Writers have emphasized this point dramatically. Questioning such an activity tends to provoke bewildered resentment and may be experienced as an insult. Interference with carrying it out, whether or not the ritual value is conscious to the user, is experienced as threatening.[27] Interference with rituals was extremely disturbing in the experiments cited. The rituals had developed in the face of unpredictable events and had reduced the rats' nervous symptoms. When the rituals were prevented, other rituals appeared together with severe disturbance. Autistic children seem less tolerant of interference with their rituals than other children or adults. How much their behavior is disturbed by interference is unknown.

Some of the autobiographies indicate prevention of rituals in infancy, and the tenacity of autistic children's parents suggests that they have gone to considerable lengths to prevent those rituals that interfered with their purposes. The parents' and children's first confrontation over the children's rituals usually involved eating. The coercive power of food refusal, with the risk of malnutrition and starvation, gave infants leverage they did not have in other areas and made the struggle grim for the mothers. The usual result was that mothers of autistic children eventually yielded and accepted eating rituals. Probably, rituals that were less threatening to the parents were prevented.

Disturbance in laboratory animals and people often follows a similar course. Stressful training fosters ritual. If stress is limited and ritual permitted, a stable adaptation develops that reduces disturbance and that is thought to forestall extreme disturbance. If stress increases or ritual is prevented, breakdowns occur. Ritual continues to be a basic part of the more-handicapping adaptations that then develop in laboratory animals and in adults after they have become schizophrenic. Perhaps a similar sequence occurs in autistic and retarded children.

Children who retained the symptoms typical of autism but who were rediagnosed as schizophrenic during adolescence often were classified under the subdivision of catatonia. As this diagnostic practice suggests, the symptom clusters identifying autism and catatonia are much the same, with the main difference being age. The two are typified by ritual, unresponsiveness, immobility, muteness, echolalia, negativism, posturing, stereotyped movements, occasional excitement, and failure to take rudimentary care of oneself. Kraepelin noted that catatonics who do not talk sometimes answer questions by singing or writing; so do autistic children.[28] Like autistic children, catatonic adults give a false impression of being oblivious to events. The cataleptic behavior and rituals of catatonics have been interpreted as means of inhibiting their rather strong arousal by external stimuli. Similarly, close study of autistic children shows that they are more aroused by external stimuli than other children and that they do much to inhibit themselves.[29] If there is a continuity between autistic children and catatonic adults, much of the vast literature on schizophrenia may prove relevant to autism.

Catatonic adults used to be considered the most intriguing of mental patients. Psychiatrists often chose them for demonstration to students as wonders and as models of schizophrenia. Study of catatonics was difficult, however, because they were uncommunicative and few in number. The modern literature on them is scanty. Arieti, the best known theorist on schizophrenia in the United States, was exceptional in continuing to emphasize catatonia as its basic form.[30]

In Arieti's formulation, the core of catatonia and of schizophrenia as a whole is negativism. The concept of negativism came into psychology from nineteenth-century descriptions of psychotic adults. It refers to behavior ranging from lack of cooperation to outright defiance and doing the opposite of what is asked. It includes saying "no," not answering questions or complying with requests, seeming not to hear, pretending not to understand, ignoring people, avoiding physical contact, and withdrawing. The concept was extended to include behavior common in toddlers and then extended by Arieti to include the primitive, diffuse inhibition or inactivity seen in neonates. He defined primitive negativism as an inhibition of impulses or of reflexive responding. Thus, it is resistance of one's own behavior. Pavlov's concept of cerebral inhibition is similar.[31] He studied catatonic patients and likened their behavior to that of the dogs in whom he induced disturbance by stressful training. He suggested that the symptomatic behavior of both groups was due to cerebral inhibition, and this idea has been applied to autism.[32]

In the first weeks of life, some infants become stiff; others, limp. Either way, they are unresponsive. The inhibition has been attributed to various stresses—to frustration generally and to awkward handling and overstimulation by mothers. Some observations suggest more specifically that the inhibition is a reaction to intrusive, demanding, and conflict-arousing stimulation. *Intrusive* means that stimulation interrupts an activity in which an infant is already engaged or hinders the infant from initiating an activity other than the one called for by the stimulation. *Demanding* means that action by an infant is urged frequently or strongly. Inhibition has been attributed particularly to demands that are abrupt, contradictory, and coercive. *Conflict-arousing* means that a stimulus arouses a tendency both to make a response and not to make it or a tendency to make a response simultaneously with an incompatible response. Frequent stimulation of this sort causes frequent and increasingly prolonged periods of inhibition in infants. Much inhibition has also been attributed particularly to coercive feeding, restricted movement, intrusive caressing and fondling, teasing, inconsistent cues and reinforcements, and premature training.[33]

Automatic or reflexive response to stimuli is characteristic of living things. For Arieti, the interruption of automatic responding by inhibition is the most primitive adaptation to the environment, the prototype of catatonia. Inhibition is evidently adaptive when it brings repetitive, futile behavior to an end. If an environmental change renders useless a response that was once effective, for a creature to continue making the response until exhausted would not be adaptive. Selective inhibition of the response allows for a partially learned, new response or an old, long-unused response to be made instead of a strongly established response.[34] Thus, inhibition is helpful in dealing with change.

Selective inhibition (negativism) is commonly thought to begin in the second year. At that time, it is vigorous and unmistakable, but it begins early in the first year, as in food refusal or holding food in the mouth without swallowing. In the second year, negativism is aroused particularly by demands. The more demands caretakers make, the more negativistic infants become. That seems as true of autistic children as of others.[35]

A common parental reaction to negativism in a two-year-old is increased demand accompanied by coercion to comply. The usual effect is still more negativism. After such a sequence, when negativism has become strongly established, gentle requests that can be met easily also are resisted, and the child may appear generally negativistic. Nonetheless, the negativism is not diffuse; the child remains active and responsive to the environment, except for requests and demands from the caretaker.

Autistic children evidently show more-diffuse inhibition than others as neonates and far more negativism in the first year, particularly in food refusal. By the time toilet training is begun, whether or not it is taught in a stressful way, most of the children are so negativistic that training is likely to go badly. For the same reason, many autistic children resist training in

speech, dressing, or table conduct in the second year. They resist any training
that is initiated by parents rather than by themselves. Many parents soon
realize that their autistic children learn easily what they choose to learn while
they resist training initiated by parents.

As infants mature, their capacities for hostility develop and complicate
their resistance. When that happens, parents are correct in viewing negativism as spite. Two-year-olds who are otherwise normal may negate remarks
that do not call for an answer or are not directed at them. They may resist
everything parents ask or suggest, even when it is something they would
otherwise like to do. In addition, they may begin an activity on their own
and stop it when encouraged to go on by their parents.

These reactions are common in autistic children. At the extreme, when
told to do something by her mother that she was already doing, one child
stopped and became immobile for twenty minutes. She reacted the same way
to correction and to being asked a question.[36] Some parents learn not to
encourage, praise, or even acknowledge their autistic children's accomplishments lest the activity be discontinued and not tried again for months.

In addition, autistic children sometimes do the opposite of what is
asked. When children who are otherwise normal do that, their parents may
recognize hostility in the behavior, implied understanding of what is wanted,
and competence to do it. But experience often has led parents to conclude
that their autistic children are incompetent—that they do not understand
what is asked of them. When that happens, doing the opposite may not be
seen as showing competence.

Saying "no" and doing the opposite are ordinarily punished, while passive resistance is not, which thereby conditions passive resistance. Diffuse
inhibition also may be conditioned. Children who stop doing something
when asked to do it and then become immobile for some time may be
thought to be in a state of altered consciousness and not pressed or punished.
Unresponsive children appear not to have heard or understood their parents'
request. If their unresponsiveness has been consistent enough for the parents
to conclude that the children are defective, the negativism may be rewarded
by withdrawal of parental demands. Negativism declines in normal children
after the third year. Its continuation is associated with severe compulsivity
and psychosis.

To return to catatonia, it may be considered a primitive adaptation
insofar as inhibition is pervasive and little behavior occurs that is not ritual.
It seems a combination of diffuse inhibition and selective negativism. Some
catatonics appear to be responsive and even compliant. They allow their
bodies to be molded into any position and hold a position for hours. Some
mimic what is said to them or imitate movements of authority figures, at
times with striking accuracy. Despite the compliance and suggestibility of
this behavior, it traditionally has been considered negativistic for reasons

evident when the functions of the behavior are examined.[37] Neither repeating a question instead of answering it nor repeating a command instead of obeying it are compliance. When one person initiates an activity with another, the responder is expected to complete the action of the initiator. Only occasionally is the action completed by mimicking it. An exception is handshaking, in which extending the hand calls for an identical response. In most cases, the initiator's purpose is defeated by imitation.

Mimicry plays an important role in infancy, before speech is of much use. Mothers can instruct their infants to do something by doing it themselves. Many infants are highly imitative, and their mimicry of sounds and movements is relied on by mothers in teaching them speech, games, and eating. Waxy pliability is also helpful to mothers in diapering, dressing, and bathing infants. Therefore, the pliability and mimicry of catatonic people may be regressive forms of compliance.

During the age of negativism, however, pliability and mimicry take on oppositional functions. They lend themselves to passive hostility and may be particularly useful against adults who do not tolerate open defiance. At this age, if a child is told to do something and remains still, the mother may give a push or move the child's hands or feet, trying to get the child started doing what she wants. Pliability at this point can be as effective as stiffening in not doing what is demanded, but pliability is more confusing to a mother and less likely to be punished than stiffening. Similarly, repeating her command instead of declining may confuse her. Not many months earlier, imitating her words was a cooperative act and gratified her. She will not be sure that imitation at this time is defiant. Thus, pliability and imitation at this age may have the form of compliance and the function of resistance.

In catatonic adults, pliability and imitation do not comply with demands being made at the time. On the contrary, the behavior persists despite severe punishment. Arieti saw the negativism of catatonics as the result of a history of excessive parental demand and control. As children, they responded by being pleasing, dutiful, and successful in school. However, they were only outwardly compliant, rebelling secretly. Finally, with their schizophrenic breakdowns, their rebellion became partially overt. Their symptoms involved regression to negativism and diffuse inhibition combined with compliance.[38]

The history that Arieti presented as typical for catatonics also has been found in many studies of schizophrenia as a whole and resembles histories of autistic children. Another link is the finding that adult schizophrenics showed autistic behavior in childhood—shyness, withdrawal, unresponsiveness, lack of emotion, narrow interests, and extreme compulsivity.[39] In contrast to autistic children, those who became schizophrenic later in life developed speech normally.

The picture of mothers found in studies of schizophrenics is much like

Kanner's picture of mothers of autistic children—cold, detached, compulsive, and perfectionistic. They made extreme demands upon those of their infants who grew up to be schizophrenic—notably, in toilet training. The mothers began training early—some of them, before the infants could sit—with much use of cathartics, suppositories, and enemas.[40] This was the beginning of *"persistent instillation of . . . high expectations for achievement and perfection."*[41]

In the early years, the children performed remarkably well. Thus, a typical statement by a mother was, "There was nothing wrong with him; he was the best child, he worshiped me, he was the least trouble of all my children, the easiest to be trained."[42]

The typical mother dominated and overprotected her preschizophrenic child and discouraged contact with others.[43] She regulated the child to a great extent, curbing spontaneity, self-expression, and autonomy. The mother's special involvement with the child who became schizophrenic in adolescence or adulthood often began at birth. Her investment in the child was enormous. A typical mother's statement was, "I took him with me wherever I would go. He was my whole life."[44]

The pattern of mother-child relationships described was found to distinguish schizophrenics from their nonschizophrenic siblings. While such rearing is often pathogenic, most children who are their mothers' favorites and intimates and are subject to heavy regulation and high expectations do not become schizophrenic. Many of them become creative geniuses in the arts and sciences and superior performers in other callings, while they retain autistic traits in their adult lives. Others become driven adults whose lives are more ordinary.[45]

Data by which to distinguish the determinants of one outcome over another are lacking. One possibility is that stressful language training is more disturbing than comparable training of toileting and other skills, for reasons touched on earlier. Another possibility is that unresponsiveness is rewarded by some parents. In the case of Dibs, extraordinary pressure to learn in the second year was confined largely to verbal skills. Dibs tried to evade the pressure by busying himself with other activities, fleeing, and hiding when his mother sought to train him and by appearing not to hear or understand her. Being busy, fleeing, and hiding did not stop her. Only when he appeared not to hear or understand did she withdraw her demands, thus rewarding this behavior.

Perhaps such selective reinforcement is the critical element in autism. Autistic children act as if they cannot hear or understand what their caretakers say, and their caretakers are misled by this behavior.[46] Hearing is the principal sense by which training in language and other intellectual functioning is given to infants. Another observation that bears on this hypothesis is that the children respond to demands by adults with increased autistic behavior.[47] Any behavior that gives the appearance of being deaf and unresponsive may have the effect of getting stressful demands withdrawn. Any such behavior thereby will be rewarded.

In addition, when the appearance of being deaf and not understanding spoken words is convincing, the demands are not made as often as before. Thus, the child avoids demands and is reinforced further; and avoidance training ordinarily leads to behavior that is extremely stable despite measures to counter it.

Dibs' early resistance to training demands was active and fairly obvious; his eventual resistance was passive. Thus, the interaction described also may be construed as training in passivity and inactivity.

In the circumstances described, a chaotic, mutually distressing situation may be stabilized by a parent reaching the conclusion that a child has a serious defect (deafness or incompetence). The conclusion may lead to behavior in the parent and child that is mutually reinforcing. A suspicion of defect or incompetence may not stabilize the situation. The parent is likely to withdraw training demands temporarily and then renew them erratically for some time until a conviction of defect is established. Such a conviction is aided by a diagnosis—an authoritative statement that a child cannot do better. The diagnosis and the accompanying advice encourage the parent to accept the child's nonperformance. However, few diagnoses—especially mental diagnoses—provide a convincing answer to nagging questions about whether or not a child can do better, and autism is a particularly ambiguous one.

Ability, Will, and Role

What a child can or cannot do—the question of ability—has been a major concern of psychologists since the turn of the century. Many tests have been devised to measure intelligence and other abilities and have been received enthusiastically but have been recognized later as measuring only performance.

Diagnoses have not been designed to provide answers about ability but nonetheless have been used for that purpose. Limitations of the diagnosis of retardation were touched on earlier. Compulsions often are defined as irresistible impulses. Nonetheless, people often resist their compulsions. The diagnosis of alcoholism has been used socially and legally as proof that certain people cannot stop drinking. Nonetheless, active alcoholics do stop drinking for days or months, and people who have not had a drink for years are still called alcoholics. In short, diagnoses of mental or emotional conditions imply sickness and inability to behave differently, but the people designated by them do behave differently. The self-contradictions inhere in using diagnoses as indicators of ability.

At the simplest levels of common parlance, the question of whether or not a child can do better seems very meaningful and answerable. Professionals, although aware of philosophical difficulties in the question, have put the difficulties aside and tried to answer simply. The usual answer has been that the children are incapable, while a few professionals have concluded that they are pretending.[48] *Pretending* means deliberately misleading people. Writers have used phrases like *acts as if deaf* to describe autistic children without specifying whether or not the act was conscious.

The philosophical difficulties that were put aside, however, are fundamental. The difficulties and a challenging solution are illustrated by a problem posed to military psychiatrists during World War II. During the war, military administrators in the United States became concerned that growing numbers of servicemen were pretending to be psychotic in order to evade combat or to be discharged. Psychiatrists were asked to identify those who feigned psychosis so they could be punished, while those identified as genuinely psychotic would be treated or discharged. The psychiatrists concluded that only psychotic people would feign psychosis. Therefore, the pretence was evidence of psychosis, and the presumed distinction between genuine and feigned psychosis was invalid.

The conclusion flew in the face of traditional and psychiatric thought and common sense. It won limited acceptance, perhaps because it anticipated a trend toward social analysis of mental disturbance. In the following decades, concepts of mental disturbance and diagnostic practices were subjected to more-rigorous analyses than had been done before. In the light of those analyses, the conclusion of the military psychiatrists may be taken as an implicit definition: a psychotic person is one whose outward behavior is psychotic, one who acts psychotic in life. The consciousness, deliberation, or purpose of a person's behavior are irrelevant to the diagnosis. Such a definition obviates the difficulty of ascertaining whether or not a person is pretending, and it obviates the more-basic difficulty of acertaining whether or not a person can behave differently or better at any given time than the person behaves. Another advantage of the definition is that it is translated easily into operational terms and is pragmatic in application. Perhaps the most important advantage of the definition is its accuracy. Traditional definitions, although closer to the popular concept of psychosis, give a misleading impression of how clinicians diagnose psychosis and of the nature of people who receive the diagnosis.

In the popular concept, shared by clinicians and lay people, almost everyone who is designated as psychotic is not pretending, not consciously acting psychotic, and cannot do better. In addition, few people designated as psychotic are believed capable of role playing at all. Nonetheless, study has shown that many and perhaps most people designated as psychotic play the role of a psychotic person. They play it with varying degrees of consciousness and with considerable skill. That does not mean that people designated as psychotic are necessarily clearer about questions of ability, role, will, and pretense than other people. As Scheff noted, "Apparently it was sometimes difficult for them to tell whether they were playing the role or the role was playing them," and they were often confused by their own behavior.[49]

Stupidity as Role Behavior

Apparent deafness, typical of autistic children in their early years, does not serve well as the basis for an enduring adaptation. To be accepted and reinforced, apparent deafness must be reasonably consistent, and consistent deafness puts a child at disadvantage. The child must be equally deaf to "Who was the first president?" and "Who wants ice cream?" Many gratifications are lost. By contrast, apparent stupidity need not be as consistent and allows for much gratification, including forbidden gratification not available to competent children.[50] In short, behavior indicating deafness is punished while behavior indicating stupidity is more often rewarded. Therefore, in the circumstances described, stupidity is likely to replace deafness as an adaptation to stressful training.

Some consistency in an apparent defect is required for it to be accepted. Beyond consistency in specific acts, it is necessary to integrate the defective behavior with other behavior, to live substantially as a defective person. To be accepted and reinforced over a long period, the defective behavior must become part of a large, integrated pattern—a role.

In discussing incompetence, the words *apparent, misleading, acting* or *playing* a role, and *simulating* or *pretending* connote varying degrees of deliberation. Assessing deliberation or consciousness in people, especially in those who hardly speak, involves difficulties that are unnecessary here. It will be assumed that incompetent role behavior is not necessarily deliberate—no more deliberate than role playing in ordinary people's everyday life, as is indicated by observations like "He is a tiger in the office and a pussycat at home." Each person plays a number of roles, and the one played at any time is determined largely by setting and circumstances. Roles are learned by reinforcement and imitation and are maintained in their settings by reinforcement. In playing different roles in different settings, people are behaving largely unconsciously and habitually rather than in calculating ways. But the degree of consciousness is less important in understanding behavior than are people's conditioning histories.

Role playing connotes intelligence and may require it in the theater. In daily life, insofar as it is conditioned and imitative behavior, little intelligence is required. Role playing is well within the range of many people diagnosed and institutionalized as retarded. Educators and clinicians have long known that normal children, bright children, and even geniuses have simulated incompetence so well that their parents and teachers were convinced that they were stupid. Harder to credit is the fact that many children have played the role to such an extent that they were placed in institutions for the retarded where they remained much of their lives.[51] In addition, much of the behavior of institutionalized retarded and schizophrenic people considered typical of them is conditioned by the institutions and may not be shown when the inmates are outside. Other behavior is conditioned in the home, before institutionalization.[52]

The difference between genuine and simulated retardation is considered so great conceptually and in specific cases that professionals should have no difficulty making the distinction. But the difficulty persists. Writers of the distant past made little effort to distinguish between them, even conceptually. A major effort to distinguish was made during this century, and in the United States, the field of clinical psychology developed largely to meet the need of educators to separate retarded, psychotic, and normal children so that each group could be worked with separately. In due course, many definitions of intelligence and retardation were developed, but none proved scientifically satisfactory.

In the early part of the century, the concept of pseudofeeblemindedness was used for children who appeared to be retarded but were not. Problems in defining it led to its abandonment: upon analysis, "it becomes apparent that the question of whether an individual is 'really' defective is a meaningless one."[53]

The conceptual problem is illustrated by the fact that many workers are convinced that autistic children are basically retarded, while others are convinced that they are intelligent. The history of the concept of stupidity helps put the confusion about the intelligence of autistic children in perspective.

Among the antecedents of modern concepts of retardation and pseudoretardation, especially related to people who show flashes of intelligence, are the traditional figures of the clown and fool. Foolishness is an elusive concept, common in myth and fairy tale as a device by which children and childish adults outwit older, more-powerful adversaries. They get away with it by a pretense of stupidity.[54] Foolishness usually means a vague combination of stupidity and madness, but normal people often play the fool, and Jesus was said to. While retardation is a grave matter, particularly in technological societies, clowning has a playful aspect and includes the use of trickery to deceive normal people. Nonetheless, by tradition, the clown was a depressed, hopeless person. The clown's ancestor, the court fool or jester, a more-complex figure, is the source of much of the literature on the character and function of people to whom these terms have been applied.[55]

The male figure of the court fool traditionally embraced contradictions found in descriptions of autistic children. The fool was stupid but spoke extraordinary truths. He seemed out of touch with much that happened around him but made telling observations. He was clumsy but showed remarkable dexterity. He was full of fears but was reckless. He existed by the pleasure of the king but was negativistic and hostile. He displayed himself or masturbated openly, but his sexuality was pointless because he was not involved in intimate relationships or procreation. He was asocial and isolated, but he affected people dramatically. He played a role that they required and defined, but they were mystified by him. Being recognized as a fool enabled him to make a fool of them without being punished. Alternately, he was victim and perpetrator, and the essence of his character was paradox. Which side was real and which was simulated remained a puzzle.[56]

The paradox intrigued people. They were captivated, drawn into his foolish play, amused, moved, and ridiculed. He held up a mirror to people in which they were mocked in a number of ways because his foolishness was a caricature of theirs. But they tended not to be aware of the comparison because he was so outlandish that people were distracted from themselves and their ordinary concerns.

People seem to have become fools in different ways. In the European court, the role was filled by psychotic and retarded people and normal ones. Each of them served the same purpose, and little distinction was made among them.[57] The key feature of different kinds of fools in history was that they played the role, and that is the main feature in some recent analyses of retardation, as exemplified by the following definition: "A mental retardate is one who occupies the status of the mental retardate in one or more of the social systems in which he participates."[58] The system in which most children have that status is the educational system. For many, it is the only system in which they have such status, and when they leave school they are no longer identified as retarded and may live normal lives.[59]

Identification of retarded functioning as role behavior has won little acceptance among clinicians generally but is compatible with specialists' analyses of the concept of retardation, as in the above definition. The idea that retardation was caused simply by organic defects, which became prominent in this century, was limited in application by the fact that most retarded children had no discernible organic impairment. For the minority with evident impairment, the impairment ceased to be considered causal in the way it had been. Instead, the view of specialists is that Down's syndrome and a number of other organic conditions that are identified in neonates affect the interaction of child and parent in ways that usually (but not necessarily) cause the children to have atypical developmental experiences. In turn, the experiences foster retarded functioning.

Such an explanation is more compatible than the former one with specific cognitive peculiarities found recently in retarded children and with some older observations. Many retarded children are rather negativistic and ritualistic, and catatonic behavior has long been reported in them. In addition, early precocity has been reported in many before their decline in mental functioning.[60] And many continue to show normal and occasionally superior intelligence after institutionalization.[61] In the past, deafness was reported to be common in retarded children and thought to be the cause of their retardation. As with autistic children, careful testing showed normal hearing in most cases, and apparent deafness may be classified with other simulated defects in retarded children.

Idiot Savants

Among the retarded, fascination has long centered on a minority that possess special skills. Writers on autism have identified them as the autistic children of the past, before the concept of autism came into use.[62] Given the self-contradictory name *idiot savants,* they were mostly male children (and sometimes adults) who appeared to be grossly retarded except in one skill. Some did well enough in their specialty to have careers as performers. The best-known did arithmetic so fast and accurately that they seemed superhuman to audiences that were unaware of the tricks they used.

Psychologists made it a point to study these children. Unfortunately, their reports provided rather little background information: "in the entire literature of the idiot savant there is not a single acceptable personality description of the parents."[63] One report—the most extensive by far in the literature—did provide incidental information about the mother and her relationship with her idiot savant son.[64] The mother was a highly intelligent teacher who gave up her career to devote herself totally to her only child at his birth. From early infancy—long before abnormality was suspected—she made careful, detailed observations of his behavior, producing a voluminous record.

The boy was precocious at first, beginning to speak at six months, mastering toilet training in the first year, and passing other developmental milestones early. However, his use of language increased so slowly that by eighteen months retardation was suspected and the diagnosis subsequently was established. His mother wrote that in his fourth year he was incapable of turning a doorknob or going to the bathroom unaided. In the tenth year he was described as still unable to take off his shoes and socks.

As was usual at the time (1945), this nonperformance was taken as evidence of innate handicap, while the boy continued to show superior accomplishments in memory, arithmetic, and music. The clinicians who studied him noted that the boy's teacher found him to be "uncooperative ... stubborn, and willfully disobedient." They juxtaposed the observation that he was "wholly incapable of learning by instruction" with the observation that he taught himself, and they still did not consider if the impression he gave of stupidity was misleading.[65]

In nursery school he seemed oblivious to the presence of other children and indifferent to them. His mother seemed to be the only person to whom he was attached and whose reactions concerned him, and he could not bear separation from her. (His father seemed to have been remote from mother and child.)

Rimland said the parents of idiot savants were very bright, well-educated professionals, like parents of autistic children.[66] Some of the other cases have scant details that indicate unusually close relationships with mothers and that imply extensive intellectual training in infancy. Some writers suggested that the poor functioning and special skills resulted from heavy parental demands during infancy or "over-exploitation" of the children, and a few writers emphasized that the special skills helped idiot savants avoid action and made their experience predictable.[67]

In short, the literature on idiot savants provides limited information about why they behaved as they did, but it brings into focus the puzzle of people who show a combination of stupid and intelligent behavior. Some idiot savants were clearly geniuses. One became a successful artist but continued the life-style of a retarded person, begging his food and sleeping in railroad stations.[68] Traditionally, idiot savants have been classified as retarded no matter how intelligent they were because they followed the style or role of retarded people.

The concept of idiot savant—the idea that retardation and genius are closely related and can coexist in one person—was rooted in traditional ideas. Through the years, some scientists have suggested that retardation and genius are hard to tell apart and have a common organic basis—that they are caused by the same genes or the same diseases. Parents have explained having a retarded child by pointing to a genius in the family.[69] Rimland's theory that autism is caused by genes that produce genius is in this tradition.

Many retarded people and geniuses have formative experiences in common—specifically, stressful training. Training stress that fosters the highest performance is very close to stress that causes performance to stop. Many successful artists and other superperformers show both effects; they alternate between periods of superb productivity and periods of inactivity—of seeming inability to produce anything. One study of geniuses found "a dreadful urgency in the lives of [their] parents which makes them difficult for the children to endure."[70] Many of the children were so hard pressed to learn by their parents that they became slow learners. Sixty percent had serious school problems and were considered dull by their teachers. Some were considered retarded.[71]

Successful training under high stress produces geniuses with autistic features. Many geniuses have been so devoted to their solitary work, so oblivious, indifferent, and isolated, as to be considered basically asocial. The traditional association of these features with genius probably results from their early training. Autistic geniuses, then, may be people whose training resulted in limited disabilities—autistic features without the integrated pattern of incompetence.

The thesis of this chapter is that many people designated as schizophrenic, retarded, and autistic have similar adaptations to early stresses. Their attention to cues is deviant and limited. As a result, they often see things differently than other people do and they are handicapped in dealing with many aspects of life. And their handicaps are increased by being incorporated in roles of incompetence.

Part III
Pieces of the Puzzle

The main hypotheses have been advanced, and the focus now shifts to features of autism. From what I have presented and from additional data and hypotheses, the principal symptoms of autism will be explained. The three symptoms that Kanner chose to define autism—ritual (chapter 12), isolation (chapter 13), and language defect (chapter 14)—will be taken up at length. Then a number of other behaviors will be discussed briefly in chapter 15, including eating and sleeping disturbances, sensory anomalies, self-stimulation, erotic behavior, and altered consciousness.

12 The Superstitious Child: Ritual and Other Compulsive Behavior

In the controversial, shifting picture of autism over the years, one symptom has remained fixed and clear—compulsive behavior. The definition of compulsive behavior and the fact that it is prominent in every austistic child are undisputed. In these respects, it is unique among the symptoms of autistic children. It is also the most human of their symptoms, the one by which they have most in common with other people. By contrast, isolation and lack of speech have nonhuman connotations.

General knowledge about compulsive behavior is applicable to autistic children if their rituals have similar functions and arise under similar conditions as the rituals of others. Some writers have suggested that autistic children's rituals are distinctive. Kanner's observation that the rituals served to prevent their environment from changing has become part of the definition of autism. Prevention of environmental change or maintenance of predictability is also seen in other behavior of autistic children—preferring obscure words that mean the same thing every time to common, simple words that change in meaning according to context and deterring adults from rearranging furniture or changing routines. Other activities enable autistic children to detect slight changes. They observe carefully and use aids in remembering.

> [A] persistent and often frenetic need for arrangement is displayed vividly in the autistic child's behavior with objects. When presented with an unstructured group of objects, he usually tries to impose some arbitrary order on them.[1]

By such means, they can say if anything has been removed or moved in a room they have been in once and not seen again for months. Concern about environmental change, seen in such behavior, has been verified experimentally.[2] But that does not set autistic children apart from other people. Prevention of change or maintenance of predictability is a common function of compulsive behavior in people.

Some clinicians have suggested that autistic children use rituals to control or tyrannize their parents and thereby differ from other compulsive people. In psychoanalytic theory, compulsive rituals serve primarily to control oneself. But the emphasis is more theoretical than factual. Many rituals of children diagnosed as compulsive but not autistic also serve to tyrannize their parents. And, according to Abraham, compulsive people "completely refuse to accommodate to others, but require others to comply with their rituals."[3] This is an exaggeration in regard to most compulsive people, but it indicates that, in this respect too, autistic children are like other compulsive people.

The rituals of compulstive people are associated with compulsive character traits: negativism, stubbornness, holding back, orderliness, and collecting or hoarding things. These traits typify autistic children. Compulsive speech patterns (repetitive, literal, pedantic) also are found in autistic children who speak.

By definition, autistic and compulsive children are very different. Autism is a psychotic disturbance; compulsivity, a neurotic one. But in fact, compulsive children are substantially autistic. They prefer solitary play and lack peer relationships. They appear unemotional and robotlike. Some move so little that they appear catatonic. Smelling objects, preferring smell over vision, making errors in distinguishing right from left, and reversing words and letters are common in compulsive children. They also have "specialized, oddball interests, to the exclusion of all other activities or areas of thought," like idiot savants; and most are boys.[4] The main difference is that children diagnosed as compulsive speak competently.

Autistic and compulsive children also have similar parents. According to a major study of compulsive children, their parents are an elite group. They also seem cold, withdrawn, socially isolated, hypercritical, and proud. They try to rear the children to be perfect and boast about the children's superiority, despite their evident handicaps.[5]

In short, except for speech, children diagnosed as autistic and compulsive are similar. They are specifically alike in their rituals and other compulsive behavior, and their critical early experiences may be similar. The findings cited in chapters 9 and 10 that training with unreliable cues and reinforcements causes ritual may apply to them. And what is known about compulsive children may apply to autistic children.

For several decades, the main theory of compulsive behavior has been the psychoanalytic theory. It is fairly well worked out and may be modified and extended in the light of recent data. Psychoanalysts have focused on premature and harsh toilet training as causes of compulsivity. Such training was reported in many cases of autism, and Bemporad suggested that it is associated with both compulsivity and autism.[6] However, many autistic children did not have premature or harsh toilet training.

The experiments described in chapter 10 support occasional clinical observations in suggesting that the development of compulsivity may have less to do with the skill being trained than with how rigorously training is done.[7] The experiments also indicate that the effects of stressful training are determined by prior experience. Specifically, rigorous training is particularly likely to have adverse effects when negativism and ritual are already present.

The formal structure of the psychoanalytic theory of compulsivity does not require that the critical training experience involve toilet functions. Toilet training still is emphasized because early findings on the development of compulsivity were incorporated in the general theory of psychosexual development. In that theory, compulsivity results from fixation in the anal stage of development. There are advantages in treating compulsivity as a broader, more-basic adaptation associated with primitive cognitive or ego functions.

Toilet training was found to be critical in the past because of the value placed on early mastery in Victorian and post-Victorian society. To be toilet trained was the principal virtue attainable by infants. It meant to be clean and human, in God's image, while its lack meant to be dirty, shameful, and animalistic. Therefore, in many homes, toilet functions were the first to be trained rigorously—the first major step in socializing infants. Toilet training signaled the end of being a carefree animal; it marked the beginning of responsibility and of conformity to civilized standards.

Parents imposed other demands and social conventions on infants but not with the same arbitrariness and force. For example, feeding schedules sometimes were established in the first months. However, eating and toileting demands differed significantly. Infants who were hungry but were not given food could not err by eating at the wrong time. In addition, when given food, they were not required to hold back. Toilet training was exceptional in that infants who had urges to urinate or defecate and could do so were required to hold back. They could err by not holding back and be punished.

During this century, the value society placed on such cleanliness declined. Mental-health professionals and pediatricians advised against early, rigorous toilet training, and fewer parents attempted it. Meanwhile, concern with other functions increased. Victorians had been less concerned about infant feeding and speech. Breastfeeding was the norm and was indulgent, with milk remaining the primary or only food of infants until they were much older than at present. Thus, early feeding rarely involved changes. Feeding by set schedules with frequently changed diets became popular during this century, along with growing concern about sterility of food, scientific diets, and good eating habits. Parental effort to control infant diets and eating habits resulted in intense struggles between child and parent at mealtime in many homes; but eating is a simple task that requires little learning. Perhaps for that reason and because parents may yield more to infants' rituals and negativism in eating, experiences in eating do not seem as directly or fully involved in the eventual adaptations of autistic children as experiences in speech training.

Parents' growing concern with infant speech as an indicator of intelligence, their corresponding devotion to early verbal training, and their disappointment at lack of precocious speech, combined with the inherent difficulties of learning to speak, give speech training added importance.

Today, speech is probably the first complex skill that many parents train rigorously, and speech training is the first main socializing experience of many children.

Verbal training is more complex and arbitrary than toilet training. The forms that words take and the meanings assigned to them are social conventions that vary from one language to another. Biologically, it makes no difference whether the word *tall* refers to tallness or shortness. The same applies to rules of grammar and usage.[8] The arbitrariness of language and the changes in meaning that words undergo make speech the most problematic of skills to train. In addition, by comparison to speech, toilet use has few difficult cues and rules. Parents may regulate when and where infants eliminate, but they do not correct elimination in nearly as many ways as they correct speech. The impact of early training will be explored in the light of certain assumptions about the nature of human infants.

Basic Compulsivity

From his studies of adult behavior, Marris concluded that prevention of change was a universal human activity of primary importance in mental functioning. The conclusion is supported by observations and experiments showing young infants' gratification when sequences are repeated and distress when deviations occur. The data were obtained in Czechoslovakia, Switzerland, and the United States.[9] Corroboration in more-varied cultures is needed before maintenance of predictability is established as universal. I will assume that maintenence of predictability is present in the first weeks of life and includes the following:

> *Associative learning:* Sequences of events that are close together in time and that are repeated foster "expectations" that when the first occurs, the second will follow. At least two kinds of sequences are included: (1) a sequence of two environmental events and (2) a sequence of an act by the infant followed by an environmental event.

> *Gratification in sameness:* Repetition of a learned sequence is gratifying and rewards behavior that produces the sequence.

> *Distress at deviation:* Deviation from a learned sequence is distressing and punishes behavior that produces the deviation.

> *Restorative mechanisms:* Deviation elicits a number of mechanisms that serve to increase predictability. They may already be present or may develop in a situation of much deviation. Any behavior that restores predictability will be reinforced. The basic mechanisms probably include denial and ritual and may combine with the mechanism of negativism.

I have called the combination of these functions *basic compulsivity,* and see it as a determinant of infant behavior that persists through old age. It influences adaptations in the formative years, so that most or all children grow up to be compulsive adults. Not only people with compulsive character or symptoms but also hysterical, phobic, depressed, manic, schizophrenic, psychopathic, and normal people are basically compulsive. If their compulsivity is not apparent, it may become prominent when changes in their situation or challenges to their rituals occur.

If deviation is extreme, young infants may become inactive. Older ones may become depressed or catatonic, with minimal learning or acting on the environment. Less deviation may result in an elaboration of compulsive mechanisms, in

> [A]n attempt (albeit an illusory one) to deal with man's essential powerlessness and helplessness in both his control over his own physical being and over the physical world around him..... Fantasy or realistic manipulation of oneself and the outside world maintains an illusion of greater control over one's life than is actually so....[10]

The illusion of control permits renewed efforts to act on the environment. Although limited by denial, ritual, and isolation of mental processes, much learning remains possible despite compulsive traits.

Predictability of experience in early life depends largely on one aspect of the environment—the caretaker, who mediates the impact of much of the rest of the environment on an infant. For adults as well as children, attachments provide "the principle of regularity on which our ability to predict our own behavior and the behavior of others depends."[11] But young children seem most dependent on such regularity.[12] Those infants who are attached to only one person become extremely dependent on the person for predictability of their experience. If the person behaves erratically or is absent, their experience becomes unpredictable.

Control

In dealing with unpredictability, people have most control over themselves, moderate control over some people and things in their immediate environment, and little control over other parts of the environment and the future. Autistic children are unusually self-controlled. Observers are surprised by their impassiveness in the face of sudden, loud noises and painful injuries. The children also achieve considerable control over their parents and physical things in their homes. However, "controlling oneself and the universe requires rigid control of one's emotions. All emotional responses must be either dampened, restrained, or completely denied." Inasmuch as compulsive people cannot eliminate feelings entirely from their experience, they displace feelings onto insignificant or meaningless activities and thus "appear to be uninvolved emotionally with significant people or events while grossly over-involved with minutiae."[13]

Magic usually is considered to have a positive function—to make things happen—but that is truer of magic shows than of using magic in life. Kanner and others concluded that autistic children's rituals served primarily to prevent things from happening. In this respect, their rituals are similar to religious ones and to superstitions in general. Prevention of change or return to the status quo are the usual goals. Religious offerings in human history have had more to do with propitiating angry gods to withhold punishment than with bribing generous ones to bestow favors. *Shalt nots* have outnumbered *shalts* because "primitive gods are not good; they are dreaded and dreadful, and worship of them consists chiefly in placating them."[14]

Positive or acquisitive rituals tend to be abandoned because of their lack of efficacy, but preventive rituals are retained because they seem to work. Like real acts of avoidance, they are rewarded by nonoccurrence of expected punishment. A child who employs a ritual every evening to prevent death during the night will find the ritual has been effective on every awakening. Indeed, if one expects to die and takes poison daily with the idea that it prevents death, the measure will seem to work as long as one lives. Many rituals are of this sort, and the more they are used to prevent an unlikely occurrence, the more they are strengthened. Bettelheim considered the rituals of autistic children to be used mainly to prevent serious harm or death to themselves and their parents and destruction of the world.[15] Insofar as that is true, their rituals would be rewarded by nonoccurrence of those events.

Use of preventive rituals does not depend only on such apparent success. They are also self-reinforced by virtue of their effectiveness in controlling anxiety and forbidden thoughts and impulses. Positive rituals may be retained also because they serve to control such thoughts and impulses.

If the idea that autistic children's rituals are largely preventive is true, it follows that the children are usually apprehensive. Autistic children do not tell about their apprehensions, but apprehensiveness has been inferred by many parents and clinicians from the children's manner and behavior. It has been confirmed by a small number who talked about their behavior after successful treatment as it has by catatonic adults when they resumed speaking.[16]

While prevention of harm is the main function of rituals, other functions they have for neurotic and normal chidren and adults may also be relevant to autism. Some rituals provide safe gratification that substitutes for forbidden impulses. Hostile impulses may be controlled by elaborate rituals that inconvenience other people, as by keeping them waiting or requiring them to change plans. Thus, rituals that prevent directly hostile acts may be indirectly hostile.

In addition, dangerous or forbidden acts can be rendered safe in the mind of the user if preceded by ritual. Preliminary rituals are common in primitive cultures and persist today. Two kinds of preliminary rituals were found by Werner to be common in normal children.[17] One is *sacrificial:* by renonuncing something desirable, doing something unpleasant or self-punitive, or humiliating oneself, one pays a price and is permitted to engage in forbidden acts. The most common form of renunciation is refusal of food. Unpleasant or self-punitive acts include hitting oneself, head banging, and self-mutilation. Self-humiliation is accomplished by clumsiness and shows of stupidity, as in the role of fool. Whether or not autistic children do these things as sacrifices that permit them to engage in forbidden acts is unknown.[18] They engage in forbidden acts much of the time, including flagrantly sexual ones. Sacrificial behavior tends to be disarming. Perhaps that is why the children escape punishment by parents and others for behavior that commonly is punished.

Werner called the second kind of preliminary ritual *achievement ritual.* One engages in an activity with the idea that, if done flawlessly, success in an undertaking may be expected. The ritual is oracular—it results in an omen. If favorable, one may act. If unfavorable, one waits and repeats the ritual. For example, one may recite silently the states and their capitals in alphabetical order. If done correctly, one may then fall asleep with assurance of surviving the night. In purely mental rituals, the omen is produced by the subject. One may also use a physical object, as in tossing a coin or plucking the petals of a daisy, after designating one outcome as a favorable sign. A person may carry a favorite coin or other special object for use when omens are needed or make use of objects at hand. Children use drops of water. For example they may watch raindrops run down a window to see which one reaches the bottom of the glass first. They may count the number of drops that come out of a faucet when it is turned off.

If the risk seems great or the taboo powerful, the criterion for a favorable omen may be set high—for example, five successive heads; two recitations of the states. The more compulsive a person becomes, the more carefully the rituals may be performed. At the extreme, an error or even a pause means that the recitation must begin again. The result can be continuing repetition of rituals and no action.

Autistic children's memory and calendar tricks and arithmetic calculations may serve as mental preliminary rituals. Some of the children's repetitive activities with objects also may serve—for example, spinning objects or putting things in motion and observing them.

The earlier a ritual develops, the more primitive are the thought processes associated with it and the more resistant they are to change. According to Werner, rituals developed early in life tend to operate as all-or-none chains in which no distinction is made between essential and nonessential elements. They become highly stereotyped.

Prediction

Prediction is an aid to control and is most desired when control seems impossible. For example, since hurricanes cannot be controlled, weather forecasting enables people to take protective measures. When they cannot protect themselves, they at least can brace themselves if they can anticipate what is coming. In that respect, prediction can be control.

And in difficult circumstances, prediction may be given priority over control. Most people prefer knowing what is coming over not knowing and can withstand expected stresses better than unexpected ones. Experiments have shown that people and laboratory animals prefer electric shock that results from their behavior to shock over which they have no influence. They also prefer shock to be immediate rather than delayed, and they prefer a certain, immediate shock to an uncertain situation in which they may be able to prevent shock. In difficult circumstances, animals give up trying to improve their situation in terms of getting more food and less shock if improvement makes the situation less predictable.[19] Many of the rituals of autistic children reflect a similar adaptation. Except for preventing change, the children do little to master events or to change their lives; rather, they devote much of their energy to making events predictable.

Autistic children deal with internal threats similarly. Compulsive people avoid their anxiety-provoking thoughts and impulses by repetitive, ritualistic activities, but these activities can be interrupted by external events, particularly by events that catch them off guard. Therefore, making the environment stable or at least predictable helps them control themselves and avoid impulsive action. Besides ritual, vigilance and altered consciousness help them not to be surprised into responding.

In summary, the compulsive behavior of autistic children is much like the compulsive behavior of other children and adults. It probably serves the same functions and arises from the same types of causes. Autistic children use peculiar rituals, and the peculiarity may be attributable to the early onset and unchanging character of the rituals. The psychoanalytic term *anal character* seems unduly specific. Most anal traits are better described as compulsive. With some exceptions (interest in feces and symbolically related materials), anal traits are associated also with early or rigorous training of urinary control and speech and perhaps of other skills. In autistic children, speech training is probably critical in the development of severe compulsivity.

13 The Child behind the Wall: Isolation and Unresponsiveness

The most important symptom of autism historically is the behavior called isolation. Its primacy is shown in both Kanner's choice of the term *autism*, a synonym of *isolation*, as the name of the condition and the same choice by clinicians from among the many names advanced during this century. Kanner assumed that isolation was the single, basic symptom and that all other autistic behavior resulted from it. His assumption gained acceptance since it was consistent with Western thinking about normality and abnormality. A century ago, when Kraepelin organized modern knowledge about the nature of mental abnormality, his basic symptom was also isolation. Kraepelin's word for it was *indifference*. He concluded that children who were to become abnormal later first developed indifference, behaving as if they lived in their own worlds.[1]

The importance attached to isolation goes back at least to Aristotle, who considered socialization to be the critical feature of human nature. An individual who had human form but was not social, "an isolated piece" who was indifferent to society and stood apart from it, was not human. His concept has remained at the core of Western thought for 2,000 years:

> Possibly the primary axiom that underlies the psychiatric conception of the schizophrenic is that there is some fundamental and undeniable way in which he differs from the rest of mankind. More is implied here than that the schizophrenic is an... individual defining the negative end of an adjustment continuum; he seems to be on another unnamable and terrifying continuum altogether, one that ordinary men never encounter except perhaps in their dreams..... It is almost as if he had defected from the human race to join another antideluvian one, for his schizophrenia renders him other and less than human.

> The chronic schizophrenic is intriguing because he negates many criteria which have been used to distinguish men from other animals..... he violates so many functional definitions of man....[2]

The same idea contributes to people's impressions that autistic children are not human.

The Good Baby

As noted, Kanner and others concluded that autistic children developed isolation because their parents isolated them. Specifically, most of the parents

195

reported leaving their autistic children quite alone for hours at a time during the early or middle part of the first year. They were left when awake, and the explanation usually given was that they were good babies, content to be alone, amusing themselves by solitary play. In general, they were described as quiet, calm, and self-reliant babies who rarely fussed or cried and made few demands of their caretakers. As one father wrote:

> Ann was a good baby. An exceptionally good baby. She cried when she was hungry—and that was all. As the weeks rolled by EVERYONE remarked on just how good she was. She would lie in her pram for hours at a time and it was easy to forget she was even there.[3]

The mother of another autistic child said he was so good that "we didn't know we had him."[4] The literature contains similar comments by clinicians: "She was a 'good' baby, content to be left alone in her crib. She rarely cried, and consequently was picked up only for feedings."[5] Such reports were so frequent that being a good baby was cited as a feature of autism.[6]

Other parental behavior also was seen to have an isolating effect. Parents ignored autistic children when they were present and talked about them as if they were absent. And parents handled them in an aloof manner and prevented them from interacting with other people.[7] Eisenberg and Kanner said that many autistic children adopted impenetrable aloneness "because they have been abandoned to vegetation," and reported that the parents were gratified by the result.

> Parents initially pleased by the child's "goodness"—that is, his ability to occupy himself for long periods without requiring attention—later become distressed by the persistence of this isolation when they observe that their arrival and departure are matters of indifference to the child.[8]

To clinicians, however, the infants' goodness was an early sign of autism, retardation, or other serious problems.[9]

The idea that being left alone caused isolation in autistic children was challenged by parents and clinicians who said the reverse was true. The children were left alone in early infancy because they were isolated.[10] In many cases, parents explained leaving the children alone by citing the children's indifference or aversion to people and their preference for solitude.

The two interpretations are not easily reconciled, and the phenomenon of isolation in autistic children is more complex than either one. First, not all of the good babies were indifferent or averse to people. Most were responsive to their parents when with them. When alone and their parents returned, many infants greeted them eagerly. They did not necessarily prefer solitude, and some preferred to be with their parents. What they had in common was acceptance of solitude. Thus, the explanation of leaving an infant alone because it was isolated did not apply to the majority.

Second, the explanation that the infants were left alone because they were good is insufficient. Being good is not, in itself, a reason for leaving an infant alone. A substantial number of nonautistic children are good babies but are not left alone.

Many mothers of young infants are heavily burdened. Those who have not recovered from the physical ordeal of delivery or are ill, those who have other children to care for besides the infant and have cooking and house-cleaning to do, and those who suffer postpartum breakdowns understandably might take advantage of the many opportunities a good baby provides to catch up on other chores, to rest, or to enjoy the company of adults. However, most mothers of autistic children were not in such a situation. The middle of the first year is far enough after delivery for full recovery. Illness and clinical postpartum breakdown have not been reported in the mothers. A large proportion of them had no other children to care for, and domestic help in infant care, cooking, and cleaning was available to them. Many did not make use of such help, but that was their preference. Thus, their situation does not explain leaving the children alone.

Reacting to good babies by leaving them alone or forgetting them would also be understandable in mothers who had little interest in them or who wished to be rid of them. Both of these attitudes were attributed to the mothers by Kanner, Bettleheim, and other clinicians, but reasons for rejecting the attributions were given in earlier chapters. On the contrary, most of the mothers seemed to be very involved with their autistic children during their infancy. Many arranged to be secluded with them. Many viewed them not only as talented and having future potential but also as already beautiful, graceful, and golden. It would seem that mothers with such feelings would have wanted to look at their infants, touch them, and hold them much of the time (as some of them did). In addition, if the babies were good, they should have been all the more attractive to their parents. In the circumstances, the statement that a baby was good and consequently was picked up only for feedings requires explanation.

Third, the thesis of Kanner and others that leaving an infant alone fosters isolation requires qualification. Experiments and observations cited in chapter 8 suggest that leaving a waking infant alone may arouse distress and proximity seeking. On the caretaker's return, attachment behavior occurs—nonrecognition after a long absence or repeated absences and deterring absence at subsequent signs of the caretaker's imminent departure. These reactions were not reported in autistic children who were good babies.

Let us assume that autistic children were left alone beginning at a few weeks after birth, or well before attachment had developed. At this age, if not engaged with the caretaker at the time, most infants are not disturbed by the caretaker's departure. If absences were timed judiciously, longer and longer absences might be tolerated as the infants matured. Perhaps that is one way that good babies develop. In itself, such development might be benign, but autistic effects would be likely, as follows. Assuming that the infants got little handling, they would not accommodate to it, and aversion to handling would persist or increase (see next section). The infants then would be un- cuddly, would not adapt themselves to being picked up, and would stiffen or squirm when held. In addition, having little contact with their caretakers, the infants' development of attachment would be hindered, and consequently, their tolerance of novelty and their communication and learning would be limited.

A sequence by which goodness develops has been suggested. Another possibility is that goodness is an inborn trait associated with autism, but that seems unlikely if, as Benjamin reported, tolerance of the caretaker's depar- ture is found in the great majority of neonates.[11] A more likely explanation is that goodness is simply conditioned. One couple decided before their son was born that infant crying was undesirable. The father, a graduate student in psychology, devised a simple extinction method. Whenever the infant cried, no matter how long or loud, he and his wife did not respond. Only when the infant was not crying did they approach, pick him up, play with him, or feed him. The regimen was established after he came home from the hospital. Within two weeks, he had stopped crying fully. I visited when he was three months old and sat talking for hours with his parents while the door was open to the room where the baby lay, awake much of the time. He was rather quiet. When we, at our initiative, went in to him, he became ac- tive, moving, gurgling, and smiling. He was a typical good baby.

The only demands this infant made were those that his parents had chosen to recognize. They, not he, signaled when his needs were to be met. Although quite undemanding, he was responsive. His social behavior was vigorous and finely timed to the receptivity of his parents. Except for his goodness, he seemed normal. Nonetheless, for reasons touched on earlier, such training is not recommended.

However goodness arises, subsequent events will be decisive in an in- fant's psychological development. Goodness need not reduce infant- caretaker interaction that fosters attachment and consequent development. A young infant who does not cry is at a disadvantage in learning to commun- icate. During the middle of the first year, the disadvantage can be overcome by parental imitation and reinforcement of other sounds—gurgles and bab- bling. Thus, later speech development is not precluded by goodness.

The question that remains about autistic children who were good babies is why they were left alone. Kanner and others found that parents of autistic children were particularly determined to have good or well-behaved children and trained them accordingly.[12] However, there is more to the idea of the good baby than an easy, well-behaved child. Although a good baby can be created by training, it typically has been considered a gift rather than the product of rearing or heredity. The good baby brings praise to the mother for being favored by the deity who bestows such favors.

Crying is associated so strongly with early infancy, that the idea of a baby who does not cry is miraculous and ominous. The ancient "Riddle" song in which the singer gives his love "a baby with no crying" suggests something unattainable and extraordinarily desirable. The other two gifts to his love are a cherry without a pit and a chicken without a bone—unnatural things. Because they are unnatural, having them implies supernatural intervention. The wish for a good baby has transcendental implications.

The associated idea of leaving a young infant quite alone suggests ancient myths and mysteries. Since early times, infants have been prepared for greatness by being left alone. Spartans left their infants to expose them to the rigors of nature and thereby to insure that only the noblest survived. Abandoning an infant in the wilderness was so common in heroic myths as to be characteristic of the infancy of heroes to be.[13] The Bible, mythology, and folklore perpetuate the idea of abandonment as a step toward greatness.

The fantasies of parents that their autistic children were destined for heroic, supernatural careers were described earlier. Having a good baby can be seen as a step in realizing such a destiny.[14] Therefore, the perception of one's baby as good may be influenced by the fantasy. And leaving one's baby alone may symbolize the mythical abandonment that is a step toward greatness. The fantasy is probably the underlying connection between perceiving one's infant as good and leaving the infant alone. Kanner described a mother in whom the fantasy was conscious: she left her baby alone in order to make it perfect.[15]

The Spartan ideal was renewed to an extent in the teachings of psychologists and pediatricians that dominated child-rearing manuals in the United States between World Wars I and II. Mothers were advised not to pick up babies or to respond to their cries between feedings.

One further speculation is that some autistic children may have been left to themselves not because they were good but because they were "bad." Kanner suggested that autistic children were overly erotic to the point of frequent orgasm and a number of writers made similar observations (see chapter 15). In some cases, the eroticism began in infancy. Insofar as arousal or erotic acts were or seemed to be stimulated by parents' presence, that would have been sufficient reason for many parents to have avoided contact with the children and to have repressed the reason.

Infantile eroticism or the perception of it by mothers has been reported in those who hide their children away (chapter 6). A similar reaction to this perception seems likely in those mothers who experienced their autistic children as wild animals in early infancy. Perceiving infants as highly sexual also might account for other things mothers did with their autistic children— holding them stiffly at a distance from their bodies, handling them in ways that minimized skin-to-skin contact, and expressing discomfort in such contact. Writers have explained this behavior as due to maternal inhibition, coldness, and animosity toward the children. It may be explained better as a reaction to perceiving the children as highly sensual or sexual.

Handling of Neonates

A different explanation is suggested for those autistic children reported to have been left alone because they preferred solitude in the first few months. I assume that the observed preference does not reflect pleasure in solitude since nothing is known about infants of that age to support the idea. It is early for infants to be able to manipulate inanimate objects so that they generate predictable sequences. Therefore, a waking neonate left alone can do little more than passively observe an unmoving environment.

One action possible at that age is to make the visual field move by turning the head from side to side. Head turning is among the most advanced, best synchronized acts by which neonates can interact with the environment. Eye movement is also present, and visual pursuit is used from the first days to organize experience, but head turning continues for some time to be better coordinated. To speculate, waking neonates left alone in an unmoving environment would seem likely in time to find head turning as a main way of producing repetitive sequences of stimulation. Other activities having that effect—rocking, head banging, and head rolling—have been reported in the second half-year and require further maturation (see chapter 15). Thus, it would seem likely for head turning to precede these activities. And skill in head turning might lead to pleasure in being left alone.

However, neither head turning nor any activity except sucking by which neonates might gratify themselves has been reported in the first months. Therefore, I assume that an observed preference for solitude at this time reflects aversion to caretakers. A number of ways that aversion develops have been touched on. The one that seems most generally applicable and most likely in cases of autism is aversion that results from awkward, distant handling of neonates.

Such handling is common, particularly in inhibited women with their first babies and in fathers generally. It is unusually common in mothers of autistic children. The effect on ordinary infants is that they do not anticipate being picked up or resist it actively. When held, they stiffen, arch, go limp, or wriggle and seem averse to the adult holding them. In short, the effect is behavior common in autistic children during infancy.

These observations had been interpreted in the past in the light of the long-established idea that being held and handled in certain ways is naturally pleasing, soothing, and gratifying to infants, but that idea is now in question. Similarly, it had been thought that animal young also were soothed and gratified by handling (gentling), but that is not the immediate effect. Mammalian young are averse to handling at first. It is stressful, stimulates adrenal and brain activity and growth, and eventually leads to adaptation to the stimulation. It also leads to superior adaptability to new situations. Similar benefits result from stimulation in infancy that is the opposite of gentle—electric shocks and exposure to cold. Early stresses of these kinds have been reported to foster tolerance for later stress and reduced susceptibility to disturbance.[16]

There is a bit of evidence that the same may be true of human infants and that familiar techniques for comforting neonates may be effective for unexpected reasons. For example, rocking a baby's head and providing something to suck on have been considered soothing ministrations. Instead of soothing, however, they have been found to excite neonates. The excitement inhibits crying and other distress reactions and thereby may reinforce parents for providing the stimulation. The same effect sometimes is achieved by stimulation considered aversive—loud noises, throwing infants in the air, and hitting them. Like "gentled" animals, "soothed" babies learn faster during and after infancy.[17]

In the light of these findings, I suggest the following hypotheses.

First, babies reared in seclusion with limited contact with their mother or left to themselves much of the time are likely to be frightened by novel stimuli, susceptible to emotional disturbances, and handicapped in socialization and learning. Second, some newborn babies are averse to being touched, caressed, or picked up. For them to become adapted to handling and to form normal attachments, they need considerable handling even though they are upset by it at first.

A number of parents and clinicians have concluded that autistic children of all ages need to be treated like neonates who are averse to handling; that is, verbal and physical contact should be made with them even though the children avoid it and are upset by it. It is thought that perseverance by parents eventually will overcome the children's aversion. However, the common reaction of parents to aversive infants is "active rejection or even what would be better described as protective isolation."[18] If this is true, infant development depends upon caretakers not being deterred by what they may experience as rebuffs. That is particularly difficult for mothers who are sensitive to rejection or are depressed, as most are during the neonatal period.

These ideas are in conflict with traditional psychoanalytic thought about the need to protect infants from intrusive stimulation. It was thought that they were born with a protective barrier or stimulus threshold. When overstimulated, the threshold increased, limiting reception of further stimulation. Bernfeld's view was that infantile resistance to being picked up or held was a mild form of freezing seen in animals when in danger:

> The most radical defense against the disturbing or disagreeable outer-world is the suspension of perception, the breaking off of relations with the outer-world: falling asleep, fainting, somnolent states and similar manifestations.[19]

He considered apathy a basic form of this defense.

The defense was not considered sufficient, however. Therefore, mothers were advised to intervene and to protect their infants from strong stimulation. Failure to do so was considered neglect, and doing the opposite— providing strong or intrusive stimulation—was considered pathogenic. Frequent overstimulation was thought to foster chronically raised thresholds—conditioned withdrawal.

In short, data and theories about stimulation of young infants are inconsistent, and further study is needed. The popular view that handling and holding neonates is pleasantly soothing may be incorrect. And the idea that intrusive stimulation is harmful may be incorrect in one respect. Intrusive handling and holding of neonates until they develop tolerance for it may be necessary for the development of normal behavior.

An alternative formulation may be derived from the ideas of Mahler to reconcile some of these findings.[20] Neonates react to prolonged need or tension by apathy or torpor. Presumably, that is an innate reaction. If it occurs repeatedly, it will be aroused by shorter and shorter periods of distress, by milder distress, and finally by cues that precede distress. In time, apathy will become chronic and psychosis will result. In contrast, if caretakers intervene to gratify needs and relieve tension, neonates develop an "expectation" that intervention will occur. That "expectation" enables neonates to tolerate longer and longer periods of need or tension without becoming apathetic.

Relieving neonates under high tension is difficult and requires persistence. Agitated thrashing may increase when they are picked up or held and may continue for some time, giving the impression that they are struggling to get free. Some parents interpret this behavior as anger toward them and withdraw. Others leave neonates to cry themselves out. Still others try to gratify or relieve before distress is evident. None of these approaches has the desired effect. To develop tolerance of distress, neonates must experience the distress and have it relieved. Such an experience also begins socialization.

A corollary hypothesis is that when neonates become apathetic before relief comes, their apathy should be interrupted by strong, prolonged stimulation even if they are averse to it.

The Course of Isolation

Various courses of isolation were reported in autistic children. Parents described some as unresponsive from birth. Others were said to have first shown detachment and preference for solitude in the middle or latter half of the first year. Still others were said to have been vivacious, golden, responsive babies until they changed tragically in the second or third years. In addition, the onset of isolation was reported to have been gradual in some cases and sudden in others, following an identifiable trauma or for no apparent reason.

Some writers have taken the different histories to mean that the name *autism* has been applied to two or more conditions. Others have tried to reconcile the different kinds of histories by discounting one or another. For example, it has been suggested that all of the children were isolated from birth but that some of the parents did not realize it or were gratified temporarily by the children's undemanding ways. Denial of problems in one's children clearly occurs. It has also been suggested that children who were normal in early childhood were described retrospectively by parents as having been abnormal. Some parental reports of isolation from early infancy have been contradicted by observations of other relatives, neighbors, and clinicians. For example, Dibs' and Elly's mothers reported them to be unresponsive during infancy, when their grandmothers found them to be responsive.[21]

Nonetheless, the assumption here is that each type of history has its place in autism and that different onsets refer to different behaviors grouped under the heading of isolation. Findings and interpretations discussed at various points in the book are summarized as follows.

Unresponsiveness in the first days (torpor) usually is caused by obstetric drugs given mothers during labor and by other birth traumas. In the following weeks, diffuse inhibition occurs as an unconditioned reaction to a variety of stresses.[22]

At eight weeks, deviations by caretakers from their usual responses to their infants cause rejection of the caretakers and withdrawal. By then, aversion to being picked up, held, or handled may appear as a reaction to insufficient or awkward handling. Aversion may be accompanied by avoidance of adults and subsequently by not assuming an anticipatory position for being picked up.

At a few months, the absence of attachment behavior or its slowness to develop may be noted—lack of recognition of the caretaker and of the various behaviors that bring or keep caretaker and infant together. By twenty weeks, gaze aversion is common in normal infants and seems a reaction to inattention by caretakers or their deviating from the usual responses they make to their infants. Gaze aversion sometimes is accompanied by refusal of objects offered by caretakers.[23] Gaze aversion occurs particularly when mothers who used to smile back at their smiling infants no longer do. Also, general lack of facial expressiveness by mothers toward their infants fosters expressions of puzzlement, staring at their own hands, and avoidance of eye contact while directing quick glances at the mothers.

In the second half-year, infants who are alone much of the time develop solitary play and interest in and even attachment to inanimate objects and their bodies.[24] Emerging skills in manipulating objects and in stimulating themselves (rocking, head banging) provide a variety of ways to create predictable sequences and to induce sensations and altered consciousness (chapter 15). Rituals also may be elaborated. A result of these activities is reduced interest in and response to people. In addition, developing attachment to caretakers may result in negative attachment behavior toward them after being left alone.

In the second year, stressful training may foster avoidance of the trainer, as well as negativism and immobility. Verbal and other communication may be reduced and deafness simulated. These may result in an infant appearing out of touch.

The older infants are, the more likely they are to be separated from their attachment figures and to show separation reactions after reunion that give the impression of lack of attachment. The births of siblings also contribute to hostility and withdrawal during the toddler years. All of these are probably elements in what has been called isolation.

During the second and third years, parents' concerns about infants' isolation and other peculiarities are likely to turn into serious worry. Parents may now make intense, prolonged efforts to reach their children but encounter the powerful negativism typical of the age. When parents describe autistic children as unreachable and untouchable, their words reflect the failure of long, painful effort. Some of the books written by parents focus on these struggles: unreachability is reflected in the titles *The Child in the Glass Ball* and *The Siege*. One parent spoke for many in describing his son as "encapsulated behind an invisible and seemingly impenetrable wall."[25]

These behaviors differ in detail, meaning, and causes. Parents may not emphasize the distinctions; rather, they may group the behaviors together and seek one explanation for them. If they do, each of the behaviors will contribute to the global impression of isolation in a child, who will seem increasingly isolated as time passes. In addition, different children—one who is averse to handling, another who is showing attachment behavior, and still another who is engrossed in self-stimulation—will be taken to be showing different onsets of the same phenomenon.

Insofar as parents try to find one remedy for different kinds of behavior, little success is possible. And insofar as parents react to different behaviors the same way, the behaviors may take on a functional unity; they may be integrated into a pattern or role.

14   The Inscrutable Child: Communication

Inadequate speech does not have as central or clear a place in autism as ritual and isolation. Inability to talk often has been defined as basic in autism, and some workers have hypothesized it to be the basic symptom, with other symptoms as secondary phenomena—as adaptations to the inability.[1] In diagnostic practice, however, inadequate speech is not basic. Many autistic children develop speech in infancy and then stop talking. For them, the absence of speech is secondary to other developments. In addition, a speaking child can be diagnosed as autistic, and some are. Finally, many nonspeaking autistic children do become speakers, but they retain the diagnosis of autism. By contrast, ritual and isolation are inseparable from autism. Children who are not ritualistic or isolated are not diagnosed as autistic, and children who stop being ritualistic or isolated are no longer considered autistic. Thus, whatever definition or theory of autism clinicians assert, their practice implicitly puts ritual and isolation but not speech at the heart of the concept of autism.

Nonetheless, speech occupies a key position in socialization and mental functioning. The importance of speech training in the development of compulsivity was suggested in chapter 12. No other lack or peculiarity is as upsetting to most parents of autistic children as inadequate speech. The parents may notice, ignore, or explain away other deficiencies, but the recognition that their children do not speak or are not progressing in speech is usually what moves them to go beyond family physicians and pediatricians and to undertake the round of consultations that leads to a diagnosis of autism. In addition, the role parents play in teaching speech may serve as a model for understanding autism. More is known about language training and development in autistic children than about any other aspect of their rearing.

Other parents also prize speech as their infants' most important skill. Many watch carefully to see how it will develop. The onset of speech particularly reassures apprehensive parents that their children are not defective.

The importance attached to speech is imbedded in our cultural heritage. Some psychologists and philosophers have considered language the highest achievement of civilization and the most distinctive human faculty. Although philosophers have stressed socialization and reason more than language as faculties that set humans apart from other species, a better case can be made for language. Social living and reason are found in other species; language is not. Descartes observed, "it is a very remarkable thing that there are no men, not even the insane, so dull and stupid that they cannot put words together in a manner to convey their thoughts."[2] This is not quite true, but the converse is true. No animal is known to have put words or comparable symbols together to convey its thoughts.

The association of language with human nature may explain why people who do not speak are apt to be considered nonhuman and treated accordingly. It may also explain why absence of language in a child is unnerving to parents. Their fantasies about having a monster—whether subhuman or superhuman—seem to come true when they have a child who does not speak.

People define themselves when they speak. They indicate who and what they are and what their relationship with the hearer is. The less people say, the more of a gap they leave for others to fill imaginatively. Autistic children's lack of speech has led adults to attribute to them a lack of sensation, emotion, responsiveness, and relatedness, as well as the more-fanciful qualities discussed earlier. The children have allowed others to define them. They have not contradicted adults who regarded them as deaf, blind, or lacking in feelings.

The symptomatic speech of adult schizophrenics, even when nonsensical, can be analyzed as statements about themselves and their relationships with others. Catatonic schizophrenics, insofar as they do not speak, leave people mystified and intrigued. Other schizophrenics, like autistic children, speak in peculiar ways that often leave listeners puzzled about whether they have been spoken to or not. More precisely, schizophrenic adults use words meaningfully to convey thoughts, but they also use words to convey the impression that they are not communicating.[3]

Analyses that have illuminated the speech of adult schizophrenics may be extended to autistic children if they, too, use words in such complex ways. The idea that the children do so goes against the conclusion of most workers that the children cannot speak. The children's speaking ability has been the subject of vigorous controversy. As noted earlier, the concept of ability has yet to be defined sufficiently to permit scientific answers to questions of whether people are capable or incapable of doing things that they do not do. However, the question of how competently autistic children speak bears on the analyses to be presented, and will be answered in detail.

Most autistic children develop some speech by the age of one. Many of them stop speaking between one and three, often after being separated from their mothers. Some begin speaking again and stop again. Others begin to speak early and do not stop, but they do not progress either. Their language remains primitive, and they appear not to learn new words. A few begin to speak within the first two years and progress to ordinary speech.

Those who do not begin to speak in infancy and those who begin but stop or fail to progress comprise the group with little or no speech in the preschool years—the great majority. Between the ages of five and ten, many of them progress toward competent speech. Some start to speak then at a rudimentary level, as if just learning. Others immediately show considerable vocabularies, subtlety in making distinctions, and mastery of grammar. The first words known to have been spoken by one child were, "I hear that President Kennedy has been assassinated by a man named Oswald in Texas."[4] Thus, many show that they had been learning during the years in which they appeared not to be.

Linguistic skill is shown in other odd ways. Some autistic children speak only in emergencies or on other special occasions. Some speak to one person and not to another. One spoke to his reflection in the mirror but not to people. One talked sensibly only when awakened at night. A number spoke more sensibly when running a high fever than when well.[5]

Many autistic children acquire language in atypical ways. Some who do not seem to learn speech from parents or teachers do learn from television or machines. Some are reported to teach themselves to read or write. They may read *The New York Times* or even scientific journals but not speak. Some who show no progress in the language spoken around them learn foreign or sign languages.[6]

Before using speech conventionally, most autistic children use words in ways that parents and clinicians classify as nonspeech: they mimic what others say; they sing; they spell aloud words that they do not say. These uses have been considered nonspeech on the assumption that they had no communicative function when used by autistic children. The children were thought neither to understand words they repeated nor even to understand that sounds had a communicative function. They were thought to reproduce sounds mechanically, as parrots or recording machines do. The impression of mechanical speech was intensified by those children who accurately mimicked the original speaker's pronunciation, tone, and inflection and by those who repeated things in a flat, machinelike tone. Some continued to use a dehumanized tone when the words were their own, thus misleading people into thinking they were still mimicking.[7]

Autistic children do not mimic everything they hear. Like people and unlike machines, they are selective and what they select has been shown on occasion to constitute meaningful communication. The same applies to lines they sing. In addition, details of their mimicry show grasp of meaning and grammar.[8] And many parents recognize their children's mimicry as distinctive communication and rely on it in everyday dealings with the children.

Insofar as some of the children's mimicry and singing conveys messages and their spelling rather than saying of words is usually meaningful, a substantial part of the children's use of words that has been classified as nonspeech may be communication. If this and other questionable speech (obscure metaphor, incomplete sentences) is added to the occasional normal speech of autistic children who are considered non speakers, most of them may be said to speak occasionally—enough for patterns to be found in their silences and their omissions of speech elements. Once it is clear that children do speak, although infrequently, their silences are interpretable as interpersonal behavior rather than simply as characteristics of the children. Usually, silence is an event between two people. It is often a reaction against pressure from another person to speak.[9]

The question of autistic children's speech has been posed narrowly here. In general, the more-evident fact is the absence of speech and the questionable relevance of what the children do say. As communication, their speech is grossly defective and bizarre—far below the norm during the preschool years. Most say little that qualifies as conventional communication. Much of their use of words differs from other children's in quantity, timing, style, content, and context. It frustrates adults insofar as it is obscure, confusing, incomprehensible, inaudible, and not what is expected. For these reasons, it has not been accepted as speech at times when it had a communicative function. However, if a definition like Descartes' is used and the question is Have autistic children been known to use combinations of words to answer questions, to make requests, and to comment on what is happening around them?, the answer is that almost every one of them has.

Silences and questionable speech can be misconstrued easily. Meaning can be read into them when none is present, and meaning can be missed. Kanner suggested that everything said by autistic children was meaningful.[10] Most writers have treated deviant use of words by autistic children as meaningless. In an unusual example, a therapist described his methodical training of a completely silent autistic boy to speak by imitation. After extensive training, the boy began to repeat *go* when the therapist said it. Then the boy said what sounded like *daddy,* apparently addressed to the therapist. This was the boy's first spontaneous word in three years. Nonetheless, the therapist did not reinforce it. Instead, he insisted that the boy say *go.* The boy became silent again and did not even say *go.*

Here, the therapist's rejection of speech was deliberate because it deviated from his lesson plan. Usually, autistic children's deviant speech is rejected because it is not understood. Either way, the result is that the children's speech is discouraged. Ironically, it is discouraged by people who wish to foster speech in the children and who may devote great effort toward that end.

The study of schizophrenic adults took a major step when Bleuler showed that their seemingly nonsensical speech was meaningful and communicative. Kanner made a start in exploring the meaning of autistic children's seemingly nonsensical speech. But interpretation of deviant language is difficult when few words are used. Given the choice of reading too much or too little into the words of autistic children, it would seem more constructive to risk the former.

Echolalia

Among the speech deviations of autistic children, the best known is mimicry of adults' speech, usually called *echolalia*. The question of why they mimic adults may be approached from studies of echolalia in adults and nonautistic children.

Echolalia has been considered an expression of either a positive attitude toward the person imitated or a negative attitude. On the positive side, imitation is sometimes flattering and deferential, signifying that the person imitated is superior. It may represent an effort to ally oneself with the speaker's authority and to make use of the speaker's powers.

A slight twist turns imitation into the opposite—subtle defiance. Imitation may be used to deal with unwelcome demands. It is a token response that gives nothing. Stengel interpreted echoing of demands to be refusal disguised as compliance.[11] Catatonic adults who engage in echolalia are thought to be self-absorbed and to repeat what is said as a token response that may appease others sufficiently to prevent further intrusion. Such an echo is like the "Yes, dear" of a spouse who is not listening but manages to satisfy the other enough to be allowed to continue not to listen, to continue some solitary activity. The same idea has been advanced about autistic children in relation to their parents.[12]

People who ask a question or make a demand tend to require some response—at least an acknowledgement—and echolalia can serve as a minimal response. It has been interpreted as a response to pressure to talk, particularly in autistic children, and especially as a response to demands for precocious speech.[13] As a response to such pressure, echolalia is minimally compliant: words are demanded; words are given.

Imitation can be disarming. Parents ordinarily reward it in infants just beginning to speak. Mimicry of parents by older children may be hostile also. To parents, children operate on a level vaguely between rudimentary and sophisticated speech. Consequently, parents have difficulty in distinguishing imitation that is truly compliant from hostile mimicry. Such parental uncertainty provides hostile children with a margin of safety. If children are considered dull, socially deficient, or disturbed, the margin is wide.

The ideas of disarming behavior and veiled hostility suggest intelligence and social sophistication beyond the toddler level. However, such uses of mimicry may develop out of infantile echolalia by conditioning. Echolalia appears in many autistic children as it does in normal children in the first year. It is considered a precursor of normal speech. Whether its onset is innate or conditioned is not known, but its continuation into late infancy, when most children are using it less and less, may be conditioned simply by rewarding it. To suggest a sequence leading to heavy use of echolalia in the second year, early training of speech may be divided into three phases: (1) At first, parents reward mimicry of sounds. (2) Gradually, they make reward contingent on mimicking words only. At this time, parents say words for their infants to repeat. (3) Then, appropriate use is required, and mimicry is no longer acceptable.

When phase 3 teaching is done too early, the result may be phase 2 learning; that is, teaching word meaning before a child is ready results in the acquisition of words without meaning. In addition, if a parent rewards mimicry in place of understanding, as by teaching rote memorization of lists, a child also will be learning an adaptation he or she can use later when under pressure to master difficult material—to substitute an inferior skill for the required one, mimicry for speech. Imitation is momentarily effective in meeting demands, but its applicability is narrow. Reliance on imitation provides little adaptability for the future and may be an obstacle to learning higher skills.[14] Later, when a parent insists on meaningful speech from a child whose verbal repertoire is mainly echolalic, the child may stop using words at all.

Autistic children are subject in infancy to considerable pressure for verbal performance. The usual effects of such pressure are mimicry, rote learning, and compulsiveness, specifically in the use of words—behaviors common in these children.[15] By mimicry and rote memorizing, autistic children achieve remarkable feats in infancy. They reproduce songs, prayers, and various lists—scores of words without meaning.

By contrast, learning to name objects is a phase 3 procedure. Learning to name musical pieces combines phases 2 and 3. Some meaning is involved insofar as each name is distinctively associated with a piece of music. However, the individual words the infant learns (*March, Overture, Number, One, Suite,* as well as the composer's names) are devoid of ordinary meaning as words at this time. They are learned more as sounds than words. In addition, learning them may interfere with learning words meaningfully. Insofar as the musical names happen to be common words or be similar to them, their use to identify music may interfere with learning the common meaning.[16] For example, *Opus One* will not usually be the first piece played; a musical *Suite* is not sweet to the taste. Confusion resulting from such training is not ordinarily significant but may become serious if followed by stressful training.

Hostility becomes a part of the interaction between autistic children and their parents in the second year and more so in the third. Negativism is a common response to demand in normal children at this age. Echolalia, which once gratified a parent, lends itself to negativistic use in the face of parental demands. For example:

Parent: Give me that!

Child: Give me that!

Parent: Where did you put your mittens?

Child: Where did you put your mittens?

The effect can be exasperating.

The gap between imitation and meaningful speech is great. Imitation requires discrimination of what has just been said and nothing more. The criterion for a correct response is simple; a child knows exactly what is wanted. To answer the question What is this? (while listening to a record) is more difficult. It requires discrimination of the question, recognition of the peice, and remembering the name associated with it. Here, too, the criterion for a correct response is fairly simple. The child knows what is wanted, whether or not the name is remembered. If it is remembered, the answer can be given. It is a much simpler question than others commonly asked of young children. What do you want to eat?, for example, has no simple criterion for a correct answer. To be correct, a child usually will have to take into account what was just said, who said it, and where it was said, as well as what the child wants. Different answers are correct if it was asked by mother or a stranger on the street or if asked at breakfast, lunch, dinner, or between meals. If mealtime is not far off, a correct answer is something that a caretaker would not consider likely to spoil the child's appetite. By contrast, the question What is the capital of Massachusetts? is far simpler. It always has the same answer.

These factors have been drawn out to emphasize the point that verbal skills developed in the second year vary greatly in complexity. A parent may not see much difference between naming a capital and saying what one wants to eat. The parent may even believe that the former shows more intelligence than the latter. Therefore, the parent may conclude that a child who can identify a dozen symphonies and capitals should be able to say what he or she wants. Frustrated by an incorrect response or silence to what appears to be a simple question, the parent may punish the child and demand a correct verbal response. Then the child is likely to respond with negativism, echolalia or other regressive behavior.

A final point is that when preoccupied or confused, ordinary children and adults echo what people say in order to fix the words in their minds until they can grasp the meaning and deal with it.[17] Autistic children find many ordinary things confusing and develop rituals to limit their confusion. Echolalia would seem to lend itself to ritualization in the circumstances.

Specific Omissions

Autistic children who speak commonly do not use the words *yes, I, mama, daddy,* and their equivalents. Other elements of speech are also lacking, but these stand out as early words that parents are particularly interested in having their children learn. Also, the children continue not to use these words long after they have mastered more-difficult ones.[18]

Nonuse of specific words by the children has been attributed to their lack of relevant concepts. This explanation is least applicable to nonuse of *yes.* The function of affirmation or consent is within the range of competence usually attributed to autistic children. The functional meanings of *yes* and *no* are established much earlier than the words. In the first year, infants develop selective use of gestures or sounds to indicate affirmation or refusal, and these prespeech elements of communication are abstract and symbolic. They are functionally equivalent to speech. For example, if infants use a distinctive gurgle in the affirmative when asked if they want food, a toy, or to be picked up, and if they do not use the gurgle at other times, then the gurgle may be functionally equivalent to the word *yes*.

Autistic children affirm and refuse by body language during the first few years. After they have extensive vocabularies, many repeat an adult's question to affirm but still do not say *yes*. Thus, autistic children who convey the meaning of yes and use many other words continue not to use the sound "yes."

Not saying *yes* is particularly suggestive in those who do say *no*. Parents reward *yes* more than *no*. In ordinary children, the negativistic phase is often marked by a great increase of *no* and a decline in *yes*. Since autistic children are rather negativistic, their nonuse of *yes* has been taken as negativism.

Another early function of speech is to ask for things. Distinctive vocalizing to ask for things has been reported as early as two months. *Mama* often functions as a request before it becomes a name for mother. In a one-year-old, *mama* may be the equivalent of *get* (accompanied by pointing). Many autistic children are competent in making wishes known. They may take their parents by the hand and lead them to where a desired object is to be gotten. One autistic child did this even when it required traversing a long, complex route that she had seen only once before.[19] However, autistic children who express wishes this way and have extensive vocabularies neither use simple words like *get* nor name the object desired. Others, who do name what they wish, nonetheless express their wishes strangely. For example, an autistic child who wants a cookie may say, "You want a cookie."

Nonuse of *I* has been classified under the heading of *pronominal reversal* because the children often say *you* when *I* would be correct. Some researchers had thought the autistic children also used *I* in place of *you*. The latter substitution is found rarely, if ever. The main finding is that *I* is lacking, along with *me, my,* and *mine*. The phenomenon seems an omission rather than a reversal.

Use of *you* where *I* is expected is partly attributable to echolalia. A typical answer by an autistic child to a parent's question is repetition of the question. When a parent asks, "Do you want a cookie?" and a child affirms by saying, "Do you want a cookie?," the *you* is accounted for by the mimicry. However, in mimicking sentences that contain *I,* some autistic children omit it or substitue *you*. In addition, *I* is lacking in their spontaneous verbalizations. Thus, echolalia does not fully account for the absence of *I, me, my,* and *mine* from autistic children's speech.

The main interpretation of nonuse of *I, mama,* and *daddy* has been that the children did not understnd what the words meant. Observers thought the children did not use personal pronouns because they had no sense of themselves.[20] They thought the children did not say *mama* because they did not distinguish their mothers from their fathers or other people. In support of this idea, it was noted that some called their mothers *daddy*.

The assumptions in this explanation are questionable. Children commonly use words for which they lack concepts, as do adults; and autistic children are thought to do this more than other children, as in echolalia. However, autistic children echo *I* and *mama* less than they echo other words. In addition, many of the children evidently have concepts for words they do not use. For example, a boy who did not say *daddy* spelled the word to refer to his father.[21] Another nonuser of *daddy* referred to his father as, "That man who sleeps with her, has bacon and eggs in the morning, that man.[22] In such instances, lack of words or concepts is not the problem; rather, nonuse of the words is selective avoidance.

The idea that nonuse is selective avoidance is supported by failure of efforts to condition autistic children to say *I* and *yes* as meaningless sounds. Some who began to utter a number of other sounds as a result of conditioning still did not say *I* and *yes*.[23]

Some of these threads are illustrated by the case of an autistic girl who hardly spoke English, the language of her parents. (Among the peculiarities of her English was use of *you* in place of *I*.) Her grandmother also hardly spoke English and had invented her own language combining Italian with broken English. The girl spoke competently to her grandmother in that language, but when her parents addressed her in it, she did not reply.[24] In general, the details of cases provide the strongest evidence for selective avoidance, and the context in which avoidance occurs suggests its function.

Literalness and Metaphor

Some autistic children are voluble, using large vocabularies. Nonetheless, adults find their speech confusing, with mutual frustration and misunderstanding. (The speech of compulsive children similarly has been found to be confusing and misleading.)[25] The difficulty has been identified as overly literal language by some writers and as overly metaphorical language by others. Both attributions are confirmed by selected samples of the children's speech. The same overuses have been reported in adult schizophrenics' speech.

The apparent contradiction is probably due to typing people. Overuse of literal speech or metaphor is understandable in context. All people use a

mixture of literal and metaphorical speech. Whether their speech is perceived as normal or abnormal in either respect depends upon its relationship
to what precedes it or what is called for. Detailed study of adult schizophrenics has shown that they were overly literal on tasks that called for metaphor
and that they were overly metaphorical on tasks that called for literal responses. Similarly, they were often literal when speaking to someone who
was being metaphorical and vice versa. Thus, on the whole, they were not
categorically too literal or too metaphorical; their speech was deviant in relation to the expectations of others.

The same is true of autistic children. Their speech does not conform to
the speech of adults with whom they converse. When adults speak literally,
the children may respond metaphorically and vice versa. A person who is
speaking metaphorically tends to find a literal response disconcerting. If
such responses occur often, an exasperated speaker may type the responder
as overly literal. In short, the excess literalness and metaphor attributed to
autistic children may be explainable as deviation from whichever is expected
at the time.

The function of unexpected literalness may be suggested by its effects on
the hearer, as in the following responses by autistic children:

Asked what he would do if he cut himself, a boy answered, "Bleed."

Asked what he was going to do after getting up from the table, a boy
replied, "Stand on the floor."

Told to put something down, a child put it on the floor.

A father referred to hanging pictures as being on the wall. His son corrected him by saying that the pictures were near the wall (not on it).[26]

In the first two examples, the answers are not responsive to the questioner's
intent. They are disconcerting as well as seemingly evasive. In the third example, the child obeys an instruction, but the result is not what the adult
wanted. In the last one, the result of literal construction is that the child cor-
rects or criticizes the adult.

The examples taken together suggest that the children may be enjoying
jokes at the adults' expense, as nonautistic children commonly do. The following example is typical five-year-old use of literalness. A teacher told a
boy in Eugene's class to put on his shoes. Eugene remarked that the boy had
sneakers with him, not shoes. The teacher replied, "I meant, 'Put on your
sneakers'." Eugene retorted, "I already have my sneakers on."[27]

Eugene was not autistic, and his humor may be considered beyond the
competence even of older autistic children. Teasing and humor are thought
of as sophisticated functions, but that seems largely a reflection of adult bias.
The elements of teasing and humor are primitive mental processes, easily conditioned. Systematic observation indicates the presence of both in ordinary

infants.[28] There is no basis in data for assuming that evasion, teasing, and humor are beyond autistic children's intelligence, and there is no proof that such behavior is in their repertories. The point here is that taking metaphors literally does not require sophistication and is found in young children. It is one of the first forms of children's verbal humor.

Adults are caught off guard by being taken literally because many metaphors, idioms, and other commonplace phrases are so habitual that adults use them without awareness of their lack of literal precision. Young children are adept at pointing out "errors" in such use and often do so by pretending to take what adults say at literal face value. Correcting people (item 4) is fairly open hostility. A more-covert form is to go along with what is said and to carry it to an absurd conclusion (item 3).

Each of these forms of word play enables children to turn the tables on adults. The wittier and more indirect their play is, the more likely children are to escape punishment. Jokes are a means of saying things that would be punished if expressed in another way. Adults consider many jokes beyond the understanding of children without realizing that the reverse is also true. Adults do not understand much children's humor, thereby giving children an advantage. An example is the category of moron jokes. Superficially, the moron is the butt of the humor. An unsuspecting parent may join the child who tells such a joke in laughing at the moron. Another parent may discourage jokes that make fun of handicapped people. The principal target of these jokes is not the moron, however; it is the rule-making adult. The moron violates a taboo and gets away with it under the cloak of stupidity. The child who tells the joke vicariously breaks the same taboo and gets away with it. A well-known older moron in children's fiction is Amelia Bedelia. Moronic literalness is her main way of relating to people. She uses it to wreak havoc in the homes and lives of her sensible superiors. For example, told to strip the bed sheets, she tears them into strips. Her superiors are the victims. She, the heroine, the one with whom children identify, gets away with her mischief.

In short, adults usually underestimate the humor of young children as to its guile and hostile motives. Literalness that mocks is a major element in the humor and requires rather little sophistication. Children's literal speech has been attributed to premature demands for language competence.[29] To the extent that such demands foster resentment, the hostile use of literalness would seem a likely outlet. Literalness is also a means of resisting adult questions and demands. Autistic children are extremely negativistic. In many instances, their parents sense resistance and hostility in the children's literalness. Probably, much of their literalness is evasive, negativistic, or hostile.

Similarly, responding with metaphor when literal speech or action is expected can have evasive and hostile uses. Metaphors disguise what is said to make it ambiguous. That is a principal use of metaphors in ordinary conversation; they enable people to speak without necessarily committing themselves to what is said. The function is most obvious in those metaphors called euphemisms. By employing a euphemism, the speaker avoids saying what is being said. Sexual intercourse is referred to as *going to bed, having a relationship,* or *being intimate* because the phrases are ambiguous. The speaker derives a measure of security in touching on embarrassing or forbidden matters by using words that can be taken to refer to something else. If a statement is made ambiguously, the hearer has the choice of how to take it. Obscureness serves the same function. The less understandable a metaphor is to the hearer, the less the speaker is held responsible. Thus, a metaphor that is obscure and that appears to be irrelevant and not directed to the hearer provides much freedom from responsibility.

When a child is evading a question, it is helpful to disguise the evasion. That may be accomplished by disguising the ambiguity of the reply because blatant ambiguity may not be tolerated. If asked by a parent, "Did you break that?" a reply of "Yes and no" or "I'm not going to say" is likely to be punished. Silence also is not acceptable in a child known to talk. By contrast, the response "Do birds sing?" may put off the questioner effectively. The parent may wonder if the child understood the question, what the response means, and whether the child was replying to the question or was off in a private reverie. By the time the adult considers the possibilities, it may no longer seem worth the bother of trying to pin down the child. Thus, bizarre metaphor and echolalia have in common a disarming as well as frustrating effect.

When metaphors are obscure but hint at something relevant, they function as riddles. Bettelheim concluded that autistic children use language mainly to pose riddles for adults.[30] Whether or not that is the children's intention, most clinicians and parents experience the children as enigmatic. To solve a riddle or deal with an enigmatic child on the basis of understanding requires deviation from habitual modes of thought. Riddles do not yield to the first or most obvious attempts. The riddles posed by the speech of adult schizophrenics have been studied by communication analysis and the decoding of symbols. The analysis will be extended to some aspects of autistic children's speech.

Self-Effacement

Disguise of content by metaphor is compounded by autistic children's other speech peculiarities and by their impassive silences. On the whole, it is hard to hear what autistic children say and to understand what one hears. They mutter, stress the wrong syllable, or reverse syllables. They use flat tones and no inflection or simple, rhythmic inflection (singsong). They address remarks to the wall and fall silent before completing a thought. They answer a question with a question and sometimes say the opposite of what adults think they mean. The children offer no help in interpreting their scant productions. An adult who wishes to understand usually faces a difficult job.

The following case makes a convenient starting point for analyzing meanings of the children's deviant speech.[31]

Marcia was mute. While in treatment, she began to use words. Like many autistic children, her first sentences were in song—in particular, she repeated "Why can't the English teach their children how to speak?" over and over. Marcia's mother was an Englishwoman who had moved to the United States. She was the English person in Marcia's life. Thus, the words may have referred to her mother and herself (a child who did not speak). Let us assume that this was so. Inasmuch as Marcia had not spoken during the twelve years of her life, the implied indictment of her mother was rather serious. It was indirect, however, and its gravity was mitigated in several ways. It was a question rather than a statement. It was sung, and what one sings is not taken as seriously as what one says. The words were not her own, and she and her mother were not identified as the persons whom the song was about. In addition, Marcia did not sing the song to her mother. In short, Marcia did not indicate that she was communicating. People who knew her situation inferred that her song was meaningful; but that was their idea, not necessarily hers.

Similarly, the boy who was asked to subtract four from ten and said "I'll draw a hexagon" did not indicate that he was communicating. He did not acknowledge that he had understood the question or even that he had heard it. He did not make clear whether his comment was related to the question. He offered to perform without doing so. The questioner had an opportunity to puzzle out all these things. Therefore, the next move was up to the questioner. Many speech peculiarities that characterize autistic children can be construed similarly, as communicating without appearing to.

Haley analyzed adult schizophrenics' speech as largely consisting of a series of denials that they are communicating. In normal conversation, a complete message contains the following:

Acknowledgment of a prior message or context,

Identification of the speaker,

Identification of the intended hearer,

Some definition of the relationship between them,

The content or message,

A question about whether the intended hearer received or understood the message.

Commonly, the text is explicit; the other elements may be conveyed without words and are sometimes omitted. For example, one's manner and tone (respectful, affectionate, businesslike) may define the relationship. Haley noted that a list of ways of denying the elements of a message is a list of the symptoms of schizophrenia. He added:

> The schizophrenic not only avoids defining his relationship with another person, he also can be exasperatingly skillful at preventing another person from defining his relationship with him. It is such responses which give one the feeling of not being able to "reach" a schizophrenic.[32]

His analysis fits young autistic children even better than schizophrenic adults in that more elements are omitted or ambiguous in the children's speech.

1. *Context.* There is no acknowledgement of having heard what was said to the child or of any other context. The hearer does not know if the child is responding to something just said, to something from the past, or to nothing but private thoughts. (When the hearer's words are repeated, context is indicated, but then the child seems not to have originated the message.)

2. *Identification of the speaker.* There is no reference to oneself, as by saying *I, me, in my opinion.* The speaker seems hardly to identify with the words used, as by spontaneity and personal style in choice of words, tone, or rhythm. On the contrary, even when the words are the child's, they often sound as if they are not.

3. *Identification of the hearer.* There is no reference to the hearer, as by name, title, or saying *you* or *listen,* or walking over to the hearer, looking at the hearer, or touching the hearer. On the contrary, the child avoids the presumed hearer's eyes, looks past the hearer, or seems to be talking to the wall. When the child says *you,* it may not seem to be an identification of the hearer.

4. *Definition of the relationship.* Rather than indicating a relationship, the child acts as if the hearer is absent or is inanimate, and therefore no person-to-person relationship applies.

5. *The content.* Content is fragmented and disguised. Requests to finish what the child began or to clarify what he or she said are not met.

6. *Verification of receipt.* The child neither checks to see if the hearer has heard or understood nor seems to wait for an answer. Instead, the child may turn or walk away. A sign by the hearer that a message has been understood may upset the child.[33] If the hearer replies, the child may not indicate having heard the reply.

The analysis was derived from the speech of schizophrenic adults, most of whom had demonstrated conversational skills at some time in their lives. Autistic children seem well described by this analysis in that their behavior lacks the same elements omitted in adult schizophrenics' speech. However, that is not evidence that the children are actively omitting the elements. First it is necessary to show that the missing behavior is in the children's repertory. Most clinicians believe that it is not. The behavior is beyond the social awareness usually attributed to the children.

Reasons for considering complex, misleading behavior within their range have been touched on and will be elaborated. Whether or not the children deliberately create misleading impressions is not known and is not essential to this analysis. What is clear is that they engage in behavior that has misleading effects. They act as if they are deaf, blind, unable to understand, unaware of what is going on around them, and insensitive to pain and punishment when none of these things is true. However, misleading behavior may be conditioned and engaged in without awareness.

On the whole, autistic children's behavior is inconsistent. They show many of their skills only occasionally, which causes people to believe the skills are absent. Behavior that gives the impression of being unresponsive to what is said to them has been shown to be highly responsive by close observation and analysis of film: "the behavior of autistic children is just as oriented to the social context and interacting other as the behavior of normals."[34] The behavior usually is not what adults expect; nonetheless, it is related to context.

Considerable evidence shows that the children distinguish who they are talking to and that they are being listened to. As noted, some react negatively to signs that the hearer understands them, showing concern about the effects of their communication, although they otherwise may act unconcerned. In addition, they talk differently to different people, according to the nature of the relationship.

Some of the behaviors in Haley's analysis of communication are among the most primitive. They are found in young infants and are learned as simple responses, requiring no linguistic or social skill. The defects attributed to autistic children would not hinder them from looking at a person who is talking to them or listening to them. And the impression they give of not looking at people is misleading. They do look but do it so quickly and surreptitiously that adults are not aware of being looked at.[35]

Finally, as noted, most autistic children show full language repertories. The occasions may be rare, but on some occasions they talk sensibly to grandparents, neighbors, or strangers if not to their parents. They talk in emergencies, in the middle of the night, or when feverish. DesLauriers and Carlson said that many autistic children appear normal to everyone except their mothers. The statement is incorrect on its face and undoubtedly is an exaggeration. But many autistic children do appear more normal and occasionally fully normal to some strangers.[36] If their occasional communicative speech is added up, most of them can be said to show the range of behavior specified in Haley's analysis. Therefore, the usual absence of this behavior may be selective omission.

In short, analysis of autistic children's speech suggests that they avoid the appearance of communicating. They do not identify themselves as individuals or as partners in relationships. They do not call attention to themselves, at least not directly. Even when their speech is intrusive and arresting, they convey the impression that their words are not their own. Much of their communcation is self-effacing.

I have suggested that autistic children are born to the greatest of expectations, the heaviest of responsibilities. Their self-effacement may be interpreted as a reaction against those burdens as well as against specific training demands. Much of their behavior suggests that they have done nothing and will continue to do nothing. It is construable as a denial of guilt, a statement of helplessness, and a reminder not to expect anything of them.

Evasion

Selective response usually is assumed in the case of an adolescent or adult who ignores requests. People around them say, They only hear what they want to. They ignore things, consciously and unconsciously. They may even be indulged, as when a woman explains for her child or husband, "It's no use trying to talk to him now. John doesn't hear anything when he's watching television." If people are oblivious too often, the indulgence may be withdrawn unless they act deaf consistently and are thought to be deaf. For that to happen, they must appear deaf even when no demands are being made of them. That is what autistic children do. They are not fully consistent, and an objective observer is not misled for long. But they are consistent enough to be accepted as deaf on occasion by physicians, audiologists, and parents.[37]

Some autistic children enact deafness impressively. They are not tricked by verbal offers, and they do not flinch at sudden, loud noises. Others are inconsistent, much like ordinary children and adults with selective hearing. Their parents are aware of the inconsistency but may develop imaginative, complex theories to explain intermittent hearing.[38]

Hearing is a toddler's main way of receiving instruction and demands. That is probably why hearing seems to be the most defective sense in autistic children. The account by Dibs' mother shows how avoidance of specific demands can lead to avoidance of all verbal contact. As a result of his mother's heavy training of him, testing him, and demanding that he perform, he began to avoid her. He hid under furniture or left the room, but she kept after him. Then he developed the appearance of not hearing her. When she accepted the idea that he could not hear or understand her—when he appeared grossly defective—she reduced her demands. Her tenacity did not allow for selective unresponsiveness. To respond on any one occasion would betray the fact that he was ignoring her demand on another.

Unremitting demands, including the use of subtlety and force to elicit performance up to the point at which the children appeared grossly defective, have been reported in some cases of autism.[39] Parents who trained their children that way provided contingencies of demand, punishment, and reward that fostered generalized nonresponse to sound.

Appearing not to see serves to confirm the impression of not hearing. Ordinarily, people addressed look at the speaker. Thus, looking indicates having heard. Conversely, people who do not wish to respond are in a better position not to if they avoid eye contact. Gaze aversion in autistic children has been attributed to avoidance of readiness to respond.[40]

Pain is ordinarily a powerful motivator. Autistic children have been described as untrainable because they are indifferent to punishment. Animals, from primates to simple creatures, are motivated by pain and therefore can be trained by punishment. Behaviorists have used punishment effectively with autistic children, which proves that they are not really an exception. Nonetheless, autistic children act as if they were impervious to pain to such an extent that their parents are misled.

Punishing children (as distinct from attacking them) may be justified insofar as it promotes discipline or learning. Therefore, in punishing children, one expects certain effects. The long-range effect is change in the children's behavior. The immediate effect is crying or other signs that show the children have experienced pain and that, therefore, future change is likely. Thus, the children's cries are immediate reinforcement to the parents for punishing them; and immediate reinforcement is more effective than delayed reinforcement. In other words, if children show no distress when punished, their parents will not believe the punishment is effective and, therefore, justified and will tend to stop punishing them. In turn, the children will be reinforced for not showing distress.

This is a simplified analysis. Parents react in various ways to crying or its absence when punishing children. Some are frustrated by its absence and increase the punishment to make the children cry. Other parents feel guilty when children cry and stop the punishment. Still others give additional punishment for crying. Each group, by its reaction, sets up different reinforcement contingencies and conditions different responses to punishment in children. Thus, whether crying or its absence is conditioned depends upon a parent's personality. Relevant observations on the behavior of parents of autistic children are lacking. If the parents are like most parents, signs of distress in their children reward them for administering punishment, and the absence of such signs leaves them confused about how to proceed.

Autistic children have been described here as creating impressions, misleading adults, being evasive, playing roles, teasing, and expressing hostility in disguised ways. These terms suggest awareness and sophistication not usually considered present in autistic children. I have argued that the children are more aware and sophisticated than is usually thought. Nonetheless, the terms used suggest too much. The terms were used because they are the usual terms for describing the behavior. Their inaccuracy in describing autistic children is much the same as their inaccuracy in describing normal adults. For example, manipulative behavior in adults is not necessarily conscious, planned, or an indicator of high social skills. On the contrary, it is usually unconscious and habitual, and may be conditioned in people of low intelligence. I have suggested ways in which such behavior may be conditioned in autistic children at various points. The idea that autistic children consider their situation and decide upon the role behavior that they will adopt is unlikely; rather, their complex role behavior probably is conditioned gradually in infancy by a series of experiences.

15 Additional Pieces: Eating, Sleeping, Sensory Anomalies, Self-Stimulation, Sexuality, Seizures

Some of the many symptoms or phenomena associated with autism that were left aside during the main presentation are explored in this chapter. The symptoms are a miscellany, ranging from obvious, typical behavior (food refusal and selective eating) to behavior hypothesized to be common in autistic children but not yet verified (self-induced seizures). They were chosen because it is possible to explain them and because the explanations may have broad implications for autism.

Most of the topics discussed in this chapter have not been addressed by current theories of autism. The kinds of theories developed recently that posit defects of sensation, cognition, association, memory, and communication do not cover behavior such as sleep disturbances and exhibitionism. These behaviors are also not accounted for in older theories of parental neglect, rejection, "refrigeration," or hatred of the children.

Alimentary Disturbances

The first crisis in rearing many children, and particularly autistic children, occurs in feeding. Common manifestations are difficulty in feeding, food refusal (and later selective eating), vomiting, diarrhea, colic, and celiac. Each of them has been taken as a sign of organic defect. For example, neonatal difficulty in feeding has been associated with mental retardation due to congenital disease. However, the association occurs only in the neonatal period; later, the difficulty subsides in organically retarded infants. Persistent difficulty in feeding and the other manifestations are regarded by clinicians as signs of disturbance in the infant-caretaker relationship.[1] The presumption of psychological causes in alimentary disturbances is stronger than in other disturbances of infancy.

The primacy of feeding crises is probably attributable to the combined sensitivities of infants and mothers. As noted, neonates depend on repetition of familiar experiences. Many seem particularly sensitive to changes of food and feeding methods and react by food refusal. Older infants whose attachment has developed react to separation and to a variety of changes in their mothers' behavior by food refusal. After reunion, they may accept other kinds of care from their mothers but refuse to be fed. Separation and loss cause depression, which often reduces appetite. Infants show more than disinterest, however. Many vigorously refuse food from substitute caretakers when separated and, after reunion, refuse it from their mothers while they accept it from others.

The responsiveness of the alimentary system and its probable special sensitivity to feeding changes is matched by mothers' sensitivity to the effects of their feeding. Long identified primarily as feeders, mothers tended to see their worth reflected in their children's acceptance of their food and in weight gain. During the middle of the century, when scientific diet was advocated and babies were weighed daily, mothers' concerns about their success as feeders became extreme, and they reacted strongly to their infants' alimentary behavior. Presumably, their reactions provided rewards and punishments to their infants.

Gastrointestinal upset is a common reaction of children and adults to a variety of stresses. The alimentary system not only responds to alimentary stimuli but also functions as part of a person's general adaptive repertory. The system is equipped at birth for varied behavior, and its sensitivity to events gives it a focal position in early interaction. Its functions can be influenced extensively and can have a powerful influence on mothers.

In many homes, a feeding crisis begins in the week after mothers return from the maternity ward and take over care of their infants. The weight loss that is normal in the first week alarms many mothers and rivets their attention to feeding. Moderate encouragement to eat usually has the desired effect on neonates of increasing their intake, but coercion to eat commonly has the opposite effect—food refusal and, thus, failure to thrive. Food refusal in humans and animals is associated with negativism; it is to be expected in circumstances that foster negativism.

Selective eating, a later development, may be accounted for partially by negativism. In addition, many of the food choices of autistic children—milk (particularly from a bottle), mashed and chopped foods—suggest regression and may be a reaction to stress. Perhaps the food selectivity of autistic children is regressive attachment behavior with the function of eliciting the care given young infants.

In short, many of the circumstances described in earlier chapters that cause exaggerated concern with predictability, disturbed attachment, and negativism would foster eating disturbances specifically. Almost all children get over alimentary disturbances in time as their relationships with their caretakers improve or their conflicts are transferred to other functions. In some, food refusal and selective eating recur in adolescence or early adulthood. Anorexic adolescents and autistic children have many similarities of behavior and experience.[2]

Sleep Disturbances

Sleep disturbances common in autistic children—difficulty in falling asleep, waking in terror, and long periods of wakefulness—are also taken by clinicians to be psychogenic. The concern aroused in parents is heightened when wakefulness is accompanied by head banging or crib rocking. But even without the violence, sleep disturbances tend to elicit care giving. The parents participate in lengthy bedtime rituals or sit up with the children and hold them. Thus, the children's nocturnal activities have proximity-seeking and maintaining effects and may be attachment behavior.

Nonautistic children have similar sleeping disturbances with the same effects on their parents. Waking up screaming is not rare, and milder disturbances are so common that they have been considered typical at a year and a half or two. Nonetheless, their cause and function are psychologically meaningful, and they may be followed by disturbance severe enough to be classified as psychosis or retardation. According to Fraiberg, one of the main causes of sleeping disturbances is stressful training. This is consistent with the sleeping disturbances found in animals after stressful training. The other main cause is separation, with sleeping disturbances beginning then or after reunion.[3] The latter finding supports the idea that sleeping disturbances are attachment behavior and are specific to the relationship with the attachment figure. A connection between separation and sleeping disturbances has long been inferred by clinicians who suggested that going to bed is experienced by children as symbolic or actual separation. Therefore, children with disturbed attachments are likely to be particularly upset when going to bed.

Peculiar Sensory Function

Autistic children use their senses in strange ways. Their failure to respond to stimuli perceptible to others has been attributed to subnormal or supernormal acuities; and their perception of stimuli imperceptible to others has been attributed to supernormal acuity. Defects in receiving or assimilating information were hypothesized by writers who considered the incompetence of the children to be innate and basic to autism. In contrast, autism has been explained on the basis of supernormal acuity.[4]

Many workers believed the children had abnormal acuities on the basis of parental reports, behavior when examined, audiometric tests, and a famous report on acuities that was widely misconstrued. For some years, the article by Bergman and Escalona was cited as a basic source in the literature on autism. It was considered hard data, obtained by objective measurements of sensory acuities, but the authors had not measured sensory function. They had relied on parents' impressions and their own observations.[5]

Through the years, increasingly sophisticated audiometry has shown normal hearing acuity in autistic children, and other sensory defects attributed to them have not been confirmed. Most of the children evidently have normal acuities. Their apparent subnormal and supernormal acuities have been interpreted here as consequences of selective attention and selective response.

The children's reliance on peripheral vision over focal vision has hardly been addressed. Perhaps it reflects their surreptitious observation of people and general vigilance.

Their limited use of hearing and vision and overuse of touch, smell, and taste have been addressed by a number of hypotheses. One is that the children use proximal (near) senses rather than distant ones because of some innate or acquired cause. However, the separation of their senses on this basis is inaccurate. While the underused senses of hearing and vision are distant, another underused sense—pain—is proximal. Similarly, the overused senses of touch and taste are proximal, but the other overused sense—smell—is classified as a mixed or distant sense. Thus, division of the senses into proximal and distant does not correspond to the children's selective use.

Another hypothesis is that autistic children use primitive senses rather than mature ones. Such preference has been attributed to an innate, animal-like quality and to regression to infantile behavior. Again, the division is inaccurate. It is true that young infants rely on touch and taste, but evidence that they use smell is lacking. On the contrary, young infants seem oblivious to most odors.[6] In addition, the idea that young infants do not use hearing and vision has been disproven; these senses are active in the first days of life and hearing plays a major role in neonatal adjustment. Therefore, the division into primitive or regressive versus mature senses does not reflect actual development in the use of senses.

Earlier, I suggested that hearing and vision are underused because they are the main senses by which parents get infants' attention and give formal training. Resistance to training and to responding generally, therefore, involves these senses. Similarly, resistance to training may involve nonresponse to pain.

Another hypothesis is that parental use of difficult or inconsistent cues fosters selective use of senses. Let us assume that the most problematic cues for autistic children are those used in directing, instructing, and training them—hearing and vision. Let us assume further that parents give unintended cues that are simpler or more reliable. Stressful training fosters attention to trainer cues—to unintended behavior that reveals attitudes, expectations, or hidden information. In the circumstances, children may learn to rely on cues such as their parents' perspiration, skin temperature, muscle tension and tiny involuntary movements, pulse, and respiration rate—cues perceived by smelling, touching, and mouthing people. This hypothesis is consistent with an observation that retarded children, known to rely on trainer cues, have similar sensory preferences.[7]

The Sensual Child

The isolation of autistic children is augmented by their highly repetitive activities. When spinning objects or rocking, they are less responsive than usual and may seem to be self-absorbed, hypnotized, or actively shutting out the world. Some of the activities seem pleasurable (swaying, rubbing, stroking); others are painful and destructive (head banging, hair pulling). But either kind may result in dreaminess or excitement, sometimes mounting to a peak and followed by relaxation.

The activities have most often been called *self-stimulation*, sometimes in a purely descriptive sense (they provide stimulation to the children) and sometimes in an erotic sense. Some of the activities are rhythmic. Others are neither rhythmic nor accompanied by overt excitement. Nonetheless, they have been classified as autoerotic on theoretical grounds. Observers have inferred that they are done because of the sensations they arouse, even when the children do not show signs of being stimulated. But the word *autoerotic* has been used also as if it did not necessarily mean sexual. A few writers have described the activities as explicitly sexual but have given them only passing mention. Probably, the activities vary in function and not all functions need to be found in every autistic children.

Rocking and head banging begin during infancy, usually at about six months. They also occur in a substantial minority of nonautistic children and have been studied more than other self-stimulating activities. Rocking is usually done on a flat surface but is done also on the mother's body. The infant rocks forward and back on hands and knees for minutes or hours at a time. Similarity of the movement to infantile pelvic thrusting identified as sexual raises the possibility that rocking is part of an innate sexual repertory. Sexual arousal while rocking has been observed.[8] After the first year, rocking may also be done sitting or standing, and some children use chairs for it.

Rocking need not trouble parents in itself, but it has troublesome effects. Parents become concerned that children who rock in bed get insufficient sleep. Vigorous rockers make their cribs and beds shake, bounce, and move across the floor. The noise is often upsetting to the family. In addition, rocking is the usual means by which children bang their heads. They position themselves so that each rocking cycle causes their heads to strike something hard—a crib board or a wall. The banging is essential, not incidental. If parents move children who bang away from crib sides or walls, the children move back. If parents line the hard surface with cushions, the children move them aside or find unpadded surfaces to strike. Head banging is sometimes done so hard that it raises concern about damage to the brain.[9] Head bangers who do not become autistic are, like autistic children, predominantly firstborn, boys (3.5 to 1), solemn, high strung, compulsive, especially sensitive to sound, and precociously talented in music.[10]

Although children rock and bang after they learn to speak, they have not explained their behavior. Interpretations depend on observers' impressions of the behavior and on correlating it with events that precede, accompany, and follow it. Rocking has been interpreted as a self-soothing activity. Infants are thought to do for themselves, in their caretakers' absence, what the caretakers have done for them.[11] In addition, by doing what their caretakers did, infants are thought to be symbolically restoring the absent caretakers. These ideas are consistent with observations that rocking occurs when caretakers are absent at times of distress. Rocking commonly occurs when children are put to bed, which many children find upsetting. Anxiety at such times has been interpreted as a reaction to separation.

These interpretations are based on the assumption that rocking is a pleasing, comforting, relaxing motion—at least when done gently. Vigorous rocking and rocking accompanied by head banging would not fit here. However, as noted earlier, gentle rocking may be arousing or exciting to some infants.

Vigorous rocking and banging often appear to be accompanied by rising tension. Parents sometimes get the impression that the activity is carried on as long as possible, until the child drops off to sleep from exhaustion. Another possibility is that the movements continue to satiation or to orgasm followed by relaxation. Still another possibility is that the movements are continued until the child is fully distracted from stressful inner or external stimulation (pain, anxiety, parental demands). In addition, rocking and banging probably induce alterations of consciousness.

During self-stimulation, children are less responsive to external stimuli and particularly to training. Insofar as they are also giving themselves pleasure and pain, self-stimulating children are relatively impervious to parental reward and punishment. They have in effect substituted themselves for their parents as suppliers of pleasure and pain. Ferster suggested that autistic children are unresponsive to people because much of their behavior is self-reinforced by erotic and other sensual effects of what they do. He concluded that, short of physical restraint, parents are not ordinarily in a position to gain control over the rewards and punishments experienced by the children.[12]

Additional meanings of self-stimulation are suggested by the situations that precipitate it. Normal children rock and bang when:

Depressed or grief stricken;

Frustrated;

Mastering a new skill;

Confined in a limited space;

Restricted as to movement;

Left alone for long periods;

Left, as by the caretaker's walking out of the room;

Put to bed;

Awakening;

Weaned abruptly;

Deprived of the mother or her attention at weaning.

Rocking and banging are also reported in infants when their mothers are angry.[13]

A number of these situations can be grouped as separation from mother. Waking may be related to separation insofar as a child then becomes aware of the mother's absence. Limitation of space and movement commonly occur when a child is put in a crib or playpen, which usually signals interruption of contact with its mother. In addition, the stronger the bond with the mother is and the more stimulation the mother gives, the more self-stimulation occurs during separation from her. And the mother's return often ends the self-stimulation.

Sex and Affection

The idea that the self-stimulating activities of autistic children are sexual goes against the prevailing image of them as sexless and affectionless. Because this image is well established, the meaning of their behavior will be discussed in detail. Rocking and other infantile activities seem to have a number of functions. Therefore, the discussion begins with behavior of older autistic children that is sexual on its face. By school age, many autistic children stimulate their genitals with their fingers, have orgasms, and engage in sexual play with other children and with adults, sometimes accompanied by explicit sexual talk. Many of the children also engage in behavior that ordinarily is classified as affectionate but that tends not be when done by autistic children. Specifically, they kiss and caress their parents. Some do it

more often, more intensely, and more openly than most children. When
noted, their sexual and affectionate behavior is usually explained away. One
writer noted that kissing their parents was common in autistic children but
said it showed unpredictability in their behavior rather than affection.[14] In
the following description, demonstrative behavior was used to illustrate the
opposite of affection: "he climbed up on her as if she were a chair; he rubbed
himself on her, stood on her lap, embraced her head, her arm, waist—not
affectionately but as if she were inanimate."[15] This boy also masturbated
openly and opposed his mother's plans to remarry.

The following vignette was used to typify parent-child interaction in
autism: "Tommy was under his mother's skirt. He had dropped his trousers
and was masturbating. In addition, he was poking at [her] genitals. She
stood frozen and unmoving with tears in her eyes. Pleadingly she asked the
psychologist, 'What shall I do?'"[16] The quotation is taken out of context. The
aspect of parent-child interaction that it was chosen by the authors to exemplify was maternal confusion and failure to give direction to children. The
authors did not discuss sexuality as an aspect of the children's behavior.

In one of the most extensive studies, autistic children were described as
follows:

> They are often embarrassingly direct in their curiosity about or attack on
> adults' breasts or genitalia. Most often after five or six years of age, they
> may show startling seductiveness in their body posturing, the sensuousness
> of their stroking touch, or, more rarely, their verbal requests or invitations
> for genital contact . . . .[17]

This report is not exceptional in referring to sexual behavior in autistic
children; it is exceptional in discussing the behavior.

Denial of sexuality in young children is not limited to those who are
autistic.[18] The historical denial of children's sexuality seems relevant in
understanding its denial and its meaning in autistic children. Of the ideas
Freud advanced at the turn of the century, none offended his medical colleagues as much as attribution of sexuality to infants, and he was ostracized
for it. At the same time that infant sexuality was vehemently denied, however, bizarre medical treatments were adopted to root it out—metal restrain-
ing devices, blistering of thighs and genitals, circumcision, cauterization or
surgical removal of the clitoris, and occasionally, full castration. These practices, commonly applied to infants, declined rapidly in the United States
during this century but were still found in the 1940s while the denial of infant
sexuality continued.[19] Not until the Kinsey report in 1948 were infant erections recognized to any extent. The report also described: "rhythmic body
movements with distinct penis throbs and pelvic thrusts, an obvious change
in sensory capacities, a final tension of muscles . . . . a sudden release with
convulsions."[20]

In the 1960s, such infant behavior was reported to involve mothers: "In a moment of apparent delight, the child clasps the mother, perhaps while lying relaxed upon her breast. Throwing his arms about her neck, nuzzling her chin, he begins rapid, rotatory pelvic thrusts." This report was not accepted, however. The author was dismayed to find that many clinicians regarded him as "daft" and tried "to persuade me gently that I have misinterpreted some innocent rhythmic play activity or some non-specific rocking or tension relieving behavior."[21]

For centuries, masturbation in children had been considered extremely evil and harmful. In 1855, an editorial in a medical journal in the United States concluded:

> In my opinion, neither the plague, nor war, nor smallpox, nor a crowd of similar evils, have resulted more disastrously for humanity than the habit of masturbation: it is the destroying element of civilized society.[22]

The psychological reason for the horror and prohibition of masturbation probably lies in its association with incest.[23] Masturbation is usually thought of as a solitary, asocial, and even antisocial act. As such, it fits with the image of autistic children. But psychoanalysis has shown that people's masturbatory guilt is rooted in incest fantasies. In addition, masturbation in young children is often exhibitionistic, directed at adults.[24] The effects on adults are often dramatic. All parents have been said to be revolted by their children's masturbation.[25] While the statement is exaggerated, intense emotions are aroused in many parents at the sight. One of the emotions is guilt, as shown by parents' insistence in past generations that their children learned to masturbate outside the home.

Parents' efforts to prevent masturbation and to promote cleanliness were joined in the idea that masturbation was caused by dirty genitals. A common remedy—thorough washing of children's genitals—complicated the situation insofar as the washing stimulated the children.

Of the sexual activities reported in autistic children, masturbation is by far the most frequent. If all the behavior called autoerotic is included as masturbation, then masturbation occupies much of the children's time. Kanner concluded that their rhythmic self-stimulation was masturbation because of the children's appearance when engaged in it:

> These actions and the accompanying ecstatic fervor strongly indicate the presence of *masturbatory orgastic gratification*.[26]

Masturbation has been considered a diagnostic feature of autism.[27] The most distinctive thing about autistic children's masturbation is that it is often done in front of others and sometimes is clearly directed at particular people. It is more frankly exhibitionistic than in other children.[28]

In elaborating a sensitive topic, it would be well to have a firm base and to be able to proceed from it in a convincing way. Unfortunately, the base is limited. There is little information about why autistic children engage in so much sexual activity and about whether or not parental interest in the children is expressed in sensually stimulating ways. A few indications of connections have been published.[29] But taboos that are still powerful make it unlikely that much more relevant data will be obtained in the near future. Therefore, the gap between the parents' interest and the children's sexuality can be bridged only by generalizing from the few cases that provide intimate data. The context in which the limited parent-child data may be interpreted is the marriage into which the children are born.

The marriage described by Dibs' mother was one of mutual respect and admiration with minimal sensual gratification. Kanner and other writers similarly described cool, distant marriages in cases of autism. If the picture is correct, most parents of autistic children obtained little sensual gratification in marriage. Many were profoundly disappointed and some went for years without intercourse with their spouses.[30] Lacks of this sort are common enough, but in most such marriages, at least one partner seeks gratification outside marriage, and divorces are frequent. A distinctive feature of the marriages of these parents is the rarity of affairs or divorces—much less than in the general population. The parents seem not to have sought sensual gratification with other adults.

The possibility that the parents' affectionate, erotic interests along with their ambitious hopes became focused in their autistic children will be considered next. If it is true, it does not mean that the parents intended to encourage sensual behavior in their children. Some did so half consciously, as Elizabeth's father did in playing with her in ways that he knew excited her (chapter 2). Most did not intend it. The protests of the woman described earlier whose son masturbated under her skirt are not in question. One mother bathed with her son regularly until he was three, but stopped when she noticed that he was having erections in the tub.[31] Another gave her son a book of nudes in suggestive poses, believing that he was incapable of grasping their sexual meaning. Another invited her son to look at and touch her breasts and vulva, intending to further his sexual education. A father lay on his bed regularly with his daughter on top of him, face to face, clasping her tightly to his body so that she could not move, while the mother inserted an enema syringe into the girl. And many of the parents took their autistic children to bed with them. Sometimes the reason was that the children were frightened in the night. Sometimes it was that the parents were lonely while their spouses were away. The parents' reasons make no difference here. It is a fair presumption that these experiences were erotically stimulating to the children. Parents who are devoted to their children and engage in such activities tend to have children who masturbate frequently.[32]

I know of only two cases in which parents expressed gratification in the sexual behavior of their autistic children. A father who came to me spoke admiringly of his six-year-old daughter's sexual power—her ability to masturbate up to fifty times a day. A mother boasted about her favorite son, the one who was autistic, "He can touch my breasts, do things to me like a man, but then he soils himself like a baby."[33] More common parental reactions are confusion, shock, and paralysis. Still more common is the absence of a clear reaction; many parents seem not to notice the children's sexual behavior.

Some parents complain about their children's sexuality and unintentionally reveal fantasies thereby. To illustrate, a mother complained that when she dressed or undressed, her autistic seven-year-old son would seize her breasts and squeeze them. She lived alone with her only child. There had been no men in her life since she was widowed in her son's infancy. Nonetheless, she regularly wore attractive clothes that drew particular attention to her breasts and was seductive in other ways without being aware of it.[34] Her unconscious fantasy was suggested by her reaction to her son's touching her breasts. When that happened, he seemed very large and powerful and she felt paralyzed and unable to move until he stopped. The awe of him that she expressed verged on boasting.

The inference that many of the parents stimulate their autistic children erotically leaves the question of how it is done. Instances like those cited are found only in a minority of cases and usually involve older autistic children. But the hypersexuality of autistic chldren appears in infancy, a time when sexual data are hard to obtain. Stimulation of infants that is clearly erotic from a parent's viewpoint is rare. However, many acts that are not intended to be erotic may be experienced sexually by infants. For an infant, touching of genitals may be much the same whether a parent is expressing affection or cleansing the area. Erotic experiences occur incidentally to a number of activities with nonsexual purposes—bathing, diapering, dresssing, feeding, spanking, and giving enemas. In view of the taboo on conscious genital stimulation, nonsexual activities may be the main ones that determine the erotic experiences of infants. In addition, insofar as they have nonsexual purposes, such activities lend themselves to conscious and unconscious expression of affection toward infants.

Spanking has received particular attention from clinicians as an activity in which punishment and affection often blend together in a child's experience, particularly in slapping of buttocks. In addition, parents often give affectionate pats and gentle slaps on the buttocks while diapering or dressing infants.[35]

Enemas have long been considered erotic and frightening to young children. Frequent enemas were reported in many cases of autism.[36]

Among daily activities that have erotic possibilities, bathing may be particularly relevant here. Compulsive parents tend to wash their infants' genitals the most, to continue the practice as the children grow older, and to be particularly horrified when the children became sexually aroused by it.[37] Compulsive mothers who are self-conscious about cleaning infants' genitals but who are determined to do it tend to scrub vigorously. Their manner may show that the activity is serious and devoid of pleasure. Nonetheless, vigorous scrubbing of genitals often means more erotic stimulation rather than less.

Erotic stimulation of children also may occur in activities considered affectionate and nonerotically sensual. For example, some parents spend much time touching their autistic children while grooming them—smoothing their clothes, brushing their hair.[38] The fact that many parents consider their autistic children extraordinarily beautiful suggests infatuation, with much looking and admiring. One study of mothers filmed together with their autistic children in infancy showed a great amount of sensual stimulation—holding infants for long periods, holding them tightly, rubbing or stroking them hard, nibbling them, and most of all, grooming them.[39]

The emphasis here on sensual and erotic stimulation of autistic children may lend itself to misconstruction. Such stimulation goes against cultural values and has been criticized sharply by psychological theorists from the time of Freud and Watson to the present as harmful to children. Therefore, it may be worth emphasizing that there is no competent evidence that such behavior in itself is harmful to children. Erotic attachment to one's children is normal; the absense of sensual, erotic elements in a mother's love of her baby would be abnormal.[40]

Erotic stimulation can cause problems if coupled with other events. If one arouses a child and then punishes the child for being aroused, disturbance is likely. Thereafter, arousal without punishment may be stressful to the child. Or if arousal of the child is accompanied by an expectation that the child fulfill the parent, taxing the child beyond his or her level, disturbance is likely. Studies of children whose symptoms were primarily sexual showed that the symptoms reflected parental fantasies, and a common thread was parental seductiveness followed by frustration of the children. Open masturbation by children was particularly common when there was serious but not necessarily obvious discord between the parents.[41]

A parent who stimulates a child without being aware of it is likely to be shocked by the child's arousal and to punish the child. However, awareness by the parent of erotic aspects of the relationship does not ensure consistent treatment of the child, as in the following example.[42].

A mother of an autistic boy had concluded long before his birth that no one cared for her and that she would not care for anyone. Her attitude toward her husband was contemptuous. But when her son was born, she gave up her resolution, staying up with him at night, clutching him tightly to her. They remained inseparable as he grew older. She excluded her husband from her life more than before, and the boy slept in her bed. Consciousness of her arousal did not deter her, but when her son's arousal became evident in his open masturbation, she became very upset and sent him to boarding school.

As this case shows, parents may find behavior that they have fostered intolerable, even when it meets strong needs of theirs. Erotic gratification can be an element of a parent-child relationship that makes for extreme closeness, but frankly erotic behavior in a child usually leads to abrupt withdrawal by the parent.

Age and the manner in which eroticism is expressed determine parental reactions to it. Jackson noted that many mothers coolly permit masturbation in infants but are upset by it when the children are two or more. He inferred that mothers think infants are merely enjoying physical sensations but that older boys are having sexual fantasies involving the mothers while masturbating. If so, the mothers may be right. Masturbating infants usually appear self-absorbed, but two-year-olds may accompany their masturbation by affectionate and erotic gestures toward their parents.[43] The indication in the gestures that the masturbation involves or is directed toward the parents is likely to alarm them.

In summary, the sexuality of autistic children has been particularly difficult for parents and clinicians to deal with and for writers to discuss. The children's extraordinary sexuality is probably a result of extraordinary closeness to a parent. Sexuality intensifies the relationship for both but makes it difficult to sustain.

Altered Consciousness and Self-Induced Seizures

The word paroxysm has been used occasionally in the literature of autism to describe a peak of sensual excitement, sometimes accompanied by quivering. The same word had been used much earlier to refer to excitement caused by disease, particularly in epilepsy. Epilepsy has a peculiar history in that it has been called the *Divine Disease*, associated with eroticism and genius, and treated by clitoridectomy and castration.[44] Reasons for the association are obscure.

The rhythmic self-stimulating activities of autistic children are known to be hypnotic, to alter consciousness, and to induce seizures in nonautistic people.[45] *Altered consciousness* may be defined as consciousness that is not usual and that affects most or all of a person's perceptions and reactions. Altered states differ; of particular concern here are those alterations classified as trances and seizures (including the initial aura). A *seizure* is an alteration of consciousness accompanied by epileptiform brain waves. The term *seizure* is sometimes used to refer to its most violent form—convulsions followed by unconsciousness. But the extent of an alteration of consciousness, as experienced by the subject or observed by another, is not a criterion of whether the alteration is a seizure. The mildest form, called an *absence*, may last only a second and pass unnoticed by observers and by the person who has the seizure. Most seizures fall between the extremes and are marked by:

Bizarre movements, including posturing and limb flapping;

Muteness;

Unresponsiveness;

Apparent deafness and blindness;

Insensitivity to pain;

Obliviousness to surroundings;

Unfocused gaze, gaze aversion, and staring.

These behaviors are, of course, typical of autistic chldren. In addition, while engaging in activities known to induce seizures, autistic children appear excited and sometimes ecstatic or dreamy. Meltzer concluded that autism is induced stupor.[46]

Activities that produce flickering light are particularly effective in causing seizures. Autistic children frequently engage in such activities. They seem particularly susceptible to flicker; and flicker is rewarding to them, more so than to nonautistic children.[47] Therefore, it seems likely that autistic children have seizures that do not come to physicians' attention, that are not verified by electroencephalographic recordings, and that therefore go unreported. If so, knowledge about seizures and their induction should bear on autism.

Activities that induce seizures also cause dizziness, and many people find dizziness unpleasant. In addition, the idea of seizures, particularly in the form of convulsions, is negative. Therefore, it may be surprising to many people that others would voluntarily induce them. But according to Focher, dizziness—at least in the aspect of giddiness—is pleasurable to most people and accounts for enjoyment in rocking, swinging, dancing, and amusement-park rides. Focher suggested that pleasure in seizures, especially in the early phase, is related to the dizziness that accompanies them. Sexual fantasies and orgastic feelings have been reported during seizures. Dostoyevsky, an epileptic, wrote that "seizures created happiness that defied description and was worth the rest of one's life"[48]

Common activities of autistic children known or believed to alter consciousness and to induce seizures include:

Rocking, rolling, and swaying;

Staring at the sun or bright lights;[49]

Watching television;

Staring at unmoving objects;

Staring beyond objects (defocusing);

Rubbing and scratching oneself and objects, particularly corrugated or textured surfaces;

Biting oneself, pulling one's hair, or any act that produces steady or pulsating pain;

Starving oneself;

Concentrating on one's body functions;

Obsessive thinking;

Doing mental arithmetic and memory tricks;

Listening to music;

Dancing and whirling;

Flapping one's limbs;

Hyperventilating.

Most lights in the United States flicker at sixty cycles per second. Television screens also flicker, and channel switching and detuning increase the inductive effect. Reading and scanning printed matter also cause flicker. In addition, a steady light source can be made to flicker by eye movements or blinking.[50]

Rocking and other movements are indirectly hypnotic. If done with open eyes and fixed gaze, they have the effect of making objects around one flicker. Even with eyes closed, flickering light gets through the lids.[51] In addition, rocking stimulates the vestibular function of the ear, causing dizziness and other sensations and alterations of consciousness.

Adults who do what autistic children do experience altered consciousness. One mother imitated her autistic child in an attempt to understand and reach him. Staring at fluorescent lights made her eyes defocus. Rocking gave her a "fogged" feeling. "She began to enter his world in a way she found beautiful and enriching. In these movements and their repetition, there was a hypnotic calm that would come over her."[52]

Of the kinds of stimulation that alter consciousness, flicker has been studied the most. It is also the most powerful in producing violent seizures. Prolonged flicker is not necessary. Seizures can result from a single burst of light, as by drawing back curtains in a dark room, switching on a light, or opening one's eyes in bright light. They can also result from entering a dark room, switching off a light, or closing one's eyes.[53]

Autistic children seem particularly adept in finding or creating flicker. Among the spinning objects they stare at are wheels and records, and some of them become skilled in making dishes and other unlikely objects spin. Many carry with them a small object attached to a string (as hypnotists used to) and take it out from time to time and set it spinning or swinging. Probably the most common activity of autistic children that causes flicker is wiggling their fingers or waving their hands near their eyes. They also scan corrugated, striped, or checkered surfaces; switch lights on and off; and look at moving water and other glistening objects.

Ancient Greeks and Romans knew that flicker brought on seizures, and they used a spinning potter's wheel in sunlight to diagnose epilepsy. Similarly, clinicians have tested children for autism by having them look at a spinning top. The clinicians did not specify that the resultant behavior in autistic children—posturing, hand flapping, and twirling—were seizures.[54]

People have different susceptibilities, but seizures can be induced in all by sufficiently intense, prolonged stimulation. Moderate flicker induces altered consciousness in most or all people.[55] The intensity of the subjective experience and the magnitude of the electroretinographic and electroencephalographic reactions depend upon whether people try mentally to augment or to inhibit the experience. The full range of seizures can be self-induced.

Children are more sensitive to flicker than adults, and almost all people found to self-induce seizures are children. Little is known about them. The scant literature presents general observations, largely about the techniques used and the effects induced. Psychological data are lacking except that a substantial number of these chldren are retarded.[56] The following is the only psychological case history I found.[57]

Ned, a ten-year-old only child, had been self-inducing seizures since he was five. He was withdrawn but rather demanding of his mother and was found to be very immature but not psychotic. His main technique was looking at or through a window screen, and sometimes he used a checkered or striped pattern found in clothes or a tablecloth. His seizures usually consisted of periods of one to forty-five minutes of staring through a window screen while his arms and head shook. Occasionally, he induced complex movements (psychomotor seizures) and, rarely, convulsions. His electro-encephalogram was typical of epileptic children.

At first he denied sexual arousal or fantasies, but in psychotherapy he told about being preoccupied with sex and that when aroused he went to a screen and induced a seizure, during which he had elaborate erotic visions.

His mother was compulsive and perfectionistic, considered her husband inadequate, and had little involvement with people other than Ned. With Ned, she was overindulgent and intimate, continuing to be involved in his bathing, undressing in front of him, and sleeping with him when her husband was away on trips.

When Ned was five, her frustration with her husband came to a peak, as did the inconsistency of her behavior toward the boy. At this time, particularly upset at one of her husband's departures, she directed her anger and her needs for security and gratification at Ned more than ever. The boy then began to induce seizures.

Self-inducing nonautistic children resemble autistic children in various ways. Even when not self-inducing, some are mute and generally unresponsive. During seizures, some are not responsive to ordinary speech but respond when spoken to sharply.[58]

Clinicians have inferred that autistic children's self-stimulation causes altered consciousness. Specific self-induction of seizures has not been reported in autistic children to my knowledge, but some cases are suggestive of it. For example, Jimmy, a first child, was described by his mother as normal until he was two—responsive, friendly, talkative. Then his mother left to have a second child. On her return, Jimmy confused her with the woman who had cared for him during her absence. His speech diminished, and by three he had stopped talking. Meanwhile, he became preoccupied with waving his hand or a toy in front of his eyes, apparently interested in the flicker effect and enjoying the sensation it produced.[59]

Children are self-conscious and evasive about inducing seizures in themselves, much as they are about masturbation. When questioned, most deny they do it and show guilt. Many who derive obvious pleasure deny the pleasure. When caught inducing, they say they cannot help themselves. Some claim to dread the seizures and may well do so, as they dread masturbation. Children and parents fear that seizures cause mental retardation. Nonetheless, and despite threats and punishment for doing it, children continue to self-induce.

Besides providing gratification, self-induction has interpersonal functions. Control of parental behavior by the threat or use of seizures and avoidance of parental demands seem the most common.[60]

The extent to which autistic chldren have epileptiform brain waves remains to be determined. Electroencephalograms have been given to many of them as part of routine neurological examinations, and abnormal patterns were found only in a minority—not enough to characterize the group as having epileptic tendencies. Presumably, the electroencephalograms were done during ordinary consciousness and sleep and not while the children were engaging in self-stimulation.

Full-blown seizures (psychomotor seizures and convulsions) do not appear to be more common in young autistic children than in normal children. As the children grow older, full-blown seizures do exceed the normal rate: estimates range from 12 percent to 42 percent of autistic children having seizures, compared to estimates of 1 percent to 11 percent in unselected children.[61]

In summary, much behavior of autistic children is construable as inducing altered consciousness or resulting from it. Altered consciousness can be self-induced in infancy. Therefore, the onset of self-induction in infancy may be an element in the unresponsiveness and isolation that are the mark of autism. Self-induction and sexual self-stimulation have some behaviors in common and may arise from similar conditions.

16 Retrospect and Prospect

I have presented many ideas here, from theories resting on extensive data to hypotheses with only isolated findings behind them. Autistic behaviors have been interpreted in a variety of ways. For example, rocking has been suggested as a means of alleviating internal distress, reducing external demand, producing sexual gratification, inducing seizures, and soliciting care. Although behaviors often have multiple functions, not all the hypotheses are likely to prove valid or even consistent with each other. Consistency and the development of a unitary explanation have not been the goals; rather, I have tried to include whatever seemed promising.

It is premature to choose among the hypotheses. Relevance to autism remains to be demonstrated for those based on inferred experiences in infancy. Whether the experiences occurred in enough cases to be significant is unknown because clinicians taking histories have not asked about them. Some were reported incidentally by clinicians and by parents writing about their autistic children. However, systematic inquiry is needed to verify the hypotheses. Another hindrance is that some of the experiences involve behavior so quick, subtle, or unexpected that it may be missed without special observation techniques or slow-motion analysis of filmed interaction. Nonetheless, from my impressions of the research on which they are based, some hypotheses seem particularly likely to hold up, and they may suggest future developments in the study of autism.

The Basis of Autistic Development

Attachment

The foundation for hypotheses about attachment and separation is strong. It consists of extensive observations and experiments done with various species in addition to humans. The concepts are reasonably well defined and measurable. the data have been gathered with care under a variety of conditions and cohere well. There seems to be little question that autistic children form disturbed attachments in infancy and have severe separation reactions. There also are substantial indications of experiences in their early infancies that are likely to foster disturbed attachment. Attachment theory is likely to hold up, and its relevance to autism seems likely to be confirmed.

Conditioning

Similarly, research on reinforcement schedules and contingencies is extensive and involves a variety of species and well-defined, measurable concepts. Study of experimentally induced disturbance is fairly extensive, but some of it is not clearly defined, leaving important questions. The relevance of conditioning and induced disturbance to autistic children is unclear. Some reports indicate much noncontingent reinforcement in their experience. However, the occurrence of intermittent and delayed reinforcement, nonoccurrence of expected reinforcement, difficult or shifting cues, and coerced responding is largely inferred.

Compulsivity

The psychology of ritual and other compulsive behavior is fairly well worked out. The idea that the cause is premature or stressful toilet training seems too restrictive. Toilet training evidently was involved for many autistic children, but premature, stressful speech training probably was involved in most cases.

Study of basic compulsivity—of neonatal observation of sequences of events, gratification in predictability, distress at deviations, and elaboration of behavior that increases predictability—is new. The need for predictability in neonates seems likely to prove valid because it fits with a variety of findings. If valid, the need for predictability may prove to be a primitive mechanism that underlies different behaviors: neonatal distress caused by change of caretaker or of caretaking routines, attachment and separation phenomena, learning difficulties and the development of maladaptive learning sets, compulsive character and symptoms, and depression and psychosis. If valid, basic compulsivity should be at the core of autism.

Gentling

Human and some animal infants seem to require much early handling, holding, and body-to-body contact for normal development. Beyond this generalization, major questions remain. The young of some species are averse to such stimulation at first, but continued stimulation results in adaptation with many benefits. This finding seems particularly relevant to autistic children. Whether or not similar aversion is common in human neonates is unknown. Mothers receive contrary advice about handling resistive neonates, and research in this area is needed badly. Whether or not such aversion is innate in autistic children, it is common in their infancy and may be overcome by insistent or coercive contact.

Explanatory ideas have been taken from diverse fields. Their integration into a unified theory of autism may require a conceptual breakthrough to reconcile different kinds of theories. Meanwhile, the ideas may be linked in an approximate developmental sequence.

The Development of Autism

Although infant attachment develops after a few months, its course is influenced by events as early as the first days of life. Maternal attachment is present at birth or soon after, with sensitivity to what appear to be rebuffs by a neonate. Consequently, mothers' distress at the unresponsiveness of neonates who are depressed from residual effects of obstetric drugs or overexcited or inactive because of stress may persist, causing tentativeness toward the infants and limited response to them. Limited, awkward, or distant handling of neonates will foster aversion to being held. In turn, mothers will react negatively to infants' aversion. Thus, by the time infants are mature enough to develop attachment, their development may be hindered by reactions conditioned in themselves and in their mothers.

At any age, erratic or unpredictable experience will have adverse effects on infants, and their reaction will depend on their maturity and history. In the neonatal period, their chief reactions may be crying, diffuse inhibition, food refusal, and gastrointestinal disturbance. When older, their reactions will include other refusal or resistance, ritual, and the elaboration of highly controlling techniques for interacting with the environment. If reactions to unpredictability develop before or during the growth of infant attachment, they will hinder its course. The reactions may also affect caretakers adversely.

By the middle of the first year, such effects may result in aversion to contact with caretakers, long periods of diffuse inhibition, specific negativism in a number of functions, serious feeding difficulties, and disturbed attachment. At this time, many parents of autistic children, in response to some of this behavior or for other reasons, leave the infants alone much of the time they are awake. Being left alone further limits the growth of attachment, limits interchanges that are precursors to language development and other social behavior, limits experience and learning generally, and fosters solitary activities. The self-stimulation of some of the activities alters consciousness, further reducing infant responsiveness.

In the second half-year, disturbed attachment and limited experience cause learning handicaps, intolerance of change, and specific fears. Thus, infants are poorly prepared for the rigorous training that begins then or in the second year. Ordinary training may prove highly stressful to them, arousing massive resistance, ritual, token responding, and fixity of behavior. Attainments in verbal and other skills may be erratic and tenuous insofar as resistive tendencies remain high, with limited perseverance and flexibility in handling stressful tasks. Failure will lead to substitution of less-mature skills in place of those called for and to perseveration of unsuccessful behavior. Rituals and other compulsive behavior will increase. The combination of failure, unpredictability of experience, and fear of novelty will foster preoccupation with activities that increase predictability.

In addition, by the second year, disturbed attachment will cause extreme reactions to absences and separations. The persistence of these reactions as well as lack of progress or regression in speech and other skills soon will become seriously alarming to parents, if they have not already.

Such a sequence can lead to a clearly autistic pattern in the second year—a pervasive developmental handicap defined by the following:

Heightened attachment behavior, ineffectiveness of the attachment figure as a safe base for exploring novel stimuli, and heightened vulnerability to separation;

Preoccupation with activities that increase predictability of experience, including ritual and other compulsive behavior;

Conditioned helplessness with selective attention to cues, inefficient learning sets, and perseveration of unsuccessful behavior;

Diffuse inhibition and specific negativism, avoidance of training, and token responding;

Self-stimulation and periods of altered consciousness.

A number of indirect effects may be inferred. Each of these patterns limits learning, and in combination they make for retarded functioning. In addition, avoidance of training tends to involve the appearance of incompetence. Thus, children may take on the role as well as the intelligence of a retarded child. Finally, some of the patterns, combined with aversion to being held and avoidance of the trainer, give the global picture of isolation and unresponsiveness that are at the heart of the concept of autism.

These patterns should not be taken as a specific or typical sequence leading to autism; rather, they form a composite that contains more varied and concentrated autistic development than is found in most cases. While most of these patterns occur in autistic children, they do not usually occur in such a systematic progression. The combination of patterns leading to autism may be conceptualized as a railroad. One may get on a train at any point in infancy or the toddler period. If one does not get on by then, sufficient normal development may occur to preclude autism as a reaction to later stresses. Early in the trip, the train runs slowly with stops, and one may get off. But after a time, as the different branches merge into the main line, the train runs as an express. The branches represent different kinds of autistic development—negativism, disturbed attachment, and so forth. Thus, autistic development may begin at different ages and follow different pa'hs for a time. Later, the paths intertwine, leading to an outcome that is similar for children who started out in different ways.

This sequence may account for the development of autism entirely on the basis of psychological knowledge. If the average neonate had these experiences, autism would be the likely outcome. I do not mean to suggest that I have identified all causes here or that all causes of autism are psychological. Two qualifications are worth emphasizing. First, the psychological paths to autism described in this book are also physiological in that all behavior is behavior of organisms. Perception, memory, integration, and response are mediated by parts of organisms. Second, the beginnings of the paths may be physiological.

To illustrate, one infant developed an ear infection soon after birth that apparently caused him to cry much of the time and to respond poorly to being held and fed. The infection was undetected for some time; presumably, it caused pain and deafness. As the infection spread, he became critically ill and was hospitalized when a month old. During the hospitalization, his parents were not allowed to have contact with him. When he returned, he was alert and responsive to his parents. But he gradually became unresponsive and self-absorbed, and in his second year, he was fully autistic.[1]

The parents' description of his first year indicated no other unusual events except the father's awe of the boy since his birth. The father perceived him to be both defective and divine and was deeply involved with him. No data to connect the baby's illness and hospitalization to his subsequent autism were provided. The following inferences are based on what ordinarily happens in such circumstances.

During the first month, the infant's unresponsiveness was attributable to high arousal from pain. His attention to environmental stimuli was probably minimal, and he may have been unable to hear his parents' voices. Therefore, his opportunities to learn sequences and to familiarize himself with his caretaker (the mother) were minimal. In addition, crying and other behavior that can be conditioned as precursors of language were not rewarded. Then, in the hospital, he was cared for by rotating shifts of nurses, causing frequent and unpredictable changes in his care. Therefore, he was probably disturbed by the time of his reunion with his mother.

She had had a month with him during which he was generally unresponsive and her ministrations were ineffective. That alone is a severe stress. Then, she was separated from him and told he might die and, if he recovered, that he might be permanently deaf. In the circumstances, a typical reaction of mothers is to mourn the baby as dead, become detached, turn to other interests, and be unprepared to deal with the baby on reunion. (This mother had other demanding interests—notably her two daughters.) The customary apprehensions of mothers in the circumstances—of the baby returning as a stranger, of being unable to provide care—probably were exacerbated by this mother's experience of failure in caring for him before separation.

Whether or not these events occurred in this case is unknown. The parents did not report them. Nonetheless, for them not to have occurred would have been extraordinary. In the circumstances, an infant and mother would come to reunion and to the ensuing phase of developing infant attachment at a serious disadvantage. This infant appeared not to form an attachment.

Had the events described occurred when the infant was seven months old and developing normally, the result might have been the same, although by a somewhat different path. Having developed familiarity with his environment, predictability in his daily routine, and attachment to his mother, he would have experienced the weeks of pain, deafness, and his mother's failure to relieve him as a major change. Going to the hospital would have been another change combined with separation. On his return, his attachment would probably have been manifested in rejection of his mother. For his mother too, the ear infection would have been a change. Her formerly effective behavior toward her infant would no longer have worked. And she too would have been disturbed by the separation. At its end, expecting her healthy baby to return to her as he had been before the infection, she would have been shocked and confused by his not recognizing her, avoiding her, and seeming not to hear her. If she were unsuccessful in winning him over after reunion, aversive reactions might have persisted in both, together with regression in the baby.

If he were still older when the infection began, he could describe the experience and get immediate medical attention and relief. However, other stresses that are difficult for an infant to communicate or are not dealt with effectively can disrupt attachment and foster autism in older infants.

When an organic first cause is involved, the course of autistic development probably will still be psychological insofar as experiences critical in autism are tied to the interaction of infant and caretaker. In that respect, my view is similar to those of Wing and of DesLauriers and Carlson.[2] They hypothesized an organic first cause and a psychological course leading from it to autism. They saw organic defect influencing caretakers adversely so that they did not provide experiences necessary for normal development. If, despite the defect, the caretakers did provide the experiences, the children developed normally.

Such organic and psychological formulations lead to some of the same implications for the near future. Whichever first cause or causes prove true, study of the children's experience will still be essential to the understanding of their behavior and to the development of preventive and remedial programs.

The possible implications of this and other formulations of autism go far beyond the children diagnosed as autistic and their families. Many topics require study. As relevant knowledge grows, the classification system for disturbed children will be revised to reflect functional mechanisms. Then, I believe, autistic children will be grouped together with many children now diagnosed as compulsive, schizophrenic, retarded, and minimally brain damaged. A much larger fund of knowledge will be brought to bear in working out the meaning and causes of autistic behavior and in tracing variations of it, and what researchers learn will have preventive, therapeutic, and educational implications for a much larger group.

Endnotes

A few references have been omitted to avoid possible embarrassment to writers, including those who are parents of autistic children.

Introduction

1. Rimland (1964).
2. O'Gorman (1967, p. vii).
3. La Vietes (1972, p. 1413).
4. "A substantial minority of all severely retarded individuals have autism or a related condition" ("Childhood Autism" 1980, p. 761). See also Baker (1979); Benda (1954, 1959); Bender (1959a); Bergman, Waller, and Marchand (1951); Bernstein and Menolascino (1970); Chess (1970); Chess and Hassibi (1971); Cutts (1957); Delacato (1974); Eveloff (1960); Freeman et al. (1979); Garfield and Affleck (1960); Hutt and Gibby (1965); Le Vann (1950); Menolascino (1970b); Pollack (1958); Richards (1951); Robinson and Robinson (1965); Schain and Yannet (1960); Valente (1971); Webster (1963, 1970); Wortis (1958).
5. Phillips (1957, p. 118). "[T]he ever-increasing fragmentation of present-day treatment and research is tending to isolate all aspects of autism from each other—indeed, workers engaged in these different aspects generally have very little if any contact with those outside their own narrow sphere" (Shaberman 1971, p. iii).
6. Cohen (1973, p. 728).
7. Rochlin (1973, p. 218).
8. Newson and Newson (1963, p. 13).
9. For example, book-length cases cited later include two diagnosed as aphasic and one diagnosed by Kanner as retarded rather than autistic: Junker (1964); Kastein and Trace (1966); Murray (1967). The three children showed the features of autism and have become part of the literature of autism.
10. Lovaas and Newsom (1976). See also Kanner (1973b).
11. See chapter 1 and Szasz (1970).
12. Rimland (1964); see also Paluszny (1979).
13. An exception was Ferster (1966a, 1966b, 1968).
14. Deykin and MacMahon (1980).
15. Arieti (1974).

Chapter 1   The Child of God

1. Kanner (1954c, 1962); Menolascino (1970b).
2. Ritvo (1976).
3. "More than six hundred thousand of these lonely aliens have been institutionalized for life .... because they are frightening us" (Delacato 1974, p. 2). See also Menolascino (1970b); Sarason and Doris (1969); Wolfensberger (1969).

4. See Bettelheim (1967) on feral children, Wing (1972) on changelings, and Wing (1966) on extraterrestrial creatures.

5. Wing (1972, p. 6).

6. Erikson (1963, p. 169).

7. van Krevelen (1960, p. 99).

8. Bettelheim (1967, pp. 234–238). See also DesLauriers and Carlson (1969); Kaufman et al. (1959); Mahler and Elkisch (1953); Reiser (1963).

9. Delacato (1974, pp. vii–ix).

10. DesLauriers and Carlson (1969). Their title, "Your Child Is Asleep," and section headings are taken from the New Testament: Mark (5), Luke (8), and Matthew (9).

11. Becker (1974, p. 770). See also Hagamen (1980); La Vietes (1972).

12. Kanner (1941a, 1941b).

13. Bruch (1959).

14. Kanner (1948a, p. 725).

15. Kanner (1954d, p. 384).

16. Kanner (1949, 1954b, 1954d).

17. Kanner (1949, p. 420). See also Kanner and Lesser (1958). For the opposite finding, see Deykin and MacMahon (1980); Finegan and Quarrington (1979); Fish and Alpert (1962); Goodwin (1971).

18. Kanner (1952).

19. Statements made in 1968 (Kanner 1973a, pp. 139 and 138) and 1969 (quoted by Rimland 1972, p. 52).

20. Kanner (1973c).

21. The Talmud (in Kanner 1964, p. 6).

22. Kanner (1943).

23. Morgan (1981, p. 15).

24. King (1975, p. 674).

25. Wing (1966, pp. 38 and viii). See also Condon (1977); Ferster (1966b); Morgan (1981); Sarason and Doris (1969).

26. Rimland (1964). See also Moore and Shiek (1971); O'Gorman (1967); Tustin (1972).

27. Campbell (1956); Raglan (1949); Rank (1959); Victor (1973).

28. Harding (1971); Money-Kyrle (1965); Taylor (1970).

29. Harding (1971, p. 118); Delacato (1974). On fickleness, see Kanner (1949, 1954d); Rank (1955). On destroying, see Bettelheim (1967); Craig (1978); Kanner (1951).

Chapter 2   The Autistic Child

1. Ritvo (1976).

2. Taken from DesLauriers and Carlson (1969).

3. Kanner (1972, p. 707).

4. Despert (1965); Ornitz (1973, 1976); Ornitz and Ritvo (1968); Wing, O'Connor, and Lotter (1967); Ney (1979); Pearson (1947).

5. Bergman and Escalona (1949); Haka-Ikse (1974); Hefferman (1955); Hoberman and Goldfarb (1963).

6. Bettelheim and Sylvester (1949); Bradford and Carter (1974); Creak (1968); Clancy, Dugdale, and Rendle-Short (1969); Daneel (1974); Hefferman (1955); Reiser (1963); Rendle-Short (1967).

7. DesLauriers and Carlson (1969).

8. Park (1967, p. 21).

9. Kanner (1944).

10. Soddy (1964, p. 525).

11. Ibid.

12. Shaberman (1971, p. iv).

13. Szurek (1956); Brask (1959). To van Krevelen (1960, p. 102), "the most essential trait is the unexpected, the unpredictable in the child's behavior." To Kugelmass (1970, p. 3), "The study of the autistic child is like the pursuit of one's shadow. It moves each time you move, and changes shape from moment to moment."

14. Wing (1972).

15. For a detailed description of early development, see Bender and Freedman (1952); Ornitz and Ritvo (1968). Anthony (1958) presented a complex course. See also Sucharewa (1967).

16. But see Ross (1974).

17. Rimland (1968) suggested that the diagnosis is changed because the children's behavior changes "rather suddenly" when they are five and a half and is no longer autistic. See also Morgan (1981). However, most clinicians have not reported such a change.

18. "The basic nature of [autism] is so intimately related to the basic nature of childhood schizophrenia as to be indistinguishable from it. ... I do not believe that there is any likelihood that early infantile autism will at any future time have to be separated from the schizophrenias" (Kanner 1949, pp. 419–420). See also Kanner (1948a, 1954c); Havelkova (1968); Marsh (1977); Menolascino (1970a).

19. Bartel and Guskin (1971); Bogdan and Taylor (1976); Braginsky and Braginsky (1971); Clarke and Clarke (1975b); Dexter (1958, 1964); Garfield and Affleck (1960); Menolascino (1970b).

20. See note 4 in introduction. Chess (1970) suggested that retarded children who do not appear psychotic differ from psychotic children by their conformity and obedience.

21. NIMH (1973, p. 6).

22. Rimland (1964, p. 1).

23. Eisenberg (1966); DeMyer (1979); Kanner (1948b, 1949, 1954c, 1965); Menolascino and Eaton (1967).

24. Rendle-Short (1967); Wing (1972).

25. Spitz (1945, 1954); Spitz and Wolf (1946); and chapter 8.

26. Antonovic (1972) likened autism to depression.

27. Chess, Thomas, and Birch (1966).

28. Wenar (1963) reviewed studies of parental accuracy. See also Bowlby (1973); Chassell (1938); Garfinkel (1967); Goddard, Broder, and Wenar (1961); Haggard, Brekstad, and Skard (1960); Kitsuse (1968); Maccoby and Masters (1970); McCord and McCord (1961); Macfarlane (1935); McGraw and Molloy (1941); Manson (1964); Newton (1955); Pyles, Stolz, and Macfarlane (1935); Robbins (1963); Robertson (1962, 1965); Smith (1958); Thomas, Chess, and Birch (1968); Wenar, Handlon, and Garner (1962); Wolff and Chess (1965). On histories furnished by mothers of

schizophrenics, see Garmezy (1967); Johnson et al. (1956); Prout and White (1956).

29. On unresponsiveness, Churchill and Bryson (1972); Coffey and Umbarger (1967); Kaufman et al. (1959); King (1975); Massie (1975); Park (1967). On other inaccuracies, Boatman and Szurek (1960); Bullard et al. (1968); Call (1974); Despert (1965); Fabian (1954); Lewis and Van Ferney (1960); Moe, Waal, and Urdahl (1960); Ornitz and Ritvo (1976); Pavenstedt and Andersen (1952); Reiser (1963); Soddy (1964); Speers and Lansing (1965).

30. Lewis and Van Ferney (1960, p. 510).

31. Fabian (1954). See also Bettelheim (1967); Ferster (1968); Haggard, Brekstad, and Skard (1960); Rank (1949).

Chapter 3   A Retarded Genius

1. Axline (1964) presented the case without psychological or medical terms, without a list of symptoms or a diagnosis. Her behavior descriptions indicated autism, and the case became part of the literature of autism although some writers argued against its inclusion (e.g., Park 1976).

2. Axline, V.M., *Dibs: In Search of Self,* p. 21. Copyright © 1964 by Houghton Mifflin Company. Used by permission.

3. Ibid, p. 64.

4. Ibid, p. 64–65.

5. Ibid, p. 66.

6. Ibid, p. 67.

7. Such reactions are common according to Kaufman et al. (1959); Szurek and Berlin (1973). See also Kanner's (1952) observation that parents sabotage treatment.

8. Axline (1964, p. 137).

9. Balint (1965); Goshen-Gottstein (1966); Klein, Potter and Dyk (1950).

10. Axline (1964, p. 137).

11. Ibid, p. 140.

12. Ibid, p. 138.

13. Ibid, p. 139.

14. Copeland (1974); Kastein and Trace (1966); Kaufman (1976); Park (1967).

15. Kanner (1943).

16. Schreibman and Koegel (1975). See also Woodward, Siegal, and Eustis (1958).

Chapter 4   The Special Child

1. Park (1967, p. 12).

2. Ibid, pp. 3, 5, and 20.

3. Greenfeld (1972, p. 19).

4. Kastein and Trace (1966, pp. 22, 26).

5. Most published cases give little on parental backgrounds, and some give nothing. The information relevant here has not been inquired for routinely by clinicians and parents have not thought to volunteer it. With these limitations, published

case material bears on this chapter as follows. Group data consistent with the hypotheses are in Despert (1951); Lordi and Silverberg (1964); Speers and Lansing (1968). Single cases that fit or indicate some of the factors listed are in Axline (1967); Bettelheim (1967, case of Laurie); Bruch (1959); Call (1963a); Copeland (1974); Despert (1965); Foy (1970); Greenfeld (1972); Junker (1964); Kastein and Trace (1966); Kaufman (1976); Kotsopolous (1976); McDougall and Lebovici (1969); Murray (1967); Nagelberg, Spotnitz, and Feldman (1958, case no. 1); Park (1967); Pavenstedt (1955); Rochlin (1953); Ross (1955); Rothenberg (1977, case of Chaim); Sperling (1954); Susz and Marburg (1978). Cases with limited family data that suggest the presence of the factors are in Bergman (1971); Bosch (1970, case of Richard); Brazelton (1961); Brazelton, Young, and Bullowa (1971); de Souza (1960, case L); Despert (1952); Eickhoff (1952); Kanner (1948a, cases of Dennis, Catherine); Kris (1962); Langdell (1967); Mahler (1968, cases of Barry, George, Violet, Benny); Putnam, Rank, and Kaplan (1951); Sander (1964); Scheerer, Rothmann, and Goldstein (1945); Szurek (1956); Waal (1955). Cases with scant data that suggest the factors or that indicate a situation in which the factors would be likely are in Beach (1957); Beckett et al. (1956); Bender (1955); Berlin (1973a); Bettelheim (1955, case of Mary; 1967, cases of Joey, Marcia); Blank, Smith, and Bruch (1943); Blau (1962); Bosch (1970, cases of Hans, Dieter); Bradley (1942); Eberhardy (1967); Elkisch (1968, case of Kenneth); Elles (1962); Eveloff (1960); Fabian (1951); Fisher (1975); Frijling-Schreuder (1969, case of Alfie); Gajzago and Prior (1974); Gerard and Overstreet (1957); Gurevitz (1952); Harms (1952); Heuyer, Lebovici, and Roumajon (1955); Kanner (1943, cases of Don, Frederick; 1952); Kestenberg (1952); Knowlton (1954, 1955); Kupferman (1971); Langer (1952); Lewis and Van Ferney (1960); Little (1947); Lourens and Dorman (1972); Morrow and Loomis (1955); Moser (1967); Pavenstedt (1961, cases of Laureen, Nora); Pavenstedt and Andersen (1952); Putnam (1948); Rank and Kaplan (1951); Rochlin (1973); Shapiro, Huebner, and Campbell (1974); Slimp (1950); Speers and Lansing (1965); Sperling (1951, case of Paul; 1954); Sterba (1936); Stutte and Dauner (1971); Sylvester (1945); Thomas (1966, cases of Basil, Norma); Tustin (1972, case of John); Wilcox (1956).

6. Junker (1964). See also Foy (1970).

7. Murray (1967, p. 19).

8. Kaufman (1976, p. 118).

9. Ibid.

10. Autistic children's mothers are older than the average (Finegan and Quarrington 1979; Gillberg 1980).

11. Arajarvi, Alanen, and Viitamaki (1964); Beck and Nunnally (1965); Bettelheim (1967); Betz (1945); Boatman and Szurek (1960); Lordi and Silverberg (1964); Mandel et al. (1971); "Mothers-to-Be's Anxiety" (1977); Olin (1975); O'Moore (1972); Reiser (1963); Savage (1968); Speers and Lansing (1965, 1968). Baker (1967, p. 11) noted that a child conceived as a replacement for a lost child is usually the subject of inordinate expectations, particularly to "make up for all the suffering [the mother] had as a result of the loss of the first. This will almost certainly spoil the relationship from the beginning." The same would apply to a child conceived or perceived as a replacement for a lost parent or distant husband. Traditionally, women have been advised to have a baby to replace a miscarried fetus or a child who died young or to cement a shaky marriage. The advice may help women through a

difficult time, but having a baby in such circumstances puts a stress on the unfolding relationship, and the advice is likely to have undesirable long-range consequences.

12. Freud (1970). See also Lidz (1973); Weissman and Paykel (1972).

13. Arajarvi, Alanen, and Viitamaki (1964); Bettelheim (private communication 1971); DesLauriers and Carlson (1969); Despert (1951); Goldfarb et al. (1970); Kupferman (1971); Meltzer (1974); Rank (1955). On maternal depression causing autism, Ferster (1973); Goshen (1963); Miller (1974); Savage (1968); Senn and Solnit (1968); Starr (1954); Stone (1970); Tustin (1972).

14. Ruttenberg (1971, p. 165). See also Craig (1978).

15. Greenberg (1971, p. 410). See also Betz (1945).

16. Goldfarb et al. (1970).

17. Lidz (1968); Murphy (1973b).

18. Bart (1972, pp. 134, 140). See also Weissman and Paykel (1974).

19. On other causes of experiencing a child as special, see Baker (1967); Illingworth and Illingworth (1972); Sears, Maccoby, and Levin (1957).

20. Baker (1967); Barsch (1968); Ehlers (1966); Love (1973); Powdermaker (1953); Ryckman and Henderson (1965); Scott and Ashworth (1967); Sharlin and Polansky (1972); Sperling (1955); Staver (1953); Waterman (1948); Woodward, Jaffe, and Brown (1970); Woodward, Siegal, and Eustis (1958); Worchel and Worchel (1961).

21. La Barre (1972).

22. Michaels and Shucman (1962, p. 572).

23. Hunt (1967, p. 33).

24. Murray (1967, pp. 71 and 189).

25. Kaufman (1976, p. 118).

26. Knowlton and Burg (1955).

27. Rothenberg (1977, p. 111). See also Copeland (1974); Greenfeld (1978).

28. As an ancestor, Greenfeld (1972); Murray (1967). As a deity, Foy (1970); Kaufman (1976); Murray (1967).

29. On the parent as a missionary, Crawley (1971); Dewey (1971); Everard (1980); Foy (1970); Greenfeld (1978); Junker (1964); Kaufman (1981); Murray (1967); Park (1976). Some parents were identified as would-be prophets by Ackerley (1979). Tustin (1972) suggested that messianic fantasies were typical in the parents.

30. Copeland (1974). See also Kaufman (1976, 1981).

31. Kringlen (1967); Pollin et al. (1966); Pollin, Stabenau, and Tupin (1965); Stabenau and Pollin (1968). Also Bowen (1960); Broussard (1977); Kaufman et al. (1959); and chapter 11.

32. Kanner (1949, p. 423). See also Despert (1965); Freedman (1954); Freedman and Bender (1957); Gajzago and Prior (1974); Reiser (1963); Shaberman (1971); Vaillant (1962).

33. Rimland (1964). See also Morgan (1981).

34. Kanner (1944; 1949, p. 423; 1972).

35. Despert (1965); Schreibman and Koegel (1975). See also Lomas (1967a); Rowe (1959).

36. Lomas (1967a) suggested that parents who hid autistic children considered them sexually evil.

37. Despert (1970). See also Rowe (1959).

38. McDougall and Lebovici (1969).
39. D'Ambrosio (1970, p. 59, 64).
40. Searles (1960); and see Brody and Axelrod (1978) on denial of maternal love.

Chapter 5 The Coming of the Child

1. Jarvis (1962). See also Zilboorg (1931).
2. Blakely (1940).
3. Masters and Johnson (1966). See also Colman and Colman (1971). Less desire for sex is also reported.
4. Brew and Seidenberg (1950, p. 411). See also Benedek (1970); Colman and Colman (1971).
5. Shainess (1966, pp. 47, 48).
6. Jones (1970); Wolff (1970). Some depression usually occurs in relatively good circumstances (Colman 1969).
7. A remarkably low rate of separation and divorce in parents of autistic children has been noted. Insofar as the parents are not evidently happier in their marriages than other people, the explanation that having autistic children serves to keep parents together may be valid (Selvini Palazzoli et al. 1978).
8. See note 11 in chapter 4.
9. Eliade (1943); Konig (1963); La Barre (1972); Taylor (1970); Victor (1973).
10. Solnit and Stark (1961).
11. McBride (1973).
12. Dershimer (1938, p. 323).
13. McBride, A.B. *The Growth and Development of Mothers.* Harper & Row, Publishers, Inc., 1973, pp. 19–27. Reprinted by permission. This selection is not balanced by the maturer, more-realistic thoughts in the original.
14. Harding (1971); Taylor (1970).
15. Dershimer (1938, pp. 320–321). See also Klein, Potter, and Dyk (1950); Mannoni (1972).
16. Brew and Seidenberg (1950); Colman and Colman (1971); Mannoni (1972); Speers and Lansing (1968). See also Freedman (1969); Lomas (1967a, 1967b); Pipineli-Potamianou (1975).
17. See especially Copeland (1974); Foy (1970); Kastein and Trace (1966); Kaufman (1975).
18. Speers and Lansing (1968). See also Foy (1970); Greenfeld (1972).
19. Doering (1977); Mehl (1977).
20. Colman and Colman (1971); Doering (1977).
21. Baker (1967); Crammond (1954); Doering (1977); Scott and Thomson (1956).
22. Doering (1977); Klaus and Kennell (1982b); Klein, Potter, and Dyk (1950). An exception, the specific fear during pregnancy that the woman herself will harm her fetus or infant, is associated with negative outcomes; see Colman and Colman (1971); Ferreira (1960); Zilboorg (1928).
23. Baker (1967); Crammond (1954); Scott and Thomson (1956).
24. Wolff (1969a).
25. de Beauvoir (1964); Wolff (1969b).

Chapter 6   The Beginning

1. Bloom (1964).
2. Call (1964); Gunther (1961); Solkoff et al. (1969).
3. Barnard (1981).
4. Bonica (1967); Broussard (1979); Broussard and Hartner (1970); Buxbaum (1979); Crawford (1972); Douglas (1963); Ferreira (1960); Flowers (1967); Galton (1978); Kennell (1978); Leiderman (1974); Levy (1958); Lidz (1968); Macfarlane (1977); McBryde (1951); Provence and Lipton (1962); Sander (1962); Stechler (1964); Thoman, Leiderman, and Olson (1972); Thoms (1962); Ucko (1965); Whiten (1977); Wolff (1969a).
5. Carithers (1951); Irvine (1974).
6. Barnett et al. (1970); DiVitto and Goldberg (1979); Field (1979); Herzog (1979); Kaplan and Mason (1960); Kennell and Klaus (1982); Klaus and Kennell (1982b); Korner (1978); Leiderman (1974); Leifer et al. (1972); Macfarlane (1977); Minkowski and Amiel-Tison (1974); Oppe (1960); Reid (1961); Siqueland (1973); Solkoff et al. (1969); Trause, Klaus, and Kennell (1982). As a result of separation, breastfeeding was rare. A recent finding is that the milk of mothers of premature neonates is unusually rich in nitrogen, which the babies particularly need.
7. Bonica (1967); Brackbill (1977); Crawford (1972); Dunbar (1944); Flowers (1967); Kron, Stein, and Goddard (1966); Moir (1974); Newton and Newton (1962); Among the effects are EEG anomalies.
8. Lester (1981).
9. Newson and Newson (1963).
10. Lewis (1973, p. 671).
11. Chess (1966, p. 18). See also Lester (1981); Szurek (1969).
12. Bell and Ainsworth (1972); Broussard (1979); Bruch (1961, 1962b); Korner (1973); Pavenstedt (1968); Pawlby (1977); Schwarz (1979); Szurek (1969); Yarrow (1963). On stereotyping as a cause of disturbance, Coleman, Kris, and Provence (1953); Scott and Ashworth (1967, 1969).
13. Ribble (1941, 1944); Szurek (1969).
14. Ainsworth (in Bowlby, 1969, p. 320). See also Call (1975); Massie (1977); Provence and Lipton (1962); Silberstein, Blackman, and Mandell (1966); Wolff (1969a).
15. DeMyer, Bryson, and Churchill (1973).
16. Jay (1965). See also Rosenblatt (1967).
17. Kulka, Fry, and Goldstein (1960, p. 563). See also Silberstein, Blackman, and Mandell (1966).
18. Wing (1972, p. 58). See also Des Lauriers and Carlson (1969); Kulka, Fry, and Goldstein (1960); Mahler, Pine, and Bergman (1975); Schopler (1962); Tinbergen and Tinbergen (1972, 1983).
19. Ainsworth (1967a); Aldrich (1942); Bloomfield (1962); Call (1975); Drillien (1964); Feldstein (1928); Gunther (1955); Hytten, Yorston, and Thomson (1958); Illingworth and Illingworth (1972); Lidz (1968); Newson and Newson (1962, 1963); Salber, Stitt, and Babbott (1959).
20. Escalona (1965); Chess (1970); Zaslow and Breger (1969).
21. DesLauriers and Carlson (1969); Wing (1972).

22. Bloom (1964); Call (1964, 1975); Dunn and Richards (1977); Gunther (1961); Kagan, Kearsley, and Zelazo (1978); Moss (1968); Rebelsky and Hanks (1971); Solkoff et al. (1969); Thompson (1960).

23. Schwarz (1979, p. 881).

24. Dershimer (1938). See also Bergler (1964); Dyer (1963); McBride (1973).

25. Deutsch (1945).

26. McBride (1973, p. 33).

27. de Beauvoir (1964, p. 509). See also Wolff (1969b).

28. Wolff (1969a).

29. Deutsch (1945).

30. Especially Junker (1964); Kaufman (1976); Murray (1967).

31. Wolff (1969a).

32. Goldfarb et al. (1970). See also DesLauriers and Carlson (1969); Kessler (1966); Pitfield and Oppenheim (1964); Wing (1972).

33. Macfarlane (1977).

34. Prechtl (1965); Trevarthen (1977).

35. Ainsworth (1963, 1979); Richards (1971); Rubenstein (1967); Rutter (1972); Schwarz (1979); White (1973).

36. For example, Kanner (1949, 1951); Kastein and Trace (1966).

37. Stone, Smith, and Murphy (1973, p. 4). Until recently, the opposite was believed.

38. Brazelton et al. (1975); Dember and Earl (1957); Lewis and Brooks (1974); Macfarlane (1977); Mundy-Castle and Anglin (1973); Papousek (1969, 1970, 1978); Papousek and Papousek (1977); Spitz (1950); Stone, Smith, and Murphy (1973); Watson (1966, 1978).

39. Bruner (1968, 1977); Condon and Sander (1974); Newson (1977); Papousek and Papousek (1977); Pawlby (1977); Schaffer (1977); Stone, Smith, and Murphy (1973); Terhune (in Brazelton et al. 1975); Trevarthen (1974, 1977); Walters and Parke (1965).

40. Sander (1962); Wolff (1969a).

41. Park (1974, p. 18). See also Call (1975); Condon (1977); Condon and Sander (1974); Macfarlane (1977); Main (1977); Papousek and Papousek (1977); Sander (1969); Sperling (1950); Trevarthen (1977).

42. Korner and Grobstein (1966); Korner and Thoman (1970); Mundy-Castle and Anglin (1973); Watson (1966, 1972).

43. Ainsworth, Bell, and Stayton (1972); Brackbill et al. (1966); Escalona (1965); Kennell (1978); Korner and Grobstein (1966); Korner and Thoman (1970); Kris (1962); Mahler, Pine, and Bergman (1975); Ribble (1938, 1941, 1944, 1945); Robertson (1962); Senn (1948); Stone, Smith, and Murphy (1973); Szurek (1969); Yarrow and Pedersen (1972).

44. Birns, Blank, and Bridger (1973); Brackbill (1973); Wolff (1973b).

45. Sander (1962); Coleman, Kris, and Provence (1953); Murphy (1973); Szurek (1969).

46. Brackbill and Thompson (1967, p. 582).

47. Bell and Ainsworth (1972); David and Appell (1969); Ribble (1941, 1944); Sander (1962); Schwarz (1979); Stewart (1953); Szurek (1969).

48. LeMasters (1957).

49. Goldfarb, Braunstein, and Scholl (1959); Goldfarb et al. (1970). See also Broussard (1979); Douglas (1956); Fabian and Donohue (1956); Goshen (1963); Greenberg (1970); Haka-Ikse (1974); Meyers and Goldfarb (1961); Pitfield and Oppenheim (1964); Reiser (1966); Schopler and Reichler (1971); Weissman and Paykel (1974); Weissman et al. (1971).

50. Zilboorg (1928, 1929); Frumkes (1934); Linn and Polatin (1950); Lomas (1959, 1960b, 1967a); Ostwald and Regan (1957); Smalldon (1940); Yalom et al. (1968). For contrary findings, see Hamilton (1962).

51. Lomas (1959, 1960b, 1967a).

52. Kanner (1949, 1954d).

53. Ibid.

54. Smalldon (1940). See also Brew and Seidenberg (1950); Hamilton (1962); Yalom et al. (1968).

55. Brazelton (1961, p. 510).

56. Prugh and Harlow (1962); Reiser (1966); Smolen (1965).

57. Goshen (1963, pp. 170-171). See also Ack (1966); Appell and David (1961); Bernstein and Menolascino (1970); Berrini and Tommazzolli (1972); Coleman and Provence (1957); Dalton and Epstein (1963); David (1967); Ferster (1973); Fraiberg (1968, case of Robbie); Kaplan (1969); Staver (1953); Woodward, Jaffe, and Brown (1970).

58. Goshen (1963, p. 172).

Chapter 7   The Relationship

1. Rochlin (1961), p. 460).

2. Ainsworth (1962); Bowlby (1973); Dizmang (1969); Freud and Burlingham (1973); Hansburg (1972); Mahler (1961): Patton and Gardner (1963); Ribble (1965); Scott (1963); Sroufe (1979); Yarrow (1968).

3. On evacuation of English children, see Alcock (1948); Burlingham and Freud (1942); Freud and Burlingham (1943); Hansburg (1972). On mother-infant separation and hospitalization, see Dennis (1973); Provence and Lipton (1962); Spitz (1945, 1957); Spitz and Wolf (1946). On the Iowa experiments, Skeels (1966); Skeels and Dye (1939); Skeels et al. (1938); Skodak (1938, 1939, 1950). For related experiments with autistic children, Dundas (1964); O'Gorman (in "The Halt and the Blind" 1958). See also Whalen and Henker (1971). On animal separation, Seay, Hansen and Harlow (1962); Suomi and Harlow (1972).

4. Rutter (1972); Walters and Parke (1963).

5. Bronfenbrenner (1968). See also Lakin (1957); Manson (1964); Spitz (1951); Thompson and Melzack (1956); Wenar, Handlon, and Garner (1960).

6. Fox (1969b); Hamburg (1969); Scott (1963).

7. Hersher, Richmond, and Moore (1963).

8. "Dr. Jacobi stated that no baby lived more than three months in the Randall's Island institution" (Shaw 1915, p. 184). Such facts were suppressed. For example, Hamill (1915) cited a foundling hospital with a death rate of "100 percent" for infants less than one year old that officially reported only 11 percent mortality. See also Bakwin (1942); Chapin (1915); Dennis (1973); Dennis and Najarian (1957); Knox (1915); Mead (1962); Spitz (1945).

9. Bowlby (1973); Bronson (1968); Mahler, Pine, and Bergman (1975); Shirley (1942).

10. Rochlin (1961). Inability to profit from experience has been attributed to autistic children and posited as the core of adult schizophrenia (see note 30 in chapter 10) and of psychopathic personality.

11. Breger (1974); Maccoby and Masters (1970); Sroufe and Waters (1977); Waters (1978).

12. Parkes (1972, p. 13). See also Ainsworth (1963, 1979); Bowlby (1973); Erikson (1973).

13. Robinson and Robinson (1965).

14. Speers and Lansing (1965, case of Walter); Zaslow and Breger (1969). On relationships between hostility and attachment-inducing behavior in animals, see Lorenz (1963).

15. Parkes (1972).

16. Benjamin (1963).

17. Engel (1962).

18. Ferenczi (1950).

19. Ainsworth (1963, 1979). See also Caldwell et al. (1970); Stayton, Hogan and Ainsworth (1971).

20. Spiro (1965).

21. Kaufman (1970); Schaffer (1965); Schaffer and Emerson (1968).

22. Richards (1971, p. 38). See also Ainsworth (1963, 1979); Bruner (1968, 1977); Lewis and Goldberg (1969); Pawlby (1977); Rubenstein (1967); Rutter (1972); Schwarz (1979); Stayton and Ainsworth (1973); Stayton, Hogan, and Ainsworth (1971); White (1973); Yarrow et al. (1973).

23. Massie (1978a).

24. Hoffman (1974); Rutter (1972).

25. Hoffman (1974).

Chapter 8   The Strained Relationship

1. Bowlby (1952, 1969).

2. O'Gorman (1967); Erikson (1963); Mahler (1958, 1961). See also Boatman and Szurek (1960); Bowley and Gardner (1969); Dundas (1964); Evans-Jones and Rosenbloom (1978); Lourie (1954); Mannoni (1972); Morrow (1959); O'Moore (1972); Reiser (1963); Tustin (1972); Williams (1956); Williams and Harper (1974); Zaslow and Breger (1969). The implication of abandoning a young child elicits strongly worded positions: "All authors regard object loss as the critical factor in the origin of these serious disturbances." (Rochlin 1953, p. 289); "[T]he campaign on the evils of mother-child separation is just another attempt by men to shackle women to the home" (Rutter 1976, p. 154). On separation in older autistic children, see Green (1970). Spiro (1965) attributed autistic features of commune-reared children, including avoidance of speech to separations from caretakers and parents. See also Geber (1962).

3. O'Gorman (1967, p. 3).

4. O'Moore (1972, p. 117).

5. Putnam, Rank, and Kaplan (1951, p. 43).

6. Susz and Marburg (1978, p. 151).

7. Mahler (1961); Tustin (1972); Zaslow and Breger (1969).

8. Freud (1943); Main (1977).

9. On the child remaining at home or the environment remaining the same except for the caretaker's absence, see Deutsch (1959); Kennell and Bergen (1966); Robertson and Robertson (1971); Spiro (1965); Spitz and Wolf (1946). On mother being with her child in the hospital or other new environment, see Alcock (1948); Ballard et al. (1982); Bowlby (1969); Fagin (1966); Main (1958); Matic (1957).

10. Ribble (1965); Stone, Smith, and Murphy (1973).

11. Marris (1974, pp. 2, 4).

12. See note 38 in chapter 6.

13. Denenberg, Ottinger, and Stephens (1962). On other switching of caretakers, Moore (1968).

14. Gelinier-Ortigues and Aubry (1955); Rochlin (1973).

15. On animal separation, see Hersher, Moore, and Richmond (1958); Hinde and Davies (1972); Kaufman (1970); Leifer (1972). In Moore's (1968) experiments with goats and sheep, separation or other interference with attachment caused depression in mothers, in which infants were rejected or passively tolerated. On human separation, see Kennell and Klaus (1982); and note 6 in chapter 6.

16. Fox (1969b); Maccoby and Masters (1970).

17. Muscular tension with body arching also has been reported (Ribble 1945).

18. Benjamin (1963); Papousek and Papousek (1977).

19. Wolff (1969b). See also Main (1977); Papousek and Papousek (1977); Solomon (1980).

20. Infants who have little human contact become attached to television sets by nine weeks of age; removal of the sets seriously disrupts their behavior, according to Cairns (Stone, Smith, and Murphy 1973).

21. Engel (1962, p. 33).

22. Ribble (1945, 1965).

23. Benjamin (1963); Wolff (1969b).

24. From a review of research by Engel (1962, p. 51).

25. Bowlby (1960, p. 22). See also Bowlby, Robertson, and Rosenblith (1952).

26. Parkes (1969, p. 88).

27. Stengel (1939, 1943).

28. Schaffer (1967).

29. For example, Stewart (1953, cases of Carol and Eric), and on monkeys, Hinde and Spencer-Booth (1971).

30. Ainsworth and Wittig (1969). See also Ainsworth and Bell (1970); Wolff (1969b).

31. Kellogg and Kellogg (in Bowlby 1973, p. 58). According to Bowlby (1960a), nothing causes more-violent hatred of mother than separation. See also Solnit (1970).

32. Mahler, Pine, and Bergman (1975).

33. Spelke et al. (1973).

34. Spitz (1945, 1965); Spitz and Wolf (1946). See also Meyers (1974).

35. Arsenian (1943).

36. Kaufman (1970); Rosenblum and Alpert (1974). On related studies of dogs, see Fox (1969b).

37. Bowlby (1960a, 1969); Deutsch (1959); Micic (1962); Schaffer and Callendar (1959); Yarrow (1961); and, especially, Burlingham and Freud (1942); Heinicke and Westheimer (1965).

38. Frijling-Schreuder (1969, p. 322). See also Rochlin (1953); Tustin's (1972) exemplary case of John.

39. On depression and autism, see Antonovic (1974); Edelson (1966); Ferster (1966a, 1966b); Haggerty (1959); Langdell (1973); Meyers (1974); Olin (1975). See also Anthony (1975); Engel and Reichsman (1958); Mittelman (1954); Poznanski and Zrull (1971).

40. Brown (1968, p. 435). On depression in children not bereaved, see Cytryn and McKnew (1972, 1974); Harrington and Hassan (1958); Langdell (1973); Lesse (1968); Marris (1974); Mendelson, Reid, and Frommer (1972).

41. Thus, Lindemann (1944), a specialist on bereavement, noted his surprise in finding children whose parents died to be preoccupied, guilty, angry, cold toward people, and prone to physical illness. He found the reaction was long delayed in some children, which is also true of some adults. See also Arthur and Kemme (1964); Birtchnell (1969); Bowlby (1960a); Brown (1972); Dizmang (1969); Freud and Burlingham (1943); Malmquist (1972).

42. Sandler and Joffe (1965).

43. Volkart and Michael (1957, p. 289).

44. Clinicians identified depression in adults that was not obvious as masked depression, and the concept was extended to children: See Cytryn and McKnew (1974); Glaser (1967); Harrington and Hassan (1958); Keeler (1954); Meyers (1974); Mittelman (1954); Rie (1966); Sandler and Joffe (1965); Sperling (1959); Toolan (1962, 1975). The concept of masked depression seems to fit autistic children well. On depression in infants, see Davidson (1968); Engel and Reichsman (1958); Langdell (1973); Spitz (1954); Toolan (1962).

45. Sandler and Joffe (1965, p. 89) referred to the "widespread adult conspiracy to deny any state in the child which smacks of depression—and to take active steps ... to persuade the child that he is not unhappy" in contrast to willingness to recognize and seek help for children's phobias, obsessions, or antisocial behavior. See also Malmquist (1972); Sperling (1959).

46. In an unusually detailed study of separation, Heinicke and Westheimer (1965, p. 336) noted that the behavior they found would ordinarily indicate depression, but concluded that "this label is not appropriate to children so young."

47. Parkes (1972); Solnit (1970).

48. Volkart and Michael (1957).

49. Bowlby (1969, p. 27).

50. Bowlby, Robertson, and Rosenblith (1952).

51. Bowlby (1969).

52. Bowlby (1973).

53. Erikson (1963).

54. Marris (1974). See also Parkes (1972).

55. On good relationships leading to traumatic separation, see Spitz and Wolf (1956). Murphy (1962, p. 51) reported, "The boys with severe separation problems had erotically excited relations with their mothers." For other studies of the prior mother-child relationship as a factor in separation reactions, see Ainsworth (1962,

1979); Ainsworth, Bell, and Stayton (1973); Bowlby (1952, 1960b, 1973); Britton (1969); Deardon (1970); Hansburg (1972); Heinicke and Westheimer (1965); Maccoby and Masters (1970); Mead (1962); Pill (1970); Ribble (1945); Rutter (1972); Spelke et al (1973); Stacey (1970); Stayton and Ainsworth (1973); Tennes and Lampl (1966); Yarrow and Goodwin (1977). Freud and Burlingham (1943) suggested that maternal behavior beforehand had little to do with reaction to separation.

56. Gofman, Burkman, and Schade (1957). See also Bergmann (1965); Fineman (1958); Heinicke and Westheimer (1965); Kennell and Bergen (1966); Leifer et al. (1972); Moore (1957); Parkes (1972); Vernon et al. (1965). Loss of a child is an extreme stress and often leads to parental divorce.

57. Bosch (1970); Slimp (1950).

58. Freud (1970); Heinicke and Westheimer (1965); Vernon et al. (1965).

59. Alcock (1948).

60. Freud (1970); Heinicke and Westheimer (1965, case of Owen). See also Howells and Layng (1956).

61. Heinicke and Westheimer (1965, p. 101).

62. Heinicke and Westheimer (1965).

63. Freud (1970).

64. Kanner (1949, 1952); Wing (1972); Zaslow and Breger (1969). See also DesLauriers and Carlson (1969); DeMyer, Hintgen, and Jackson (1981); Tinbergen and Tinbergen (1983); Welch (1983).

65. Trevarthen (1974).

66. Rochlin (1953); Tustin (1972). See also Bowlby (1952); Engel (1962); Freud (1970); Freud (1963); Geber (1958); Patton and Gardner (1972); Reiser (1963); Robertson (1965); Stewart (1953, cases of Carol and Stephen); Williams and Harper (1974). Geleerd (1958) suggested that autistic children experience the mother's brief absence or diminution of love (whether real or only perceived by the child) as loss of the mother.

67. Robertson (1965, p. 113).

68. Junker (1964, pp. 137, 139).

Chapter 9   Stresses in Learning

1. Junker (1964, p. 178).

2. Scott (1963).

3. Buxbaum (1970); McCandless (1976); Rubinstein et al. (1959); Whiting and Child (1953).

4. Wing (1972). See also Park (1967); Webster (1980).

5. Axline (1967); Ferster (1968); Goldfarb et al. (1970); Greenberg (1971); Kanner (1943, case of Don); Scheerer, Rothmann, and Goldstein (1945); Zaslow and Breger (1969).

6. Burtt (1941). See also Condon (1977); Condon and Sander (1974).

7. Newson and Newson (1963, pp. 119–120). Twenty percent of the mothers began toilet training in the second month.

8. Boatman and Szurek (1960, p. 413). See also Goshen (1963); MacDougall and Lebovici (1969); and, especially, parents' accounts by Everard (1980) and Kastein and Trace (1966).

9. Masserman (1943).

10. Schaffer (1974) suggested that deviation from any familiar experience evokes fear.

11. Infant handling by depressed mothers has been touched on at various points. On stimulation, reward, and deprivation by depressed mothers, see Haka-Ikse (1974).

12. Voyat (1980).

13. Speers and Lansing (1965, 1968). See also Lidz (in Lennard, Beaulieu, and Embry 1965). According to Salzman (1973), parents like those described by Kanner typically deal with their children by selective inattention.

14. Ferster (1966b).

15. Clark (1974); Fay (1971); Lovaas, Koegel, and Schreibman (1979); Menyuk (1964); Rutter and Mittler (1972); Trevarthen (1974).

16. Clark (1974); Morris (1957); Provence and Lipton (1962).

17. Ferster (1966b, p. 319).

18. Selvini Palazoli et al. (1978).

19. Speers and Lansing (1965, p. 145).

20. Ferster (1968, p. 228). See also Ekstein (1966); Ferster (1966a); Freedman (1954); Goldfarb, Braunstein, and Scholl (1959); Greenberg (1971); Kastein and Trace (1966); Kaufman et al. (1959); Speers and Lansing (1965).

21. Colby (1973).

22. Wing (1977). My impression from the autobiographies is similar. See also Goldfarb (1970); Park (1974); Schopler and Reichler (1971); Schreibman and Koegel (1975); Webster (1980).

23. Lantz (1945); Goldstein (1959).

24. Dewey (1971); Everard (1980).

25. Clark (1974).

26. Axline (1967); Ferster (1966a); Krasnogorski (1925).

27. Aldrich (1942). See also Krasnogorski (1925); Mahrer (1956).

28. Lewis and Goldberg (1969). See also Ainsworth (1967); Eaton and Weil (1955); Mahrer (1956); McCandless (1976); Moss (1973); Newson (1977); Papousek (1970); Robson (1967); Rutter (1972); Schwarz (1979); Stayton, Hogan, and Ainsworth (1971); Watson (1972, 1973); Yarrow and Goodwin (1965).

29. Mahrer (1956).

30. On preference for immediate punishment, see Seligman (1968); Seligman, Maier, and Solomon (1971).

31. Metz (1965). And autistic children's learning is greatly improved by making reinforcements functionally related to their behavior, according to Williams, Koegel, and Egel (1981).

32. Papousek (1978); Sackett (1965); Watson (1978); Wyckoff (1952).

33. Engberg et al. (1972); Ney (1973); Seligman (1968, 1975). See also Ainsworth and Bell (1969); Erikson (1963); Ferster (1966b); Stone, Smith, and Murphy (1973); Streissguth and Bee (1972); Watson (1973); Weisberg (1963); Yarrow and Pedersen (1972).

34. Speers and Lansing (1965, p. 144; 1968, pp. 341, 344). According to Beadle (1970), "The majority of autistic children have exceptionally intelligent, perfectionist, coldly objective, and unemotional parents; and it is thought that dutiful but joyless mothering—without warmth, interest, or responsiveness to the baby—convinces the

child that he is powerless to act upon the environment in his own behalf, so he just gives up the effort" (p. xix). Beadle suggested that this view was common though not necessarily her own.

35. Kanner (1943); Kanner and Lesser (1958).

36. Ferster (1968) suggested that prevention of interaction was typical in autism. See also Bruch (1959); Gardner et al. (1968); Greenberg (1971); Kris (1962).

37. Speers and Lansing (1965, p. 144).

38. Goshen (1963).

39. For example, Wing (1970, 1972).

40. Kanner (1949, 1954a); Despert (1965). See also Cruikshank and Paul (1971); Morgan (1936).

41. Ferster (1966b, 1968); Gardner et al (1968); Goldfarb, Braunstein, and Scholl (1959); Kanner (1949, 1954a); Lourens and Dorman (1972); Lovaas (1971); Lovaas et al. (1965); Patterson and Reid (1970); Sander (1962; 1964, case of Ned); Sarvis and Garcia (1961); Scheff (1966); Sperling (1951); Staver (1953); Vogel (1958). Problem behavior can be rewarded in a more-general way. Many children whose ordinary or constructive behavior elicits little parental interest succeed in getting interest by problem behavior. Parental interest and attention are themselves rewarding and may perpetuate behavior that parents deplore (Wahler 1976).

Chapter 10   The Impossible Task

1. Fletcher (1895).

2. Kimble (1961, p. 441).

3. Kurtsin (1969).

4. Krasnogorski (1925).

5. Solomon, Kamin, and Wynne (1953); Solomon and Wynne (1954).

6. Moore (1958).

7. Cook (1937).

8. Bateson et al. (1956).

9. Maier (1939). On a related experiment with deer, see Liddell (1955). See also Moore (1968).

10. Maier (1961). See also Hamilton (1962); Johnson (1969); Wyckoff (1952). Horses are easily trained to respond to riders' cues and also are easily disturbed by inconsistent cues. A changeable rider "will reduce a normally calm horse to such a state of nervous tension that one can hardly believe it is the same animal—it seems to lose all power of reason" (Croft 1951, p. 585).

11. Ruesch (1957, p. 129).

12. Morrison, Miller, and Mejia (1971, p. 512). See also Cowan, Hoddinott, and Wright (1965); Despert (1965); Tinbergen and Tinbergen (1976).

13. Cowan, Hoddinott, and Wright (1965); Jose and Cohen (1980); Ney (1979); Sussman and Sklar (1969); Volkmar and Cohen (1982). See also Wallace (1975); Zaslow and Breger (1959). For a contrary finding, see Clark and Rutter (1977).

14. For example, in the following vignette, the mother was not aware of her inconsistency. She had come to visit her son. "He was glad to see her and impulsively put his arm around her shoulders, whereupon she stiffened. He withdrew his arm, and she asked, 'Don't you love me any more;' He then blushed, and she said, 'Dear,

you must not be so easily embarrassed and afraid of your feelings' " (Bateson et al. 1956, pp. 253–254).

15. Goldfarb, Levy, and Meyers (1972); Goldfarb, Yudkowitz, and Goldfarb (1973); King (1974); Olin (1975); Pitfield and Oppenheim (1964); Rice, Kepecs, and Yahalom (1966).

16. Mavity (1982, p. 3). Another wrote of "enormous pressure" (Kastein and Trace 1969).

17. Kanner (1943, 1949). See also Bettelheim (1967); Boatman and Szurek (1960); Cameron (1958); Copeland (1974); Foy (1970); Freedman (1954); Gibson (1968); Kaufman (1976); Slimp (1950); Tustin (1972); Webster (1970, 1980); Wing (1972).

18. Pitfield and Oppenheim (1964).

19. Broadhurst (1961).

20. Maier (1961, pp. 27, 28). On insoluble tasks fostering restricted use of cues, see Bainbridge (1973).

21. On preference for predictable shock over a less-predictable situation in which shock is avoidable, see Seligman (1968); Seligman, Maier, and Solomon (1971).

22. Some rats were coerced not by electric shock or an air jet but by hunger. Deprived of food, their only way to obtain it was to jump to the platform. A substantial minority of them did not jump and starved to death (Maier 1961).

23. Marquart (1948). See also Patrick (1934).

24. Thornton and Jacobs (1971). See also Averill and Rosenn (1972); Dweck and Reppucci (1973); Hiroto (1974).

25. Seligman (1974).

26. Bandura (1982); Garber and Seligman (1980); Overmier and Seligman (1967); Richter (1957); Seligman (1975); Tryon (1976).

27. Seligman (1974, 1975). See also Bibring (1953, 1968); Davis (1970); Lichtenberg (1957); Melges and Bowlby (1969); Miller and Seligman (1973); Rie (1966); Schmale (1958); Serban (1975). Ferster (1966a) suggested a connection among the kind of reinforcement contingencies discussed, depression in adults, and autism. Tustin (1972) saw autism as an adaptation to depression. See also Heard (1973); Oswald (1959).

28. Marris (1974, p. 14). See also Blatz (1966); Flint (1959).

29. An exception is the limited application of sociological analysis of group function and deviance to mental disturbance and retardation (next chapter).

30. Chapman (1966); Chapman and McGhie (1964); Devereux (1939); Garmezy (1967); Kornetsky and Mirsky (1966); Mendel (1974); Shakow (1963); Silverman (1964, 1967); Will (1967). See also Arieti (1955, 1966); Beck (1972); Becker (1964, 1968); Binswanger (1963); Bogdanov (1973); Burnham (1965, 1969a); Burton (1974); Chapman (1956); Henry (1971); Hoskins (1931); Jenkins (1952); Laing (1969); Lidz (1973); Makita and Okonogi (1969); Noyes and Kolb (1958); Oswald (1959); Payne (1961); Pious (1949); Rashkis and Singer (1959); Rodnick and Garmezy (1957); Rosenbaum (1970); Singer (1967).

31. White (1965, p. 207).

32. Bettelheim (1967, p. 46).

33. Rimland (1964, p. 79, italics in original).

34. Goldfarb, Mintz, and Stroock (1969, p. 6). See also Bemporad (1979); Cleland (1936); Ferrara and Hill (1980); Green and Schechter (1957); Greenbaum (1970);

Hermelin (1968); King (1975); Koegel and Egel (1979); Ornitz and Ritvo (1976); Rochlin (1973).

35. Baker and Ward (1971); Bensberg (1962); Blum (1958); Cromwell (1963); DeVellis and McCauley (1979); Heber (1964); Heilman (1950); Hirsch (1959); Hutt and Gibby (1965); McCandless (1964); Zigler (1972).

Chapter 11   Adaptations

1. For example, Bruner (1968); Ganz (1968).

2. Studies of learning processes and strategies in retarded children were summarized by Cromwell (1963); Denny (1964); O'Connor and Hermelin (1963); Robinson and Robinson (1970); Zigler (1972). See also Barrett and Lindsley (1962); Bensberg (1962); Berkson (1963); Birnbrauer (1976); Clarke and Clarke (1975b); Gardner (1966); Heber (1964); Hermelin and O'Connor (1958); Luria (1963); O'Connor (1970); O'Connor and Hermelin (1961); Rosenberg (1963); Stevenson (1963); Zeaman (1965); Zeaman and House (1963).

3. Harlow (1949).

4. Ibid.

5. Zeaman (1965).

6. Zigler (1968, 1971).

7. Hutt et al. (1965); Hutt and Ounsted (1966); Morrison, Miller, and Mejia (1971); Wallace (1975).

8. Webster et al. (1973, p. 343).

9. Gantt et al. (1966).

10. Rosenthal and Jacobson (1968).

11. Barsch (1968); Pitfield and Oppenheim (1964).

12. See note 2.

13. Mavity (1982).

14. St. Clair (1966).

15. For example, Foy (1970); Kastein and Trace (1966).

16. Bainbridge (1973).

17. Frith (1972); Kessler (1966); Koegel and Schreibman (1977); Koegel and Wilhelm (1973); Lovaas et al. (1971); Reynolds, Newsom, and Lovaas (1974); Rincover (1978). See also Arick and Krug (1978); Cleland (1936); Friedman (1961); Frith (1970); Hermelin and O'Connor (1970); Hewett (1965); Lourens (1973); Lovaas, Koegel, and Schreibman (1979); Wing (1972). On retarded children's use of cues, see Barrett and Lindsley (1962); Bensberg (1962); Clarke and Clarke (1965b); Denny (1964); Zeaman (1965); Zigler (1972).

18. Hermelin and O'Connor (1975).

19. Kanner (1946); Dewey (1971, p. 84). See also Bogdanov (1973); Everard (1980).

20. Koegel and Wilhelm (1973).

21. Everard (1980); Morgan (1981).

22. Haley (1963).

23. Maier (1933).

24. Wing (1972, p. 72). See also Frith (1972); Metz (1965).

25. Kagan (1966).

26. Birch and Walker (1966).

27. Garfinkel (1967); Langer (1948); Marris (1974).

28. Kraepelin (1915). See also Jackson (1950); Kanner and Eisenberg (1955); Kupferman (1971); Laufer and Gair (1969). Other similarities include repeating questions instead of answering them, other mimicry, food refusal, self-mutilation, apparent insensitivity to stimuli, open masturbation, and other autoerotic behavior. On the continuity between autism in early childhood and catatonia or other forms of schizophrenia later, see Bender and Faretra (1972); O'Gorman (1967); Ornitz and Ritvo (1968); Weil (1953a).

29. Hutt et al. (1965); Hutt and Hutt (1970).

30. Arieti (1974). See also Boyer (1956); Kahlbaum (1974); and, especially, Chapman (1966).

31. Pavlov (in Arieti 1974). Levy's (1955, 1956) view of the constructive function of negativism and its role in schizophrenia is similar to Arieti's. See also Berlyne (1960); Bernfeld (1929); Solomon (1980).

32. Sucharewa (1967).

33. Arieti (1974); Bakwin and Bakwin (1966); Call (1975); English and Pearson (1945); Illingworth (1949); Jersild (1940); Levy (1955, 1956); Macfarlane, Allen, and Honzik (1962); Meek (1933); Moloney (1951); Ribble (1945); Webster (1970).

34. Davis (1970).

35. Tustin (1972). See also Benjamin (1942); Kanner (1944).

36. Plant (1941). See also Bettelheim (1967, case of Marcia); Park (1967).

37. Carluccio, Sours, and Kolb (1964); Chapman and McGhie (1964); Noyes and Kolb (1958). The "robot-like conformity" of autistic children is extremely primitive negativism according to Ruttenberg (1971, p. 173).

38. Arieti (1955). See also Breger (1974).

39. Alanen (1966); Kraepelin (1919); Ricks and Nameche (1966); Treadway (1920).

40. Tietze (1949). See also Abrahams and Varon (1953); Alanen (1958); Arthur and Schumann (1970); Beckett et al. (1956); Beckett et al. (1963); Bowen (1960); Brodey (1959); Dworin and Wyant (1957); Frazee (1953); Freeman and Grayson (1955); Gerard and Siegel (1950); Haley (1965); Hill (1955); Karon and Rosberg (1958); Lidz (1973); Lidz and Cornelison (1965); Lidz et al. (1957); Lidz and Lidz (1952); Lyketsos (1959); Lomas (1967b); McGhie (1961); Prout and White (1950); Ricks and Nameche (1966); Rowe (1959); Scott and Ashworth (1967); Summers (1976); Waring and Ricks (1965); Wolman (1970).

41. Lu (1961, p. 138, italics in original).

42. Tietze (1949, p. 60).

43. Lu (1961). See also Mahler, Pine, and Bergman (1975).

44. Gerard and Siegel (1950), p. 57). They found an unusually intense and sometimes exclusive mother-child relationship in 91 percent of their sample and in none of the comparison group.

45. Besdine (1968, 1971); Victor (1973).

46. "In all instances it could be established that hearing as such was not defective" (Kanner 1948a, p. 717). On the misleading effect, see Eberhardy (1967); Kessler (1966). DesLauriers and Carlson (1969) said that many autistic children appear

normal to people other than their mothers. See note 36 in chapter 14. In addition, autistic children observed without their awareness show competence not seen at other times (Tinbergen and Tinbergen 1983), and their highest intelligence may be shown in mischief (Jose and Cohen 1980).

47. Hamblin et al. (1971).

48. Cain in (Wax 1973); Pearson (1947).

49. Scheff (1966, p. 58). See also Braginsky, Braginsky, and Ring (1969); Charny (1975); Helfand (1956); Jones (1964); Laing (1965); Ludwig and Farrelly (1966); Pollin et al. (1966); Scheff (1968); Selvini Palazzoli et al. (1978); Vogel and Bell (1960); Zarlock (1966).

50. Ack (1966); Mahler (1942); Staver (1953); Webster (1973); Weisskopf (1951); Welsford (1966).

51. Braginsky and Braginsky (1971); Dexter (1960); Mannoni (1972); Mercer (1973); Morgan (1936); Rheingold (1964); Shotwell (1945).

52. On retarded behavior conditioned by institutions, see Braginsky and Braginsky (1971); Guskin (1963); Stein and Susser (1971). On retarded behavior conditioned in the family, see Philips (1967). Also Grunebaum et al. (1962); Halpern and Halpern (1966).

53. Cantor (in Hutt and Gibby 1965, p. 40).

54. Braginsky and Braginsky (1971, p. 48, italics in original) wrote in connection with retarded children: "The power of the adult or parent is *legitimate power*, ordained to them by society and sanctioned by law and custom. The power that children can employ, however, is *subversive* in nature ... achieved primarily by undermining and violating the adult power system in subtle and usually disguised ways." Compare Delacato's (1974) observation that autistic children induce terror in adults by violating their laws.

55. On stupidity, see Mahler (1942); Staver (1953); Webster (1973); Weisskopf (1951). On bungling and clumsiness, Freud (1960). On fools, La Barre (1972); Zucker (1954). Shamanistic clowns were sometimes mute, had speech peculiarities, insenstivity to stimuli, negativism, and other traits found in autistic children. Lommel (1967) reported autistic features in them before they became shamans and that they induced seizures in themselves. See also Eliade (1943); Parsons and Beals (1934). For a theoretical comparison of shamans and schizophrenics, see Silverman (1967).

56. Willeford (1969) also suggested that despite the fool's solitary, self-sufficient ways and indifference to people, his foolish show was symbolically directed to his mother.

57. "The fool is, in short, a silly or idiotic or mad person, or one who is made by circumstances (or the actions of others) to appear a fool in that sense, or a person who imitates for nonfools the foolishness of being innately silly or made to look so" (Willeford 1969, p. 10). See also Delacato (1974); Love (1973).

58. Mercer (1973, p. 27).

59. Charles (1957); Kirman (1968); Schmidt (1946, 1949); Woodward, Jaffe, and Brown (1970); Woodward and Siegal (1957).

60. In 1907, Weygandt characterized the behavior of retarded people as catatonic (Bartmeier 1925). See also Earl (1934); Garfield (1963); MacGillivray (1956); Soddy (1964); Woodward, Jaffe, and Brown (1970). On early precocity, see Mahler, Pine, and Bergman (1975); Sperber (1974); Stendler (1950).

61. Agnew (1972); Bartel and Guskin (1971); Birnbrauer (1976); Capobianco (1962); Charles (1957); Cromer (1974); Heber and Garber (1972); Keener (1952); Mein and O'Connor (1960); O'Connor and Hermelin (1961, 1963); Osborn (1961); Potter (1970); Rensberger (1977); Schmidt (1946); Webster (1970); Whalen and Henker (1971).

62. Tustin (1972, p. 132) said many workers considered idiot savants to be "'recovered' autistic children." See also Bakwin and Bakwin (1966); Goodman (1972); Menolascino (1970a); Rimland (1974, 1977).

63. Sarason and Gladwin (in Sarason and Doris 1969, p. 436).

64. Scheerer, Rothmann, and Goldstein (1945). Goldstein (1959) subsequently identified the boy as autistic.

65. Scheerer, Rothmann, and Goldstein (1945, p. 4).

66. Rensberger (1977).

67. "Over-exploitation" was the word of Anastasi and Levee (1960) who also saw it as fostering special talents in autistic children. See also Goldstein (1959); Horwitz et al. (1965); Jones (1926); Luria (1968); Minogue (1923); Nurcombe and Parker (1964); Plank and Plank (1954); Rosen (1953).

68. Lindsley (1965).

69. Kagan and Moss (1962); Mandelbaum and Wheeler (1967); Mannoni (1972); O'Gorman (1967); Rimland (1964, 1977); Savage (1968); Tustin (1972).

70. Goertzel and Goertzel (1962, p. 8). See also Besdine (1968, 1971); Buxbaum (1970); Greenacre (1958, 1962); Hollingworth (1942); Honzik (1967); Illingworth (1966); Keiser (1969); Kelly (1970); Rossi (1968); Schaefer (1972); Winterbottom (1958).

71. Dali, de la Fontaine, de Maupassant, Edison, Einstein, Benjamin Franklin, Gauguin, Samuel Johnson, Jung, Paderewski, Picasso, Poe, Rodin, Bernard Shaw, Percy Shelley, Thackeray, and Tolstoy among the best known.

Chapter 12   The Superstitious Child

1. Morgan (1981, p. 22).

2. Ferrara and Hill (1980).

3. Abraham (1968, p. 376). See also Jones (1950; Salzman (1973).

4. Adams (1973, p. 8). See also Abraham (1968); Jones (1950).

5. Adams (1973).

6. Bemporad (1980).

7. Salzman (1973). See also Cameron (1947).

8. This had been the prevailing view among linguists and psychologists until Chomsky's (1965, 1968) theory of innately determined language structure.

9. Marris (1974); and note 38 in chapter 6.

10. Salzman (1973, p. viii).

11. Marris (1974, p. 37).

12. Arthur and Kemme (1964); Werner (1957).

13. Salzman (1973, pp. 30, 31).

14. Briffault (1959, p. 237).

15. Bettelheim (1967).

16. Ibid.

17. Werner (1957). See also Langer (1948); Victor (1973).
18. On self-humiliation in autistic children, see Speers and Lansing (1965).
19. Seligman (1975).

Chapter 13   The Child behind the Wall

1. Anastasiadis (1963).
2. Braginsky, Braginsky, and Ring (1969, pp. 31–32). Schooler and Parkel (in Braginsky, Braginsky, and Ring, p. 32).
3. Copeland (1974, p. 9, capitals in original).
4. Tustin (1972, p. 143).
5. Schopler (1962, p. 193). See also Kupferman (1971).
6. Paluszny (1979); Rimland (1974).
7. Boatman and Szurek (1960); Call (1963, 1975); Creak (1968); Despert (1965); Ferster (1968); Kanner (1943, 1952); Kaufman et al. (1959); King (1975); Kupferman (1971); Massie (1975, 1977, 1978b); Schopler (1962); Speers and Lansing (1965, case of Walter).
8. Eisenberg (1967, p. 1434). Similarly, Eisenberg and Kanner (1956).
9. Illingworth (1966); Prugh (1951); Ribble (1938); Webster (1970).
10. For example, Creak (1968).
11. Benjamin (1963).
12. Kanner (1949); Kupferman (1971). Laing (1965) found the desire for and fostering of the good baby in cases of children who became schizophrenic adults. Many studies of schizophrenic adults indicate that, when young, they were the good children in their families (chapter 11). See Brody and Axelrad (1970, p. 137) on mothers who "express maternal pleasure only in regard to the infants being undemanding."
13. Anthony (1974b); Raglan (1949); Rank (1959); Victor (1973).
14. McBride (1973).
15. Kanner (1949).
16. Fox and Stelzner (1966). See also Bernstein (1955); Denenberg (1978); Rueg-amer, Bernstein, and Benjamin (1954); Thompson and Melzack (1956).
17. Bridger and Birns (1968). There seems to be an optimal level of arousal beyond which infants become less receptive to stimulation and learning.
18. Creak (1960, p. 43). See also DesLauriers and Carlson (1969); Rothenberg (1977); Tinbergen and Tinbergen (1983); Welch (1983); Wing (1972).
19. Bernfeld (1929, p. 27).
20. Geleerd (1958); Mahler, Pine, and Bergman (1975).
21. Axline (1965); Park (1967). See also Gardner et al. (1968); King (1964); King and Ekstein (1967); Szurek (1956); Williams and Harper (1974). Kaufman et al. (1959) considered the avoidance of contact attributed to the children to be a projection of parents' attitudes. For example, "Mrs. T complained that the child would not tolerate physical closeness to her. However, at the clinic, when the child came close ... she placed her arm stiffly on the chair in front of her, literally making a fence between the two of them, so that the child could not get near" (p. 463). King (1975) noted similar patterns.

22. Fox (1969a). Freedman (1954) spoke of fetal torpor as part of an immature physiological organization attributed to autistic children.

23. Bruner (1968); Trevarthen (1977). On conditioned gaze aversion, see Massie (1975); Richards (1971).

24. Scott (1968).

25. Kaufman (1976, p. 2). The titles are from Junker (1964) and Park (1967).

Chapter 14   The Inscrutable Child

1. Churchill (1978); DeMyer (1975); Oxman, Webster, and Konstantareas (1980); Ricks and Wing (1975); Rutter (1968, 1971b); Webster (1980).

2. Limber (1977, p. 280).

3. Haley (1959, 1963); Laing (1965, 1969); Sagarin (1973).

4. Alvarez (1972, p. 54). Kaufman (1976) described a child who went from using 7 words to 75 in a week.

5. van Krevelen (1960); Robinson (1961); Campbell (1980); Sullivan (1980). One child was silent for ten years, spoke a sophisticated sentence, and never spoke again (O'Gorman 1952). See also Bartolucci and Albers (1974); Benda (1960); Bettelheim (1967); Caparulo and Cohen (1980); Creak (1970); Goldfarb, Braunstein, and Lorge (1956); Goldfarb, Goldfarb, and Scholl (1966); Kanner (1946, 1957); Morgan (1981); Rudikoff (1972); Weiland and Legg (1964); Wing (1972).

6. Arnold (1960); Bemporad (1979); Cobrinik (1974); Colby (1973); Creak (1970); DeMyer (1971); Goodwin (1971); Furneaux (1966); Oxman, Webster, and Konstantareas (1980); Rimland (1964, 1977). Miller and Miller (1973) took twenty mute, severely autistic children and taught all of them a sign language. Of related interest are Agnew (1972); Rozin, Poritsky, and Sotsky (1971); Wilcox (1956, case of Maria).

7. For example, Freedman (1969, case of Ann).

8. Lenneberg (1964) reported observations of autistic children relying on linguistic knowledge (pronunciation, syntax, and meaning) as aids in repeating what they heard, as other people do. See also Buium and Stuecher (1974). On the children's echolalia having a communicative function, see Prizant and Duchan (1981).

9. Heard (1973); Morrison, Miller, and Mejia (1971).

10. Kanner (1946). See also Wing (1972).

11. Stengel (1947).

12. Haworth and Menolascino (1968).

13. Ibid.; Morehead and Morehead (1974); Premack and Premack (1974); Ruesch (1957). See also Curcio and Paccia-Cooper (1981); Fkstein (1966); Ekstein and Caruth (1969); Fay (1971); Hackett (1968); Kanner (1972); Peckarsky (1952); Prizant and Duchan (1981).

14. Morehead and Morehead (1974).

15. On verbal training of autistic children, see Eisenberg and Kanner (1956); Hackett (1968); Kanner (1943); Mandel et al. (1971); Peckarsky (1952); Wilcox (1956); Zaslow and Breger (1969). On the effects of such training, see Ruesch (1957); Wieder (1966).

16. Kanner (1948).

17. Stengel (1947).

18. "[T]he autistic child can learn to say 'heptagon' more easily than 'mother' or 'I'. (Rudikoff 1972, p. 67). See also Charney (1980).

19. Junker (1964). Mahler, Pine, and Bergman (1975) suggested that leading or pulling mother instead of asking for something was a manifestation of separation anxiety.

20. Bettelheim (1967); Wing (1972). See also Fay (1979).

21. Bettelheim (1967, case of Joey).

22. Despert (in Straight, 1954, p. 8). Having the concept of mama while not using the word was shown in Hewett's (1965) case. Selective avoidance was detailed by Park (1967). See also Charney (1980); Fay (1971); Webster (1963).

23. There is disagreement about the effects of such conditioning on autistic children. See Bartak and Rutter (1974); Bettelheim (1967); Rutter (1968); Zaslow and Breger (1969).

24. Wilcox (1956, case of Maria).

25. Adams (1972, 1973).

26. The examples are from Savage (1968, p. 85); Wing (1972, p. 18); and two from Kanner (1944, p. 215).

27. Wolfenstein (1954, p. 56).

28. Newson (1977). Many other functions, formerly considered beyond them, have been found in young infants (Stone, Smith, and Murphy 1973).

29. Kanner (1957); Ruesch (1957).

30. Bettelheim (1967); Hamblin et al. (1971). On adult schizophrenic speech as riddles, see Lorenz (1957); also Bateson et al. (1956); Haley (1959).

31. Bettelheim (1967).

32. Haley (1959, p. 330).

33. Ekstein (1966); Ruttenberg (1971).

34. Sussman and Sklar (1969, p. 799) See also Boatman and Szurek (1960); Churchill and Bryson (1972); Hutt and Hutt (1970); Hutt and Ounsted (1966, 1970).

35. Castell (1970); Furneaux (1966); Hutt and Ounsted (1966); Richer and Coss (1976); Wing (1972).

36. DesLauriers and Carlson (1969). See also Axline (1967); Beams (1967); Everard (1980); Fearnside (1967); Junker (1964); Kastein and Trace (1966); Lasscock (1967); Park (1967); Wing (1966).

37. See Myklebust (1965) on psychic deafness in relation to parental demand.

38. For example, Eberhardy (1967).

39. Bettelheim (1967); Foy (1970); Kastein and Trace (1966); Park (1967).

40. Bettelheim (1967); Hutt and Ounsted (1966).

Chapter 15   Additional Pieces

1. Levy (1955); Maier (1939).

2. Bruch (1970, 1973, 1978).

3. Fraiberg (1950).

4. Ney (1979); Pearson (1947).

5. The phraseology of Bergman and Escalona (1949) contributed to misconstruction of their report.

6. Macfarlane (1975).

7. O'Connor and Hermelin (1963).

8. "It is of course well known that rocking with the thighs pressed together is a common method of masturbation in infancy" because the thighs press against the genitals (FitzHerbert 1952, p. 331). See also Brody (1960); Kinsey, Pomeroy, and Martin (1948); Kleeman (1976); Levine (1951); Lewis (1965); Spitz and Wolf (1949). Lourie (1949) disagreed.

9. Kravitz et al. (1960 p. 203).

10. Ilg and Ames (1955); Kravitz et al. (1960).

11. Escalona (1963).

12. Ferster (1966b).

13. On grief and depression, see Bowlby (1961); Spitz (1953). On frustration, Levy (1944). On separation, Brody (1960); Levine (1951); Silberstein, Backman, and Mandell (1966); Spitz (1953); Spitz and Wolf (1949); Thomas (1961). On weaning, FitzHerbert (1952). On mother's anger, Furer (1964).

14. Furer (1964). On kissing and caressing, see also Bosch (1970); O'Gorman (1967).

15. Rochlin (1953, p. 293).

16. Goldfarb et al. (1970, p. 159). See also Putnam, Rank, and Kaplan (1951), Craig (1978).

17. Boatman and Szurek (1960, p. 396). See also Benda (1960); Bettelheim (1956; 1967, case of Joey); Bosch (1970); Brask (1959); Kanner (1943, case of Paul; 1952, case of Jay); Klein (1960); Morgan (1981); O'Gorman (1967); Reiser (1963); Ross (1955); Ruttenberg et al. (1966); Schachter, Meyer, and Loomis (1962); Speers and Lansing (1965); Sylvester (1945); Thomas (1966); Tustin (1972); Weil (1953a); Weitman (1973); Wergeland (1964); Wing (1972). Fabian and Holden (1951) considered sexual behavior so common in autistic children as to be a diagnostic criterion.

18. Sears, Maccoby, and Levin (1957).

19. Duffy (1963); Richards (1930); Spitz (1952); Szasz (1975).

20. Kinsey, Pomeroy, and Martin (1948, p. 177).

21. Lewis (1965, p. 372). He also questioned mothers and found that one in seven reported such behavior, but they showed embarrassment and seemed not to consider the behavior sexual. See also Halversan (1938); Kaufman (1970); Kleeman (1976); Korner (1969); Sears, Maccoby, and Levin (1957). Bowlby (1969) said such thrusting in primate infants had an attachment function.

22. Duffy (1963, p. 246). See also Richards (1930); Spitz (1952); Taylor (1970). Among the diseases said to be caused by masturbation was autism (Sinkler 1892).

23. Attribution of the taboo to divine revelation was incorrect since Onan's biblical sin involved coitus interruptus rather than masturbation.

24. Fenichel (1945); Galenson and Roiphe (1976); Spitz (1952); Tausk (1951).

25. Levine (1951).

26. Kanner (1943, p. 246, italics in original). Starr (1954) referred to "unremitting autoerotic activity"; Mahler and Elkisch (1953) to "paroxysms of excitement" that, however, struck them more as mechanical than sexual. See also Furer (1964); Kanner (1944).

27. Ruttenberg et al. (1966).

28. Boatman and Szurek (1960); Bosch (1970); MacDougall and Lebovici (1969); O'Gorman (1967); Reiser (1963); Shaberman (1971); Speers and Lansing (1966); Weil (1953).

29. Bosch (1970); Craig (1978); Rank (1955); Speers and Lansing (1965); and individual cases later in the section.

30. Bettelheim (1967); Kanner (1949, 1951); Sperling (1954); Szurek and Berlin (1973).

31. This and the following examples are from MacDougall and Lebovici (1969); Staver (1953); Hellman (1954); Bettelheim (1967, case of Marcia). For other cases with reported or implied erotic stimulation, see Eveloff (1960); Frijling-Schreuder (1969); Gerard and Overstreet (1957); Goldfarb et al. (1970); Green (1970); Greenberg (1970); O'Gorman (1967); Putnam, Rank, and Kaplan (1951); Park (1967); Rothenberg (1977, case of Chaim); Sperling (1954); Thomas (1966, case of Basil). See also Alanen (1966).

32. Spitz (1962); Spitz and Wolf (1946). See also Mittelman (1955). The mother-infant seclusion common in cases of autism in itself would tend to foster mutual overstimulation. In turn, overstimulation tends to foster sudden withdrawal by mothers (Hellman 1954).

33. Rothenberg (1977, p. 110).

34. For related observations, see Speers and Lansing (1965).

35. Brody (1960) suggested that infants rock in order to present their buttocks to be slapped—that they are conditioned to rock by mothers who slap their buttocks affectionately. See also Silberstein, Blackman, and Mandell (1966).

36. Bettelheim (1967). See Burton (1974) on anal intimacies and schizophrenia.

37. English and Pearson (1945, p. 115) noted, "The child therefore is being stimulated by his mother but at the same time has to repress any physical reaction." See also Jackson (1958); Levine (1951); Rheingold (1964).

38. Bosch (1970, Hans, who received such attentions, masturbated openly; see also the cases of Dieter and Karl). See also Bettelheim (1967, case of Laurie); Ross (1955).

39. Greenberg (1971).

40. Tausk (1951); Freud and Burlingham (1973); Galenson and Roiphe (1976). Call (1963), Despert (1951), and MacDougall and Lebovici (1969) suggested that conflict about erotic feelings toward autistic children resulted in parental rejection of them or avoidance of sensual contact. Arousal by parents tends to result in giving children contradictory cues.

41. Giffin, Litin, and Johnson (1969); McCord, McCord, and Thurber (1962).

42. Sperling (1954).

43. Jackson (1958); Galenson and Roiphe (1976).

44. Temkin (1971).

45. Evans (1961); Solnit (1968).

46. Meltzer (1974). A typical observation is, "He spent most of his time ... with his fingers fanning in front of his eyes, apparently totally preoccupied ... to the exclusion of all else about him" (Berlin 1973a, p. 529). According to DeMyer, Bryson, and Churchill (1973), this kind of staring in early infancy particularly distin-

guishes autistic children from normal children. Kaufman (1975, p. 37) listed "hypnotic preoccupation with spinning, rocking, and repetitive movements" as a diagnostic feature. Bettelheim (1967) stressed fascination with spinning objects. See also Everard (1980); Kanner (1943); Ornitz (1971, 1976); Ornitz and Ritvo (1968); Ruttenberg et al. (1966); Speers and Lansing (1964); Wergeland (1964).

47. Colman et al. (1976); Frankel et al. (1976).

48. In Focher (1965, p. 513). See also Andermann (1971); Gottschalk (1956); Harley, Baird, and Freeman (1967); Hutchison, Stone, and Davidson (1958); Mitchell, Falconer, and Hill (1954); Olds (1958). Babies have been rocked since early times because of the hypnotic effect.

49. Exposure to the sun was once considered a cause of autism (Sinkler 1892).

50. Oriental people have long used chanting to alter consciousness. Autistic children do not chant in the usual sense, but their speaking rhythm has been found to resemble chanting (Goldfarb, Braunstein, and Lorge (1956).

51. Many children are more sensitive to flicker when their eyes are closed than open (Bower 1963); Pantelakos, Bower, and Jones (1962).

52. Kaufman (1976, p. 51).

53. Bickford and Klass (1969); Bower (1963); Schwab (1956); Symonds (1959).

54. Ornitz and Ritvo (1976). See also Ornitz (1970, 1971).

55. Bickford and Klass (1969); Ulett (1951); Walter and Walter (1949).

56. Earl (1934); Focher (1965); Jeavons and Harding (1975).

57. Gottschalk (1956).

58. Bickford, Daly, and Keith (1953); Klapatek (1959).

59. Cunningham and Dixon (1961). See also Lewis and Van Ferney (1960); Speers and Lansing (1965, case of Tina; see also case of Bob).

60. Gastaut (1958); Libo, Palmer, and Archibald (1971). On self-induction as a defense against double-bind demands, see King (1970).

61. Creak (1963); Lotter (1974); Rimland (1973); Rutter and Bartak (1971); Schain and Yannet (1960); Verhees (1976). Seizures have been found common in autistic children's infancy (Goodwin 1971), but that may not be abnormal (Milner 1955).

Chapter 16   Retrospect and Prospect

1. Kaufman (1976).

2. Wing (1972); DesLauriers and Carlson (1969).

Bibliography

The following abbreviations are used in the bibliography.

A	= American	Medl	= Medical
Abn	= Abnormal	Medn	= Medicine
Ann	= Annual	Men	= Mental
Arch	= Archives	Ner	= Nervous
B	= Books	Ortho	= Orthopsychiatry
Beh	= Behavior, Behavioral or Behaviour	P	= Press
		Ped(s)	= Pediatric(s)
Br	= British	Pgical	= Psychological
Ch	= Child	Pgist	= Psychologist
Chn	= Children	Pgy	= Psychology
Clin	= Clinic(s) or Clinical	Psa	= Psychoanalysis or Psychoanalytic
Def	= Deficiency		
Dev	= Development or Developmental	Ptric	= Psychiatric
		Ptrica	= Psychiatrica
Dis	= Disease(s)	Ptry	= Psychiatry
Disor	= Disorders	Q	= Quarterly
Exp	= Experimental	Rec	= Record
Genet	= Genetic	Rep	= Reports
Genr	= General	Res	= Research
I	= International	Sci	= Science(s)
J	= Journal	Soc	= Society
JACS	= Journal of Autism and Childhood Schizophrenia	U	= University or Universities
JADD	= Journal of Autism and Developmental Disorders		

Abraham, K. Contributions to the Theory of the Anal Character. In *Selected Papers*. Basic B, 1968.

Abrahams, J. and Varon, E. *Maternal Dependency and Schizophrenia*. IUP, 1953.

Ack, M. Julie. *Psa Study Ch*, 21: 127–149, 1966.

Ackerley, M. Book Review. *JADD*, 9: 129–130, 1979.

Adams, P.L. Family Characteristics of Obsessive Children. *A J Ptry*, 128: 1414–1417, 1972.

————. *Obsessive Children*. Brunner/Mazel, 1973.

Agnew, P. 13 Retarded Children Learn to Read Spontaneously. *Star-Ledger* (Newark, N.J.), Jan. 11, 1972, p. 22.

Ainsworth, M.D. The Effects of Maternal Deprivation. In *Deprivation of Maternal Care*. World Health Organization, 1962.

————. The Development of Infant-Mother Interaction among the Ganda. In Foss, B.M. (Ed) *Determinants of Infant Behaviour*. Methuen, Vol. 2, 1963.

————. *Infancy in Uganda*. Johns Hopkins P, 1967a.

————. Patterns of Infantile Attachment to Mother. In Brackbill, Y. and Thompson, G.G. (Eds) *Behavior in Infancy and Early Childhood*. Free P, 1967b.

Ainsworth, M.D. and Bell, S.M. Attachment, Exploration, and Separation. *Ch Dev*, 41, 49–67, 1970.

Ainsworth, M.D., Bell, S.M. and Stayton, D.J. Individual Differences in the Development of Some Attachment Behaviors. *Merrill-Palmer Q*, 18: 123–143, 1972.

————. Individual Differences in Strange-Situation Behavior of One-Year-Olds. In Stone, L.J., Smith, H.B. and Murphy, L.B. (Eds) *The Competent Infant*. Basic B, 1973.

Ainsworth, M.D. and Wittig, B.R. Attachment and Exploratory Behavior of One-Year-Olds in a Strange Situation. In Foss, B.M. (Ed) *Determinants of Infant Behaviour*. Methuen, Vol. 4, 1969.

Alanen, Y.O. The Mothers of Schizophrenic Patients. *Acta Ptrica Neurologica Scandinavica*, 33: Supp. 124, 1958.

————. The Family in the Pathogenesis of Schizophrenic and Neurotic Disorders. *Acta Ptrica Scandinavica*, 42: Supp. 189, 1966.

Alcock, T. Conclusions from Psychiatric Work with Evacuated Children. *Br J Medl Pgy*, 21: 181–184, 1948.

Aldrich, C.A. Ancient Processes in a Scientific Age. *A J Dis Chn*, 64: 714–722, 1942.

Alvarez, A. Children in the Shadows. *Parents' Mag*, Mar. 1972, p. 54.

Anastasi, A. and Levee, R.F. Intellectual Defect and Musical Talent. *A J Men Def*, 64: 695–703, 1960.

Anastasiadis, Y.S. A Study on the Psychopathological Influence of Parental Environment on Neurotic and Schizoid Patients. *Acta Psychotherapeutica*, 11: 370–390, 1963.

Andermann, F. Self-induced Television Epilepsy. *Epilepsia*, 12: 269–275, 1971.

Anthony, E.J. An Experimental Approach to the Psychopathology of Childhood Autism. *Br J Medl Pgy*, 31: 211–225, 1958.

————. The Syndrome of the Psychologically Invulnerable Child. In Anthony, E.J. and Koupernik, C. (Eds) *The Child in His Family*. Wiley, Vol. 3, 1974.

————. Childhood Depression. In Anthony, E.J. and Benedek, T. (Eds) *Depression and Human Existence*. Little Brown, 1975.

Antonovic, O.H. Depressive Elements in Early Childhood Schizophrenia. In Annell, A.L. (Ed) *Depressive States in Childhood and Adolescence.* Halsted, 1972.

Appell, G. and David, M. Case Notes on Monique. In Foss, B.M. (Ed) *Determinants of Infant Behaviour.* Methuen, Vol. I, 1961.

Arajarvi, T., Alanen, Y.O. and Viitamaki, R.O. Psychoses in Childhood. *Acta Ptrica Scandinavica,* 40: Supp. 174, 1964.

Arick, J.R. and Krug, D.R. Autistic Children. *A J Men Def,* 83: 200–202, 1978.

Arieti, S. *Interpretation of Schizophrenia.* Brunner, 1st ed, 1955; Basic B, 2nd ed, 1974.

––––––– . Creativity and its Cultivation. In *American Handbook of Psychiatry.* Basic B, Vol. 3, 1966.

Arnold, G.E. Writing instead of Speaking. *Current Problems Phoniatry Logopedics,* 1: 155–162, 1960.

Arsenian, J.M. Young Children in an Insecure Situation. *J Abn Social Pgy,* 38: 225–249, 1943.

Arthur, B. and Kemme, M.L. Bereavement in Childhood. *J Ch Pgy Ptry,* 5: 37–49, 1964.

Arthur, B. and Schumann, S. Family and Peer Relationships in Children with Paranoid Delusions. *Ch Ptry Human Dev,* 1: 83–101, 1970.

Averill, J.R. and Rosenn, M. Vigilant and Nonvigilant Coping Strategies and Psychophysiological Stress Reactions during the Anticipation of Shock. *J Personality Social Pgy,* 23: 128–141, 1972.

Axline, V.M. *Dibs.* Houghton Mifflin, 1964.

Bainbridge, P.L. Learning in the Rat. *J Comparative Physiological Pgy,* 82: 301–307, 1973.

Baker, A.A. *Psychiatric Disorders in Obstetrics.* Blackwell, 1967.

Baker, A.M. Cognitive Functioning of Psychotic Children. *Exceptional Chn,* 45: 344–348, 1979.

Baker, B.L. and Ward, M.H. Reinforcement Therapy for Behavior Problems in Severely Retarded Children. *A J Ortho,* 41: 124–135, 1971.

Bakwin, H. and Bakwin, R.M. *Clinical Management of Behavior Disorders in Children.* Saunders, 3rd ed, 1966.

Balint, A. Love for the Mother and Mother Love. In Balint, M. *Primary Love and Psycho-Analytic Technique.* Liveright, 1965.

Ballard, R.A., Leonard, C.H., Irvin, N.A., and Ferris, C.P. An Alternative Birth Center in a Hospital Setting. In Klaus, M.H. and Kennell, J.H. (Eds) *Parent-Infant Bonding.* Mosby, 2nd ed, 1982.

Bandura, A. Self-Efficacy Mechanisms in Human Agency. *A Pgist,* 37: 122–147, 1982.

Barnard, K.E. An Ecological Approach to Parent-Child Relations. In Brown, C.C. (Ed) *Infants at Risk.* Johnson & Johnson, 1981.

Barnett, C.R., Leiderman, P.H., Grobstein, R. and Klaus, M.H. Neonatal Separation. *Peds,* 45: 197–205, 1970.

Barrett, B.H. and Lindsley, O.R. Deficits in Acquisition of Operant Discrimination and Differentiation Shown by Institutionalized Retarded Children. *A J Men Def,* 67: 424–436, 1962.

Barsch, R.A. *The Parent of the Handicapped Child.* Thomas, 1968.

Bart, P.B. Depression in Middle-Aged Women. In Bardwick, J.M. (Ed) *Readings on the Psychology of Women.* Harper & Row, 1972.

Bartak, L. and Rutter, M. The Use of Personal Pronouns by Autistic Children. *JACS,* 4: 217–222, 1974.

Bartel, N.R. and Guskin, S.L. A Handicap Is a Social Phenomenon. In Cruikshank, W.H. (Ed) *Psychology of Exceptional Children and Youth.* Prentice-Hall, 3rd ed, 1971.

Bartmeier, L.H. Psychoses in the Feebleminded. *J Psycho-Asthenics,* 30: 314–322, 1925.

Bartolucci, G. and Albers, R.J. Deictic Categories in the Language of Autistic Children. *JACS,* 4: 131–141, 1974.

Bateson, G., Jackson, D.D., Haley, J. and Weakland, J. Toward a Theory of Schizophrenia. *Beh Sci,* 1: 251–265, 1956.

Beach, W.B. Psychosis in Childhood. *Northwest Medn,* 56: 438–442, 1957.

Beadle, M. *A Child's Mind.* Doubleday, 1970.

Beams, M. Discussion. In Eszenyi, D. (Ed) *Autism.* Autistic Children's Assn S Australia, c1967.

Beck, S.J. Bimodality in Schizophrenia. *Br J Medl Pgy,* 45: 221–232, 1972.

Beck, S.J. and Nunnally, J.C. Parental Attitudes in Families. *Arch Genr Ptry,* 13: 208–213, 1965.

Becker, E. *The Revolution in Psychiatry.* Free P, 1964.

————. Socialization, Command of Performance, and Mental Illness. In Spitzer, S.P. and Denzin, N.K. (Eds) *The Mental Patient.* McGraw-Hill, 1968.

Becker, R.D. Childhood Psychosis by Leo Kanner. *A J Men Def,* 78: 770–771, 1974.

Beckett, P.G.S., Robinson, D.B., Frazier, S.H., Steinhilber, R.M., Duncan, G.M., Estes, H.R., Litin, E.M., Grattan, R.T., Lorton, W.L., Williams, G.E. and Johnson, A.M. The Significance of Exogenous Traumata in the Genesis of Schizophrenia. *Ptry,* 19: 137–142, 1956.

Beckett, P.G.S., Senf, R., Frohman, C. and Gottlieb, J.S. Energy Production and Premorbid History in Schizophrenia. *Arch Genr Ptry,* 8: 155–162, 1963.

Bell, S.M. and Ainsworth, M.D. Infant Crying and Maternal Responsiveness. *Ch Dev,* 43: 1171–1190, 1972.

Bemporad, J.R. Adult Reflections of a Formerly Autistic Child. *JADD,* 9: 179–197, 1979.

Benda, C.E. Psychopathology of Childhood. In Carmichael, L. (Ed) *Manual of Child Psychology.* Wiley, 2nd ed, 1954.

————. Childhood Schizophrenia, Autism and Heller's Disease. In Bowman, P.W. and Mautner, H.V. (Eds) *Mental Retardation.* Grune & Stratton, 1960.

Bender, L. The Development of a Schizophrenic Child Treated with Electric Convulsions at Three Years of Age. In Caplan, G. (Ed) *Emotional Problems of Early Childhood.* Tavistock, 1955.

Bender, L. and Faretra, G. The Relationship between Childhood Schizophrenia and Adult Schizophrenia. In Kaplan, A.R. (Ed) *Genetic Factors in "Schizophrenia."* Thomas, 1972.

Bender, L. and Freedman, A.M. A Study of the First Three Years in the Maturation of Schizophrenic Children. *Q J Ch Beh,* 4: 245–272, 1952.

Benedek, T. The Psychobiology of Pregnancy. In Anthony, E.J. and Benedek, T. (Eds) *Parenthood.* Little Brown, 1970.

Benjamin, E. The Period of Resistance in Early Childhood. *A J Dis Chn,* 63: 1019–1079, 1942.

Benjamin, J.D. Further Comments on Some Developmental Aspects of Anxiety. In Gaskill, H.S. (Ed) *Counterpoint.* IUP, 1963.

Bensberg, G.J. Concept Learning in Mental Defectives as Function of Appropriate and Inappropriate "Attention Sets." In Trapp, E.P. and Himelstein, P. (Eds) *Readings on the Exceptional Child.* Appleton-Century-Crofts, 2nd ed, 1972.

Bergler, E. *Parents Not Guilty!* Liveright, 1964.

Bergman, A. "I and You." In McDevitt, J.B. and Settlage C.F. (Eds) *Separation-Individuation.* IUP, 1971.

Bergman, M., Waller, H. and Marchand, J. Schizophrenic Reactions during Childhood in Mental Defectives. *Ptric Q,* 25: 294–333, 1951.

Bergman, P. and Escalona, S. Unusual Sensitivities in Very Young Children. *Psa Study Ch,* 3–4: 333–352, 1949.

Bergmann, T. *Children in the Hospital.* IUP, 1965.

Berkson, G. Psychophysiological Studies in Mental Deficiency. In Ellis, N.R. (Ed) *Handbook of Mental Deficiency.* McGraw-Hill, 1963.

———. Abnormal Stereotyped Motor Acts. In Zubin, J. and Hunt, H.F. (Eds) *Comparative Psychopathology.* Grune & Stratton, 1967.

Berlin, I.N. A Clinical Note on the Reversibility of Autistic Behavior in a 20-Month-Old Child. In Szurek, S.A. and Berlin, I.N. (Eds) *Clinical Studies in Childhood Psychoses.* Brunner/Mazel, 1973a.

Berlin, I.N. Intrapersonal, Interpersonal, and Impersonal Factors in the Genesis of Childhood Schizophrenia. In Szurek, S.A. and Berlin, I.N. (Eds) *Clinical Studies in Childhood Psychoses.* Brunner/Mazel, 1973b.

Berlyne, D.E. *Conflict, Arousal, and Curiosity.* McGraw-Hill, 1960.

———. Soviet Research in Intellectual Processes in Children. In Society for Research in Child Development. *Cognitive Development in Children.* U Chicago P, 1970.

Bernfeld, S. *Psychology of the Infant.* Kegan Paul Trench Trubner, 1929.

Bernstein, A. Some Relations between Techniques of Feeding and Training during Infancy and Certain Behavior in Childhood. *Genet Pgy Mono,* 51: 3–44, 1955.

Bernstein, N.R. and Menolascino, F.J. Apparent and Relative Mental Retardation. In Menolascino, F.J. (Ed) *Psychiatric Approaches to Mental Retardation.* Basic B, 1970.

Berrini, M.E. and Tommazzolli, C.M. Depressing Aspects of Mental Inhibition and Pseudoretardation. In Annell, A.L. (Ed) *Depressive States in Childhood and Adolescence.* Halsted, 1972.

Besdine, M. The Jocasta Complex, Mothering and Genius. *Psa Rev,* 55: 259–277 and 574–600, 1968.

———. The Jocasta Complex, Mothering and Women Geniuses. *Psa Rev,* 58: 51–74, 1971.

Bettelheim, B. Schizophrenia as a Reaction to Extreme Situations. *A J Ortho,* 26: 507–518, 1956.

———. *The Empty Fortress.* Free P, 1967.

Bettelheim, B. and Sylvester, E. Physical Symptoms in Emotionally Disturbed Children. *Psa Study Ch,* 3–4: 353–368, 1949.

Betz, B.J. A Psychiatric Children's Ward. *A J Nursing,* 45: 817–821, 1945.

Bibring, E. The Mechanism of Depression. In Greenacre, P. (Ed) *Affective Disorders.* IUP, 1953.

———— . The Mechanism of Depression. In Gaylin, W. (Ed) *The Meaning of Despair*. Aronson, 1968.

Bickford, R.G., Daly, D. and Keith, H.M. Convulsive Effects of Light Stimulation in Children. *A J Dis Chn*, 86: 170–183, 1953.

Bickford, R.G. and Klass, D.W. Sensory Precipitation and Reflex Mechanisms. In Jasper, H.H., Ward, A.A. and Pope, A. (Eds) *Basic Mechanisms of the Epilepsies*. Little Brown, 1969.

Binswanger, L. Introduction to Schizophrenie. In *Being in the World*. Basic B, 1963.

Birch, H.G. and Walker, H.A. Perceptual and Perceptual-Motor Dissociation. *Arch Genr Ptry*, 14: 113–118, 1966.

Birnbrauer, J.S. Mental Retardation. In Leitenberg, H. (Ed) *Handbook of Behavior Modification and Behavior Therapy*. Prentice-Hall, 1976.

Birns, B., Blank, M. and Bridger, W.H. The Effectiveness of Various Soothing Techniques on Human Neonates. In Stone, L.J., Smith, H.B. and Murphy, L.B. (Eds) *The Competent Infant*. Basic B, 1973.

Birtchnell, J. The Possible Consequences of Early Parent Death. *Br J Medl Pgy*, 42: 1–12, 1969.

Blakely, S.B. The Psychology of Pregnancy. *Trans A Assn Obstetricians, Gynecologists, Abdominal Surgeons*, 53: 151–160, 1940.

Blank, H.R., Smith, O.C. and Bruch, H. Schizophrenia in a Four Year Old Boy. *A J Ptry*, 100: 805–810, 1943.

Blatz, W.E. *Human Security*. U Toronto P, 1966.

Blau, A. The Nature of Childhood Schizophrenia. *J Ch Ptry*, 1: 225–235, 1962.

Bloom, B.J. *Stability and Change in Human Characteristics*. Wiley, 1964.

Bloomfield, A.E. How Many Mothers Breast Feed? *Practitioner*, 188: 393–396, 1962.

Blum, L.H. Not All Are Definitely Defective. *Men Hygiene*, 42: 211–223, 1958.

Boatman, M.J. and Szurek, S.A. A Clinical Study of Childhood Schizophrenia. In Jackson, D.D. (Ed) *The Etiology of Schizophrenia*. Basic B, 1960.

Bogdan, R. and Taylor, S. The Judged, not the Judges. *A Pgist*, 31: 47–52, 1976.

Bogdanov, E.I. A Study of the Influence of Immediately Past Experience on Visual Perception in Schizophrenia. *Pgical Abstracts*, 50: 1, 1973.

Bonica, J.J. *Principles and Practice of Obstetric Analgesia and Anesthesia*. F.A. Davis, Vol. I, 1967.

Bosch, G. *Infantile Autism*. Springer, 1970.

Bowen, M. A Family Concept of Schizophrenia. In Jackson, D.D. (Ed) *The Etiology of Schizophrenia*. Basic B, 1960.

Bower, B.D. Television Flicker and Fits. *Clin Peds*, 2:134–138, 196

Bowlby, J. *Maternal Care and Mental Health*. World Health Org, 2nd ed, 1952.

———— . Grief and Mourning in Infancy and Early Childhood. *Psa Study Ch*, 15: 9–52, 1960a.

———— . Separation Anxiety. *I J Psa*, 41: 89–113, 1960b.

———— . Childhood Mourning and Psychiatric Illness. In Lomas, P. (Ed) *The Predicament of the Family*. IUP, 1967.

———— . *Attachment and Loss*, Vol. 1: *Attachment*. Basic B, 1969a.

———— . The Effects on Behaviour of Disruption of an Affectional Bond. In Thoday, J.D. and Parkes, A.S. (Eds) *Genetic and Environmental Influences on Behaviour*. Oliver & Boyd, 1969b.

———— . *Attachment and Loss*, Vol. 2: *Loss*. Basic B, 1973.

Bowlby, J., Robertson, J. and Rosenbluth, D. A Two-Year-Old Goes to the Hospital. *Psa Study Ch*, 7: 82–96, 1952.

Bowley, A.H. and Gardner, L. *The Young Handicapped Child.* Livingstone, 2nd ed, 1969.

Boyer, L.B. On Maternal Overstimulation and Ego Defects. *Psa Study Ch*, 11: 236–256, 1956.

Brackbill, Y. The Long-Term Effects of Obstetric Medication on Cognitive Functioning and Response. Paper read at Obstetrical Management Infant Outcome Conf, New York, Nov. 16, 1977.

Brackbill, Y., Adams, G., Crowell, D.H. and Gray, M.L. Arousal Level of Neonates and Preschool Children under Continuous Auditory Stimulation. *J Exp Ch Pgy*, 4: 178–188, 1966.

Brackbill, Y. and Thompson, G.G. (eds.) *Behavior in Infancy and Early Childhood.* Free P., 1967.

Bradford, L.J. and Carter, T. Pseudo-Hearing Losses. Paper read at A Assn Ptric Svcs Chn, New York, Nov. 23, 1974.

Bradley, C. Biography of a Schizophrenic Child. *Ner Ch*, 1: 141–171, 1942.

Braginsky, D.D. and Braginsky, B.M. *Hansels and Gretels.* Holt Rinehart Winston, 1971.

Braginsky, B.M., Braginsky, D.D. and Ring, K. *Methods of Madness.* Holt Rinehart Winston, 1969.

Brask, B.H. Borderline Schizophrenia in Children. *Acta Ptrica Neurologica Scandinavica*, 34: 265–282, 1959.

Brazelton, T.B. Psychophysiologic Reactions in the Neonate. *J Peds*, 58: 508–512, 1961.

Brazelton, T.B., Tronick, E., Adamson, L., Als, H. and Wise, S. Early Mother-Infant Reciprocity. In Ciba Foundation. *Parent-Infant Interaction.* Elsevier, 1975.

Brazelton, T.B., Young, G.G. and Bullowa, M. Inception and Resolution of Early Developmental Pathology. *J Ch Ptry*, 10: 124–136, 1971.

Breger, L. *From Instinct to Identity.* Prentice-Hall, 1974.

Brew, M.F. and Seidenberg, R. Psychotic Reactions Associated with Pregnancy and Childbirth. *J Ner Men Dis*, 111: 408–423, 1950.

Bridger, W.H. and Birns, B. Experience and Temperament in Human Neonates. In Newton, G. and Levine, S. (Eds) *Early Experience and Behavior.* Thomas, 1968.

Briffault, R. *The Mothers.* Allen & Unwin, 1959.

Britton, R.S. Psychiatric Disorders in the Mothers of Disturbed Children. *J Ch Pgy Ptry*, 10: 245–258, 1969.

Broadhurst, P.L. Abnormal Animal Behaviour. In Eysenck, H.J. (Ed) *Handbook of Abnormal Psychology.* Basic B, 1961.

Brodey, W.M. Some Family Operations and Schizophrenia. *Arch Genr Ptry*, 1: 379–402, 1959.

Brody, S. Self-Rocking in Infancy. *J A Psa Assn*, 8: 464–491, 1960.

Brody, S. and Axelrad, S. *Anxiety and Ego Formation in Infancy.* IUP, 1970.

——— . *Mothers, Fathers, and Children.* IUP, 1978.

Bronfenbrenner, U. Early Deprivation in Mammals. In Newton, G. and Levine, S. (Eds) *Early Experience and Behavior.* Thomas, 1968.

Bronson, G.W. The Fear of Novelty. *Pgical Bull*, 69: 350–358, 1968.

Broussard, E.R. Primary Prevention Program for Newborn Infants at High Risk for Emotional Disorder. In Klein, D. and Goldston, S. (Eds) *Primary Prevention.* DHEW, 1977.

————. Assessment of the Adaptive Potential of the Mother-Infant System. *Seminars in Perinatology,* 3: 91–100, 1979.

Broussard, E.R. and Hartner, M.S.S. Maternal Perception of the Neonate as Related to Development. *Ch Ptry Human Dev,* 1: 16–25, 1970.

Brown, F. Bereavement and Lack of a Parent in Childhood. In Miller, E. (Ed) *Foundations of Child Psychiatry.* Pergamon, 1968.

Brown, F. Depression and Childhood Bereavement. In Annell, A.L. (Ed) *Depressive States in Childhood and Adolescence.* Halsted, 1972.

Brown, G.T. Schizophrenia in Children. *J Indiana St Medl Assn,* 53: 1906–1916, 1960.

Brown, J.L. Follow-up of Children with Atypical Development (Infantile Psychosis). *A J Ortho,* 33: 855–861, 1963.

Bruch, H. The Various Developments in the Approach to Childhood Schizophrenia. *Acta Ptrica Neurologica Scandinavica,* 34: Supp. 130, 5–27, 1959.

————. Transformation of Oral Impulses in Eating Disorders. *Ptric Q,* 35: 458–481, 1961.

————. Falsification of Bodily Needs and Body Concept in Schizophrenia. *Arch Genr Ptry,* 6: 18–24, 1962a.

————. The Constructive Use of Ignorance. *Bull Assn Psa Medn,* 2: 19–23, 1962b.

————. Family Background in Eating Disorders. In Anthony, E.J. and Koupernik, C. (Eds) *The Child in His Family.* Wiley, Vol. 1, 1970.

————. *Eating Disorders.* Basic B, 1973.

————. *The Golden Cage.* Harvard U P, 1978.

Bruner, J.S. *Processes of Cognitive Growth.* Clark U P, 1968.

————. Early Social Interaction and Language Acquisition. In Schaffer, H.R. (Ed) *Studies in Mother-Infant Interaction.* Academic P, 1977.

Buium, N. and Stuecher, H.U. On Some Language Parameters of Autistic Echolalia. *Language Speech,* 17: 353–357, 1974.

Bullard, D., Glaser, H.H., Heagarty, M.C. and Pivchik, E.H. Failure to Thrive in the "Neglected" Child. *Ann Prog Ch Ptry Ch Dev,* 540–544, 1968.

Burlingham, D. and Freud, A. *Young Children in War-Time.* Allen & Unwin, 1942.

Burnham, D.L. Separation Anxiety. *Arch Genr Ptry,* 13: 346–358, 1965.

————. Child-Parent Relationships which Impede Differentiation and Integration. In Burnham, D.L., Gladstone, A.I. and Gibson, R.W. *Schizophrenia and the Need-Fear Dilemma.* IUP, 1969a.

————. Schizophrenia and Object Relations. In Burnham, D.L., Gladstone, A.I. and Gibson, R.W. *Schizophrenia and the Need-Fear Dilemma.* IUP, 1969b.

Bursten, B. and D'Esopo, R. The Obligation to Remain Sick. In Scheff, T.J. (Ed) *Mental Illness and Social Processes.* Harper & Row, 1967.

Burton, A. The Alchemy of Schizophrenia. In Burton, A., Lopez-Ibor, J.J. and Mendel, J.W.M. *Schizophrenia as a Life Style.* Springer, 1974.

Burtt, H.E. An Experimental Study of Early Childhood Memory. *J Genet Pgy,* 58: 435–439, 1941.

Buxbaum, E. The Parents' Role in the Etiology of Learning Disturbances. In *Troubled Children in a Troubled World.* IUP, 1970.

————. Modern Woman and Motherhood. In Karasu, T.B. and Socarides, C.W. (Eds) *On Sexuality,* IUP, 1979.

Caldwell, B.M., Wright, C.M., Honig, A.S. and Tannenbaum, J. Infant Day Care and Attachment. *A J Ortho,* 40: 397–412, 1970.

Call, J.D. Interlocking Affective Freeze between an Autistic Child and his "As-If" Mother. *J Ch Ptry,* 2: 319–344, 1963a.

———. Prevention of Autism in a Young Infant in a Well-Child Conference. *J Ch Ptry,* 2: 451–459, 1963b.

———. Newborn Approach Behaviour and Early Ego Development. *I J Psa,* 45: 286–294, 1964.

———. Autistic Behavior in Infants and Young Children. In Kelley, V.F. (Ed) *Practice of Pediatrics.* Harper & Row, Vol. 1, 1974.

———. The Adaptive Process in Early Infancy. In Anthony, E.J. (Ed) *Explorations in Child Psychiatry.* Plenum, 1975.

Cameron, K. A Group of Twenty-Five Psychotic Children. *Acta Paedopsychiatrica,* 25: 117–122, 1958.

Cameron, N. *The Psychology of Behavior Disorders.* Houghton Mifflin, 1947.

Campbell, J. *The Hero with a Thousand Faces.* Meridian, 1956.

Campbell, M. Response. *JADD,* 10: 237–238, 1980.

Caparulo, B. and Cohen, D.J. Response. *JADD,* 10: 239–240, 1980.

Capobianco, R.J. Reasoning Methods and Reasoning Ability in Mentally Retarded and Normal Children. In Trapp, E.P. and Himelstein, P. (Eds) *Readings on the Exceptional Child.* Appleton-Century-Crofts, 1962.

Carithers, H.A. Mother-Pediatrician Relationship in the Neonatal Period. *Peds,* 38: 654–660, 1951.

Carluccio, C., Sours, J.R. and Kolb, L.C. Psychodynamics of Echo-Reactions. *Arch Genr Ptry,* 10: 623–629, 1964.

Castell, R. Physical Distance and Visual Attention as Measures of Social Interaction between Child and Adult. In Hutt, S.J. and Hutt, C. (Eds) *Behaviour Studies in Psychiatry.* Pergamon, 1970.

Chapin, H.D. A Plea for Accurate Statistics in Infants' Institutions. *Trans A Ped Soc,* 27: 180–185, 1915.

Chapman, J. The Early Symptoms of Schizophrenia. *Br J Ptry,* 112: 225–251, 1966.

Chapman, J. and McGhie, A. Echopraxia in Schizophrenia. *Br J Ptry,* 110: 365–374, 1964.

Charles, D.C. Adult Adjustment of some Deficient American Children. *A J Men Def,* 62: 300–304, 1957.

Charney, R. Pronoun Errors in Autistic Children. *Br J Disor Communication,* 15: 39–43, 1980.

Charny, I. The New Psychotherapies and Encounters of the Seventies. *Reflections,* 10: #3, 1–17, 1975.

Chassell, J. Family Constellation in the Etiology of Essential Alcoholism. *Ptry,* 1: 473–504, 1938.

Chess, S. Psychiatry of the First Three Years of Life. In Arieti, S. (Ed) *American Handbook of Psychiatry.* Basic B, Vol. 3, 1966.

———. Temperament and Children at Risk. In Anthony, E.J. and Koupernik, C. (Eds) *The Child in his Family.* Wiley, Vol. 1, 1970.

Chess, S. and Hassibi, M. Behavior Deviations in Mentally Retarded Children. *Ann Prog Ch Ptry Ch Dev,* 353–366, 1971.

Chess, S., Thomas, A. and Birch, H.G. Distortions in Developmental Reporting

Made by Parents of Behaviorally Disturbed Children. *J Ch Ptry,* 5: 226–234, 1966.

Childhood Autism and Related Conditions. *Br Medl J,* 761–762, 1980.

Chomsky, N. *Aspects of the Theory of Syntax.* MIT P, 1965.

Chomsky, N. *Language and Mind.* Harcourt Brace World, 1968.

Churchill, D.W. *Language of Autistic Children.* Winston, 1978.

Churchill, D.W. and Bryson, C.Q. Looking and Approach Behavior of Psychotic and Normal Children as a Function of Adult Attention or Preoccupation. *Comprehensive Ptry,* 13: 171–177, 1972.

Clancy, H., Dugdale, A. and Rendle-Short, J. The Diagnosis of Infantile Autism. *Devl Medn Ch Neurology,* 11: 432–442, 1969.

Clark, E.V. Some Aspects of the Conceptual Basis for First Language Acquisition. In Schiefelbusch, R.L. and Lloyd, L.L. (Eds) *Language Perspectives.* U Park P, 1974.

Clark, P. and Rutter, M. Compliance and Resistance in Autistic Children. *JACS,* 7: 33–48, 1977.

Clarke, A.M. and Clarke, A.D.B. Criteria and Classification of Subnormality. In *Mental Deficiency.* Free P, 3rd ed, 1975a.

————. Experimental Studies. In *Mental Deficiency.* Free P, 3rd ed, 1975b.

Cleland, C.A. Schizoid Trends in Children. *Canadian Medl Assn J,* 34: 514–518, 1936.

Cobrinik, L. Unusual Reading Ability in Severely Disturbed Children. *JACS,* 4: 163–175, 1974.

Coffey, H.S. and Umbarger, C.C. The Nature of Childhood Autism and Schizophrenia. In Coffey, H.S. and Wiener, L.L. *Group Treatment of Autistic Children.* Prentice-Hall, 1967.

Cohen, D.J. The Medical Care of Autistic Children. *Peds,* 51: 278–280, 1973.

Colby, K.M. The Rationale for Computer-Based Treatment of Language Difficulties in Nonspeaking Autistic Children. *JACS,* 3: 254–260, 1973.

Coleman, R.W., Kris, E. and Provence, S. A Study of Variations of Early Parental Attitudes. *Psa Study Ch,* 8: 20–47, 1953.

Coleman, R.W. and Provence, S. Environmental Retardation (Hospitalism) in Infants Living in Families. *Peds,* 19: 285–292, 1957.

Colman, A.D. Psychological State during First Pregnancy. *A J Ortho,* 39: 788–797, 1969.

Colman, A.D. and Colman, L.L. *Pregnancy.* Herder & Herder, 1971.

Colman, R.S., Frankel, F., Ritvo, E. and Freeman, B.J. The Effects of Fluorescent and Incandescent Illumination upon Repetitive Behaviors in Autistic Children. *JACS,* 6: 157–162, 1976.

Condon, W.S. A Primary Phase in the Organizing of Infant Responding Behaviour. In Schaffer, H.R. (Ed) *Studies in Mother-Infant Interaction.* Academic P, 1977.

Condon, W.S. and Sander, L.W. Neonatal Movement Is Synchronized with Adult Speech. *Sci,* 183: 99–101, 1974.

Cook, S.W. A Survey of the Methods Used to Produce "Experimental Neurosis." *A J Ptry,* 95: 1259–1276, 1939.

Copeland, J. *For the Love of Ann.* Ballantine, 1974.

Cowan, P.P., Hoddinott, B.A. and Wright, B.A. Compliance and Resistance in the Conditioning of Autistic Children. *Ch Dev,* 36: 913–923, 1965.

Craig, E. *One, Two, Three.* McGraw-Hill, 1978.

Crammond, W.A. Psychological Aspects of Uterine Dysfunction. *Lancet,* 267(2): 1241–1245, 1954.

Crawford, J.S. *Principles and Practice of Obstetric Anaesthesia.* Blackwell, 3rd ed, 1972.

Crawley, C. The Irish Society for Autistic Children. In Park, C.C. (Ed) *Research and Education.* NIMH, 1971.

Creak, M. Schizophrenia in Early Childhood. *Acta Paedopsychiatrica,* 30: 42–47, 1963.

———. Psychosis in Childhood. In Miller, E. (Ed) *Foundations of Child Psychiatry.* Pergamon, 1968.

———. Diagnostic and Treatment Variations in Child Psychoses and Mental Retardation. In Menolascino, F.J. (Ed) *Psychiatric Approaches to Mental Retardation.* Basic B, 1970.

Croft, P.G. Some Observations on Neurosis in Farm Animals. *J Men Sci,* 97: 584–588, 1951.

Cromer, R.F. Receptive Language in the Mentally Retarded. In Schiefelbusch, R.L. and Lloyd, L.L. (Eds) *Language Perspectives.* U Park P, 1974.

Cromwell, R.L. A Social Learning Approach to Mental Retardation. In Ellis, N.R. (Ed) *Handbook of Mental Deficiency.* McGraw-Hill, 1963.

Cruikshank, W.M. and Paul, J.L. The Psychological Characteristics of Brain-Injured Children. In Cruikshank, W.M. (Ed) *Psychology of Exceptional Children and Youth.* Prentice-Hall, 3rd ed, 1971.

Crum, J.E. Social Learning and Reinforcement History. In Walters, C.E. (Ed) *Mother-Infant Interaction.* Human Sciences, 1976.

Crumley, F.E. and Blumenthal, R.S. Children's Reactions to Temporary Loss of the Father. *A J Ptry,* 130: 778–782, 1973.

Cunningham, M.R. and Dixon, C. A Study of the Language of an Autistic Child. *J Ch Pgy Ptry,* 2: 193–202, 1961.

Curcio, F. and Paccia-Cooper, J. Response Sets in Autistic Echolalia. *Perceptual Motor Skills,* 53: 78, 1981.

Cutts, R.A. Differentiation between Pseudo-Mental Defectives with Emotional Disorders and Mental Defectives with Emotional Disturbances. *A J Men Def,* 61: 761–772, 1957.

Cytryn, L. and McKnew, D.H. Proposed Classification of Childhood Depression. *A J Ptry,* 129: 149–155, 1972.

———. Factors Influencing the Changing Clinical Expression of the Depressive Process in Children. *A J Ptry,* 131: 879–881, 1974.

Dalton, J. and Epstein, H. Counseling Parents of Mildly Retarded Children. *Social Casework,* 44: 523–530, 1963.

D'Ambrosio, R. *No Language but a Cry.* Doubleday, 1970.

Daneel, A.B. Early Childhood Autism. *S Afr Medl J,* 48: 28–30, 1974.

David, M. and Appell, G. Mother-Child Relationship. In Howells, J.G. (Ed) *Modern Perspectives in International Child Psychiatry.* Oliver & Boyd, 1969.

Davidson, J. Infantile Depression in a "Normal" Child. *J Ch Ptry,* 7, 522–535, 1968.

Davis, D.R. Family Processes in Mental Retardation. *A J Ptry,* 124: 340–350, 1967.

———. Depression as Adaptation to Crisis. *Br J Medl Pgy,* 43: 109–116, 1970.

Deardon, R. The Psychiatric Aspects of the Case Study Sample. In Stacey, M., Dearden, R., Pill, R. and Robinson, D. *Hospitals, Children and their Families.* Routledge & Kegan Paul, 1970.

de Beauvoir, S. The Second Sex. Knopf, 1964.

Delacato, C.H. *The Ultimate Stranger*. Doubleday, 1974.

Dember, W.N. and Earl, R.W. Analysis of Exploratory, Manipulatory, and Curiosity Behaviors. *Pgical Rev,* 64: 91–96, 1957.

DeMyer, M.K. Discussion. In Churchill, D.W., Alpern, G.D. and DeMyer, M.K. *Colloquium on Infantile Autism*. Thomas, 1971.

———. The Nature of the Neuropsychological Disability in Autistic Children. *JACS,* 5: 109–128, 1975.

———. *Parents and Children in Autism*. Winston, 1979.

DeMyer, M.K., Bryson, C.Q. and Churchill, D.W. The Earliest Indicators of Pathological Development. *Res Pubn Assn Res Ner Men Dis,* 51: 298–332, 1973.

DeMyer, M.K., Hingtgen, J.N. and Jackson, R.K. Infantile Autism Reviewed. *Schizophrenia Bull,* 7: 388–451, 1981.

Denenberg, V.H. Paradigms and Paradoxes in Views of the Infant. In Thoman, E.B. and Trotter, S. (Eds) *Social Responsiveness of Infants*. Johnson & Johnson, 1978.

Denenberg, V.H., Ottinger, D.R. and Stephens, M.W. Effects of Maternal Factors upon Growth and Behavior of the Rat. *Ch Dev,* 33: 65–71, 1962.

Dennis, W. *Children of the Creche*. Appleton-Century-Crofts, 1973.

Dennis, W. and Najarian, P. Infant Development under Environmental Handicap. *Pgical Mono,* 71: Whole no. 536, 1957.

Denny, M.R. Research in Learning and Performance. In Stevens, H.R. and Heber, R. (Eds) *Mental Retardation*. U Chicago P, 1964.

Dershimer, F.W. A Study in the Cause and Prevention of Functional Mental Disease. *A J Ortho,* 8: 302–328, 1938.

DesLauriers, A.M. and Carlson, C.F. *Your Child is Asleep*. Dorsey, 1969.

de Souza, D.S. Annihilation and Reconstruction of Object-Relationship in a Schizophrenic Girl. *I J Psa,* 41: 554–558, 1960.

Despert, J.L. Thinking and Motility Disorder in a Schizophrenic Child. *Ptric Q,* 15: 522–536, 1941.

———. Some Considerations Relating to the Genesis of Autistic Behavior in Children. *A J Ortho,* 21: 335–347, 1951.

———. Treatment in Child Schizophrenia. In Bychowski, G. and Despert, J.L. (Eds) *Specialized Techniques in Psychotherapy*. Basic B, 1952.

———. *The Emotionally Disturbed Child*. Brunner, 1965.

Deutsch, H. *The Psychology of Women*. Grune & Stratton, Vol. 2, 1945.

———. A Two Year Old Boy's First Love Comes to Grief. In Jessner, L. and Pavenstedt, E. (Eds) *Dynamic Psychopathology in Childhood*. Grune & Stratton, 1959.

Devereux, G. A Sociological Theory of Schizophrenia. *Psa Rev,* 26: 315–342, 1939.

DeVellis, R.F. and McCauley, C. Perception of Contingency and Mental Retardation. *JADD,* 9: 261–270, 1979.

Dewey, M. Dick. In Park, C.C. (Ed) *Research and Education*. NIMH, 1971.

Dexter, A.L. A Social Theory of Mental Deficiency. *A J Men Def,* 62: 920–928, 1958.

———. Research on Problems of Mental Subnormality. *A J Men Def,* 64: 835–838, 1960.

————. On the Politics and Sociology of Stupidity in our Society. In Becker, H.S. (Ed) *The Other Side*. Free P, 1964.

Deykin, E.Y. and MacMahon, B. Pregnancy, Delivery, and Neonatal Complications among Autistic Children. *A J Dis Chn*, 134: 860–864, 1980.

DiVitto, B. and Goldberg, S. The Effects of Newborn Medical Status on Early Parent-Infant Interaction. In Field, T.M. (Ed) *Infants Born at Risk*. SP Books, 1979.

Dizmang, L.H. Loss, Bereavement, and Depression in Childhood. *I Ptry Clin*, 6: #2, 175–195, 1969.

Doering, S.G. Coping with Childbirth. Paper read at Obstetrical Management Infant Outcome Conf, New York, Nov. 16, 1977.

Douglas, G. Psychotic Mothers. *Lancet*, 270(1): 124–125, 1956.

————. Puerperal Depression and Excessive Compliance with the Mother. *Br J Medl Pgy*, 36: 271–278, 1963.

Drillien, C.M. *The Growth and Development of the Prematurely Born Infant*. Williams & Wilkins, 1964.

Duffy, J. Masturbation and Clitoridectomy. *J A Medl Assn*, 186: 246–248, 1963.

Dunbar, F. Effect of Mother's Emotional Attitude on the Infant. *Psychosomatic Medn*, 6: 156–159, 1944.

Dundas, M.H. Autistic Children. *Nursing Times*, 60: 138–139, 1964.

Dunn, J.B. and Richards, M.P.M. Observations on the Developing Relationship between Mother and Baby in the Neonatal Period. In Schaffer, H.R. (Ed) *Studies in Mother-Infant Interaction*. Academic P, 1977.

Durham. M.S. Pandora's Box. *J Ch Ptry*, 11: 255–269, 1972.

Dweck, C.S. and Reppucci, N.D. Learned Helplessness and Reinforcement Responsibility in Children. *J Personality Social Pgy*, 25: 109–116, 1973.

Dworin, J. and Wyant, O. Authoritarian Attitudes in Mothers of Schizophrenics. *J Clin Pgy*, 13: 332–338, 1957.

Dyer, E.D. Parenthood as Crisis. *Marriage Family Living*, 25: 196–201, 1963.

Earl, C.J. The Primitive Catatonic Psychosis of Idiocy. *Br J Medl Pgy*, 14: 230–253, 1934.

Eaton, J.W. and Weil, R.J. *Culture and Mental Disorders*. Free P, 1955.

Eberhardy, F. A View from "the Couch." *J Ch Pgy Ptry*, 8: 257–263, 1967.

Edelson, S.R. A Dynamic Formulation of Childhood Schizophrenia. *Dis Ner System*, 27: 610–615, 1966.

Ehlers, W.H. *Mothers of Retarded Children*. Thomas, 1966.

Eickhoff, L.F.W. The Aetiology of Schizophrenia in Childhood. *J Men Sci*, 98: 229–234, 1952.

Eisenberg, L. The Classification of the Psychotic Disorders in Childhood. In Eron, L.D. (Ed) *Classification of Behavior Disorders*. Aldine, 1966.

————. Psychotic Disorders. In Freedman, A.M. and Kaplan, H.I. (Eds) *Comprehensive Textbook of Psychiatry*. Williams & Wilkins, 1967.

Eisenberg, L. and Kanner, L. Childhood Schizophrenia. *A J Ortho*, 26: 556–566, 1956.

Ekstein, R. The Acquisition of Speech in the Autistic Child. In *Children of Time and Space, of Action and Impulse*. Appleton-Century-Crofts, 1966.

Ekstein, R. and Caruth, E. Levels of Verbal Communication in the Schizophrenic

Child's Struggle against, for, and with the World of Objects. *Psa Study Ch,* 24: 115–137, 1969.

Eliade, M. *Myths, Dreams, and Mysteries.* Harper & Row, 1943.

Elkisch, P. Nonverbal, Extraverbal, Autistic Verbal Communication in the Treatment of a Child Tiquer. *Psa Study Ch,* 23, 423–437, 1968.

Elles, G. The Mute Sad-Eyed Child. *I J Psa,* 43: 40–49, 1962.

Engberg, L.R., Hansen, G., Welker, R.L. and Thomas, D.R. Acquisition of Key-Pecking via Autoshaping as a Function of Prior Experience. *Sci,* 178: 1002–1004, 1972.

Engel, G.L. *Psychological Development in Health and Disease.* Saunders, 1962.

Engel, G.L. and Reichsman, F. Spontaneous and Experimentally Induced Depressions in an Infant with a Gastric Fistula. *J A Psa Assn,* 4: 428–452, 1956.

English, O.L. and Pearson, G.H.J. *Emotional Problems of Living.* W.W. Norton, 1945.

Erikson, E.H. *Childhood and Society.* W.W. Norton, 2nd ed, 1963.

Escalona, S.K. Patterns of Infantile Experience and the Developmental Process. *Psa Study Ch,* 18: 197–244, 1963.

_____. Some Determinants of Individual Differences. *Trans NY Acad Sci,* 27: 802–816, 1965.

Evans, J. Rocking at Night. *J Ch Pgy Ptry,* 2: 71–85, 1961.

Evans-Jones, L.G. and Rosenbloom, L. Disintegrative Psychosis in Childhood. *Dev Medn Ch Neurology,* 20: 462–470, 1978.

Eveloff, H.H. The Autistic Child. *Arch Genr Ptry,* 3: 66–81, 1960.

Everard, P. *Involuntary Strangers.* Clare, 1980.

Fabian, A.A. Some Familial Considerations in Childhood Schizophrenia. *A J Ortho,* 24: 513–516, 1954.

Fabian, A.A. and Donohue, J.F. Maternal Depression. *A J Ortho,* 26: 400–405, 1956.

Fabian, A.A. and Holden, M.A. Treatment of Childhood Schizophrenia in a Child Guidance Clinic. *A J Ortho,* 21: 571–581, 1951.

Fagin, C.M. *The Effects of Maternal Attendance during Hospitalization on the Post-Hospital Behavior of Young Children.* F.A. Davis, 1966.

Fay, W.H. On Normal and Autistic Pronouns. *J Speech Hearing Disor,* 36: 242–249, 1971.

_____. Personal Pronouns and the Autistic Child. *JADD,* 9: 247–260, 1979.

Fearnside, A. Discussion. In Eszenyi, D. (Ed) *Autism.* Autistic Children's Assn S Australia, c1967.

Feldstein, G.J. A Breast and Bottle Shy Infant. *A J Dis Chn,* 35: 103–108, 1928.

Fenichel, O. *The Psychoanalytic Theory of Neurosis.* W.W. Norton, 1945.

Ferenczi, S. Stages in the Development of the Sense of Reality. In *Sex in Psychoanalysis.* Basic B, 1950.

Ferrara, C. and Hill, S.D. The Responsiveness of Autistic Children to Predictability of Social and Nonsocial Toys. *JADD,* 10: 51–57, 1980.

Ferreira, A.J. The Pregnant Woman's Emotional Attitude and Its Reflection on the Newborn. *A J Ortho,* 30: 553–561, 1960.

Ferster, C.B. Animal Behavior and Mental Illness. *Pgical Rec,* 16: 345–356, 1966a.

_____. The Repertoire of the Autistic Child in Relation to Principles of Reinforcement. In Gottschalk, L.A. and Auerbach, A.H. (Eds) *Methods of Research in Psychotherapy.* Appleton-Century-Crofts, 1966b.

———. Operant Reinforcement of Infantile Autism. In Lesse, S. (Ed) *An Evaluation of the Results of the Psychotherapies.* Thomas, 1968.

———. A Functional Analysis of Depression. *A Pgist,* 28: 857–870, 1973.

Field, T.M. Interaction Patterns of Pre-term and Term Infants. In *Infants Born at Risk.* SP Books, 1979.

Finegan, J.A. and Quarrington, B. Pre, Peri, and Neonatal Factors in Infantile Autism. *J Ch Pgy Ptry,* 20: 119–128, 1979.

Fineman, A.D. The Utilization of Child Psychiatry on a Children's Surgical Service. *A J Surgery,* 95: 64–73, 1958.

Fish, B. and Alpert, M. Abnormal State of Consciousness and Muscle Tone in Infants Born to Schizophrenic Mothers. *A J Ptry,* 119: 439–445, 1962.

Fisher, S.M. On the Development of the Capacity to Use Transitional Objects. *J Ch Ptry,* 14: 114–124, 1975.

FitzHerbert, J. Some Further Observations on Head-Banging and Allied Behaviour. *J Men Sci,* 98: 330–333, 1952.

Fletcher, W.B. Mental Development and Insanity of Children. *I Clin,* 138–147, 1895.

Flowers, C.E. *Obstetric Analgesia and Anesthesia.* Hoeber, 1967.

Flint, B.M. *The Security of Infants.* U Toronto P, 1959.

Focher, L. Convulsivinism. *J Ch Ptry,* 4: 513–520, 1965.

Fox, M.W. A Syndrome in the Dog Resembling Human Infantile Autism. *J A Veterinary Medl Assn,* 148: 1387–1390, 1966.

———. Psychomotor Disturbances. In *Abnormal Behavior in Animals.* Saunders, 1969a.

———. Socialization, Environmental Factors, and Abnormal Behavioral Development in Animals. In *Abnormal Behavior in Animals.* Saunders, 1969b.

Fox, M.W. and Stelzner, D. Behavioral Effects of Differential Early Experience in the Dog. *Animal Beh,* 14: 273–281, 1966.

Foy, J.G. *Gone is Shadow's Child.* Logos, 1970.

Fraiberg, S. On the Sleep Disturbances of Early Childhood. *Psa Study Ch,* 5: 285–335, 1950.

———. Parallel and Divergent Patterns in Blind and Sighted Infants. *Psa Study Ch,* 23: 264–300, 1968.

Frankel, F., Freeman, B.J., Ritvo, E., Chikami, B. and Carr, E. Effects of Frequency of Photic Stimulation upon Autistic and Retarded Children. *A J Men Def,* 81: 32–40, 1976.

Frazee, H.E. Children Who Later Become Schizophrenic. *Smith College Studies Social Work,* 23: 125–149, 1953.

Freedman, A.M. Maturation and Its Relation to the Dynamics of Childhood Schizophrenia. *A J Ortho,* 24: 487–491, 1954.

Freedman, A.M. and Bender, L. When the Childhood Schizophrenic Grows Up. *A J Ortho,* 27: 553–562, 1957.

Freedman, D.A. The Role of Early Mother-Child Relations in the Etiology of Some Cases of Mental Retardation. In Farrell, G. (Ed) *Congenital Mental Retardation.* U Texas P, 1969.

Freeman, B.J., Guthrie, D., Ritvo, E., Schroth, P., Glass, R. and Frankel, F. Behavior Observation Scale. *Pgical Rep,* 44: 519–524, 1979.

Freeman, R.V. and Grayson, H.M. Maternal Attitudes in Schizophrenia. *J Abn Social Pgy,* 50: 45–52, 1955.

Freud, A. The Concept of the Rejecting Mother. In Anthony, E.J. and Benedek, T. (Eds) *Parenthood.* Little Brown, 1970.

Freud, A. and Burlingham, D.T. *War and Children.* Medl War B, 1943.

———. *Infants without Families.* IUP, 1973.

Freud, S. *The Problem of Anxiety.* W.W. Norton, 1963.

———. *The Psychopathology of Every Day Life.* Hogarth, Std Ed, Vol. VI, 1960.

Friedman, G. Conceptual Thinking in Schizophrenic Children. *Genet Pgy Mono,* 63: 149–196, 1961.

Friedman, R. *Family Roots of School Learning and Behavior Disorders.* Thomas, 1973.

Frijling-Schreuder, E.C.M. Borderline States in Children. *Psa Study Ch,* 24: 307–327, 1969.

Frith, U. Studies in Pattern Detection in Normal and Autistic Children. *J Abn Pgy,* 76: 413–420, 1970.

———. Cognitive Mechanisms in Autism. *JACS,* 2: 160–173, 1972.

Frumkes, G. Mental Disorders Related to Childbirth. *J Ner Men Dis,* 79: 540–552, 1934.

Furer, M. The Development of a Preschool Symbiotic Psychotic Boy. *Psa Study Ch,* 19: 448–469, 1964.

Furneaux, B. The Autistic Child. *Br J Disor Communication,* 1: 85–90, 1966.

Gajzago, C. and Prior, M. Two Cases of "Recovery" in Kanner Syndrome. *Arch Genr Ptry,* 31: 264–268, 1974.

Galenson, E. and Roiphe, H. Some Suggested Revisions Concerning Early Development. *J A Psa Assn,* 24: Supp. 29–57, 1976.

Galton, L. For Mother and Child—Closer Encounters. *Parade,* Oct. 1, 1978, pp. 6, 8.

Gantt, W.H., Newton, J.E.O., Royer, F.L. and Stephens, J.H. Effect of Person. *Conditional Reflex,* 1: 18–35, 1966.

Ganz, L. An Analysis of Generalization Behavior in the Stimulus-Deprived Organism. In Newton, G. and Levine, S. (Eds) *Early Experience and Behavior.* Thomas, 1968.

Garber, J. and Seligman, M.E.P. (Eds) *Human Helplessness.* Academic P, 1980.

Gardner, J.E., Pearson, D.T., Bercovici, A.N. and Bricker, D.E. Measurement, Evaluation, and Modification of Selected Social Interactions between a Schizophrenic Child, His Parents, and His Therapist. *J Consulting Clin Pgy,* 32: 537–542, 1968.

Gardner, W.I. Effects of Success and Failure with Institutionalized Mentally Retarded Adults. *Pgical Rep,* 18: 779–782, 1966.

Garfield, S.L. Abnormal Behavior and Mental Deficiency. In Ellis, N.R. (Ed) *Handbook of Mental Deficiency.* McGraw-Hill, 1963.

Garfield, S.L. and Affleck, D.C. A Study of Individuals Committed to a State Home for the Retarded Who Were Later Released as Not Mentally Defective. *A J Men Def,* 64: 907–915, 1960.

Garfinkel, H. *Studies in Ethnomethodology.* Prentice-Hall, 1967.

Garmezy, N. Contributions of Experimental Psychology to Understanding the Origins of Schizophrenia. In Romano, J. (Ed) *The Origins of Schizophrenia.* Excerpta Medica, 1967.

Gastaut, H. Discussion. In Wolstenholme, G.E.W. and O'Connor, C.M. (Eds) *Neurological Basis of Behavior.* Little Brown, 1958.

Geber, M. The Psycho-Motor Development of African Children in the First Year and the Influences of Maternal Behavior. *J Social Pgy*, 47: 185–195, 1958.

———. Longitudinal Study and Psycho-Motor Development among Baganda Children. In Skard, A.G. and Husen, T. *Child and Education*. Munksgaard, 1962.

Geleerd, E.R. Borderline States in Childhood and Adolescence. *Psa Study Ch*, 13: 279–295, 1958.

Gelinier-Ortigues, M.C. and Aubry, J. Maternal Deprivation. Psychogenic Deafness and Pseudo-Retardation. In Caplan, G. (Ed) *Emotional Problems of Early Childhood*. Basic B, 1955.

Gerard, D.L. and Siegel, J. The Family Background of Schizophrenia. *Ptric Q*, 24: 47–73, 1950.

Gerard, M.W. and Overstreet, H.M. Technical Modification in the Treatment of a Schizoid Boy within a Treatment Institution. In Gerard, M.W. (Ed) *The Emotionally Disturbed Child*. Child Welfare League, 1957.

Gibson, D. Early Infantile Autism. *Canadian Pgist*, 9: 36–39, 1968.

Gillberg, C. Maternal Age and Infantile Autism. *JADD*, 10: 293–297, 1980.

Glaser, K. Masked Depression in Children and Adolescents. *A J Psychotherapy*, 21: 565–574, 1967.

Goddard, K.E., Broder, G. and Wenar, C. Reliability of Pediatric Histories. *Peds*, 28: 1011–1018, 1961.

Goertzel, U. and Goertzel, M.G. *Cradles of Eminence*. Little Brown, 1962.

Gofman, H., Buckman, W. and Schade, G.H. Parents' Emotional Response to Child's Hospitalization. *A J Dis Chn*, 93: 629–637, 1957.

Goldfarb, W. *Childhood Schizophrenia*. Harvard U P, 1961.

———. Childhood Psychosis. In Mussen, P.H. (Ed) *Carmichael's Manual of Child Psychology*, Wiley, 3rd ed, Vol. 2, 1970.

Goldfarb, W., Braunstein, P. and Lorge, I. A Study of Speech Patterns in a Group of Schizophrenic Children. *A J Ortho*, 26: 544–555, 1956.

Goldfarb, W., Braunstein, P. and Scholl, H.H. An Approach to the Investigation of Childhood Schizophrenia. *A J Ortho*, 29: 481–486, 1959.

Goldfarb, W., Goldfarb, N. and Scholl, H.H. The Speech of Mothers of Schizophrenic Children. *A J Ptry*, 122: 1220–1227, 1966.

Goldfarb, W., Levy, D.M. and Meyers, D.I. The Mother Speaks to Her Schizophrenic Child. *Ptry*, 35: 217–226, 1972.

Goldfarb, W., Mintz I. and Stroock, K.W. A Time to Heal. IUP, 1969.

Goldfarb, W., Sibulkin, L., Behrens, M.L. and Jahoda, H. The Concept of Maternal Perplexity. In Anthony, E.J. and Benedek, T. (Eds) *Parenthood*. Little Brown, 1970.

Goldfarb, W., Yudkowitz, E. and Goldfarb, N. Verbal Symbols to Designate Objects. *JACS*, 3: 281–298, 1973.

Goldstein, K. Abnormal Mental Conditions in Infancy. *J Ner Men Dis*, 128: 538–557, 1959.

Goodman, J. A Case Study of an "Autistic Savant." *J Ch Pgy Ptry*, 13: 267–278, 1972.

Goodwin, M.S. Autism, Mental Retardation, Brain Damage. In Park, C.C. (Ed) *Research and Education*. NIMH, 1971.

Goshen, C.E. Mental Retardation and Neurotic Maternal Attitudes. *Arch Genr Ptry*, 9: 168–174, 1963.

Goshen-Gottstein, E.R. *Marriage and the First Pregnancy.* Tavistock, 1966.

Gottschalk, L.R. The Relationship of Psychologic State and Epileptic Activity. *Psa Study Ch*, 11: 352–380, 1956.

Green, A.H. The Effects of Object Loss on the Body Image of Schizophrenic Girls. *J Ch Ptry*, 9: 532–547, 1970.

Green, M.R. and Schechter, D.E. Autistic and Symbiotic Disorders in Three Blind Children. *Ptric Q*, 31: 628–646, 1957.

Greenacre, P. The Family Romance of the Artist. *Psa Study Ch*, 13: 9–36, 1958.

———. The Early Years of the Gifted Child. In Bereday, G.Z.F. and Lauwerys, J.A. (Eds) *The Gifted Child (Yearbook of Education)*. Harcourt Brace, 1962.

Greenbaum, G.H.C. Regularity and Consistency in the Behaviour of Autistic Children. In Hutt, S.J. and Hutt, C. (Eds) *Behaviour Studies in Psychiatry*. Pergamon, 1970.

Greenberg, N.H. Atypical Behavior during Infancy. In Anthony, E.J. and Koupernik, C. (Eds) *The Child in his Family*. Wiley, Vol. 1, 1970.

———. A Comparison of Infant-Mother Interactional Behavior in Infants with Atypical Behavior and Normal Infants. *Exceptional Infant*, 2: 390–418, 1971.

Greenfeld, J. *A Child Called Noah*. Holt Rinehart Winston, 1972.

———. *A Place for Noah*. Holt Rinehart Winston, 1978.

Grunebaum, M.G., Hurwitz, I., Prentice, N.M. and Sperry, B.M. Fathers of Sons with Primary Neurotic Learning Inhibitions. *A J Ortho*, 32: 462–472, 1962.

Gunther, M. Instinct and the Nursing Couple. *Lancet*, 268: 575–578, 1955.

———. Infant Behaviour at the Breast. In Foss, B.M. (Ed) *Determinants of Infant Behaviour*. Methuen, Vol. 1, 1961.

Gurevitz, S. Psychotherapy of a Schizophrenic Child. *Psa*, 1: 62–73, 1952.

Guskin, S. Social Psychologies of Mental Deficiency. In Ellis, N.R. (Ed) *Handbook of Mental Deficiency*. McGraw-Hill, 1963.

Hackett, J.D. Schizophrenia—a Different, but Comparable Model. *Dis Ner System*, 29: Supp. 5, 133–143, 1968.

Hagamen, M.B. Autism and Childhood Schizophrenia. In Bemporad, J.R. (Ed) *Child Development in Normality and Psychopathology*. Brunner/Mazel, 1980.

Haggard, E.R., Brekstad, A. and Skard, A.G. On the Reliability of the Anamnestic Interview. *J Abn Social Pgy*, 61: 311–318, 1960.

Haggerty, A.D. The Effects of Long-Term Hospitalization or Institutionalization upon the Language Development of Children. *J Genet Pgy*, 94: 205–209, 1959.

Haka-Ikse, K. Child Development as an Index of Maternal Mental Illness. Paper read at Royal College Physicians Canada Conf, Montreal, 1974.

Haley, J. An Interactional Description of Schizophrenia. *Ptry*, 22: 321–332, 1959.

———. *Strategies of Psychotherapy*. Grune & Stratton, 1963.

———. The Art of Being Schizophrenic. *Voices*, 1: 133–147, 1965.

Halpern, H. and Halpern, T. Four Perspectives on Anti-Achievement. *Psa Rev*, 53: 407–417, 1966.

The Halt and the Blind. *California Men Health News*, Nov.-Dec. 1958, p. 2.

Halversan, H.M. Infant Sucking and Tensional Behavior. *J Genet Pgy*, 53: 365–430, 1938.

Hamblin, R.L., Buckholdt, D., Ferritor, D., Kozloff, M. and Blackwell, L. *The Humanization Process.* Wiley, 1971.

Hamburg, D.A. Observations of Mother-Infant Interactions in Primate Field Studies. In Foss, B.M. (Ed) *Determinants of Infant Behaviour.* Methuen, Vol. 4, 1969.

Hamill, (ni). Discussion. In Chapin, H.D. A Plea for Accurate Statistics in Infants' Institutions. *Trans A Ped Soc,* 27: 180–185, 1915.

Hamilton, J.A. *Postpartum Psychiatric Problems.* Mosby, 1962.

Harding, M.E. *Woman's Mysteries.* Putnam's, rev ed, 1971.

Harley, R.D., Baird, H.W. and Freeman, R.D. Self-Induced Photogenic Epilepsy. *Arch Ophthalmology,* 78: 730–737, 1967.

Harlow, H.F. The Formation of Learning Sets. *Pgical Rev,* 56: 51–65, 1949.

Harms, E. Two Case Histories. *Ner Ch,* 10: 19–35, 1952.

Harrington, M. and Hassan, J.M.W. Depression in Girls during Latency. *Br J Medl Pgy,* 31: 43–50, 1958.

Havelkova, M. Follow-Up Study of 71 Children Diagnosed as Psychotic in Preschool Age. *A J Ortho,* 38: 846–857, 1968.

Haworth, M.R. and Menolascino, F.J. Some Aspects of Psychotic Behavior in Young Children. *Arch Genr Ptry,* 18: 355–359, 1968.

Heard, D.H. Unresponsive Silence and Intra-Familial Hostility. In Gosling, R. (Ed) *Support, Innovation, and Autonomy.* Tavistock, 1973.

Heber, R. Personality. In Stevens, H.A. and Heber, R. (Eds) *Mental Retardation.* U Chicago P, 1964.

Heber, R. and Garber, H. An Experiment in the Prevention of Cultural-Familial Retardation. In Primrose, D.A.A. (Ed) *Proceedings of the Second Congress of the International Association for the Scientific Study of Mental Deficiency.* Swets & Zeitlinger, 1972.

Hefferman, A. A Psychiatric Study of Fifty Preschool Children Referred to Hospital for Suspected Deafness. In Caplan, G. (Ed) *Emotional Problems of Early Childhood.* Tavistock, 1955.

Heilman, A.E. Parent Adjustment ot the Dull Handicapped Child. *A J Men Def,* 54: 556–562, 1950.

Heinicke, C.M. and Westheimer, I.J. *Brief Separations.* IUP, 1965.

Helfand, I. Role Taking in Schizophrenia. *J Consulting Pgy,* 20: 37–41, 1956.

Henry, J. *Pathways to Madness.* Random House, 1971.

Hermelin, B. Recent Experimental Research. In Mittler, P.J. (Ed) *Aspects of Autism.* Br Pgical Soc, 1968.

————. Images and Language. In Rutter, M. and Schopler, E. (Eds) *Autism.* Plenum, 1978.

Hermelin, B. and O'Connor, N. The Rote and Concept Learning of Imbeciles. *J Men Def Res,* 2: 21–27, 1958.

————. *Psychological Experiments with Autistic Children.* Pergamon, 1970.

————. Rules and Structures. In Clarke, A.M. and Clarke, A.D.B. (Eds) *Mental Deficiency.* Free P, 3rd ed, 1975.

Hersher, L., Moore, A.U. and Richmond, J.B. Effect of Post Partum Separation of Mother and Kid on Maternal Care in the Domestic Goat. *Sci,* 128: 1342–1343, 1958.

Hersher, L., Richmond, J.B. and Moore, A.U. Maternal Behavior in Sheep and Goats. In Rheingold, H.L. (Ed) *Maternal Behavior in Mammals.* Wiley, 1963.

Herzog, J.M. Disturbances in Parenting High-Risk Infants. In Field, T.M. (Ed) *Infants Born at High Risk.* SP Books, 1979.

Heuyer, G., Lebovici, S. and Roumajon, Y. A Case of Psychosis in a Young Child. In Caplan, G. (Ed) *Emotional Problems of Early Childhood.* Tavistock, 1955.

Hewett, F.M. Teaching Speech to an Autistic Child through Operant Conditioning. *A J Ortho,* 35: 927–936, 1965.

Hill, L.B. *Psychotherapeutic Intervention in Schizophrenia.* U Chicago P, 1955.

Hinde, R.A. and Davies, L. Removing Infant Rhesus from Mother for 13 Days Compared with Removing Mother from Infant. *J Ch Pgy Ptry,* 13: 227–237, 1972.

Hinde, R.A. and Spencer-Booth, Y. Effects of Brief Separation from Mother on Rhesus Monkeys. *Sci,* 173: 111–118, 1971.

Hiroto, D.S. Locus of Control and Learned Helplessness. *J Exp Pgy,* 102: 187–193, 1974.

Hirsch, E.A. The Adaptive Significance of Commonly Described Behavior of the Mentally Retarded. *A J Men Def,* 63: 639–646, 1959.

Hoberman, S.E. and Goldfarb, W. Speech Reception Thresholds in Schizophrenic Children. *J Speech Hearing Res,* 6: 101–106, 1963.

Hoffman, H.S. Fear-Mediated Processes in the Context of Imprinting. In Lewis, M. and Rosenblum, L.A. (Eds) *The Origins of Fear.* Wiley, 1974.

Hollingworth, L.S. *Children above 180 IQ.* World, 1942.

Honzik, M.P. Environmental Correlates of Mental Growth. *Ch Dev,* 38: 337–364, 1967.

Horwitz, W.H., Kestenbaum, C., Person, E. and Jarvik, L. Identical Twin—"Idiot Savants"—Calendar Calculators. *A J Ptry,* 121: 1075–1079, 1965.

Hoskins, R.G. Dementia Praecox. *J A Medl Assn,* 96(2): 1209–1211, 1931.

Howells, J.G. and Layng, J. The Effect of Separation Experiences on Children Given Care away from Home. *Medl Officer,* 95: 345–347, 1956.

Hunt, D. Preface. In Hunt, N. *The World of Nigel Hunt.* Garrett, 1967.

Hutchison, J.H., Stone, F.H. and Davidson, J.R. Photogenic Epilepsy Induced by the Patient. *Lancet,* 274(1): 243–245, 1958.

Hutt, C. and Hutt, S.J. Stereotypies and Their Relation to Arousal. In Hutt, S.J. and Hutt, C. (Eds) *Behaviour Studies in Psychiatry.* Pergamon, 1970.

Hutt, C. and Ounsted, C. The Biological Significance of Gaze Aversion with Particular Reference to the Syndrome of Infantile Autism. *Beh Sci,* 11: 346–356, 1966.

————. Gaze Aversion and Its Significance in Childhood Autism. In Hutt, S.J. and Hutt, C. (Eds) *Behaviour Studies in Psychiatry.* Pergamon, 1970.

Hutt, M.L. and Gibby, R.G. *The Mentally Retarded Child.* Allyn & Bacon, 2nd ed, 1965.

Hutt, S.J., Hutt, C., Lee, L.D. and Ounsted, C. A Behavioural and Electroencephalographic Study of Autistic Children. *J Ptric Res,* 3: 181–197, 1965.

Hytten, F.E., Yorston, J.C. and Thomson, A.M. Difficulties Associated with Breast-Feeding. *Br Medl J,* 310–315, 1958.

Ilg, F.L. and Ames, L.B. *Child Behavior.* Harper, 1955.

Illingworth, R.S. Common Difficulties in Infant Feeding. *Br Medl J,* 1077–1081, 1949.

————. *The Development of the Infant and Young Child.* Williams & Wilkins, 3rd ed, 1966.

Illingworth, R.S. and Illingworth, C. *Babies and Young Children.* Churchill Livingstone, 5th ed, 1972.

Irvine, E.E. The Risks of the Register. In Anthony, E.J. and Koupernik, C. (Eds) *The Child in His Family.* Wiley, Vol. 3, 1974.

Jackson, D.D. Guilt and Control of Pleasure in Schizoid Personalities. *Br J Medl Pgy,* 31: 124–130, 1958.

Jackson, L. 'Non-Speaking' Children. *Br J Medl Pgy,* 23: 87–100, 1950.

Jarvis, W. Some Effects of Pregnancy and Childbirth on Men. *J A Psa Assn,* 10: 689–700, 1962.

Jay, P. The Common Langur of North India. In De Vore, I. (Ed) *Primate Behavior.* Holt Rinehart Winston, 1965.

Jeavons, P.M. and Harding, G.F.A. Photosensitive Epilepsy. *Clin Devl Medn,* #56, 1975.

Jenkins, R.L. The Schizophrenic Sequence. *A J Ortho,* 22: 738–748, 1952.

Jersild, A.T. *Child Psychology.* Prentice-Hall, rev ed, 1940.

Johnson, A.M. Factors in the Etiology of Fixations and Symptom Choice. In *Experience, Affect, and Behavior.* U Chicago P, 1969.

Johnson, A.M., Giffin, M.E., Watson, E.J. and Beckett, P.G.S. Observations on Ego Functions in Schizophrenia. *Ptry,* 19: 143–148, 1956.

Jones, B. The Dynamics of Marriage and Motherhood. In Morgan, R. (Ed) *Sisterhood is Powerful.* Vintage, 1970.

Jones, D.M. Binds and Unbinds. *Family Process,* 3: 323–331, 1964.

Jones, E. Anal-Erotic Character Traits. In *Papers on Psycho-Analysis.* Balliere Tindall Cox, 1950.

Jones, H.E. Phenomenal Memorizing as a "Special Ability." *J Applied Pgy,* 10: 367–377, 1926.

Jose, P.E. and Cohen, D.J. The Effect of Unfamiliar Tasks and Teachers on Autistic Children's Negativism. *J Ch Ptry,* 19: 78–89, 1980.

Junker, K. *The Child in the Glass Ball.* Abingdon, 1964.

Kagan, J. Developmental Studies in Reflection and Analysis. In Kidd, A.H. and Rivoire, J.L. (Eds) *Perceptual Development in Children.* IUP, 1966.

Kagan, J., Kearsley, R.B. and Zelazo, P.R. *Infancy.* Harvard U P, 1978.

Kagan, J. and Moss, H.A. *Birth to Maturity.* Wiley, 1962.

Kahlbaum, K.L. *Catatonia.* Johns Hopkins U P, 1974.

Kanner, L. Cultural Implications of Children's Behavior Problems. *Men Hygiene,* 25: 353–362, 1941a.

————. *In Defense of Mothers.* Thomas, 1941b.

————. Autistic Disturbances of Affective Contact. *Ner Ch,* 2: 217–250, 1943.

————. Early Infantile Autism. *Peds,* 25: 211–217, 1944.

————. Irrelevant and Metaphorical Language in Early Infantile Autism. *A J Ptry,* 103: 242–245, 1946.

————. *Child Psychiatry.* Thomas, 2nd ed, 1948a.

————. Feeblemindedness. *Ner Ch,* 7: 365–397, 1948b.

————. Problems of Nosology and Psychodynamics of Early Infantile Autism. *A J Ortho,* 19: 416–426, 1949.

————. A Discussion of Early Infantile Autism. *Digest Neurology Ptry,* 19: 158, 1951.

_____ . Emotional Interference with Intellectual Functioning. *A J Men Def,* 56: 701–707, 1952.

_____ . Discussion. *A J Ortho,* 24: 764–766, 1954a.

_____ . Discussion. *A J Ortho,* 24: 526–528, 1954b.

_____ . General Concept of Schizophrenia at Different Ages. *Proceedings Assn Res Ner Men Dis,* 34: 451–453, 1954c.

_____ . To What Extent Is Early Infantile Autism Determined by Constitutional Inadequacies? In Hooker, D. and Hare, C.C. (Eds) *Genetics and the Inheritance of Neurological and Psychiatric Patterns.* Williams & Wilkins, 1954d.

_____ . *Child Psychiatry.* Thomas, 3rd ed, 1957.

_____ . Emotionally Disturbed Children. *Ch Dev,* 33: 97–102, 1962.

_____ . *A History of the Care and Study of the Mentally Retarded.* Thomas, 1964.

_____ . *Child Psychiatry.* Thomas, 4th ed, 1972.

_____ . Early Infantile Autism Revisited. In *Childhood Psychosis.* Winston, 1973a.

_____ . Linwood Children's Center. In *Childhood Psychosis.* Winston, 1973b.

_____ . *Childhood Psychosis.* Winston, 1973c.

Kanner, L. and Eisenberg, L. Notes on the Follow-Up Studies of Autistic Children. In Hoch, P.H. and Zubin, J. (Eds) *Psychopathology of Childhood.* Grune & Stratton, 1955.

Kanner, L. and Lesser, L.I. Early Infantile Autism. *Ped Clin North A,* 5: 711–730, 1958.

Kaplan, D.M. and Mason, E.A. Maternal Reactions to Premature Birth Viewed as an Acute Emotional Disorder. *A J Ortho,* 30: 539–547, 1960.

Kaplan, F. Siblings of the Retarded. In Sarason, S.B. and Doris, J. (Eds) *Psychological Problems in Mental Deficiency.* Harper & Row, 4th ed, 1969.

Karon, B.P. and Rosberg, J. Study of the Mother-Child Relationship in a Case of Paranoid Schizophrenia. *A J Psychotherapy,* 12: 522–533, 1958.

Kastein, S. and Trace, B. *The Birth of Language.* Thomas, 1966.

Kaufman, B.N. Reaching the "Unreachable" Child. *Reflections,* 10: #5, 36–46, 1975.

_____ . *Son-Rise.* Harper & Row, 1976.

_____ . *A Miracle to Believe In.* Doubleday, 1981.

Kaufman, I., Frank, T., Heims, L., Herrick, J. and Willer, L. Four Types of Defense in Mothers and Fathers of Schizophrenic Children. *A J Ortho,* 29: 460–472, 1959.

Kaufman, I.C. Biologic Considerations of Parenthood. In Anthony, E.J. and Benedek, T. (Eds) *Parenthood.* Little Brown, 1970.

Keeler, W.R. Children's Reaction to the Death of a Parent. In Hoch, P.H. and Zubin, J. (Eds) *Depression.* Grune & Stratton, 1954.

Keener, M.R. The Man Who Might Have Been. *Training School Bull,* 49: 3–7, 1952.

Keiser, S. Superior Intelligence. *J A Psa Assn,* 17: 452–473, 1969.

Kelly, K. A Precocious Child in Analysis. *Psa Study Ch,* 25: 122–145, 1970.

Kennell, J.H. Discussant's Summary. In Thoman, E.B. and Trotter, S. (Eds) *Social Responsiveness of Infants.* Johnson & Johnson, 1978.

Kennell, J.H. and Bergen, M.E. Early Childhood Separations. *Peds,* 37: 291–298, 1966.

Kennell, J.H. and Klaus, M.H. Caring for the Parents of Premature or Sick Infants. In Klaus, M.H. and Kennell, J.H. (Eds) *Parent-Infant Bonding.* Mosby, 2nd ed, 1982.

Kessler, J.W. *Psychopathology of Childhood.* Prentice-Hall, 1966.

Kestenberg, J.S. Pseudo-Schizophrenia in Childhood and Adolescence. *Ner Ch,* 10: 146–162, 1952.

Kimble, G.A. *Hilgard and Marquis' Conditioning and Learning.* Appleton-Century-Crofts, rev ed, 1961.

King, P.D. Theoretical Considerations of Psychotherapy with a Schizophrenic Child. *J Ch Ptry,* 3: 638–649, 1964.

———. Ego Development and the Hypnosis Theory of Schizophrenia. *Psa Rev,* 57: 647–656, 1970.

———. (cited in *Clin Ptry News,* Sep. 1974, p. 2, 16).

———. Early Infantile Autism. *J Ch Ptry,* 14: 666–682, 1975.

King, P.D. and Ekstein, R. The Search for Ego Controls. *Psa Rev,* 54: 639–645, 1967.

Kinsey, A.C., Pomeroy, W.B. and Martin, C.E. *Sexual Behavior in the Human Male.* Saunders, 1948.

Kirman, B.H. *Mental Retardation.* Pergamon, 1968.

Kitsuse, J.I. Societal Reaction to Deviant Behavior. In Spitzer, N.P. and Denzin, N.K. (Eds) *The Mental Patient.* McGraw-Hill, 1968.

Klapatek, J. Photogenic Epileptic Seizures Provoked by Television. *Electroencephalography Clin Neurology,* 11: 809, 1959.

Klaus, M.H. and Kennell, J.H. The Family During Pregnancy. In *Parent-Infant Bonding.* Mosby, 2nd ed, 1982a.

———. Labor, Birth, and Bonding. In *Parent-Infant Bonding.* Mosby, 2nd ed, 1982b.

Kleeman, J.A. Freud's View on Early Infantile Sexuality in the Light of Direct Child Observation. *J A Psa Assn,* 24: Supp. 3–27, 1976.

Klein, H.R., Potter, H.W. and Dyk, R.B. *Anxiety in Pregnancy and Childbirth.* Hoeber, 1950.

Klein, M. *The Psychoanalysis of Children.* Grove, 1960.

Knowlton, P. Some Principles of Psychotherapy with Atypical Children. *A J Ortho,* 24: 789–796, 1954.

Knowlton, P. and Burg, M. Treatment of a Borderline Psychotic Five-Year-Old Girl. In Caplan, G. (Ed) *Emotional Problems of Early Childhood.* Tavistock, 1955.

Knox (ni). Discussion. In Chapin, H.D. A Plea for Accurate Statistics in Infants' Institutions. *Trans A Ped Soc,* 27: 180–185, 1915.

Koegel, R.L. and Egel, A.L. Motivating Autistic Children. *J Abn Pgy,* 88: 418–426, 1979.

Koegel, R.L. and Schreibman, L. Teaching Autistic Children to Respond to Simultaneous Multiple Cues. *J Exp Ch Pgy,* 24: 199–311, 1977.

Koegel, R.L. and Wilhelm, H. Selective Responding to the Components of Multiple Visual Cues by Autistic Children. *J Exp Ch Pgy,* 15: 442–453, 1973.

Konig, K. *Brothers and Sisters.* St. George, 1963.

Korner, A.F. Neonatal Startles, Smiles, Erections, and Reflex Sucks as Related to State, Sex, and Individuality. *Ch Dev,* 40: 1039–1053, 1969.

———. Individual Differences at Birth. In Westman, J.D. (Ed) *Individual Differences in Children.* Wiley, 1973.

_____ . Maternal Rhythms and Waterbeds. In Thoman, E.B. and Trotter, S. (Eds) *Social Responsiveness of Infants.* Johnson & Johnson, 1978.

Korner, A.F. and Grobstein, R. Visual Alertness as Related to Soothing in Neonates. *Ch Dev,* 37: 867–876, 1966.

Korner, A.F. and Thoman, E.B. Visual Alertness in Neonates as Evoked by Maternal Care. *J Exp Ch Pgy,* 10: 67–78, 1970.

Kornetsky, C. and Mirsky, A.F. On Certain Psychopharmacological and Physiological Differences between Schizophrenic and Normal Persons. *Psychopharmacologia,* 8: 309–318, 1966.

Kotsopoulos, S. Infantile Autism in Dizygotic Twins. *JACS,* 6: 133–138, 1976.

Kraepelin, E. *Clinical Psychiatry.* Macmillan, 1915.

_____ . *Dementia Praecox and Paraphrenia.* Livingstone, 1919.

Kransogorski, N.I. Conditioned Reflexes and Children's Neuroses. *A J Dis Ch,* 30: 753–768, 1925.

Kravitz, H., Rosenthal, V., Teplitz, Z., Murphy, J.B. and Lesser, R.E. A Study of Head-Banging in Infants and Children. *Dis Ner System,* 21: 203–208, 1960.

Kringlen, E. Heredity and Social Factors in Schizophrenic Twins. In Romano, J. (Ed) *The Origins of Schizophrenia.* Excerpta Medica, 1967.

Kris, E. Decline and Recovery in the Life of a Three-Year-Old. *Psa Study Ch,* 17: 175–215, 1962.

Kron, R.E., Stein, M. and Goddard, K.E. Newborn Sucking Behavior Affected by Obstetric Sedation. *Peds,* 37: 1012–1016, 1966.

Kugelmass, I.N. *The Autistic Child.* Thomas, 1970.

Kulka, A., Fry, C. and Goldstein, F.J. Kinesthetic Needs in Infancy. *A J Ortho,* 30: 562–571, 1960.

Kupferman, K. The Development and Treatment of a Psychotic Child. In McDevitt, J.B. and Settlage, C.F. (Eds) *Separation-Individuation.* IUP, 1971.

Kurtsin, I.T. Pavlov's Concept of Experimental Neurosis and Abnormal Behavior in Animals. In Fox, M.W. (Ed) *Abnormal Behavior in Animals.* Saunders, 1969.

La Barre, W. *The Ghost Dance.* Delta, 1972.

Laing, R.D. *The Divided Self.* Penguin, 1965.

_____ . *The Self and Others.* Pantheon, 2nd ed, 1969.

Lakin, M. Personality Factors in Mothers of Excessively Crying (Colicky) Infants. *Mono Soc Res Ch Dev,* 22: #1, 1957.

Langdell, J.I. Family Treatment of Childhood Schizophrenia. *Men Hygiene,* 51: 387–392, 1967.

_____ . Depressive Reactions of Childhood and Adolescence. In Szurek, S.A. and Berlin, I.N. (Eds) *Clinical Studies in Childhood Psychoses.* Brunner/Mazel, 1973.

Langer, E. A Case of Suspected Schizophrenia in a Three-Year-Old. *Ner Ch,* 10: 94–111, 1952.

Langer, S.K. *Philosophy in a New Key.* Mentor, 1948.

Lantz, B. Some Dynamic Aspects of Success and Failure. *Pgical Mono,* 59: #1, 1945.

Lasscock, E. D. Discussion. In Eszenyi, D. (Ed) *Autism.* Autistic Children's Assn S Australia, c1967.

Laufer, M.W. and Gair, D.S. Childhood Schizophrenia. In Bellak, L. and Loeb, L. (Eds) *The Schizophrenic Syndrome.* Grune & Stratton, 1969.

La Vietes, R. Discussion. *A J Ptry,* 128: 1413–1414, 1972.

Leiderman, P.H. Mothers at Risk. In Anthony, E.J. and Koupernik, C. (Eds) *The Child in his Family.* Wiley, Vol. 3, 1974.

Leifer, A.D., Leiderman, P.H., Barnett, C.R. and Williams, J.A. Effects of Mother-Infant Separation on Maternal Attachment Behavior. *Ch Dev,* 43: 1203–1218, 1972.

LeMasters, E.E. Parenthood as Crisis. *Marriage Family Living,* 19: 352–355, 1957.

Lennard, H.L., Beaulieu, M.R. and Embrey, N.C. Interaction in Families with a Schizophrenic Child. *Arch Genr Ptry,* 12: 166–183, 1965.

Lenneberg, E.H. Language Disorders in Childhood. *Harvard Educ Rev,* 34: 152–177, 1964.

Lerea, L. and Ward, B. Speech Avoidance among Children with Oral-Communication Defects. *J Pgy,* 60: 265–270, 1965.

Lesse, S. The Multivariant Masks of Depression. *A J Ptry,* 124: Supp. 35–40, 1968.

Lester, B.M. The Continuity of Change in Neonatal Behavior. In Brown, C.C. (Ed) *Infants at Risk.* Johnson & Johnson, 1981.

le Vann, L.J. The Concept of Schizophrenia in the Low Grade Mental Defective. *A J Men Def,* 54: 469–472, 1950.

Levine, M.I. Pediatric Observations on Masturbation in Children. *Psa Study Ch,* 6: 117–124, 1951.

Levy, D.M. On the Problem of Movement Restraint. *A J Ortho,* 14: 644–671, 1944.

————. Oppositional Syndromes and Oppositional Behavior. In Hoch, P.H. and Zubin, J. (Eds) *Psychopathology of Childhood.* Grune & Stratton, 1955.

————. Developmental and Psychodynamic Aspects of Oppositional Behavior. In Rado, S. and Daniels, G.E. (Eds) *Changing Concepts of Psychoanalytic Medicine.* Grune & Stratton, 1956.

————. *Behavioral Analysis.* Thomas, 1958.

Lewis, M. The Meaning of a Response or Why Researchers in Infant Behavior Should Be Oriental Metaphysicians. In Stone, L.J., Smith, H.B. and Murphy, L.B. (Eds) *The Competent Infant.* Basic B, 1973.

Lewis, M. and Brooks, J. Self, Other, and Fear. In Lewis, M. and Rosenblum, L.A. (Eds) *The Origins of Fear.* Wiley, 1974.

Lewis, M. and Goldberg, S. The Acquisition and Violation of Expectancy. *J Exp Ch Pgy,* 7: 70–80, 1969.

Lewis, S.R. and Van Ferney, S. Early Recognition of Infantile Autism. *J Peds,* 56: 510–512, 1960.

Lewis, W.C. Coital Movements in the First Year of Life. *I J Psa,* 46: 372–374, 1965.

Libo, S.S., Palmer, C. and Archibald, D. Family Group Therapy for Children with Self-Induced Seizures. *A J Ortho,* 41: 506–509, 1971.

Lichtenberg, P. A Definition and Analysis of Depression. *Arch Neurology Ptry,* 77: 519–527, 1957.

Liddell, H.S. The Natural History of Neurotic Behavior. In Galdston, I. (Ed) *Society and Medicine.* IUP, 1955.

Lidz, R.W. and Lidz, T. Therapeutic Considerations Arising from the Intense Symbiotic Needs of Schizophrenic Patients. In Brody, E.B. and Redlich, F.C. (Eds) *Psychotherapy with Schizophrenics.* IUP, 1952.

Lidz, T. *The Person.* Basic B, 1968.

————. *The Origin and Treatment of Schizophrenic Disorders.* Basic B, 1973.

Lidz, T. and Cornelison, A.R. *Schizophrenia and the Family.* IUP, 1965.

Lidz, T., Cornelison, A.R., Fleck, S. and Terry, D. The Intrafamilial Environment of the Schizophrenic Patient. *Ptry,* 20: 329–342, 1957.

Limber, J. Language in Child and Chimp. *A Pgist,* 32: 280–295, 1977.

Lindemann, E. Symptomatology and Management of Acute Grief. *A J Ptry,* 101: 141–148, 1944.

Lindsley, O.R. Can Deficiency Produce Specific Superiority? *Exceptional Chn,* 31: 225–232, 1965.

Linn, L. and Polatin, P. Psychiatric Problems of the Puerperium from the Standpoint of Prophylaxis. *Ptric Q,* 24: 375–384, 1950.

Litin, E.M., Giffin, M.E. and Johnson, A.M. Parental Influence in Unusual Sexual Behavior in Children. In Johnson, A.M. *Experience, Affect and Behavior.* U Chicago P, 1969.

Little, H.M. The Psychotic Child. *Pennsylvania Medl J,* 51: 174–178, 1947.

Lomas, P. The Husband-Wife Relationship in Cases of Puerperal Breakdown. *Br J Medl Pgy,* 32: 117–123, 1959.

———. Dread of Envy as an Aetiological Factor in Puerperal Breakdown. *Br J Medl Pgy,* 33: 105–112, 1960.

———. The Significance of Post-Partum Breakdown. In *The Predicament of the Family.* IUP, 1967a.

———. The Study of Family Relationships in Contemporary Society. In *The Predicament of the Family.* IUP, 1967b.

Lommel, A. *Shamanism.* McGraw-Hill, 1967.

Lordi, W.M. and Silverberg, J. Infantile Autism. *I J Group Psychotherapy.* 14: 360–365, 1964.

Lorenz, K. *On Aggression.* Harcourt Brace World, 1963.

Lotter, V. Factors Related to Outcome in Autistic Children. *JACS,* 4: 263–277, 1974.

Lourens, P.J.D. Early Infantile Autism. *Alabama J Medl Sci,* 10: 261–269, 1973.

Lourens, P.J.D. and Dorman, L.B. Functional Factors in the Etiology and Treatment of a Case of Infantile Autism. *Alabama J Medl Sci,* 9: 428–433, 1972.

Lourie, R.S. Studies of Bedrocking, Head Banging and Related Rhythmic Patterns. *Clin Proceedings Children's Hospital,* 5: 295–302, 1949.

———. Discussion. *Clin Proceedings Children's Hospital,* 10: 15–16, 1954.

Lovaas, O.I. Considerations in the Development of a Behavioral Treatment Program for Psychotic Children. In Churchill, D.W., Alpern, G.D. and DeMeyer, M.K. (Eds) *Colloquium on Infantile Autism.* Thomas, 1971.

Lovaas, O.I., Freitag, G., Gold, V.J. and Kassorla, I.C. Experimental Studies in Childhood Schizophrenia. *J Exp Ch Pgy,* 2: 67–84, 1965.

Lovaas, O.I., Koegel, R.L. and Schreibman, L. Stimulus Overselectivity in Autism. *Pgical Bull,* 86: 1235–1254, 1979.

Lovaas, O.I. and Newsom, C.D. Behavior Modification with Psychotic Chidren. In Leitenberg, H. (Ed) *Handbook of Behavior Modification and Behavior Therapy.* Prentice-Hall, 1976.

Lovaas, O.I., Schreibman, L., Koegel, R.L. and Rehm, R. Selective Responding by Autistic Children to Multiple Sensory Input. *J Abn Pgy,* 77: 211–222, 1971.

Love, H.D. *The Mentally Retarded Child and His Family.* Thomas, 1973.

Lu, Y.C. Mother-Child Role Relations in Schizophrenia. Ptry, 24: 133–142, 1961.

_____ . Contradictory Parental Expectations in Schizophrenia. *Arch Genr Ptry*, 6: 219–234, 1962.

Ludwig, A.M. and Farrelly, F. The Code of Chronicity. *Arch Genr Ptry*, 15: 562–568, 1966.

Luria, A.R. Psychological Studies of Mental Deficiency in the Soviet Union. In Ellis, N.R. (Ed) *Handbook of Mental Deficiency*. McGraw-Hill, 1963.

_____ . *The Mind of the Mnemonist*. Basic B, 1968.

Lyketsos, G.C. On the Formation of Mother-Daughter Symbiotic Relationship Patterns in Schizophrenia. *Ptry*, 22: 161–166, 1959.

McBride, A.B. *The Growth and Development of Mothers*. Harper & Row, 1973.

McBryde, A. Compulsory Rooming-In in the Ward and Private Newborn Service at Duke Hospital. *J A Medl Assn*, 145: 625–628, 1951.

McCandless, B.R. Relation of Environmental Factors to Intellectual Functioning. In Stevens, H.A. and Heber, R. (Eds) *Mental Retardation*. U Chicago P, 1964.

_____ . The Socialization of the Individual. In Schopler, E. and Reichler, R.J. (Eds) *Psychopathology and Child Development*. Plenum, 1976.

Maccoby, E.E. and Masters, J.C. Attachment and Dependency. In Mussen, P.H. (Ed) *Carmichael's Manual of Child Psychology*. Wiley, 3rd ed, Vol. 2, 1970.

McCord, J. and McCord, W. Cultural Stereotypes and the Validity of Interviews for Research in Child Development. *Ch Dev*, 32: 171–185, 1961.

McCord, J., McCord, W. and Thurber, E. Some Effects of Paternal Absence on Male Children. *J Abn Social Pgy*, 64: 361–369, 1962.

McDougall, J. and Lebovici, S. *Dialogue with Sammy*. IUP, 1969.

Macfarlane, J.A. Olfaction in the Development of Social Preferences in the Human Neonate. In Ciba Foundation. *Parent-Infant Interaction*. Elsevier, 1975.

_____ . *The Psychology of Childbirth*. Harvard U P, 1977.

Macfarlane, J.W. Studies in Child Guidance. *Mono Soc Res Ch Dev*, 3: #6, 1938.

Macfarlane, J.W., Allen, L. and Honzik, M.P. *A Developmental Study of the Behavior Problems of Normal Children between 24 Months and 14 Years*. U California P, 1962.

McGhie, A. A Comparative Study of the Mother-Child Relationship in Schizophrenia. *Br J Medl Pgy*, 34: 209–221, 1961.

MacGillivray, R.C. The Larval Psychosis of Idiocy. *A J Men Def*, 60: 570–574, 1956.

McGraw, M.B. and Molloy, L.B. The Pediatric Anamnesis. *Ch Dev*, 12: 255–265, 1941.

Mahler, M.S. Pseudoimbecility. *Psa Q*, 11: 149–164, 1942.

_____ . Autism and Symbiosis. *I J Psa*, 39: 77–83, 1958.

_____ . On Sadness and Grief in Infancy and Childhood. *Psa Study Ch*, 16: 332–351, 1961.

_____ . *On Human Symbiosis and the Vicissitudes of Individuation*. IUP, Vol. 1, 1968.

Mahler, M.S. and Elkisch, P. Some Observations on Disturbances of the Ego in a Case of Infantile Psychosis. *Psa Study Ch*, 8: 252–261, 1953.

Mahler, M.S., Pine, F. and Bergman, A. *The Psychological Birth of the Human Infant*. Basic B, 1975.

Mahrer, A.R. The Role of Expectancy in Delayed Reinforcement. *J Exp Pgy,* 52: 101–106, 1956.

Maier, N.R.F. An Aspect of Human Reasoning. *Br J Pgy,* 24: 144–155, 1933.

―――― . *Studies of Abnormal Behavior in the Rat.* Harper, 1939.

―――― . *Frustration.* U Michigan P, 1961.

Main, M.B. Analysis of a Peculiar Form of Reunion Behavior Seen in Some Day-Care Children. In Webb, R.A. (Ed) *Social Development in Childhood.* Johns Hopkins U P, 1977.

Makita, K. and Okonogi, K. Parental Attitude and Family Dynamics in Children's Problems in Japan. In Howells, J.G. (Ed) *Modern Perspectives in International Child Psychiatry.* Oliver & Boyd, 1969.

Malmquist, C.P. Depressions in Childhood and Adolescence. *Ann Prog Ch Ptry Ch Dev,* 507–535, 1972.

Mandel, H.P., Marcus, S.I., Roth, R.M. and Berenbaum, H.L. Early Infantile Autism. *Psychotherapy,* 8: 114–119, 1971.

Mandelbaum, A. and Wheeler, M.E. The Meaning of a Defective Child to Parents. In Rabkin, L.Y. and Carr, J.E. (Eds) *Sourcebook in Abnormal Psychology.* Houghton Mifflin, 1967.

Mannoni, M. *The Backward Child and His Mother.* Pantheon, 1972.

Manson, G. Neglected Children and the Celiac Syndrome. *J Iowa Medl Soc,* 54: 228–234, 1964.

Marquart, D.I. The Pattern of Punishment and Its Relation to Abnormal Fixation in Adult Human Subjects. *J Genr Pgy,* 39: 107–144, 1948.

Marris, P. *Loss and Change.* Pantheon, 1974.

Marsh, R.W. The Diagnosis, Epidemiology, and Etiology of Childhood Schizophrenia. *Genet Pgy Mono,* 95: 267–330, 1977.

Masserman, J.H. *Behavior and Neurosis.* U Chicago P, 1943.

Massie, H.N. The Early Natural History of Childhood Psychosis. *J Ch Ptry,* 14: 683–707, 1975.

―――― . Patterns of Mother-Infant Behavior and Subsequent Childhood Psychosis. *Ch Ptry Human Dev,* 7: 211–230, 1977.

―――― . Blind Ratings of Mother-Infant Interaction in Home Movies of Prepsychotic and Normal Infants. *A J Ptry,* 135: 1371–1374, 1978a.

―――― . The Early Natural History of Childhood Psychosis. *J Ch Ptry,* 17: 29–45, 1978b.

Masters, W.H.M. and Johnson, V.E. *Human Sexual Response.* Little Brown, 1966.

Matic, V. A Hospital without Nurses. *World Men Health,* 9: 119–123, 1957.

Mavity, I.S. How They Grow. *The Advocate* (NSAC), Mar. 1982, p. 3.

Mead, M. A Cultural Anthropologist's Approach to Maternal Deprivation. In *Deprivation of Maternal Care.* World Health Org, 1962.

Meek, L.H. Foreword. In Caille, R.K. *Resistant Behavior in Preschool Children.* Teachers College (Columbia U), 1933.

Mehl, L. Common Obstetrical Interventions. Paper read at Obstetrical Management Infant Outcome Conf, New York, Nov. 16, 1977.

Mein, R. and O'Connor, N. A Study of the Oral Vocabularies of Severely Subnormal Patients. *J Men Def Res,* 4: 130–143, 1960.

Melges, F.T. and Bowlby, J. Types of Hopelessness in Psychopathological Process. *Arch Genr Ptry,* 20: 690–699, 1969.

Meltzer, D. Mutism in Infantile Autism, Schizophrenia and Manic-Depressive States. I J Psa. 55: 297-404, 1974.

Mendel, W.M. A Phenomenological Theory of Schizophrenia. In Burton, A., Lopez-Ibor, J.J. and Mendel, W.M. *Schizophrenia as a Life Style*. Springer, 1974.

Mendelson, W.B., Reid, M.A. and Frommer, E.A. Some Characteristic Features Accompanying Depression, Anxiety and Aggressive Behaviour in Disturbed Children Under Five. In Annell, A.L. (Ed) *Depressive States in Childhood and Adolescence*. Halsted, 1972.

Menolascino, F.J. Infantile Autism. In *Psychiatric Approaches to Mental Retardation*. Basic B, 1970a.

_____ . Psychiatry's Past, Current and Future Role in Mental Retardation. In *Psychiatric Approaches to Mental Retardation*. Basic B, 1970b.

Menolascino, F.J. and Eaton, L. Psychoses of Childhood. *A J Men Def,* 72: 370-380, 1967.

Menyuk, P. Early Development of Receptive Language. In Schiefelbusch, R.L. and Lloyd, L.L. (Eds) *Language Perspectives*. U Park P, 1974.

Mercer, J.R. *Labelling the Mentally Retarded*. U Calif P, 1973.

Metz, J.R. Conditioning Generalized Imitation in Autistic Children. *J Exp Ch Ptry,* 2: 389-399, 1965.

Meyers, D.I. The Question of Depressive Equivalents in Childhood Schizophrenia. In Lesse, S. (Ed) *Masked Depression*. Aronson, 1975.

Meyers, D.I. and Goldfarb, W. Studies of Perplexity in Mothers of Schizophrenic Children. *A J Ortho,* 31: 551-564, 1961.

Michaels, J. and Schucman, H. Observations of the Psychodynamics of Parents of Retarded Children. *A J Men Def,* 66: 567-573, 1962.

Micic, Z. Psychological Stress in Children in Hospital. *I Nursing Rev,* 9: 23-31, 1962.

Miller, A. and Miller, E.E. Cognitive-Developmental Training with Elevated Boards and Sign Language. *JACS,* 3: 65-85, 1973.

Miller, R.T. Childhood Schizophrenia. *I J Men Health,* 3: 3-46, 1974.

Miller, W.R. and Seligman, M.E.P. Depression and the Perception of Reinforcement. *J Abn Pgy,* 82: 62-73, 1973.

Milner, M. The Role of Illusion in Symbol Formation. In Klein, M., Heimann, P. and Money-Kyrle, R.E. (Eds) *New Directions in Psycho-Analysis*. Basic B, 1955.

Minkowski, A. and Amiel-Tison, C. Obstetrical Risk in the Genesis of Vulnerability. In Anthony, E.J. and Koupernik, C. (Eds) *The Child in His Family*. Wiley, Vol. 3, 1974.

Minogue, B.M. A Case of Secondary Mental Deficiency with Musical Talent. *J Applied Pgy,* 7: 349-352, 1923.

Mitchell, W., Falconer, M.A. and Hill, D. Epilepsy with Fetishism Relieved by Temporal Lobectomy. *Lancet,* 267: 626-628, 1954.

Mittelman, B. Motility in Infants, Children, and Adults. *Psa Study Ch,* 9: 142-177, 1954.

_____ . Motor Patterns and Genital Behavior. *Psa Study Ch,* 10: 241-263, 1955.

Moe, M., Waal, N. and Urdahl, B. Group Psychotherapy with Parents of Psychotic and of Neurotic Children. *Acta Psychotherapeutica,* 8: 134-146, 1960.

Moir, D.D. Drugs Used during Labour. In Hawkins, D.F. (Ed) *Obstetric Therapeutics*. Bailliere Tindall, 1974.

Moloney, J.C. Some Simple Cultural Factors in the Etiology of Schizophrenia. *Ch Dev*, 22: 163–183, 1951.

Money-Kyrle, R. *The Meaning of Sacrifice*. Johnson Reprint Co., 1965.

Moore, A.U. Conditioning and Stress in the Newborn Lamb and Kid. In Gantt, W.H.(Ed) *Physiological Bases of Psychiatry*. Thomas, 1958.

————. Effects of Modified Maternal Care in the Sheep and Goat. In Newton, G. and Levine, S. (Eds) *Early Experience and Behavior*. Thomas, 1968.

Moore, B.R. When Johnny Must Go to the Hospital. *A J Nursing*, 57: 178–181, 1957.

Moore,, D.J. and Schiek, D.A. Toward a Theory of Early Infantile Autism, *Pgical Rev*, 78: 451–456, 1971.

Morehead, D.M. and Morehead, A. From Signal to Sign. In Schiefelbusch, R.L. and Lloyd, L.L. (Eds) *Language Perspectives*. U Park P, 1974.

Morgan, G.A. and Ricciuti, H.N. Infants' Responses to Strangers During the First Year. In Foss, B.M. (Ed) *Determinants of Infant Behaviour*. Methuen, Vol. 4, 1969.

Morgan, J.J.B. *The Psychology of the Unadapted School Child*. Macmillan, rev ed, 1936.

Morgan, S.B. *The Unreachable Child*. Memphis St U P, 1981.

Moriarty, D.M. *The Loss of the Loved One*. Thomas, 1967.

Morris, D. The Rigidification of Behaviour. *Pholosophical Trans Royal Soc*, Ser. B, 251: 327–330, 1966.

Morris, M.G. and Gould, R.W. Role Reversal. *A J Ortho*, 33: 298–299, 1963.

Morrison, D., Miller, D. and Mejia, B. Effects of Adult Verbal Requests on the Behavior of Autistic Children. *A J Men Def*, 75: 510–518, 1971.

Morrow, J.T. A Psychiatrist Looks at the Non-Verbal Child. *Exceptional Chn*, 25: 347–351, 367, 1959.

Morrow, J.T. and Loomis, E.A. Symbiotic Aspects of a Seven-Year-Old Psychotic. In Caplan, G. (Ed) *Emotional Problems of Early Childhood*. Tavistock, 1955.

Moser, D. The Nightmare of Life with Billy. In Rabkin, L.Y. and Carr, J.E. (Eds) *Sourcebook in Abnormal Psychology*. Houghton Mifflin, 1967.

Moss, H.A. Sex, Age, and State as Determinants of Mother-Infant Interaction. *Ann Prog Ch Ptry Ch Dev*, 73–91, 1968.

Mother-to-Be's Anxiety Linked to Autism. *Sci News*, 12: 374, 1977.

Mundy-Castle, A.C. and Anglin, J.M. Looking Strategies in Infants. In Stone, L.J., Smith, H.B. and Murphy, L.B. (Eds) *The Competent Infant*. Basic B, 1973.

Murphy, L.B. *The Widening World of Childhood*. Basic B, 1962.

————. Development in the First Year of Life. In Stone, L.J., Smith, H.B. and Murphy, L.B. (Eds) *The Competent Infant*. Basic B, 1973a.

————. Later Outcomes of Early Infant and Mother Relationships. In Stone, L.J., Smith, H.B. and Murphy, L.B. (Eds) *The Competent Infant*. Basic B, 1973b.

Murray, D.G. *This is Stevie's Story*. Abingdon, 2nd ed, 1967.

Nagelberg, L., Spotnitz, H. and Feldman, Y. The Attempt at Healthy Insulation in the Withdrawn Child. In Esman, A.H. (Ed) *New Frontiers in Child Guidance*. IUP, 1958.

Newson, L.J. An Intersubjective Approach to the Systematic Description of Mother-Infant Interaction. In Schaffer, H.R. (Ed) *Studies in Mother-Infant Interaction.* Academic P, 1977.

Newson, L.J. and Newson, E. Breast-Feeding in Decline. *Br Medl J,* 1744–1745, 1962.

Newton, N. *Maternal Emotions.* Hoeber, 1955.

Newton, N. and Newton, M. Mothers' Reactions to Their Newborn Babies. *J A Medl Assn,* 181: 206–210, 1962.

Ney, P.G. Effect of Contingent and Non-Contingent Reinforcement on the Behavior of an Autistic Child. *JACS,* 3: 115–127, 1973.

———. A Psychopathogenesis of Autism. *Ch Ptry Human Dev,* 9: 195–205, 1979.

NIMH. *Facts About: Autism.* DHEW Pub. 73-9129, 1973.

Noyes, A.P. and Kolb, L.C. *Modern Clinical Psychiatry.* Saunders, 5th ed, 1958.

Nurcombe, B. and Parker, N. The Idiot Savant. *J Ch Ptry,* 3: 469–489, 1964.

O'Connor, N. Speech and Thought in Severe Subnormality. In Society for Research in Child Development. *Cognitive Development in Children.* U Chicago P, 1970.

O'Connor, N. and Hermelin, B. Speech and Thought in Severe Subnormality. Pergamon, 1963.

———. Like and Cross Modality Recognition in Subnormal Children. *Q J Exp Pgy,* 13: 48–52, 1961.

O'Gorman, G. Discussion: Psychoses in Childhood. *Proceedings Royal Soc Medn,* 45: 800–802, 1952.

———. *The Nature of Childhood Autism.* Butterworths, 1967.

Olds, J. Discussion. In Wolstenholme, G.E.W. and O'Connor, C.M. (Eds) *Neurological Basis of Behavior.* Little Brown, 1958.

Olin, R.H. Differentiating the Psychotic Child from the Mentally Retarded Child. *Minnesota Medn,* 58: 489–492, 1975.

O'Moore, M. A Study of the Aetiology of Autism from a Study of Birth and Family Characteristics. *J Irish Medl Assn,* 65: 114–120, 1972.

Oppe, T. The Emotional Aspects of Prematurity. *Cerebral Palsy Bull,* 2: 233–237, 1960.

Ornitz, E.M. Vestibular Dysfunction in Schizophrenia and Childhood Autism. *Comprehensive Ptry,* 11: 159–173, 1970.

———. Childhood Autism. In Rutter, M. (Ed) *Infantile Autism.* Churchill Livingstone, 1971.

———. Childhood Autism. *California Medn,* 118: 21–47, 1973.

———. The Modulation of Sensory Input and Motor Output in Autistic Children. In Schopler, E. and Reichler, R.J. (Eds) *Psychopathology and Child Development.* Plenum, 1976.

Ornitz, E.M. and Ritvo, E.R. Perceptual Inconsistency in Early Infantile Autism. *Arch Genr Ptry,* 18: 76–98, 1968.

———. Medical Assessment. In Ritvo, E.R. (Ed) *Autism.* SP Books, 1976.

Osborn, W.J. Associative Clustering in Organic and Familial Retardates. *A J Men Def,* 65: 351–357, 1961.

Ostwald, P.F. and Rogan, P.F. Psychiatric Disorders Associated with Childbirth. *J Ner Men Dis,* 125: 153–165, 1957.

Oswald, I. Experimental Studies of Rhythm, Anxiety and Cerebral Vigilance. *J Men Sci,* 105: 269–294, 1959.

Overmier, J.B. and Seligman, M.E.P. Effects of Inescapable Shock upon Subsequent Escape and Avoidance Responding. *J Comparative Physiological Pgy*, 63: 28–33, 1967.

Oxman, J., Webster, C.D. and Konstantareas, M.M. The Perception and Processing of Information by Severely Dysfunctional Nonverbal Children. In Webster, C.D., Konstantareas, M.M., Oxman, J. and Mack, J.E. (Eds) *Autism*. Pergamon, 1980.

Paluszny, M.J. *Autism*. Syracuse U P, 1979.

Pantelakos, S.N., Bower, B.D. and Jones, H.D. Convulsions and Television Viewing. *Br Medl J*, 633–638, 1962.

Papousek, H. Individual Variability in Learned Responses in Human Infants. In Robinson, R.J. (Ed) *Brain and Early Behaviour*. Academic P, 1969.

———. The Infant's Fundamental Adaptive Response System in Social Interaction. In Thoman, E.B. and Trotter, S. (Eds) *Social Responsiveness of Infants*. Johnson & Johnson, 1978.

Papousek, H. and Papousek, M. Mothering and the Cognitive Head-Start. In Schaffer, H.R. (Ed) *Studies in Mother-Infant Interaction*. Academic P, 1977.

Park, C.C. *The Siege*. Harcourt Brace World, 1967.

———. *You Are Not Alone*. Little Brown, 1976.

Park, D. Operant Conditioning of a Speaking Autistic Child. *JACS*, 4: 189–191, 1974.

Parkes, C.M. Separation Anxiety. In Lader, M.H. (Ed) *Studies of Anxiety*. Headley, 1969.

———. *Bereavement*. IUP, 1972.

Parsons, E.C. and Beals, R.L. The Sacred Clowns of the Pueblo and Mayo-Yaqui Indians. *A Anthropologist*, 36: 491–514, 1934.

Patrick, J.R. Studies in Rational Behavior and Emotional Excitement. *J Comparative Pgy*, 18: 153–195, 1934.

Patterson, G.R. and Reid, J.B. Reciprocity and Coercion. In Neuringer, C. and Michael, J.L. (Eds) *Behavior Modification in Clinical Psychology*. Appleton-Century-Crofts, 1970.

Patton, R.G. and Gardner, L.I. *Growth Failure in Maternal Deprivation*. Thomas, 1963.

Pavenstedt, E. History of a Child with an Atypical Development, and Some Vicissitudes of His Treatment. In Caplan, G. (Ed) *Emotional Problems of Early Childhood*. Tavistock, 1955.

———. A Study of Immature Mothers and Their Children. In Caplan, G. (Ed) *Prevention of Mental Disorders in Children*. Basic B, 1961.

———. Development During the Second Year. In Chandler, C.A., Lourie, R.S., Peters, A.D. and Dittman, L.L. (Eds) *Early Child Care*. Atherton, 1968.

Pavenstedt, E. and Andersen, I.N. Complementary Treatment of Mother and Child with Atypical Development. *A J Ortho*, 22, 607–633, 1952.

Pawlby, S.J. Imitative Interaction. In Schaffer, H.R. (Ed) *Studies in Mother-Infant Interaction*. Academic P, 1977.

Payne, R.W. Cognitive Abnormalities. In Eysenck, H.J. (Ed) *Handbook of Abnormal Psychology*. Basic B, 1961.

Pearson, G.H.J. Discussion. *Pennsylvania Medl J*, 51: 178–179, 1947.

Peckarsky, A.M.K. Maternal Attitudes toward Children with Psychogenically Delayed Speech. Ph.D. thesis, New York U, 1952.

Philips, I. Psychopathology and Mental Retardation. *A J Ptry,* 124: 29–35, 1967.

Phillips, E.L. Contributions to a Learning-Theory Account of Childhood Autism. *J Pgy,* 43: 117–124, 1957.

Pill, R. The Sociological Aspects of the Case-Study Sample. In Stacey, M., Dearden, R., Pill, R. and Robinson, D. *Hospitals, Children and Their Families.* Routledge & Kegan Paul, 1970.

Pious, W.L. The Pathogenic Process in Schizophrenia. *Bull Menninger Clin,* 13: 152–159, 1949.

Pipineli-Potamianou, A. The Child, Vulnerable in the Mother's Desire. *Psychotherapy Psychosomatics,* 26: 211–218, 1975.

Pitfield, M. and Oppenheim, A.N. Child Rearing Attitudes of Mothers of Psychotic Children. *J Ch Pgy Ptry,* 5: 51–57, 1964.

Plank, E.N. and Plank, R. Emotional Components in Arithmetical Learning as Seen through Autobiographies. *Psa Study Ch,* 9: 274–293, 1954.

Plant, J.S. Negativism. *A J Dis Chn,* 61: 358–368, 1941.

Polan, C. and Spencer, B. Check List of Symptoms of Autism in Early Life. *W Virginia Medl J,* 55: 198–204, 1959.

Pollack, M. Brain Damage, Mental Retardation and Childhood Schizophrenia. *A J Ptry,* 115: 422–428, 1958.

Pollin, W., Stabenau, J.R., Mosher, L. and Tupin, J. Life History Differences in Identical Twins Discordant for Schizophrenia. *A J Ortho,* 36: 492–509, 1966.

Pollin, W., Stabenau, J.R. and Tupin, J. Family Studies with Identical Twins Discordant for Schizophrenia. *Ptry,* 28: 60–78, 1965.

Potter, H.W. Foreword. In Menolascino, F.J. (Ed) *Psychiatric Approaches to Mental Retardation.* Basic B, 1970.

Powdermaker, F. Preface. In Abrahams, J. and Varon, E. *Maternal Dependency and Schizophrenia.* IUP, 1953.

Poznanski, E. and Zrull, J.P. Childhood Depression. *Ann Prog Ch Ptry Ch Dev,* 455–466, 1971.

Prechtl, H.F.R. Problems of Behavioral Studies in the Newborn Infant. In Lehrman, D.S., Hinde, R.A. and Shaw, E. (Eds) *Advances in the Study of Behavior.* Academic P, Vol. 1, 1965.

Premack, D. and Premack, A.J. Teaching Visual Language to Apes and Language-Deficient Persons. In Schiefelbusch, R.L. and Lloyd, L.L. (Eds) *Language Perspectives.* U Park P, 1974.

Prizant, B.M. and Duchan, J.F. The Functions of Immediate Echolalia in Autistic Children. *J Speech Hearing Disor,* 46: 241–249, 1981.

Prout, C.T. and White, M.A. A Controlled Study of Personality Relationships in Mothers of Schizophrenic Male Patients. *A J Ptry,* 107: 251–256, 1950.

———. The Schizophrenic's Sibling. *J Ner Men Dis,* 123: 162–170, 1956.

Provence, S. and Lipton, R.C. *Infants in Institutions.* IUP, 1962.

Prugh, D.G. A Preliminary Report on the Role of Emotional Factors in Idiopathic Celiac Disease. *Psychosomatic Medn,* 13: 220–241, 1951.

Prugh, D.G. and Harlow, R.G. "Masked Deprivation" in Infants and Young Children. *Deprivation of Maternal Care.* World Health Org, 1962.

Putnam, M.C. A Case Study of an Atypical Two-And-A-Half-Year-Old. *A J Ortho,* 18: 1–7, 1948.

Putnam, M.C., Rank, B. and Kaplan, S. Notes on John. *Psa Study Ch,* 6: 38–58, 1951.

Pyles, M.K., Stolz, H.R., and Macfarlane, J.W. The Accuracy of Mothers' Reports on Birth and Developmental Data. *Ch Dev,* 6: 165–176, 1935.

Raglan, F.R.S. *The Hero.* Watts, 1949.

Rakusian, J.M. and Fierman, L.B. Five Assumptions for Treating Chronic Psychotics. *Men Hospitals,* 14: 140–148, 1963.

Rank, B. Adaptation of the Psychoanalytic Technique for the Treatment of Young Children with Atypical Development. *A J Ortho,* 19: 130–139, 1949.

———— . Intensive Study and Treatment of Preschool Children Who Show Marked Personality Deviations, or "Atypical Development," and Their Parents. In Caplan, G. (Ed) *Emotional Problems of Early Childhood.* Tavistock, 1955.

Rank, B. and Kaplan, S. A Case of Pseudoschizophrenia in a Child Workshop. *A J Ortho,* 21: 155–181, 1951.

Rank, O. *The Myth of the Birth of the Hero.* Vintage, 1959.

Rashkis, H.A. and Singer, R.D. The Psychology of Schizophrenia. *Arch Genr Ptry,* 1: 406–416, 1959.

Rebelsky, F. and Hanks, C. Fathers' Verbal Interaction with Infants in the First Three Months of Life. *Ch Dev,* 42: 63–68, 1971.

Reid, D.E. Comments on the Prevention of Prematurity. In Kowlessar, M. (Ed) *Physiology of Prematurity.* Macy Fndn, 1961.

Reiser, D.E. Psychosis of Infancy and Early Childhood, as Manifested by Children with Atypical Development. *New England J Medn,* 269: 790–798 and 844–850, 1963.

———— . Infantile Psychosis. *Men Hygiene,* 50: 588–589, 1966.

Rendle-Short, T.J. The Diagnosis of Infantile Autism. In Eszenyi, D. (Ed) *Autism.* Autistic Children's Assn S Australia, c1967.

Rensberger, B. Key Suggested to Mental Feats of Idiot Savants. *The New York Times,* Apr. 4, 1977, p. 18.

Reynolds, B.S., Newsom, C.D. and Lovaas, O.I. Auditory Overselectivity in Autistic Children. *J Abn Ch Pgy,* 2: 253–263, 1974.

Rheingold, J.C. *The Fear of Being a Woman.* Grune & Stratton, 1964.

Ribble, M.A. Clinical Studies of Instinctive Reactions in New Born Babies. *A J Ptry,* 95: 149–158, 1938.

———— . Disorganizing Factors of Infant Personality. *A J Ptry,* 98: 459–463, 1941.

———— . Infantile Experience in Relation to Personality Development. In Hunt, J.McV. (Ed) *Personality and the Behavior Disorders.* Ronald, Vol. 2, 1944.

———— . Anxiety in Infants and Its Disorganizing Effects. In Lewis, N.D.C. and Pacella, B.L. (Eds) *Modern Trends in Child Psychiatry.* IUP, 1945.

———— . *The Rights of Infants.* Columbia U P, 2nd ed, 1965.

Rice, G., Kepecs, J.G. and Yahalom, I. Differences in Communicative Impact between Mothers of Psychotic and Nonpsychotic Children. *A J Ortho,* 36: 529–543, 1966.

Richards, B.W. Childhood Schizophrenia and Mental Deficiency. *J Men Sci,* 97: 290–312, 1951.

Richards, E.L. Special Psychiatric Problems in Childhood. *J A Medl Assn,* 95: 1011–1015, 1930.

Richards, M.P.M. Social Interaction in the First Weeks of Human Life. *Psychiatria Neurologia Neurochurgia,* 74: 35–42, 1971.

Richer, J.M. and Coss, R.G. Gaze Aversion in Autistic Children. *Acta Ptrica Scandinavica.* 53: 193–210, 1976.

Richter, C.P. On the Phenomenon of Sudden Death in Animals and Man. *Psychosomatic Medn,* 19: 191–198, 1957.

Ricks, D.F. and Nameche, G. Symbiosis, Sacrifice, and Schizophrenia. *Men Hygiene,* 50: 541–551, 1966.

Ricks, D.M. and Wing, L. Language, Communication, and the Use of Symbols in Normal and Autistic Children. *JACS,* 5: 191–221, 1975.

Rie, H.E. Depression in Childhood. *J Ch Ptry,* 5: 653–684, 1966.

Rimland, B. *Infantile Autism.* Appleton-Century-Crofts, 1964.

————. On the Objective Diagnosis of Infantile Autism. *Acta Paedopsychiatrica,* 35: 146–161, 1968.

————. Comment on Ward's "Early Infantile Autism." *Pgical Bull,* 77: 52–53, 1972.

————. Childhood Psychosis, by Leo Kanner. *JACS,* 3: 88–92, 1973.

————. Infantile Autism. *Ch Personality Psychopathology,* 1: 137–167, 1974.

Rincover, A. Variables Affecting Stimulus Fading and Discriminative Responding in Psychotic Children. *J Abn Pgy,* 87: 541–553, 1978.

Ritvo, E.R. Autism. In *Autism.* SP Books, 1976.

Robbins, L.C. The Accuracy of Parental Recall of Aspects of Child Development and of Child Rearing Practices. *J Abn Social Pgy,* 66: 261–270, 1963.

Robertson, J. Mothering as an Influence on Early Development. *Psa Study Ch,* 17: 245–264, 1962.

————. Mother-Infant Interaction from Birth to Twelve Months. In Foss, B.M. (Ed) *Determinants of Infant Behaviour.* Methuen, Vol. 3, 1965.

Robertson, J. and Robertson, J. Young Children in Brief Separation. *Psa Study Ch,* 26: 264–315, 1971.

Robinson, D. *The Process of Becoming Ill.* Routledge & Kegan Paul, 1971.

Robinson, H.B. and Robinson, N.M. *The Mentally Retarded Child.* McGraw-Hill, 1965.

————. Mental Retardation. In Mussen, P.H. (Ed) *Carmichael's Manual of Child Psychology.* Wiley, 3rd ed, Vol. 2, 1970.

Robinson, J.F. The Psychoses of Early Childhood. *A J Ortho,* 31: 536–550, 1961.

Robson, K.S. The Role of Eye-to-Eye Contact in Maternal-Infant Attachment. *J Ch Pgy Ptry,* 8: 13–25, 1967.

Rochlin, G. Loss and Restitution. *Psa Study Ch,* 8: 288–309, 1953.

————. The Dread of Abandonment. *Psa Study Ch,* 16: 451–470, 1961.

————. *Man's Aggression.* Gambit, 1973.

Rodnick, E.H. and Garmezy, N. An Experimental Approach to the Study of Motivation in Schizophrenia. *Nebraska Symposium Motivation,* 5: 109–184, 1957.

Rosen, V.H. On Mathematical "Illumination" and the Mathematical Thought Processes. *Psa Study Ch,* 8: 127–154, 1953.

Rosenbaum, C.P. *The Meaning of Madness.* Science House, 1970.

Rosenberg, S. Problem-Solving and Conceptual Behavior. In Ellis, N.R. (Ed) *Handbook of Mental Deficiency.* McGraw-Hill, 1963.

Rosenblatt, J.S. Nonhormonal Basis of Maternal Behavior in the Rat. *Sci,* 156: 1512–1514, 1967.

Rosenblum, L.A. and Alpert, S. Fear of Strangers and Specificity of Attachment in Monkeys. In Lewis, M. and Rosenblum, L.A. (Eds) *The Origins of Fear*. Wiley, 1974.

Rosenthal, R. and Jacobson, L. *Pygmalion in the Classroom*. Holt Rinehart Winston, 1968.

Ross, A.O. A Schizophrenic Child and His Mother. *J Abn Social Pgy*, 51: 133–139, 1955.

———. *Psychological Disorders of Children*. McGraw-Hill, 1974.

Rossi, A.S. Transition to Parenthood. *J Marriage Family*, 30: 26–39, 1968.

Rothenberg, M. *Children with Emerald Eyes*. Dial, 1977.

Rowe, R.H. The Symptom in Past History. In Artiss, K.L. (Ed) *The Symptom as Communication in Schizophrenia*. Grune & Stratton, 1959.

Rozin, P., Poritsky, S. and Sotsky, R. American Children with Reading Problems Can Easily Learn to Read English Represented by Chinese Characters. *Sci*, 171: 1264–1267, 1971.

Rubenstein, J. Maternal Attentiveness and Subsequent Exploratory Behavior in the Infant. *Ch Dev*, 38: 1089–1100, 1967.

Rubinstein, B.O., Falick, M.L., Levitt, M. and Ekstein, R. Learning Impotence. *A J Ortho*, 29: 315–323, 1959.

Rudikoff, S. Why Some Children Don't Speak. *Commentary*, 54: 54–67, Oct. 1972.

Ruegamer, W.R., Bernstein, L. and Benjamin, J.D. Growth, Food Utilization, and Thyroid Activity in the Albino Rat as a Function of Extra Handling. *Sci*, 120: 184–185, 1954.

Ruesch, J. *Disturbed Communication*. W.W. Norton, 1967.

Ruttenberg, B.A. A Psychoanalytic Understanding of Infantile Autism and its Treatment. In Churchill, D.W., Alpern, G.D. and DeMyer, M.K. (Eds) *Colloquium on Infantile Autism*. Thomas, 1971.

Ruttenberg, B.A., Dratman, M.L., Fraknoi, J. and Wenar, C. An Instrument for Evaluating Autistic Children. *J Ch Ptry*, 5: 453–478, 1966.

Rutter, M. Psychotic Disorders in Early Childhood. In Coppen, A.J. and Walk, A. (Eds) *Recent Developments in Schizophrenia*. Headley, 1967.

———. Concepts of Autism. In Mittler, P.J. (Ed) *Aspects of Autism*. Br Pgical Soc, 1968.

———. Parent-Child Separation. In Clarke, A.M. and Clarke, A.D.B. (Eds) *Early Experience*. Free P, 1976.

Rutter, M. and Bartak, L. Cases of Infantile Autism. *JACS*, 1: 20–32, 1971.

Rutter, M. and Mittler, P. Environmental Influences on Language Development. In Rutter, M. and Martin, J.A.M. (Eds) *The Child with Delayed Speech*. Heineman, 1972.

Ryckman, D.B. and Henderson, R.A. The Meaning of the Retarded Child for His Parents. *Men Retardation*, 3: 4–7, Aug. 1965.

Sackett, G.P. Effects of Rearing Conditions upon the Behavior of Rhesus Monkeys. *Ch Dev*, 36: 855–868, 1965.

Sagarin, E. Etiquette, Embarrassment, and Forms of Address. In Birenbaum, A. and Sagarin, E. (Eds) *People in Places*. Praeger, 1973.

St. Clair, H. Manipulation. *Comprehensive Ptry*, 7: 248–258, 1966.

Salber, E.J., Stitt, P.G. and Babbott, J.G. Patterns of Breast Feeding in a Family Health Clinic. *New England J Medn*, 260: 310–315, 1959.

Salzman, L. *The Obsessive Personality*. Aronson, 2nd ed, 1973.

Sander, L.W. Issues in Early Mother-Child Interaction. *J Ch Ptry*, 1: 141–166, 1962.

————. Adaptive Relationships in Early Mother-Child Interaction. *J Ch Ptry*, 3: 231–264, 1964.

————. The Longitudinal Course of Early Mother-Child Interaction. In Foss, B.M. (Ed) *Determinants of Infant Behaviour*. Methuen, Vol. 4, 1969.

Sandler, J. and Joffe, W.G. Notes on Childhood Depression. *I J Psa*, 46: 88–96, 1965.

Sarason, S.B. and Doris, H. *Psychological Problems in Mental Deficiency*. Harper & Row, 4th ed, 1969.

Sarvis, M.A. and Garcia, B. Etiological Variables in Autism. *Ptry*, 24: 307–317, 1961.

Savage, V.A. Childhood Autism. *Br J Disor Communication*, 3: 75–88, 1968.

Schachter, F.F., Meyer, L.R. and Loomis, E.A. Childhood Schizophrenia and Mental Retardation. *A J Ortho*, 32: 584–594, 1962.

Schaefer, E.S. Parents as Educators. In Hartup, W. (Ed) *The Young Child*. Nat Assn Educ Young Chn, 1972.

Schaffer, H.R. Changes in Developmental Quotient under Two Conditions of Maternal Separation. *Br J Social Clin Pgy*, 4: 39–46, 1965.

————. Objective Observations of Personality Development in Early Infancy. In Brackbill, Y. and Thompson, G.G. (Eds) *Behavior in Infancy and Early Childhood*. Free P, 1967.

————. Cognitive Components of the Infant's Response to Strangers. In Lewis, M. and Rosenblum, L.A. (Eds) *The Origins of Fear*. Wiley, 1974.

————. Early Interactive Development. In *Studies in Mother-Infant Interaction*. Academic P, 1977.

Schaffer, H.R. and Callender, W.M. Psychologic Effects of Hospitalization in Infancy. *Peds*, 24: 528–539, 1959.

Schaffer, H.R. and Emerson, P.E. The Effects of Experimentally Administered Stimulation on Developmental Quotients of Infants. *Br J Social Clin Pgy*, 7: 61–67, 1968.

Schain, R.J. and Yannet, H. Infantile Autism. *J Peds*, 57: 560–567, 1960.

Scheerer, M., Rothmann, E. and Goldstein, K. A Case of "Idiot Savant." *Pgical Mono*, 58: no. 4, Whole no. 269, 1945.

Scheff, T.J. *Being Mentally Ill*. Aldine, 1966.

————. The Role of the Mentally Ill and the Dynamics of Mental Disorder. In Spitzer, S.P. and Denzin, N.K. (Eds) *The Mental Patient*. McGraw-Hill, 1968.

Schmale, A.F. Relationship of Separation and Depression to Disease. *Psychosomatic Medn*, 20: 259–277, 1958.

Schmidt, B.G. Changes in Personal, Social, and Intellectual Behavior of Children Originally Classified as Feebleminded. *Pgical Mono*, 60, #5, 1946.

————. Development of Social Competencies in Adolescents Originally Classified as Feebleminded. *A J Ortho*, 19: 125–129, 1949.

Schopler, E. The Development of Body Image and Symbol Formation through Bodily Contact with an Autistic Child. *J Ch Pgy Ptry*, 3: 191–202, 1962.

Schopler, E. and Reichler, R.J. Parents as Cotherapists in the Treatment of Psychotic Children. *JACS*, 1: 87–102, 1971a.

————. Psychobiological Referents for the Treatment of Autism. In Churchill,

D.W., Alpern, G.D. and DeMyer, M.K. (Eds) *Colloquium on Infantile Autism.* Thomas, 1971b.

Schreibman, L. and Koegel, R.L. Autism. *Pgy Today,* 61–67, Mar. 1975.

Schwab, R.S. Discussion. *Trans A Neurological Assn,* 79: 102, 1956.

Schwarz, J.C. Childhood Origins of Psychopathology. *A Pgist,* 34: 879–885, 1979.

Scott, E.M. and Thomson, A.M. A Psychological Investigation of Primigravidae. *J Obstetrics Gynaecology Br Empire,* 63: 502–508, 1956.

Scott, J.P. The Process of Primary Socialization in Canine and Human Infants. *Mono Soc Res Ch Dev,* 28: no. 1, 1963.

———. *Early Experience and the Organization of Behavior.* Brooks/Cole, 1968.

Scott, R.D. and Ashworth, P.L. 'Closure' at the First Schizophrenic Breakdown. *Br J Medl Pgy,* 40: 109–145, 1967.

———. The Shadow of the Ancestor. *Br J Medl Pgy,* 42: 13–42, 1969.

Scott, W.C.M. A Psycho-Analytic Concept of the Origin of Depression. *Br Medl J,* 538–540, 1948.

Searles, H.F. *The Nonhuman Environment in Normal Development and in Schizophrenia.* IUP, 1960.

Sears, R.R., Maccoby, E.E. and Levin, H. *Patterns of Child Rearing.* Row & Peterson, 1957.

Seay, B., Hansen, E. and Harlow, H.F. Mother-Infant Separation in Monkeys. *J Ch Pgy Ptry,* 3: 123–132, 1962.

Seligman, M.E.P. Chronic Fear Produced by Unpredictable Electric Shock. *J Comparative Physiological Pgy,* 66: 402–411, 1968.

———. Depression and Learned Helplessness. In Friedman, R.J. and Katz, M.M. (Eds) *The Psychology of Depression.* Winston, 1974.

———. *Helplessness.* Freeman, 1975.

Seligman, M.E.P., Maier, S.F. and Solomon, R.L. Unpredictable and Uncontrollable Aversive Events. In Brush, F.R. (Ed) *Aversive Conditioning and Learning.* Academic P, 1971.

Selvini Palazzoli, M., Cecchin, G., Prata, G. and Boscolo, L. *Paradox and Counterparadox.* Aronson, 1978.

Senn, M.J.E. Emotions and Symptoms in Pediatric Practice. *Advances in Peds,* 3: 69–89, 1948.

Senn, M.J.E. and Solnit, A.J. *Problems in Child Behavior and Development.* Lea & Febiger, 1968.

Serban, G. The Phenomenology of Depression. *A J Ptry,* 30: 355–362, 1965.

Shaberman, R.B. *Autistic Children.* Stuart & Watkins, 1971.

Shainess, N. Psychological Problems Associated with Motherhood. In Arieti, S. (Ed) *American Handbook of Psychiatry.* Basic B, Vol. 3, 1966.

Shakow, D. Psychological Deficit in Schizophrenia. *Beh Sci,* 8: 275–305, 1963.

Shapiro, T., Huebner, H.F. and Campbell, M. Language Behavior and Hierarchic Integration in a Psychotic Child. *JACS,* 4: 71–90, 1974.

Sharlin, S.A. and Polansky, N.A. The Process of Infantilization. *A J Ortho,* 42: 92–102, 1972.

Shaw (ni). Discussion. In Chapin, H.D. A Plea for Accurate Statistics in Infants' Institutions. *Trans A Ped Soc,* 27: 180–185, 1915.

Shirley, M.M. Children's Adjustments to a Strange Situation. *J Abn Social Pgy,* 37: 201–217, 1942.

Shotwell, A.M. Arthur Performance Ratings of Mexican and American High-Grade Mental Defectives. *A J Men Def,* 49: 445–449, 1945.

Silberstein, R.M., Blackman, S. and Mandell, W. Autoerotic Head Banging. *J Ch Ptry,* 5: 235–242, 1966.

Silverman, J. The Problem of Attention and Research and Theory in Schizophrenia. *Pgical Rev,* 71: 352–379, 1964.

———. Shamans and Acute Schizophrenia. *A Anthropologist,* 69: 21–31, 1967.

Singer, M.T. Family Transactions and Schizophrenia. In Romano, J. (Ed) *The Origins of Schizophrenia.* Excerpta Medica, 1967.

Sinkler, W. Insanity in Early Childhood. *U Medl J,* 5: 248–255, 1892.

Siqueland, E.R. Biological and Experiential Determinants of Exploration in Infancy. In Stone, L.J., Smith, H.B. and Murphy, L.B. (Eds) *The Competent Infant.* Basic B, 1973.

Skeels, H.M. Adult Status of Children with Contrasting Early Life Experiences. *Mono Soc Res Ch Dev,* 31: no. 3, 1966.

Skeels, H.M. and Dye, H.B. A Study of the Effects of Differential Stimulation on Mentally Retarded Children. *J Psycho-Asth enics,* 44: 114–136, 1939.

Skeels, H.M., Updegraaf, R., Wellman, B.L. ar d Williams, H.M. A Study of Environmental Stimulation. *U Iowa Studies Ch Welfare,* 15: no. 4, 1938.

Skodak, M. The Mental Development of Adopted Children Whose True Mothers are Feeble-Minded. *Ch Dev,* 9: 303–308, 1938.

———. Children in Foster Homes. *U Iowa Studies Ch Welfare.* 16: no. 1, 1939.

———. Mental Growth of Adopted Children in the Same Family. *J Genet Pgy,* 77: 3–9, 1950.

Slimp, E. Life Experiences of Schizophrenic Children. *Smith College Studies Social Work,* 21: 103–122, 1950.

Smalldon, J.L. A Survey of Mental Illness Associated with Pregnancy and Childbirth. *A J Ptry,* 97: 80–98, 1940.

Smith, H.T. A Comparison of Interview and Observation Measures of Mother Behavior. *J Abn Social Pgy,* 57: 278–282, 1958.

Smolen, E.M. Some Thoughts on Schizophrenia in Childhood. *J Ch Ptry,* 4: 443–472, 1965.

Soddy, K. The Autistic Child. *Practitioner,* 192: 525–533, 1964.

Solkoff, N., Yaffe, S., Weintraub, D. and Blase, B. Effects of Handling on the Subsequent Development of Premature Infants. *Devl Pgy,* 1: 765–768, 1969.

Solnit, A.J. A Study of Object Loss in Infancy. *Psa Study Ch,* 25: 257–272, 1970.

Solnit, A.J. and Stark, M.H. Mourning and the Birth of a Defective Child. *Psa Study Ch,* 16: 523–537, 1961.

Solomon, R.L. The Opponent-Process Theory of Acquired Motivation. *A Pgist,* 35: 691–712, 1980.

Solomon, R.L., Kamin, L.J. and Wynne, L.C. Traumatic Avoidance Learning. *J Abn Social Pgy,* 48: 291–302, 1953.

Solomon, R.L. and Wynne, L.C. Traumatic Avoidance Learning. *Pgical Rev,* 61: 353–385, 1954.

Sontag, L.W. Differences in Modifiability of Fetal Behavior and Physiology. *Psychosomatic Medn,* 6: 151–154, 1944.

Speers, R.W. and Lansing, C. Group Psychotherapy with Preschool Psychotic Children and Collateral Group Therapy of their Parents. *A J Ortho,* 34: 659–666, 1964.

_____ . *Group Therapy in Childhood Psychosis.* U N Carolina P, 1965.

_____ . Some Genetic-Dynamic Considerations in Childhood Symbiotic Psychosis. *J Ch Ptry,* 7: 329–349, 1968.

Spelke, E., Zelazo, P.R., Kagan, J. and Kotelchuk, M. Father Interaction and Separation Protest. *Devl Pgy,* 9: 83–90, 1973.

Sperber, M.A. Symbiotic Psychosis and the Need for Fame. *Psa Rev,* 61: 517–534, 1974.

Sperling, M. Children's Interpretation and Reaction to the Unconscious of their Mothers. *I J Psa,* 31: 36–41, 1950.

_____ . The Neurotic Child and His Mother. *A J Ortho,* 21: 351–364, 1951.

_____ . Reactive Schizophrenia in Children. *A J Ortho,* 24: 506–512, 1954.

_____ . Psychosis and Psychosomatic Illness. *I J Psa,* 36: 320–327, 1955.

_____ . Equivalents of Depression in Children. *J Hillside Hospital,* 8: 138–148, 1959.

Spiro, M.E. *Children of the Kibbutz.* Schocken, 2nd ed, 1965.

Spitz, R.A. Hospitalism. *Psa Study Ch,* 1: 53–74, 1945.

_____ . The Psychogenic Diseases in Infancy. *Psa Study Ch,* 6: 255–275, 1951.

_____ . Authority and Masturbation. *Psa Q,* 21: 490–527, 1952.

_____ . Aggression. In Loewenstein, R.M. (Ed) *Drives, Affects, Behavior.* IUP, 1953.

_____ . Infantile Depression and the General Adaptation Syndrome. In Hoch, P.H. and Zubin, J. (Eds) *Depression.* Grune & Stratton, 1954.

_____ . *No and Yes.* IUP, 1957.

_____ . *The First Year of Life.* IUP, 1965.

Spitz, R.A. and Wolf, K.M. Anaclitic Depression. *Psa Study Ch,* 2: 313–342, 1946.

_____ . Autoerotism. *Psa Study Ch,* 3–4: 85–120, 1949.

Sroufe, L.A. The Coherence of Individual Development. *A Pgist,* 34: 834–841, 1979.

Sroufe, L.A. and Waters, E. Attachment as an Organizational Construct. *Ch Dev,* 48: 1184–1199, 1977.

Stabenau, J.R. and Pollin, W. Early characteristics of Monozygotic Twins Discordant for Schizophrenia. *Ann Prog Ch Ptry Ch Dev,* 497–515, 1968.

Stacey, M. Practical Recommendations. In Stacy, M., Dearden, R., Pill, R. and Robinson, D. *Hospitals, Children and Their Families.* Routledge & Kegan Paul, 1970.

Starr, P.H. Psychoses in Children. *Psa Q,* 23: 544–565, 1954.

Staver, N. The Child's Learning Difficulty as Related to the Emotional Problem of the Mother. *A J Ortho,* 23: 131–140, 1953.

Stayton, D.J. and Ainsworth, M.D. Individual Differences in Infant Responses to Brief, Everyday Separations as Related to Other Infant and Maternal Behaviors. *Devl Pgy,* 9: 226–235, 1973.

Stayton, D.J., Hogan, R. and Ainsworth, M.D. Infant Obedience and Maternal Behavior. *Ch Dev,* 42: 1057–1069, 1971.

Stechler, G. Newborn Attention as Affected by Medication during Labor. *Sci,* 144: 315–317, 1964.

Stein, Z. and Susser, M. Mutability of Intelligence and Epidemiology of Mild Mental Retardation. *Ann Prog Ch Ptry Ch Dev,* 367–407, 1971.

Stendler, C.B. Sixty Years of Child Training Practices. *J Peds,* 36: 122–134, 1950.

Stengel, E. Studies on the Psychopathology of Compulsive Wandering. *Br J Medl Pgy,* 18: 250–254, 1939.

———. Further Studies on Pathological Wandering. *J Men Sci*, 89: 224–241, 1943.

———. A Clinical and Psychological Study of Echo-Reactions. *J Men Sci*, 93: 598–612, 1947.

Sterba, E. An Abnormal Child. *Psa Q*, 5: 375–414, 560–600, 1936.

Stern, D.N. A Micro-Analysis of Mother-Infant Interaction. *J Ch Ptry*, 10: 501–517, 1971.

Stevenson, H.W. Discrimination Learning. In Ellis, N.R. (Ed) *Handbook of Mental Deficiency*. McGraw-Hill, 1963.

Stewart, A.H. Excessive Crying in Infants—a Family Disease. *Problems Infancy Childhood*, 6: 138–160, 1953.

Stone, F.H. The Autistic Child. *Practitioner*, 205: 313–318, 1970.

Stone, L.J., Smith, H.B. and Murphy, L.B. (Eds) *The Competent Infant*. Basic B, 1973.

Straight, B. Schizophrenic-Like Psychoses in Children. *Clin Proceedings Children's Hospital*, 10: 6–16, 1954.

Streissguth, A.P. and Bee, H.L. Mother-Child Interactions and Cognitive Development in Children. In Hartup, W.W. (Ed) *The Young Child*. Nat Assn Educ Young Chn, 1972.

Stutte, H. and Dauner, I. Systematized Delusions in Early Life Schizophrenia. *JACS*, 1: 411–420, 1971.

Sucharewa, G.J. The Importance of Considering the Effect of Age for the Study of Fixed Rules in the Course of Schizophrenia in Children and Adolescents. (In German) *Acta Paedopsychiatrica*. 34: 307–320, 1967.

Sullivan, R.C. Why Do Autistic Children . . .? *JADD*, 10: 231–241, 1980.

Summers, F.L. Symbiosis and Conformation in the Family Relationships of Schizophrenics. *Dissertation Abs*, 36: 3630B, 1976.

Suomi, S.J. and Harlow, H.F. Social Rehabilitation of Isolate-Reared Monkeys. *Devl Pgy*, 6: 487–496, 1972.

Sussman, S. and Sklar, J.L. The Social Awareness of Autistic Children. *A J Ortho*, 39: 798–806, 1969.

Susz, E. and Marberg, H.M. Autistic Withdrawal of a Small Child under Stress. *Acta Paedopsychiatrica*, 43: 149–158, 1978.

Sylvester, E. Analysis of Psychogenic Anorexia and Vomiting in a Four-Year-Old Child. *Psa Study Ch*, 1: 167–187, 1945.

Symonds, C. Excitation and Inhibition in Epilepsy. *Brain*, 82: 133–146, 1959.

Szasz, T.S. *The Manufacture of Madness*. Delta, 1970.

———. *Ceremonial Chemistry*. Anchor, 1975.

Szurek, S.A. Psychotic Episodes and Psychotic Maldevelopment. *A J Ortho*, 26: 519–543, 1956.

———. The Child's Needs for His Emotional Health. In Howells, J.G. (Ed) *Modern Perspectives in International Child Psychiatry*. Oliver & Boyd, 1969.

Szurek, S.A. and Berlin, I.N. The Problem of Blame in Therapy with Parents and Their Children. In *Clinical Studies in Childhood Psychoses*. Brunner/Mazel, 1973.

Tausk, V. On Masturbation. *Psa Study Ch*, 6: 61–79, 1951.

Taylor, G.R. *Sex in History*. Harper, 1970.

Temkin, O. *The Falling Sickness*. Johns Hopkins U P, 1971.

Tennes, K.H. and Lampl, E.R. Some Aspects of Mother-Child Relationship Pertaining to Infantile Separation Anxiety. *J Ner Men Dis,* 143: 426–437, 1966.

Thoman, E.B., Leiderman, P.H. and Olson, J.P. Neonate-Mother Interaction during Breast Feeding. *Devl Pgy,* 6: 110–118, 1972.

Thomas, A , Chess, S. and Birch, H.G. *Temperament and Behavior Disorders in Childre;1.* New York U P, 1968.

Thomas, R. Comment. In Foss, B.M. (Ed) *Determinants of Infant Behaviour.* Methuen, Vol. 1, 1961.

———. Comments on Some Aspects of Self and Object Representation in a Group of Psychotic Children. *Psa Study Ch,* 21: 527–580, 1966.

Thompson, W.R. Early Environmental Influences on Behavioral Development. *A J Ortho,* 30: 306–314, 1960.

Thompson, W.R. and Melzack, R. Early Environment. *Scientific A,* 194: 38–42, Jan 1956.

Thoms, H. *Childbirth with Understanding.* Thomas, 1962.

Thornton, J.W. and Jacobs, P.D. Learned Helplessness in Human Subjects. *J Exp Pgy,* 87: 367–372, 1971.

Tietze, T. A Study of Mothers of Schizophrenic Patients. *Ptry,* 12: 55–65, 1949.

Tinbergen, E.A. and Tinbergen, N. Early Childhood Autism. *J Comparative Ethology,* Supp. no. 10, 1972.

———. The Aetiology of Childhood Autism. *Pgical Medn,* 6: 545–549, 1976.

Tinbergen, N. and Tinbergen, E.A. *Autistic Children.* Allen & Unwin, 1983.

Toolan, J.M. Depression in Children and Adolescents. *A J Ortho,* 32: 404–415, 1962.

———. Masked Depression in Children and Adolescents. In Lesse, S. (Ed) *Masked Depression.* Aronson, 1975.

Trause, M.A., Klaus, M.H. and Kennell, J.H. Maternal Behavior in Animals. In Klaus, M.H. and Kennell, J.H. (Eds) *Parent-Infant Bonding.* Mosby, 2nd ed, 1982.

Treadway, W.L. May Potential Insanity be Recognized in Childhood? *I Clin,* 129–138, 1920.

Trevarthen, C. Conversations with a Two-Month-Old. *New Scientist,* 62: 230–235, 1974.

———. Descriptive Analyses of Infant Communicative Behaviour. In Schaffer, H.R. (Ed) *Studies in Mother-Infant Interaction.* Academic P, 1977.

Tryon, W.W. Models of Behavior Disorder. *A Pgist,* 32: 509–518, 1976.

Tustin, F. *Autism and Childhood Psychosis.* Science House, 1972.

Ucko, L.E. A Comparative Study of Asphyxiated and Non-Asphyxiated Boys from Birth to Five Years. *Dev Medn Ch Neurology,* 7: 643–657, 1965.

Ulett, G. Discussion. *Electroencephalography Clin Neurophysiology,* 3: 380, 1951.

Vaillant, G.E. John Haslam on Early Infantile Autism. *A J Ptry,* 119: 376, 1962.

Valente, M. Autism, *Peds,* 48: 495–496, 1971.

van Krevelen, D.A. Autismus Infantum. *Acta Paedopsychiatrica.* 27: 97–107, 1960.

Verhees, B. A Pair of Classically Early Infantile Autistic Siblings. *JACS,* 6: 53–59, 1976.

Vernon, D.T.A., Foley, J.M., Sipowicz, R.R. and Schulman, J.L. *The Psychological Responses of Children to Hospitalization and Illness.* Thomas, 1965.

Victor, G. *Invisible Men.* Prentice-Hall, 1973.

Vogel, E.F. and Bell, N.W. The Emotionally Disturbed Child as a Family Scapegoat. *Psa Rev,* 47: 21–42, 1960.

Volkart, E.H. and Michael, S.T. Bereavement and Mental Health. In Leighton, A.H., Clausen, J.A. and Wilson, R.N. (Eds) *Explorations in Social Psychiatry.* Basic B, 1957.

Volkmar, F.R. and Cohen, D.J. A Hierarchical Analysis of Patterns of Noncompliance in Autistic and Behavior-Disturbed Children. *JADD,* 12: 35–42, 1982.

Voyat, G. Piaget on Schizophrenia. *J A Acad Psa,* 8: 93–113, 1980.

Waal, N. A Special Technique of Psychotherapy with an Autistic Child. In Caplan, G. (Ed) *Emotional Problems of Early Childhood.* Tavistock, 1955.

Wahler, R.G. Deviant Child Behavior within the Family. In Leitenberg, H. (Ed) *Handbook of Behavior Modification and Behavior Therapy.* Prentice-Hall, 1976.

Walter, V.J. and Walter, W.G. The Central Effects of Rhythmic Sensory Stimulation. *Electroencephalography Clin Neurophysiology.* 1: 57–86, 1949.

Walters, R.H. and Parke, R.D. The Role of the Distance Receptors in the Development of Social Responsiveness. *Advances Ch Dev Beh,* 2: 59–96, 1965.

Waring, M. and Ricks, D.F. Family Patterns of Children Who Became Adult Schizophrenics. *J Ner Men Dis,* 140: 351–364, 1965.

Waterman, J.H. Psychogenic Factors in Parental Acceptance of Feebleminded Children. *Dis Ner System,* 9: 184–187, 1948.

Waters, E. The Reliability and Stability of Individual Differences in Infant-Mother Attachment. *Ch Dev,* 49: 483–494, 1978.

Watson, J.S. The Development and Generalization of "Contingency Awareness" in Early Infancy. *Merrill-Palmer Q,* 12: 123–135, 1966.

———. Smiling, Cooing, and "The Game." *Merrill-Palmer Q,* 18: 323–339, 1972.

———. Smiling, Cooing, and "The Game." in Stone, L.J., Smith, H.B. and Murphy, L.B. (Eds) *The Competent Infant.* Basic B, 1973.

———. Perception of Contingency as a Determinant of Social Responsiveness. In Thoman, E.B. and Trotter, S. (Eds) *Social Responsiveness of Infants.* Johnson & Johnson, 1978.

Wax, D.E. Learning How to Pretend. *Br J Medl Pgy,* 46: 297–302, 1973.

Webster, C.D. The Characteristics of Autism. In Webster, C.D., Konstantareas, M.M., Oxman, J. and Mack, J.E. (Eds) *Autism.* Pergamon, 1980.

Webster, C.D., McPherson, H., Sloman, L., Evans, M.A. and Kuchar, E. Communicating with an Autistic Boy by Gestures. *JACS,* 3: 337–346, 1973.

Webster, T.G. Problems of Emotional Development in Young Retarded Children. *A J Ptry,* 120: 37–43, 1963.

———. Unique Aspects of Emotional Development in Mentally Retarded Children. In Menolascino, F.J. (Ed) *Psychiatric Approaches to Mental Retardation.* Basic B, 1970.

Weil, A.P. Certain Severe Disturbances of Ego Development in Childhood. *Psa Study Ch,* 8: 271–287, 1953.

Weiland, I.H. and Legg, D.R. Formal Speech Characteristics as a Diagnostic Aid in Childhood Psychosis. *A J Ortho,* 34: 91–94, 1964.

Weisberg, P. Social and Nonsocial Conditioning of Infant Vocalizations. *Ch Dev,* 34: 377–388, 1963.

Weisskopf, E.A. Intellectual Malfunctioning and Personality. *J Abn Social Pgy,* 46: 410–423, 1951.

Weissman, M.M. and Paykel, E.S. *The Depressed Woman,* U Chicago P, 1974.

Weissman, M.M., Paykel, E.S., Siegal, R. and Klerman, G.L. The Social Role Performance of Depressed Women. *A J Ortho,* 41: 390–405, 1971.

Weitman, S.R. Intimacies. In Birenbaum, A. and Sagarin, E. (Eds) *People in Places.* Praeger, 1973.

Welch, M.G. Retrieval from Autism through Mother-Child Holding Therapy. In Tinbergen, N. and Tinbergen, E.A. *Autistic Children.* Allen & Unwin, 1983.

Welsford, E. *The Fool.* Smith, 1956.

Wenar, C. The Reliability of Developmental Histories. *Psychosomatic Medn,* 25: 505–509, 1963.

Wenar, C., Handlon, M.W. and Garner, A.M. Patterns of Mothering in Psychosomatic Disorders and Severe Emotional Disturbances. *Merrill-Palmer Q,* 6: 165–170, 1960.

──────. *Origins of Psychosomatic and Emotional Disturbances.* Hoeber, 1962.

Werner, H. *Comparative Psychology of Mental Development.* IUP, rev ed, 1957.

Wergeland, H. Autistic Children. In Renfrew, C. and Murphy, K. (Eds) *The Child Who Does Not Talk.* Spastics Soc, 1964.

Whalen, C.K. and Henker, B.A. Play Therapy Conducted by Mentally Retarded Inpatients. *Psychotherapy,* 8: 236–245, 1971.

White, B.L. An Analysis of Excellent Early Educational Practices. In Stone, L.J., Smith, H.B. and Murphy, L.B. (Eds) *The Competent Infant,* Basic B, 1973.

White, R.W. The Experience of Efficacy in Schizophrenia. *Ptry,* 28: 199–211, 1965.

Whiten, A. Assessing the Effects of Perinatal Events on the Success of the Mother-Infant Relationship. In Schaffer, H.R. (Ed) *Studies in Mother-Infant Interaction.* Academic P, 1977.

Whiting, J.W.M. and Child, L.L. *Child Training and Personality.* Yale U P, 1953.

Wieder, H. Intellectuality. *Psa Study Ch,* 21: 294–323, 1966.

Wilcox, D.E. Observations of Speech Disturbances in Childhood Schizophrenia. *Dis Ner System,* 17: 20–23, 1956.

Will, O.A. Schizophrenia. In Romano, J. (Ed) *The Origins of Schizophrenia.* Excerpta Medica, 1967.

Willeford, W. *The Fool and His Sceptre.* Northwestern U P, 1969.

Williams, J.A., Koegel, R.L. and Egel, A.L. Response-Reinforcer Relationships and Improved Learning in Autistic Children. *J Applied Beh Analysis,* 14: 53–60, 1981.

Williams, J.F. Childhood Schizophrenia. *Medl J Australia,* 43(1): 224–226, 1956.

Williams, S. and Harper, J. A Study of Etiological Factors at Critical Periods of Development in Autistic Children. *I J Men Health,* 3: 90–99, 1974.

Wing, J.K. Diagnosis, Epidemiology, Aetiology. In *Early Childhood Autism.* Pergamon, 1966.

Wing, J.K., O'Connor, N. and Lotter, V. Autistic Conditions in Early Infancy. *Br Medl J,* 389–392, 1967.

Wing, L. *Children Apart.* Br Medl Assn, c1970.

──────. *Autistic Children.* Brunner/Mazel, 1972.

──────. Book Reviews. *JACS,* 7: 109–112, 1977

Winterbottom, M.R. The Relation of Need for Achievement to Learning Experiences in Independence and Mastery. In Atkinson, J.W. (Ed) *Motives in Fantasy, Action and Society.* Van Nostrand, 1958.

Wolfensberger, W. The Origin and Nature of Our Institutional Models. In Kugel, R.J. and Wolfensberger, W. (Eds) *Changing Patterns in Residential Services for the Mentally Retarded.* President's Committee Men Retardation, 1969.

Wolfenstein, M. *Children's Humor.* Free P, 1954.

Wolff, P.H. Mother-Infant Relations at Birth. In Howells, J.G. (Ed) *Modern Perspectives in International Child Psychiatry.* Oliver & Boyd, 1969a.

Wolff, P.H. The Natural History of Crying and Other Vocalizations in Early Infancy. In Foss, B.M. (Ed) *Determinants of Infant Behaviour.* Methuen, Vol. 4, 1969b.

Wolff, S. Behavior and Pathology of Parents of Disturbed Children. In Anthony, E.J. and Koupernik, C. (Eds) *The Child in His Family.* Wiley, Vol. 1, 1970.

Wolff, S. and Chess, S. An Analysis of the Language of Fourteen Schizophrenic Children. *J Ch Pgy Ptry,* 6: 29–41, 1965.

Wolman, B.J. Childhood Schizophrenia and Vectoriasis Praecocissima. *A J Psychotherapy,* 24: 264–277, 1970.

Woodward, K.F., Jaffe, N. and Brown, D. Early Psychiatric Intervention for Young Mentally Retarded Children. In Menolascino, F.J. (Ed) *Psychiatric Approaches to Mental Retardation.* Basic B, 1970.

Woodward, K.F. and Siegal, M.G. Psychiatric Study of Mentally Retarded Children of Preschool Age. *Peds,* 19: 119–126, 1957.

Woodward, K.F., Siegal, M.G. and Eustis, M.J. Psychiatric Study of Mentally Retarded Children of Preschool Age. *A J Ortho,* 28: 376–393, 1958.

Worchel, T.L. and Worchel, P. The Parental Concept of the Mentally Retarded Child. *A J Men Def,* 65: 782–788, 1961.

Wortis, J. Schizophrenic Symptomatology in the Mentally Retarded. *A J Ptry,* 115: 429–431, 1958.

Wortis, R.P. The Acceptance of the Concept of the Maternal Role by Behavioral Scientists. *A J Ortho,* 41: 733–746, 1971.

Wyckoff, L.B. The Role of Observing Responses in Discrimination Learning. *Pgical Rev,* 59: 431–442, 1952.

Wynne, L.C. and Singer, M.T. Thought Disorder and Family Relations of Schizophrenics. *Arch Genr Ptry,* 9: 191–198, 1963.

Yalom, I.D., Lunde, D.T., Moos, R.H. and Hamburg, D.A. "Postpartum Blues" Syndrome. *Arch Genr Ptry,* 18: 16–77, 1968.

Yarrow, L.J. Maternal Deprivation. *Pgical Bull,* 58: 459–490, 1961.

———. Research in Dimensions of Early Maternal Care. *Merrill-Palmer Q,* 9: 101–114, 1963.

———. Conceptualizing the Early Environment. In Chandler, C.A., Lourie, R.S., Peters, A.D. and Dittman, L.L. (Eds) *Early Child Care.* Atherton, 1968.

Yarrow, L.J. and Goodwin, M.S. Some Conceptual Issues in the Study of Mother-Infant Interaction. *A J Ortho,* 35: 473–481, 1965.

Yarrow, L.J. and Pedersen, F.A. Attachment. In Hartup, W.W. (Ed) *The Young Child.* Nat Assn Educ Young Chn, 1972.

Yarrow, L.J., Rubenstein, J.L., Pedersen, F.A. and Jankoski, J.J. Dimensions of

correcting.

Early Stimulation and Their Differential Effects on Infant Development. In Stone, L.J., Smith, H.B. and Murphy, L.B. (Eds) *The Competent Infant.* Basic B, 1973.

Zarlock, S.P. Social Expectations, Language and Schizophrenia. *J Humanistic Pgy,* 6: 68–74, 1966.

Zaslow, R.W. and Breger, L. A Theory and Treatment of Autism. In Breger, L. (Ed) *Clinical-Cognitive Psychology.* Prentice-Hall, 1969.

Zeaman, D. Learning Processes of the Mentally Retarded. In Osler, S.F. and Cooke, R.E. (Eds) *The Biosocial Basis of Mental Retardation.* Johns Hopkins U P, 1965.

Zeaman, D. and House, B.J. The Role of Attention in Retardate Discrimination Learning. In Ellis, N.R. (Ed) *Handbook of Mental Retardation.* McGraw-Hill, 1963.

Zigler, E. Rigidity in the Retarded. In Trapp, E.P. and Himelstein, P. (Eds) *Readings on the Exceptional Child.* Appleton-Century-Crofts, 1962.

———. Familial Mental Retardation. *Ann Prog Ch Ptry Ch Dev,* 281–299, 1968.

———. The Retarded Child as a Whole Person. In Adams, H.E. and Boardman, W.K. (Eds) *Advances in Experimental Clinical Psychology.* Pergamon, 1971.

Zilboorg, G. Post-Partum Schizophrenias. *J Ner Men Dis,* 68: 370–383, 1928.

———. The Dynamics of Schizophrenic Reactions Related to Pregnancy and Childbirth. *A J Ptry,* 8: 733–766, 1929.

———. Depressive Reactions Related to Parenthood. *A J Ptry,* 10: 927–962, 1931.

Zucker, W.M. The Image of the Clown. *J Aesthetics Art Criticism,* 12: 310–317, 1954.

Index of Names

Index of Subjects

infant, 73, 93, 176; devotion, 53, 55, 60-64, 176; disappointment, 56, 74, 84-85, 91, 93, 96, 138, 140; distraction, 134, 140; exclusive care, 63, 95, 176; expectations of infant, 84-85; fantasies, 67ff, 93; favored child, 53-64, 126; hesitancy re infant, 85-86; hiding children, 63, 93; infatuation with child, 54, 63; inhibition, 63-64; leaving infant alone, 196-199, 203; mechanical care, 59, 63, 92, 96; sacrifice, 53-54, 63-64; seclusion, 50, 63, 201; turning point in life, 53-54, 56, 60, 67ff, 92; withdrawal, 105, 118, 122-123
Performance anxiety, 170
Predictability of experience, 130, 156-162, 191, 194, 242
Prematurity, 55, 78, 98
Proximity seeking, 99, 105, 106, 125

Recklessness, 31, 107, 148
Refusal of care, 121, 124, 128
Regression, 106, 113, 124, 158, 226
Rejection of caretaker, 108, 122, 128, 131
Resistance, 152ff, 168. See also Negativism
Responding, abortive, 155ff; fixed, 153ff, 170; token, 157-159, 171, 209-211
Retardation, 35-37, 61, 165-171, 179-184
Reunion, 114, 128-129, 132-133
Riddle, 216-217
Ritual, 25-26, 124, 151, 154, 171-172, 187-194, 205. See also Compulsivity
Rocking, 122, 124, 140, 200, 203, 227-229, 237, 241

Scanning, 104, 107, 120, 124
Schizophrenia, 35-37, 153, 163, 165, 175-176, 178-179, 206, 208, 213, 214, 217-218; catatonia, 152, 159, 163, 172-175, 188, 206, 208
Searching, 120, 124
Seizures, 235ff
Self-abuse, 107, 140, 155, 193, 237
Self-effacement, 216-220
Self-stimulation, 29, 124, 227-229, 235-240
Sensory anomalies, 28, 225-227; hearing, 28,

128, 176-177, 179, 220, 226, 236; smell, 28, 188, 227; vision, 221, 226
Sensuality, 29, 227
Separation, 98, 101, 104, 106, 107, 113-136, 204, 228-229
Sexuality, 29, 63-64, 181, 199, 227, 229-235, 239; masturbation, 124, 230-231, 232, 233
Sick/sickly infant, 60-61, 111
Skills, loss of, 124, 145; special, 14, 30, 103, 182
Sleep, 31, 90, 121, 124, 225
Special child, 40, 51, 53-64, 67
Speech, 21, 137, 143-147, 189-190, 205ff; ambiguous, 216-219; echolalia, 157-158, 209-211, 212; literalness, 213-215; metaphor, 213, 215-216; opposites, 145, 174; pronouns, 211-213; silence, 208, 236
Staring, 104ff, 109, 120, 124, 236, 237
Stimulation of infant, 109, 138-139; intrusive, 109, 110, 132-133, 173, 201-202
Symptoms, 25-33, 38

Teasing, 214-215
Television, 30, 237
Toilet training, 30, 173, 176, 189
Training, 137-164; coercive, 153ff, 162, 173; correction, 139, 144-145; cues, ambivalent, 153, 155, 169; cues, changed, 153-158, 162; cues, difficult, 153, 162, 226; punishment, 139ff, 221; reinforcement, 137-150, 242; reinforcement, delayed, 147-148; reinforcement, intermittent, 144ff; reinforcement, noncontingent, 147, 148-150, 160, 162; rewarding autistic behavior, 150; stressful, 46, 49, 62, 93, 137-183, 220, 225
Twin studies, 111

Uncuddliness, 32, 78, 80-81, 122
Unresponsiveness, 27, 109, 145, 152, 169, 173, 203, 220, 228, 236, 239

Vigilance, 163, 194

Wandering, 31, 107
Withdrawal, 27-28, 121, 122-123, 127

About the Author

George Victor is a clinical psychologist. He is a graduate of Columbia University and received an M.A. from Harvard University and a Ph.D. from New York University. *The Riddle of Autism* is the result of eleven years of work. His prior book, *Invisible Men* (1973), is a study of self-alienation in men. Among his other publications are "Interpretations Couched in Mythical Imagery," an article on analytic technique in the *International Journal of Psychoanalytic Psychotherapy* (1978–1979), and the forthcoming *Hitler: The Pathology of Evil.*